STUDIES IN GERMAN LITERATURE,
LINGUISTICS, AND CULTURE
Vol. 66

Music and German Literature

Their Relationship since the Middle Ages

edited by

James M. McGlathery

CAMDEN HOUSE

Copyright © 1992 by
CAMDEN HOUSE, INC.

Published by Camden House, Inc.
Drawer 2025
Columbia, SC 29202 USA

Set in Garamond type and printed on acid-free paper.
Binding materials are chosen for strength and
durability.

ISBN: 1-879751-03-8

Library of Congress Cataloging-in-Publication Data

Music and German literature : their relationship since the Middle Ages
/ edited by James M. McGlathery.
        p. cm. -- (Studies in German literature, linguistics, and
culture ; vol. 66)
        Essays presented at a meeting held Apr. 6-9, 1989 at the
University of Illinois at Urbana-Champaign.
        Includes bibliographical references and index.
        ISBN 1-879751-03-8 :
        1. Music--Germany--History and criticism--Congresses. 2. Music
and literature--Congress. I. McGlathery, James M., 1936- .
II. Series: Studies in German literature, linguistics, and culture ;
v. 66.
ML275.M93 1992
780'.083--dc20   91-27933
                                                  CIP
                                                  MN

Contents

Illustrations

Preface

NOWHERE IN EUROPE DID the ties between music and literature become more intimate and important than in the German-speaking countries. This volume is the first collection of essays in English surveying music and German literature from the Middle Ages to this century; indeed no volume with that coverage exists in German, or any other language.

The meeting from which the volume arose was the first scholarly conference ever to survey music's relationship to German literature over the entire period of their interaction. To our knowledge, this symposium, held 6-9 April 1989 at the University of Illinois at Urbana-Champaign, was also the first to bring together in relatively large and equal numbers scholars studying music and literature both in this country and overseas. Eight of the nineteen contributors to this volume teach at universities abroad, one each in Australia, Austria, England, and The Netherlands, the remainder in Germany.

The volume's aim is to offer a broad picture of the current state of scholarly research and critical thought on the connection between German literature and music. The speakers at the meeting were asked to address their remarks to the general educated public, not to other scholars alone. The same principle has been observed in collecting the essays. It is hoped that the book will prove interesting and informative to a wide English-speaking audience.

Concern was taken to include as many of the currently prominent scholars writing on music and German literature as possible, and particularly to improve English-speakers' acquaintance with research being done by scholars writing in German. To this end, my editorial assistant Ellen Gerdeman-Klein and I have translated the essays by Göbel, Riethmüller, Salmen, Hubach, and Dümling. In addition, all German quotations have been translated, the shorter ones generally in the text, longer ones in the notes. The Introduction was written by the editor of this volume.

I would like to take this opportunity to thank the Max Kade Foundation, Inc.; the Goethe Institute, Chicago; the Consulate General of the Federal Republic of Germany, Chicago; the Austrian Institute; and the Kurt Weill Foundation, New York, for their financial support of the symposium. Gratitude is due also to the Deutsche Forschungsgemeinschaft for additional help in making attendance by scholars from Germany possible. Important funding for the symposium came also from the Chancellor of the University of Illinois at Urbana-Champaign, the College of Liberal Arts and Sciences, the School of Music, and from the Department of Germanic Languages and

Literatures, sponsor of the meeting. Invitations to the scholars represented in this volume came at the suggestion of the members of the organizing committee comprised of Professor Alexander Ringer of the School of Music, Professor Edwin Jahiel of the Unit for Cinema Studies, and the following colleagues in the Department of Germanic Languages and Literatures: Professors H. G. Haile, Marianne E. Kalinke, Herbert Knust, Ruth E. Lorbe, Karl-Heinz Schoeps, Mara R. Wade, and Rochelle Wright. Funding to make possible the volume's publication was given by the Max Kade Foundation; the Goethe Institute, Chicago; the Consulate General of the Federal Republic of Germany; and the Chancellor, the College of Liberal Arts and Sciences, and the Department of Germanic Languages and Literatures of the University of Illinois at Urbana-Champaign. Support for the editing of the volume was received from the University's Research Board. A huge debt of gratitude is owed to Kyia Miller for her patience in seeing to so many details that helped make the symposium successful, as well as to the other members of the department's office staff who assisted her: Mary Ann Hill, Antje Kolodziej, and Sarita Pankau.

James M. McGlathery

Introduction

THE RELATIONSHIP BETWEEN MUSIC and literature is emerging as one of the prominently discussed and debated subjects among literary scholars and musicologists. This volume brings together the scholarly fields of musicology and Germanistics to survey the entire history of interaction between music and German literature. Among the areas of research discussed, and which beg to be explored further, are the study of opera libretti, the history of poetry set to music, metaphorical references to music in the work of German authors since the Middle Ages, and literary authors' contributions to the formulation of our view of music in the modern period.

Much of the scholarly work on music and literature being produced today has resulted from the post-structuralist and deconstructive emphasis on the materiality of language and concerns the structural semantic affinities between the arts. This line of theoretical investigation is largely ignored in this volume. The emphasis lies instead in the area of practical criticism, especially the relationship of music and German literature in concrete cultural and historical contexts.

The contribution of the German-speaking countries to the classical music of Europe has of course been dominant, indeed overwhelming. A fascinating and intriguing question for historians of Western culture is why this should have been so. The answer cannot be found in the history of German music itself, in isolation from the specific cultural environment in which it flourished. The special nature of German culture, in turn, is best reflected in its language and literature. German composers, moreover, have tended to select products of their own linguistic and literary culture for setting to music. Conversely, in German literature more than any other, music has represented a poetic theme of major and profound significance in the works of many of its best authors.

Investigation of the early history of German literature's relationship to music is hampered by a dearth of surviving musical notation. With this difficulty fully in mind, Ronald Taylor discusses, in the first of this volume's essays, the issue of whether the poem or the music — *wort* or *wîse* — was of foremost importance in the art of the medieval minnesinger, the German troubadours. Was the poem written to fit the music, or the music to fit the poem? To what extent can the relative importance of music and the text be determined for the individual minnesinger, and what was the general practice?

The connection between music and literature in the German Middle Ages is approached differently by Hubert Heinen in his essay, but in a way that bears directly on Taylor's question. Heinen addresses the issue of the scarcity of evidence about the musical knowledge possessed by medieval

German poets. To shed light on this, he discusses examples of the use of musical terminology by these poets, and examines the probable and possible explanations for the infrequent occurrence of such terms.

The problem of explicit, uncontested evidence about the mutual interaction between music and literature remains, but is less acute, in the early modern period. In her essay, Dianne McMullen focuses on an intriguing example of such interplay, the texted galliard, a dance form that required the composer to take into consideration not only the demands of music and dance, but also the rhythms and accents of words, and the length of poetic lines. Her discussion especially concerns the relationship between these texted galliards, which in Germany appear to have enjoyed only a short life of some thirty years — from 1593 to 1622 — and the emergence of dactylic meter in German poetry that occurred in the ensuing decades.

The problem of a dearth of surviving musical texts is particularly great for the early history of German opera. Noting that except for Lieder or arias the hundreds of extant seventeenth-century German language libretti are usually the only record of performances of drama set to music at the dozens of middle and north German courts, Judith Aikin offers suggestions about what can be learned from the relatively few surviving scores, including those for the Italian operas that served as models.

With Gary Thomas's essay on the emergence and brief flowering of the so-called Baroque song in Germany from 1630 to 1660, attention shifts to the social, cultural, and ideological implications of the mixing of music and literature. Using as his example the *Aelbianische Musen-Lust* (1657) of Constantin Christian Dedekind, Thomas views this development, which may be seen to anticipate the modern Lied, in the context of the specific historical circumstances in which it arose, usually against the backdrop of the Thirty Years' War.

The cultural background of Bach's music, specifically the degree to which his compositions were determined by language, is the subject of the study by Hans Joachim Kreutzer. Here questions are addressed such as: Which types of literature did Bach find most attractive? Was he guided by personal taste or opinion? Was he free to choose the texts he set to music? Did he perhaps write some of the texts himself?

Concern with the wider historical context continues in the essay by Gloria Flaherty on theater life in Leipzig in the first half of the succeeding, eighteenth century. To supply a broad picture of this cultural activity, she discusses a variety of sources, including theater manuals, theoretical writings, memoirs, letters, and the texts of contemporary plays themselves.

The Lied as a social activity in the later eighteenth century is the subject then of Margaret Mahony Stoljar's essay. She sees the keyboard song of the 1770s and 1780s, significantly called the "Gesellschaftslied," or society song, as reflecting changing social and cultural realities in those two decades, which came to be called — with reference to German literature — the period of Storm and Stress (*Sturm und Drang*).

The philosophical side of German authors' increasing interest in music and its relation to literature is the subject of John Neubauer's essay. After reexamining the question whether Goethe was more attracted by, and oriented toward, visual as opposed to audial phenomena, Neubauer investigates the importance for Goethe of the distinction between musical sound produced by organic bodies and that by inorganic bodies, that is, between song and instrumental music.

Linguistic considerations are taken up by Helmut Göbel in asking about the language that E. T. A. Hoffmann used in writing about music. What are the stylistic characteristics that Hoffmann employed in trying to convey to his readers a sense of the achievement of the various pieces about which he wrote music reviews, including of course the famous one on Beethoven's Fifth Symphony? Above all, where did he get the sort of language he used in passages that interpret the music? To what traditions did this style of writing belong, and did Hoffmann adapt them to new purposes?

Opera's relation to the cultural history of nineteenth-century Germany, as exemplified by the development of German Romantic opera, is investigated by Ulrich Weisstein. In showing how Heinrich Marschner's opera *Hans Heiling* (1833) forms a bridge between Carl Maria von Weber's *Freischütz* (1821) and Wagner's Romantic operas of the 1840s — *Der fliegende Holländer, Tannhäuser,* and *Lohengrin* — Weisstein focuses particular attention on the type of the melancholic, Hamletian hero as reflecting contemporary artistic taste.

The nineteenth century not only marked the zenith of opera's popularity, it was also the grand period of the glorification of composers and virtuoso performers. It was the age of Wagner and Verdi, Chopin and Liszt. This worship of the artist as cultural hero gave impetus to the genre of the poem about music, the subject of Albrecht Riethmüller's essay. His example is a poem by the Hungarian-born author Nikolaus Lenau, "The Bust of Beethoven" ("Beethovens Büste"). Riethmüller discusses whether Lenau was able to capture with words the spirit and effect of the music, and thus contribute to the understanding of Beethoven's genius.

At the turn of the century, developments in literature, music, and dance may be seen to have manifested a cultural philosophy of the physical and sensual, and of freedom and individualism. Walter Salmen, in making this argument, points to Nietzsche's cult of the "super human being," the "Übermensch," as a source for this ideal, an influence he finds exemplified by Richard Strauss's symphonic poem *Also sprach Zarathustra* (Thus Spake Zarathustra, 1896). In particular, Salmen views the popularity of new forms of dancing at the turn of the century as related to the cultural ideal of a ritualistic joy of living, and includes a number of illustrations for examination from this perspective.

The problematic relationship of authors and composers to their audiences in the first decades of this century, especially the compounding of this difficulty when a combination of music and literature was involved, is suggested by Donald Daviau's analysis of the correspondence between Richard Strauss and Hugo von Hofmannsthal about creating the now definitive second version of their opera *Ariadne auf Naxos* (1916). As Daviau shows, the letters shed light on Hofmannsthal's theory of comedy, and on the divergent views and concerns of the author and composer.

The question of how opera appeals to the audience is the subject, too, of Sybille Hubach's essay. With the Strauss-Hofmannsthal collaboration again as the example, she addresses the issues of opera's undeniable appeal to the senses and the primacy of the music over the text. Her particular concern is whether, in *Der Rosenkavalier*, the author and composer have provided a deeper level of realism or higher level of transcendence than might appear on the surface, and whether the opera thus satisfies the later call by Walter Felsenstein — at the founding of the Komisches Theater in East Berlin — for a realistic musical theater, which he considered to be one that provided a genuinely human theatrical experience.

Another aspect of the difficult and complex relationship between music and literature in the twentieth century is investigated by George Schoolfield. In this essay, the case discussed is that of Rainer Maria Rilke, whose poetry may be said to be characterized by a peculiar musicality, or primal sound, that would seem not unrelated to developments in music at the time. Schoolfield analyzes Rilke's statements about his relation to music, and his pronouncements on that art, and concludes by considering the proposition that the special qualities of sound in Rilke's poetry might not have arisen had he possessed a formal background in, and knowledge of, music.

In view of the great social and political, as well as cultural, upheavals brought by the first decades of this century, Marc Weiner considers — for the period before, during, and after World War I — the connection between revolutionary developments in music and widespread sentiment for a new social and cultural order. He examines music as a motif in German fiction from 1900 to 1930 and finds it unobtrusively referring to social issues and as implying a desire for change in the status quo — a desire that emerged again in perverted form in Nazism.

The role of music as an instrument for social and political change is the subject, too, of Albrecht Dümling's essay. In view of Bertolt Brecht's well-known antipathy toward the hypnotic power of late Romantic music, Dümling considers the question of what positive value Brecht found in singing and other vocal arts, and what he saw as the importance of acoustical effect for achieving his socially and politically oriented aesthetic aims.

Steven Scher's essay, finally, returns to the dichotomy between vocal and instrumental music as having been omnipresent in aesthetic theorizing since the Enlightenment. He asks particularly whether theoretical and practical criticism will yet succeed in balancing the literary and the musical aspects of opera and other vocal music, and whether it will succeed in focusing on the tension between text and music as an important force for creativity.

We are reminded by Scher's essay of the question of the relative importance of the music and the text that Ronald Taylor raised in the opening essay, on the medieval minnesinger. Were we to pose this question with regard to vocal music as produced and enjoyed — or "consumed" — in the present day, we would be hard pressed to find our examples in the type of music that has come to be known as "classical." This is not to say, of course, that texted music of this type is no longer being produced. The age of the Lied and of opera as genres with wide appeal, however, is no more. Neither the text nor the music of present creative works in the classical, or "serious," tradition holds the same broad cultural importance as in the past. Music and poetry, to be sure, are not dead. But as objects of enthusiasm and veneration they survive rather in popular songs and musicals. These popular genres will become the objects of investigation for scholars studying the relation between music and literature in our present culture. It is therefore not surprising that in the progression of the essays offered here, the last chronologically deals with an author, Brecht, whose career was largely framed by the two World Wars.

Classical music of the past, though, has perhaps enjoyed a renaissance of sorts, and has of course never lacked for enthusiasts. Moreover, the links between classical music and literary classics were a dominant force in European culture in the period of its global ascendancy, from the sixteenth into the present century. During most of that time, from the eighteenth to the twentieth centuries, composers from the German-speaking countries — from Bach and Handel to Wagner and Richard Strauss — generally dominated the musical world. This was a period, too, in which the same was true of German authors, from Lessing and Goethe to Thomas Mann, Kafka, and Brecht. The essays presented here do not answer, or even directly address, the issue of why this should have been so, and what connection there was between German prominence in each of these arts in that period. These studies, rather, investigate various aspects of the relation between music and German literature, and in this sense offer a start toward examination of this question of central importance for an understanding of European cultural history.

The Middle Ages

The Medieval Poet-Musician: *Wort unde Wîse*

RONALD J. TAYLOR

ONE OF THE ADVANTAGES enjoyed by anybody who sets out to present a practical aspect of the secular music of the Middle Ages is the shortage of sound, uncontested evidence. Scholars who address subjects drawn from more recent centuries will usually be able to start from printed documentary sources, corrected and refined, to which they can make constant reference in order to motivate their case. Entrepreneurs of the medieval music industry are much less inhibited by the presence of unassailable data. Sometimes we feel almost as fortunate as those inspired natural scientists who say: "Never let the facts stand in the way of your theories."

Before considering some of these facts and theories, it would be appropriate, I think, to consider for a moment the aesthetic of the situation. The human object of our concern is the medieval lyric poet-musician, the Minnesinger. He composed and sang songs — usually, we assume, his own. Others, such as professional minstrels, may also have sung them. A song is a composite art-form, *wort unde wîse* — music added to poetry, though it may be the other way round, and in the Middle Ages sometimes was.

It is, however, almost inevitable, here as in any other situation where different media are drawn into a single artistic purpose, that the one or the other will assume ascendancy at any given moment. Put bluntly, a particular Minnesinger may compose highly accomplished melodies while achieving no great subtlety of poetic expression — or, *vice versa*, he may exhibit originality of poetic thought and imagination but only be capable of composing perfunctory and undistinguished tunes. The constituent elements of his art are generally unequal partners. To quote the most obvious modern parallel from the field of opera — the field *par excellence* of words-plus-music — the works of Richard Wagner are sustained by the glory and richness of their musical substance, while beneath the music lie libretti which often have the character of literary disaster areas. My point is merely that in some of the songs of the Minnesinger — or, for that matter, the Troubadours and Trouvères, their counterparts in Provence and France — the artist's concern appears to have lain chiefly in the subject-matter of his poem, whilst in others it is in the melody that his strength seems to lie. And that there is nothing to be surprised about in this.

Coming now to the nitty-gritty of the subject, I think that the first observation one must make is that whereas our stock of the poetry of Minnesang is both considerable and representative, right through from the early twelfth century to the end of the age of chivalry and courtly love, our knowledge of the corresponding music is not.[1] Of the twenty poets whose work is anthologized in *Minnesangs Frühling* only one is known to us by his music.[2] For the greatest lyric poet of the German Middle Ages, Walther von der Vogelweide, we have only two complete and three fragmentary melodies which are certainly authentic,[3] as against over one hundred poems without music. Indeed, for the age of 'high' Minnesang as a whole, the age of the greatest achievements in medieval German literature, our documentary musical evidence is woefully weak. Alongside the important Liederhandschriften of poems alone, like the Weingartner and Manessische Handschriften, there is only one comparable manuscript which also records melodies, and this — the Jenaer Liederhandschrift[4] — unfortunately contains a preponderance of highly unexciting verses by Middle and Low German *Spruchdichter* who are unknown to us from any other source. Only with the generation of Walther's younger contemporaries, men like Neidhart von Reuenthal, Tannhäuser, and Reinmar von Zweter, do we begin to acquire a reasonably comprehensive picture of the art of a particular period.

This paucity of transmission brings two consequences in its train, one considerably more interesting than the other. The less interesting, though frustrating enough for scholars, is that, with a handful of exceptions,[5] we have only one recorded source of each of the melodies known. We are thus all but denied the opportunity to produce a critical edition of a melody through the comparison of different versions, in a manner analogous to the editing of literary texts. The only checks one has on the accuracy of a particular melody as recorded are through the detection of scribal inconsistencies or incorrect musical syntax. And it has to be admitted that the ubiquitous subjective judgment plays an uncomfortably prominent part in this exercise. Attitudes become entrenched, and remain so, because there is little new argument to dislodge them. I am reminded of the nineteenth-century British socialist Robert Owen, of whom it was said that he never thought differently about a book for having read it.

More interesting than this — because it leads directly to the sociology of Minnesang and to the heart of the medieval poet-musician's artistic activity — is the question of how one should explain this fact that the overwhelming

---

[1] Ronald J. Taylor, *Die Melodien der weltlichen Lieder des Mittelalters: Darstellungsband* (Stuttgart: Metzler, 1964), pp. 23ff.

[2] I.e. Spervogel, cf. Ronald J. Taylor, *The Art of the Minnesinger* (Cardiff: Univ. of Wales Press, 1968), 1:88; 2:127.

[3] Cf. Taylor, *The Art of the Minnesinger*, 1:95–97; 2:142–47.

[4] Georg Holz, Franz Saran, and Eduard Bernoulli, eds., *Die Jenaer Liederhandschrift*, 2 vols. (Leipzig: Hirschfeld, 1901). Also *Die Jenaer Liederhandschrift: In Abbildung*, ed. Helmut Tervooren and Ulrich Müller (Göppingen: Kümmerle, 1972).

[5] E.g. Konrad von Würzburg, cf. Taylor, *The Art of the Minnesinger*, 1:36–37, and Heinrich von Ofterdingen, ibid., pp. 25–27.

majority of Minnesang manuscripts contain no melodies. Not all manuscripts, of course, have the same stature. There are large, sumptuously
illuminated and bound volumes commissioned by wealthy patrons, probably
for preservation in libraries, where expense has been no object; there are
also humbler codices, which give the impression of having been practical
song-books, used by resident or itinerant musicians. But in our present
context this distinction is not material. Nor, needless to say, is the distinction between *Minnelied* and *Spruch*, which was for some time understood
to signify that the former was sung, the latter spoken. For is not '*Spruch*,' it
was argued, cognate with '*sprechen*'? But etymology, unfortunately, does not
help us. We probably possess more melodies to *Sprüche* than to *Minne-
lieder*, but this again is an unhelpful piece of information, since in musical
terms — I shall return to this a little later — there is nothing to distinguish
the ones from the others.

So how do we confront this discrepancy between the transmission of the
Minnesinger's poems and the transmission of his melodies? And what can
our tentative explanations tell us about his art as a whole?

There are, I think, two possible interpretations. And since both lead right
to the theoretical and practical heart of the phenomenon of Minnesang, we
are in the rare and fortunate position of being able to concede that, to this
extent, it does not matter whether our interpretation is right or wrong.

One explanation for the missing melodies would take the situation at its
face value. The argument would run like this. Let us take the largest and
most splendid manuscript of medieval German lyric poetry, the so-called
Manessische Handschrift, compiled in Zurich in the first half of the
fourteenth century. It contains some seven thousand strophes by 140
different Minnesinger but not a single melody, nor was there any intention
that it should. So, we might argue, the music was not important — anyway
no longer important by the time the manuscript was compiled. Yes, there
had been melodies but the patron who commissioned the manuscript, and
perhaps also the society to which he belonged, had no interest in recording
them. He certainly could have afforded to, when one considers how much
money he has lavished on the costly parchment, the gold leaf for the
illuminations and the leather binding, not to mention labor costs. Maybe the
melodies were no longer widely known, and no competent music scribe
could be found — for copying music was a separate and rarer skill than
copying words, and the conventions of job demarcation applied. The
conclusion of this line of reasoning is that, at least in certain courts, recited
lyric had superseded, or existed alongside, sung lyric. Not to mince matters,
the music was subsidiary and dispensable. A *wîse* may come and a *wîse* may
go, but the *wort* goes on forever.

The other line of argument over the relative absence of melodies
proceeds not so much from the bare recorded facts as from what these facts
conceal — the unrecorded facts which lurk between the lines. Here our
approach would run parallel to that which one employs when reading

medieval ecclesiastical chronicles. Stern, grim-faced accounts, for example, of what ought not to be going on in monasteries constitute the strongest evidence for the conclusion that such things really are going on. The transmission of secular music in the Middle Ages depended on an oral, rather than a written tradition. A melody, especially of the simple A + A + B form so common in the medieval courtly lyric, could be more easily held in the memory than a series of often highly diversified strophes sung to that melody. And as we know, a particular musico-strophic form, a *Ton*, as it was called, could be used and re-used whenever its inventor found it suited to his needs. We even encounter the phenomenon of the medieval plagiarist, the *Tönediep* — the less-gifted Minnesinger (or he may have been just lazy) who liked the sound of his colleagues' tunes and filched them for his own purposes. Moreover, the cultivation of this music was furthered, and often, no doubt, decisively influenced, by wandering minstrels who *needed* no written record, and probably also brought elements of improvisation to their performances. Musical notation, after all, is only a mnemonic.

On this reading of the situation, the melodies of these songs were not written down because it was not necessary. They came to be recorded only when the oral tradition was flagging or on the point of dying out. The patron of the Jenaer Liederhandschrift, for example, sensing that this was happening, would have commissioned text-scribes and music-scribes to make a collection of songs for posterity — not so much, one suspects, to the greater glory of God as for the anticipated boost to his cultural reputation. The parallel to this argument is the story of the folk-song, collected at the last moment — by Cecil Sharp in England and the Appalachians and by Béla Bartók in Hungary and elsewhere — when the oral tradition is threatened with extinction under the pressure of urban industrial civilization.

One other little human point may be worth mentioning. The ability to read and write was a rare skill in the Middle Ages. Text-scribes were in considerable demand for the Church, to copy the Scriptures and commentaries thereon, sermons, Books of Hours, theological texts from the Church fathers, and so on. For them to be diverted to copy out the texts of profane songs is already to make them serve a minority interest — for Minnesang was composed by and for a cultural elite. But even more difficult to find were music-scribes. We have a number of manuscripts where a stave has been ruled at the head of a poem ready to receive the corresponding melody but has been left empty[6] — presumably because none of the music scribes employed on the manuscript knew the tune in question or did not have the source of it in front of him. A situation like this demonstrates again that although a melody may not have survived with the text of the poem to which it belonged, there originally *was* such a melody, and its non-survival is only due to an unhappy quirk of fate.

---

[6] There are many such cases in the Berlin ms. *c* of Neidhart von Reuenthal, cf. Taylor, *The Art of the Minnesinger*, 2:289.

What, then, are we to make of the music that these manuscript sources, however incomplete, have bequeathed to us, and how did the Minnesinger balance the poetic and the musical aspects of his art? Music is sound, and to try to describe sound in words is a futile exercise. Unfortunately, in an essay we cannot listen to any transcription of Minnesinger songs. But as a parallel to the dualism of our poet-musician, and in order to give some semblance of form to these remarks, I would like to put before you what seems to me a relevant and revealing musical circumstance which we can ponder without the absence of actual musical sound depriving me of all credibility. Moreover, it is a circumstance which, like some of the others we have already mentioned, lays open the whole cultural scene within which the professional Minnesinger lived his life and plied his trade.

Through the monodic music of the Middle Ages runs a demarcation line which is not only of intrinsic musical importance but also has a fundamental cultural implication. It is a line that divides the ecclesiastical from the secular. On the one side of the line belong melodies which are derived from one or other of the so-called Church or ecclesiastical modes or scales — Dorian, Phrygian, and so on — as known to us from Gregorian chant and from twelfth- and thirteenth-century polyphonic works religious in inspiration and purpose. On the other side of the line lies the 'modern' major tonality, the basic building block on which the whole tradition of Western art-music rests.[7]

For a long while it was believed that this major mode emerged in the age of the Renaissance through a gradual coalescence of certain of the ecclesiastical modes. But from investigations into medieval music, and from the history in particular of the pentatonic scale, it has for some time been clear, though perhaps not adequately appreciated, that this 'modern' major mode is the fountain-head of a secular tradition which runs parallel to the ecclesiastical tradition for almost as long as we are able to trace the course of music-making in Europe.

The significance of this dichotomy reaches far beyond the musical field, for the social and intellectual standing of the Minnesinger left them peculiarly exposed to the divided tradition. Indeed, it is an exposure that started right at the top of the social ladder. We have songs written by King Richard I of England — in French, of course, for he knew no English — and there are Middle High German love lyrics attributed to the Emperor Henry VI, son of Barbarossa — though these latter unfortunately have no melodies. The professional middle-class Minnesinger — men like Heinrich von Morungen, Reinmar, Walther von der Vogelweide, Neidhart von Reuenthal, and a host of others — are assumed to have enjoyed a measure of formal education at monastery or cathedral schools, where they could not but have come into contact with the music that accompanied the liturgical offices, the

---

[7] The far-reaching implications of this dichotomy are discussed in Taylor, *Die Melodien der weltlichen Lieder des Mittelalters: Darstellungsband*, pp. 48ff.

living music of Gregorian chant. So it would be surprising if some of the characteristics of this music had not rubbed off on men, albeit of secular interests and callings, who came within its ambience.

Another area in which a link between the Church and the education of the Minnesinger is apparent, is that of the learned vocabulary of medieval German literature. Gottfried von Strassburg, for example, praises Walther von der Vogelweide's singing by exclaiming: "Wie spaehe s'organieret!" (How skillfully he performs!)[8] He is using here a word derived from *organum*, the term used to denote the early attempts at part-writing that appear in Church music between the ninth and the twelfth century. Not only does this show Gottfried's conversance with technical musical vocabulary — which does not surprise us — but it is also a valuable indication of the way in which Walther could actually have performed his songs, namely with some form of melodic-cum-harmonic accompaniment, perhaps played on a stringed instrument such as a fiddle.[9]

I am sorely tempted at this point to slip into a discussion of the performance and interpretation of the songs of the Minnesinger. This would take me far beyond my brief on this occasion, but I would like to make just one observation which is, I think, not totally irrelevant to our concerns. We cannot realistically ever expect to know what a performance by Walther von der Vogelweide or any other Minnesinger sounded like. And even if we solved tomorrow the outstanding technical questions of transcription and so on, and could reproduce, acoustically, a twelfth-century manner of performing a song by Walther, we could never know what reactions that song aroused in a twelfth-century audience. Whatever historical knowledge we bring to bear on the music of the past, we can only hear it with the ears of the present. And although our aesthetic response may be none the less sincere and true, informed by discrimination of scholarship and subtlety of perception and taste, it would be idle to pretend that it were other than a twentieth-century response, conditioned by the total historical continuum of our musical consciousness.

But I must return from this digression to the subject that I left, namely the dichotomy of the ecclesiastical and the secular in Minnesang music, and move from the Church-influenced side of the line, the area of the melodic Church modes, to the other side. This is the rival world of the major mode — the modern major scale on which we were all brought up, with the related pentatonic idiom, the associations of which are as markedly secular as those of the Church modes are ecclesiastical.

---

[8] *Tristan*, l. 4803.

[9] On performance see Taylor, *Die Melodien* ..., pp. 59ff. Illustrations of medieval musical instruments can be found in Taylor, *Die Melodien der weltlichen Lieder des Mittelalters: Melodienband* (Stuttgart: Metzler, 1964), pp. 61ff.

But — and this is one of the most interesting aspects of the question — it is not as exclusively the province of popular and non-learned musicians as are the Church modes of those who had studied in the monastery schools. The secular tradition is open to all, learned and unlearned alike. Walther, for example, even on the scant evidence we have, can be seen to have drawn on both traditions, according, apparently, to what was best suited to his immediate purpose. His so-called *Palästinalied*, a song of pilgrimage,[10] is cast in the Dorian mode and contains a number of melodic gestures unmistakably drawn from Gregorian chant. For the political songs in his *Zweiter Philippston*,[11] on the other hand, he has written a melody in the key of F-major, with a pentatonic flavor. Nor can we leave the matter here. One of the in-dwelling characteristics of Gregorian chant is its purely melodic ethos. Plainchant melodies are not composed according to latent harmonic principles, and the same is true of secular melodies that derive from the world of plainchant. With tunes in the major mode the situation is quite the reverse. This major mode, with the harmonic framework latent in it, is the basis of the music of the Western world. And although there are isolated examples of it before the twelfth century, it is in the secular corpus of Troubadour, Trouvère, and Minnesinger music that we find the first substantial group of melodies in a major key.

We may carry the implications of this still further. Performance on musical instruments — the fiddle and plucked stringed instruments, wind instruments such as flute and shawm, the hurdy-gurdy and so on — was the particular province of secular musicians. By the laws of acoustics, when a note is struck or blown, that note contains within itself the degrees of the so-called harmonic series, which emerge in an order that gives us, first the octave and the basic fifth, the dominant, then the major triad, then, one by one, the notes of the major scale. This means that an implicit harmony is embedded in the sounds produced by instruments, which gives us another way of viewing the causal chain that links the major key, harmony, and the secular European tradition. Considerations such as these convey the historical importance that attaches to these Minnesinger songs and reveal the historical continuity that confronts us when we deal with them.

Since the early nineteenth century, when scholarship first made generally available the treasures of medieval literature, we have been able to identify with some certainty the poetic personalities of individual Minnesinger. But as far as our present knowledge goes, nowhere — or practically nowhere — do we encounter a unique musical personality, a Minnesinger or *Spruchdichter* whose melodies are unmistakably his, and his alone. To quote a specific example. We have a total of 68 melodies, found in five different

---

[10] Transcribed in Taylor, *The Art of the Minnesinger*, 1:95–96.

[11] Transcribed in Taylor, ibid., pp. 96–97.

manuscripts, ascribed to Neidhart von Reuenthal.[12] Of these sixty-eight, only seventeen belong to poems which are accepted as authentic; the remaining fifty-one poems are relegated to the limbo of "unecht." It does not necessarily follow that these fifty-one melodies are all equally "unecht" but we have hardly any inner-musical criteria, as I said earlier, for distinguishing originals from imitations. We are certainly not entitled simply to attribute the more interesting to Neidhart, then consign the remainder to the trash can labelled "Pseudo-Neidhart." For the commissioners of the manuscripts, and for the audiences who listened to the songs, there was nothing at stake and nothing to argue about. There may conceivably have been a "Neidhart-type" song which contemporary circles recognized as such, though it is virtually impossible for *us* to do so. But further than this we cannot go. It is as though a kind of mass musical anonymity had settled over the whole enterprise, as in the uniformity generated by Gregorian chant, and as, in a sense, the entire religious Middle Ages represented. It was not the subjective personality that occupied the foreground but the substance of the artist's art, and the public — not to mention the God — whose interests he was serving.

And so I draw to a close. My title contained a dualism, and I may have oscillated to and fro between the two poles of that dualism in an overly free and irresponsible way. *Wort unde wîse*, ecclesiastical versus secular, manuscripts with and without melodies, uncertainties of transcription — what do we know, what do we not know, and what shall we never know?

As I said at the beginning, there is much in this subject that cannot but remain speculative. Dualisms must be accepted for what they are. A song is in itself a problematical, heterogeneous creature, with the music climbing on to the back of the words, so to speak, which were quite content before the music arrived. "Erlkönig" and "Gretchen am Spinnrade" do not *need* Schubert. A beautiful melody may rescue a mediocre poem from oblivion but it cannot affect its poetic mediocrity; nor can a beautiful poem be made less beautiful by the supervention of a poor melody. A poem is judged by the criteria of literature, a song, by the criteria of music.

Perhaps the melodies of the Minnesinger represent a social convention rather than the art-form of song as we understand it today. Maybe for the Middle Ages the words *were* more important than the music. The last word on this subject has, I am sure, not yet been spoken. It will certainly not be mine.

---

[12] The authentic Neidhart songs are transcribed in A. T. Hatto and Ronald J. Taylor, *The Songs of Neidhart von Reuenthal* (Manchester: 1958); the inauthentic songs in Taylor, *The Art of the Minnesinger*, 1:120ff.

Making Music as a Theme in German Song of the Twelfth and Thirteenth Centuries

HUBERT HEINEN

WHEN RONALD J. TAYLOR discussed the "musical knowledge of the MHG poet" some thirty-five years ago, he sketched the parameters of an intriguing literary problem.[1] He pointed out that terms referring to music occur infrequently in the songs, and that when they do they rarely betray any sophistication. Though a few passages demonstrate a knowledge of medieval musical theory and school learning, more of the sparse mentions reflect the performance of music. When I decided to investigate musical terminology as a point of access to medieval German song, I was aware of the paucity of evidence Taylor had remarked; indeed, my subsequent perusal of many thousands of strophes from the song manuscripts up to and including the Manesse and Jena anthologies (from the first part of the fourteenth century) revealed only a few dozen pertinent references.[2] I excluded, to be sure, the numerous descriptions of bird song that comprise a part of the *locus amœnus* so ubiquitous in later minnesong. On occasion, bird song and human song do coalesce. As Walther von der Vogelweide remarks,

> sît diu vogellîn also schône
> singent in ir besten dône,
> tuon wir ouch alsô. (HMiM 51, 13 C II 6–8)[3]

(Since the birds sing so beautifully in their best melody, let's do likewise.)

---

[1] "The Musical Knowledge of the MHG Poet," *Modern Language Review* 49 (1954): 331–38. A useful introduction to music and minnesong is given in James V. McMahon, *The Music of Early Minnesang* (Columbia, South Carolina: Camden House, 1990), which appeared after the completion of this study.

[2] A number of the strophes I found are contained, as I subsequently noticed, in *Mittelalter: Texte und Zeugnisse*, ed. Helmut de Boor (Munich: Beck, 1965), (especially) I, 670–709 (where I must have first encountered many of them). I have consciously excluded evidence solely contained in later manuscripts, such as the rich Colmar song codex, since so much of it seems to reflect a different attitude toward the art and practice of music (as many scholars have observed). For the sake of consistency, I have also disregarded the evidence in the late Neidhart manuscript c, although it probably represents a special case.

[3] Abbreviations and the editions they refer to are given in the appendix. For an excellent example of the lavish description of bird song, see KLD 59 Leich III 1–13.

Even clearer is Rubin's assertion (which may contain an allusion to Walther's words):

> ir vogel, singent iuwern sanc: sô singe ich mite
> in einem süezen dône. daz was ie mîn site. (KLD 47 I 2, 5)[4]

(You birds, sing your song: then I'll sing along in a sweet melody. That was always my custom.)

I also excluded the innumerable passing assertions that a singer/persona was singing or had sung a song, unless these made explicit that singing entailed more than conveying a message.[5]

In surveying the evidence, I wanted to test several working hypotheses. The scarcity of school terms, which Taylor explains as a lack of knowledge by the poets, can also be found in the songs of those who were well familiar with other areas of the seven liberal arts; it would seem far more likely (I thought) that the singers hesitated to try their lay audience's patience with arcana lacking secular prestige. Most of the themes prevalent, especially in the didactic songs, do utilize a technical terminology with a greater appeal, e.g., many areas of theology, centering on but not restricted to the adoration of Mary, Biblical lore, liturgy and prayer, the bestiary and other areas of natural history traditionally explained theologically (including astronomy); more secular spheres such as public virtues, politics, law, feudal rights, war, geography, heraldry, clothes and jewelry, the chase, court life, courtly and chivalric literature, greeting and taking leave, drinking, dancing, the generalized nature (increasingly more specified) of the *locus amœnus*, the seasons, and even agriculture and manufacture.[6] However, the choice of these themes in preference to musical ones does not always mean that a singer was tailoring his subject matter to his audience's interests, since the

---

[4] See also, for example, SKvW 16, 4, 10; BSM XI 2, 5–7.

[5] The ubiquitous reference to the poet/performer's singing a song (which is then almost invariably characterized in terms of its content) is sometimes associated with music more directly, as in Der Helleviur 1, 1–2; Meister Rumelant IX, 1; Herman Damen IV 1, 1 and V 1, 1–2 (all in HMS III, pp. 33, 67, 164, and 167, resp.); the beginning strophe of the Wartburgkrieg (HMS II p. 1); Bruder Eberhart von Sax: BSM XXVII 1, 1–3; Der von Sachsendorf: KLD 51 VI 1, 1–3; Meister Sigeher: BS 11, 1 and BS 14, 1–2. For a full discussion of singing a new song, see Heinrich Peter Brodt, *Meister Sigeher* (= BS), 76–85. Many dawn songs begin with the watchman singing a song, but the focus is on his message; Heinrich von Frauenberg's dawn song deviates from this tradition slightly by having the watchman sing sweetly and loud (BSM XIII 1, 2). Singing is frequently simply used as a synonym for wooing, cf. Peter Frenzel, "Minne-Sang: The Conjunction of Singing and Loving in German Courtly Song," *German Quarterly* 55 (1982): 336–48.

[6] For a clear presentation of the didactic lyric, see Olive Sayce, *The Medieval German Lyric 1150–1300* (Oxford: Clarendon, 1982), pp. 408–41.

themes are often treated in such an obscure manner that the poet was clearly trying to impress rather than ingratiate himself or inform. Thus my first hypothesis was not supported by the evidence. Be that as it may, although the singer/performer repeatedly stresses that he is singing, musical terminology is accorded little attention, despite the introspective nature of much medieval German song, where what the poet/persona does, knows, and/or feels is foregrounded far beyond what we might surmise would be attractive to an audience of patrons or potential patrons.

I had other hypotheses for why the mechanics of making music, an area more accessible to a unevenly educated audience, failed as well to generate any great number of more specific descriptions as songs got more laden with detail in the course of the thirteenth century. With some of the didactic poets, especially Reinmar von Zweter, whose extensive corpus lacks any hint of a concern with music making, melody clearly has a subordinate role; the message is, in fact, the message. This hypothesis is, I feel, supported by the evidence. My other hypotheses also hold true primarily for the didactic poets. For those singers more innovative and, as far as we can determine, more musically oriented, to stress the production of music would have been to call attention to their partaking in an activity commonly associated with minstrels, professional entertainers whose place in society was precarious at best, as Walter Salmen and Antonie Schreier-Hornung point out (though, as both stress, it is as difficult for us to distinguish between a socially acceptable poet/performer and an outcast, though popular, musician as it must have been in the Middle Ages).[7] Kurt Franz describes in general the fear the didactic poets had of being confused with wandering minstrels, though he may make too absolute a distinction between the two; Burghart Wachinger, while pursuing other goals, gives a more balanced characterization of the social status of the didactic poets.[8] I also hypothesized that the poets' desire to appear learned generally caused them to slight a portrayal of the *usus* 'practice' so scorned by the theoreticians of the *artes* 'areas of

---

[7] Salmen, *Der fahrende Musiker im europäischen Mittelalter* (Kassel: Bärenreiter, 1960), reworked as: *Der Spielmann im Mittelalter,* Innsbrucker Beiträge zur Musikwissenschaft, no. 8 (Innsbruck: Helbling, 1983); Schreier-Hornung, *Spielleute, Fahrende, Aussenseiter. Künstler der mittelalterlichen Welt,* Göppinger Arbeiten zur Germanistik, no. 328 (Göppingen: Kümmerle, 1981). See also Franz Bäuml, "'Guot umb êre nemen' and Minstrel Ethics," *Journal of English and Germanic Philology* 59 (1960): 173–89.

[8] Franz, *Studien zur Soziologie des Spruchdichters in Deutschland im späten 13. Jahrhundert,* Göppinger Arbeiten zur Germanistik, no. 111 (Göppingen: Kümmerle, 1974); Wachinger, *Sängerkrieg* (= WS). Der Meißner's ranking of song above instrumental music in the praise of God (OM X 1) may be merely topical, but it does seem to echo a concern with status.

learning.'[9] Although I do not wish to abandon these latter three hypotheses (nor the first for the less overtly learned singers), they are, I fear, neither terribly original nor appropriate to much of the evidence. The thrust of my observations had best be descriptive and explicative rather than programmatic. I might also mention that a study of terms is made more difficult by the tendency of earlier editors to excise or insert them in creating their critical texts; the critical editions of Neidhart, one of the most prolific users of musical terminology, contaminate and rewrite to the point that scholars can be and have been misled, and the Lachmann/Kraus edition of Walther is not much better.[10] Even more recent editions of the thirteenth-century poets can sometimes only be used if one takes care to repair the damage done by the editor.[11]

As I surveyed the evidence, I realized that the thematization of making music is more important than the specific musical terms used.[12] Many of the more explicit mentions of making music stem not from the didactic poets, but from the Southern German minnesingers from Walther on. (The distinction Konrad Burdach made about Walther's broad talents being split between the didactic poets of the North and the minnesingers of the South, though overly general, can help to orient a discussion of the thematization of making music as well.) Rarely do we find songs that exemplify both *ars* and *usus*; the clearest example of such a song begs the question, since it is neither German nor characteristic of any genre we can find in German song of the thirteenth century, but it can serve as a roughly contemporary illustration from the *Carmina Burana* (and elsewhere) of what might have been: two strophes from a lengthy lyrical narrative on the commonplace topic of whether clerics or knights make the best lovers, here a description of Phyllis' and Flora's arrival at Amor's paradise (VCB 92, 61–62).

---

[9] As Konrad Burdach noted in "Über die musikalische Bildung der deutschen Dichter, insbesondere der Minnesänger, im dreizehnten Jahrhundert," in *Reinmar der Alte und Walther von der Vogelweide*, 2nd ed. (Halle: Niemeyer, 1928), pp. 174–94.

[10] BN is preferable to H/W N, in that it includes more texts (and also contains a wealth of information attractively presented), but it is not designed as a critical edition; Beyschlag accepts most of the H/W N emendations and presupposes the use of the H/W N apparatus.

[11] I have compared the texts in the editions cited with the manuscripts, using the standard facsimiles and diplomatic editions (cf. Günther Schweikle, *Minnesang*, Sammlung Metzler, no. 244 [Stuttgart: Metzler, 1989], pp. 1–15).

[12] The restriction to the thirteenth (and early fourteenth) century was made because virtually none of the songs clearly from the twelfth century makes more than the most general reference to music. (Hartwig von Rute's M/T MF III 1, 12 and Morungen's M/T MF XXIII 1, 1–2, 6 — possibly also Wolfram's M/T MF VI 4, 5–6 — would be the exceptions.) For a survey of music and musical performance in minnesong, see Schweikle, *Minnesang*, pp. 34–59.

Quicquid potest hominum   comprehendi mente,
totum ibi uirgines   audiunt repente,
uocum differentię   sunt illic inuentę,
sonat dyatesseron,   sonat dyapente.

(Whatever human intellect can comprehend, all that claims the ear of the girls; one hears the creation of polyphonic pieces, the fourth and the fifth sound out.)

Sonat uoces auium   modulatione pia
et buxum multiplici   dantum edit uia,
et Amoris stu<dio   plaudunt harmonia
tympanum, psalterium,   lyra, symphonia.[>]

(The voices of the birds ring out in a charming melody, the beechwood recorder emits its song from various holes, and drum, psaltery, lyre, and organistrum [hurdy-gurdy] resound, full of zeal for Amor, in harmony.)

In these strophes we have terms both from the quadrivium and from a highly sophisticated practice: "vocum differentię … inuentę" and "dyatesseron" as well as "dyapente" on the one hand, and on the other a description of flute playing unmatched in its precision in all but one German song, as well as (in a portion of the poem no longer present in the *Carmina Burana*) a less striking list of musical instruments.[13] The other nine songs of this collection for which a rapid survey revealed similar mentions of making music have far more innocuous ones, and all in all the theme seems almost as rare here as it is in the German songs (in at least one case, as a matter of fact, the impetus for the theme may have come from the German tradition).[14]

In comparison to the richness of the isolated passage, however, one of the closest equivalents among the German singers to the melding of theory and practice, a passing mention of the third art of the quadrivium by the Kanzler, is almost embarrassing in its spareness.

diu dritte menschen stimme kêret
ze sange ûf abe nu mitte nu oben nu unden;   (KLD 28 XVI 10, 13–14)

(The third turns the human voice to song: up, down, now in the middle, now above, now below.)

[13] For some comments on this poem, see Jutta Goheen, *Mittelalterliche Liebeslyrik von Neidhart von Reuental bis zu Oswald von Wolkenstein*, Philologische Studien und Quellen, no. 110 (Berlin: Schmidt, 1984), pp. 26–28.

[14] VCB 76, 2, 3; 121, 1, 1–2; 123, 1, 1–2; 163, 10, 1–4; 165, 3, 1–5; 168, 1, 4–6; 185, 6, 3–4 (macaronic: German and Latin); 216, 1, 3–4; 217, 1, 3–4 and 2, 3–8.

Here, at least, the art is related to creating a melodic line; normally the *ars musica*, if it is mentioned at all, serves only to demonstrate the singer's erudition. To be sure, Regenbogen is more expansive. However, though he stresses (in HMS II p. 309; I 4, 1–6) how the sixth art can direct performance, his overall depiction of the *artes* is that they provide a basis for proper behavior (for which he should not be accused of ignorance, since his moralization of the arts does not prove that he has failed to understand them, but merely that they only serve him as a pretext). The much-discussed reference to solmization in Meister Rumelant's attack on the Marner:

IV,6 3   Du has die museken an der hant, die sillaban an dem vinger
gemezzen, des versma die leien niht zuo sere! (WS p. 164)

(You have measured the musical notes on your hand, the syllables on your finger; therefore do not scorn the laity too much.)

has as its primary intent (one often misunderstood, I feel) the poet's implication that he is just as aware of the techniques of the schools as the Marner, who flaunts his erudition by writing in Latin as well as in German. The Marner himself certainly pays little notice to musical matters; in fact, in the only passage where he explicitly thematizes performance, he remarks that most of his audience wants to hear heroic epics (which were probably sung, albeit to a simple melody, and thus could well form part of the repertoire of a trained musician) and *König Rother*, a tale in rhymed couplets that most scholars consider to have been spoken, only occasionally desiring "hübschen minnesanc" (*courtly minnesong*) and continues "sus gât mîn sanc in manges ôre, als der mit blîge in marmel bort" (SM XV 14, 271, 279) *(thus my song goes into many a person's ear as when someone bores into marble with lead)*. Whether the public's obtuseness in failing to appreciate the singer's gifts are due to its tin ear or to his lack of musical talent cannot be discerned (although the image would suggest the latter); the Marner probably, despite his choice of image, assumes the former.

Vegeviur (= Purgatory, Flame of Pugatory: clearly a minstrel's pseudonym), in ostensible praise of the Meißner and oblique defense of the Marner, demands that the former "gebe den pfaffen ir dœne wider und singe, swaz er welle" (WS p. 159 II, 4, 7) *(give the clerics back their tunes and sing whatever he wishes)*. One interpretation of what he means is that he is demanding that the Meißner use melodies in traditional keys rather than strictly observing the church modes (most, though not all, of the Meißner's melodies are, in fact, transmitted in ecclesiastic modes).[15] The

---

[15] See Ronald J. Taylor, *The Art of the Minnesinger* (Cardiff: Univ. of Wales Press, 1968), II, 69–92. For a cautionary statement on the whole matter of distinguishing between church modes and major (or minor) keys, see Peter Frenzel, "Melody and Genre in German Courtly Singing in the Thirteenth Century," in *Genres in Medieval*

passage might also imply that the Marner, who was apparently a cleric, followed the latter course; he would then be one of the "pfaffen." However, the late, flawed, but apparently not completely spurious transmission utilized major keys — which may, of course, have been introduced as "modernizations"(see Taylor, *Art*, II, 63–69). Of course, the passage may not refer to music at all, since *dœne* can be strophic forms as well as melodies. In addition, Vegeviur himself uses the church modes exclusively: "quod licet Jovi non licet bovi?" (see Taylor, *Art*, II, 23–25, 34–35). In any case, Vegeviur also takes care to differentiate his art of song from that of the artless, who "âne kunst für manigen herren schallen" (HMS III p. 36; II[=I], 4, 7) *(make raucous noise before many lords without artistry)*, a topic joined in by others as well. For example, Der Unverzagte (= The Fearless One), who praises the proper treatment of "gernde liute" (HMS III p. 46; III 8) *(those desiring pay, e.g., minstrels)* does so (if we can take the order of strophes as a reflection of authorial intent) immediately after advising "die künste-losen edelen" *(nobles without learning or artistry)* who reward artless performers that their proper reward is beer (at the time, the least palatable beverage available and one reserved for the lower classes) and warning them that being praised by beer-swilling good-for-nothings does not spread their reputation very far (7). Obviously, for him at least, there were those singers and musicians who knew their trade and those who did not.[16]

In two sets of two strophes, Konrad von Würzburg defends the skillful singers against the less skilled ones (without, apparently, equating skill with learning), giving as an example of the latter the Meißner, whose "splendid talents" are appropriate only for the fairgrounds, where the common people await a recitation of the exploits of Ecke (SKvW 32, 166–95, 286–315), as Wachinger has observed (*Sängerkrieg*, 162–63). Each strophe develops a separate topic (it is by no means certain that they can be paired as I suggest), and I should like to focus only on one: the exemplum of the dog and the ass (166–80). When the courtly dog barked sweetly, he was rewarded, whereupon the ass brayed out in hope of similar treatment, only to be punished; in his commentary, Konrad regrets that many a nobleman, far from taking heed of the tale of the dog and the ass, rewards the artless rascal while failing to reward the "gefüegem" — i.e., the courtly and artful — man for his skill.[17] Der wilde Alexander draws on bits of tradition and biblical lore to explain mythopoetically how it has come to pass that writing

---

German Literature, ed. Hubert Heinen and Ingeborg Henderson, Göppinger Arbeiten zur Germanistik (Göppingen: Kümmerle, 1986), pp. 30–46.

[16] For a brief discussion of this topic, see Wachinger, *Sängerkrieg*, 117–18. Konrad does not use the church modes, though Taylor sees some influence of them (echoes would not be remarkable, even for an unlearned musician), *Art*, II, 138–41.

[17] For a discussion of *gefüege* in its relationship to courtly skills, especially to those of musicianship, see my "Propriety and Courtly Skills in *Tristan*," *Tristania* (forthcoming).

and singing songs and playing musical instruments, once the art of kings, has become the occupation of "ein arme diet"; when he continues that those scandalized by this degradation can alleviate it either by taking up the art themselves or by rewarding those who have done so, he is doubtless hoping his auditors will choose the latter course (KLD 1 II 12–13).

Musical erudition and/or the production of music fairly often appear in religious songs or in connection with religious topics (e.g., KLD 63 III 2; OM X 1; OM XV 4); thus Der wilde Alexander, in seeking to enhance the reputation of making music, refers to King David and to Salome (KLD 1 II 13). In his "Marienlied" Meister Sigeher personifies the "schuole" *(school)* by which he probably means the *artes*, having them, in the form of "musicâ," and the "canticâ," which are presented as a separate entity, praise Mary. When he continues that the psaltery, bells, and the organ also do so, it is not clear whether these instruments are examples of "musicâ" or yet other types of music. In any case, shortly thereafter "seitenklanc" *(the sound of strings)* and "himelsanc" *(heavenly song)* become epithets for Mary herself (BS 11–16, 27a, 29a).

Frauenlob's work can be considered the culmination of the tradition of didactic poets (certainly he regarded himself as the exemplary learned singer, as his strophe SF V 115 makes clear), and in it one can find an occasional reference not only to music as an erudite art but to making music as a sublime entertainment (e.g., SF V 122). In a poem that bears ample evidence of the poet/singer's learning and skill, the *ars musica* is briefly characterized and related to the lover's wooing of his sweetheart (the speaker) through the medium of music (SF I 18, 1–8). Two things set this passage apart: 1) the poem in question is Frauenlob's masterful "Marien-leich," and 2) the lover and his sweetheart are Christ and Mary.[18] The *leich* 'non-strophic song with intricate repetitions of sections,' which was probably a musical form more than it was a poetic one, not infrequently contains references to making music.[19] Both Frauenlob's and Rudolf von Rotenburg's (earlier) "Marienleich" (cf. KLD 49 Leich VI 62a, 64, 66–71) thematize music, the latter giving a detailed list of instruments (most of which are — though clearly viewed positively — not beautiful enough to express proper praise of Mary). Nevertheless, a mention of making music is more characteristic of a special type of *leich*, the one wholly or partially devoted to depicting the dance. For when we turn from the didactic poets

---

[18] Instructive insights into the poem are presented in Christoph März, *Frauenlobs Marienleich: Untersuchungen zur spätmittelalterlichen Monodie*, Erlanger Studien, no. 69 (Erlangen: Palm & Enke, 1987).

[19] For a general discussion of the *leich*, see Sayce, *Medieval German Lyric*, pp. 346–407. Otto von Botenlauben's "Minneleich" closes with a mention of making music, though the "seitenspil" we find there is a dubious editorial insertion (KLD 41 XI 118–19).

to the minnesingers it becomes clear that by far the most references to performing and hearing music are from dance songs.

The first reference to singing and dancing in German song is also perhaps the first clear passage transmitted in which humans are shown making music in minnesong. In the first strophe of a three-strophe song, Heinrich von Morungen situates the object of his love at a dance on the heath (M/T MF XXIII 1). From the heath the encounters are transferred to the lady's chamber and then to the battlements, and the relationship becomes ever more intense. This first example of what one might call the courtly song and dance is also the most accomplished, a situation so commonplace in the history of literature as to be less than surprising. Nevertheless, other mentions of dancing and music making in a courtly setting, such as those by Walther von der Vogelweide, Ulrich von Winterstetten, Der von Sachsendorf, and Hadlaub, are not without interest.

The strophe by Walther in the first Philipp's tune (*Ton*) deals with matters far removed from the usual pastoral setting of dances, and indeed Walther is merely using terminology from a dance song to make a sociopolitical comment (L/K WvdV 19, 37–20, 3). (It is by no means rare to have poets making oblique allusions to genres for which there are few contemporary examples.)

32   dô gieng ich slîchent als ein pfâwe swar ich gie,
        daz houbet hanht ich nider unz ûf mîniu knie:
        nû riht ich ez ûf nâch vollem werde.
37   wol ûf, swer tanzen welle nâch der gîgen!
20, 1 mir ist mîner swære buoz:
        êrste wil ich eben setzen mînen fuoz
        und wider in ein hôhgemüete sîgen.

(Then I went slinking like a peacock wherever I went; my head I hung down all the way to my knee. Now I'll pick it up in full dignity. Arise, whoever wishes to dance to the fiddle. I have recompense for my tribulation: first I will place my foot evenly and against that droop in high spirits.)

Walther's depiction of his peacock-like humility, reflected in his dipping his head, does not signal his use of a traditionally skewed emblem. As Stephen L. Wailes has made clear, Walther is not referring to traditions in his depiction of the crane and the peacock at all, but rather is making an observation from nature. As he says, "in this poem the peacock serves Walther to express both humility *and* pride," since the persona both hangs his head and raises it proudly.[20] What Wailes fails to observe is that the depiction of the crane and the peacock is part and parcel of a consistent ironic use of an image of the dance.[21] The editors since Lachmann have "corrected" the final word of the strophe, "sîgen" *(droop)*, inserting "stîgen" *(rise)* in its place. That fits 19, 34 and creates an easily understood sense, but the emendation destroys an intentional oxymoron. Walther, upon remarking in 19, 29 how his proud obsequiousness has earned him service and a warming hearth, comments that now he can bear himself haughtily. However, as the oxymoronic "sîgen," i.e., 'droop' clearly suggests, dancing to the fiddle (and singing for the dance) will not necessarily insure one's acceptance at court with its attendant high spirits; what is raised high will fall. But just as Walther's initial humility is suspect, his final dashed hopes will not remain depressed; by paralleling the gestures of this strophe to those of a dance such as the one described by Ulrich von Winterstetten (KLD 59, Leich III 115–18), Walther has created a perfect parallel to the maneuvering courtiers must engage in to prevail at court — elsewhere he remarks that "swie si [the people at court] sint, so wil ich sîn, / daz si niht verdrieze mîn" (HMiM 47,36 C' II' 9–10) *(as they are, thus I wish to be, so that they do not disdain me)* although this strophe (the crucial one for all the editors since Lachmann) may be an scribal accretion from a version of this song by Reinmar.[22] Far from giving a deeply felt report of his personal fate, something that would be of no interest to his audience, he presents a model of *urbanitas* 'courtly decorum,' a quality without which the court would collapse.[23] The conclusion of this strophe is carried forward in the strophe that follows this one in manuscript B, with its mention of a deafening cacophony at the court of Hermann von Türingen perhaps only partially attributable to heavy traffic: "Der in den ôren siech von ungesühte sî" (20,

---

[20] "The Crane, the Peacock, and the Reading of Walther von der Vogelweide 19, 29," *Modern Language Notes* 88 (1973): 947–55, here 952. Two recent essays on this song do not add anything essential to my discussion: Ursula Liebertz-Grün, "Rhetorische Tradition und künstlerische Individualität: Neue Einblicke in L. 19, 29 und L. 17, 11," and Walter Röll, "'Den phawen ofte hat überstigen des kraneches vluc': Zu L. 19, 29ff.," in *Walther von der Vogelweide: Beiträge zu Leben und Werk*, ed. Hans-Dieter Mück (Stuttgart: Stöffler & Schütz, 1989), pp. 281–97 (here 281–88) and pp. 379–90.

[21] For dancing terminology in general (she does not treat this strophe), see Ann Harding, *An Investigation into the Use and Meaning of Medieval German Dancing Terms*, Göppinger Arbeiten zur Germanistik, no. 93 (Göppingen: Kümmerle, 1973).

[22] Winterstetten's dance is a peasant one, but the language of Leich III 115–18 would seem to be intended to reflect courtly practice, probably setting off the pretensions of the parvenu peasants in the manner of Neidhart.

[23] See C. Stephen Jaeger, *The Origins of Courtliness: Civilizing Trends and the Formation of Courtly Ideals 939–1210* (Philadelphia: Univ. of Pennsylvania Press, 1985). The texts in B and C of 18, 29 through 19, 28 seem to represent two independent transmissions of one of the songs; the two strophes 19, 29 through 20, 15 are only in B, and fit together with each other better than with the other three.

4) *(He whose ears suffer from a severe malady)*. This may be the second, or a part of the second, of two songs Walther wrote in this tune, although all five politicodidactic strophes in the tune seem fairly autonomous.

Ulrich von Winterstetten, whose references to making music fall even more thickly than those of his frequent model, Neidhart, does not restrict himself to the Neidhart tradition (for that matter, neither does Neidhart, completely). In a pastoral song that lacks the sardonic bite of this tradition he enlivens the commonplaces of suing in vain for the love of an obdurate lady who turns a deaf ear to his entreaties by utilizing an evocation of the dance and of musical entertainment as a negative foil: all these delights fail to rescue him from his slough of despond (KLD 59 Lied XXIV 1, 5-8 and 2, 5-8). By chance, his sinking low spirits echo, without the oxymoronic irony, Walther's sinking high ones. In a manner reminiscent of Morungen, though without his richness, von Sachsendorf recounts how he met his love dancing.[24] From the encounter on, however, his experience is the typical one that Winterstetten also recounts: she does not return his love. His explicit discussion of singing does not derive directly from the dance, but from a self-conscious effort to thematize the intricacy of his song; it is not clear whether the mention of difficulties is intended for comic effect, with his reach clearly exceeding his grasp, or as an ironic humility formula to call attention to his virtuosity.[25] In either case, a mention of singing serves to introduce each of the strophes, though in strophes 2 and 3 the singing is content oriented, as are most such references (KLD 51 VI 1, 1–5, 2, 1–2, and 3, 1–2). Hadlaub, finally, whose inventiveness and originality in the revitalization of hackneyed clichés is remarkable, as Wolfgang Adam has demonstrated capably, is also able to follow the custom of making the pallor paler, of vitiating the energies inherent in the dance song tradition to make the resultant song more like a restrained courtly one (BSM XXVII 29, 17–20).[26] It is certainly possible that it was Hadlaub's creative energies that ebbed, but he is too consummate a connoisseur of the traditions to make that very likely.

Not all singing about singing refers to the dance, of course, as a passage from Meister Heinrich von Teschler can remind us (BSM VIII 6, 29–33), though in this example the emphasis is, as so often, more on the content than on the musicality of the singing. Even Neidhart, the master of the dance song, occasionally presents his persona for a strophe or two in the typical

---

[24] The most celebrated encounter at a dance, of course, is Walther's 74, 20, but it does not entail making music as well as dancing.

[25] Wizlaw von Rügen has a comparable song, where the mention of the difficulty seems fairly clearly to be thinly veiled self praise (T/S WvR II).

[26] *Die >Wandelunge<: Studien zum Jahreszeitentopos in der mittelhochdeutschen Dichtung*, Beihefte zum Euphorion, no. 15 (Heidelberg: Winter, 1979).

guise of the unrequited suitor, as in his "Dise trüeben tage" (BN 34 I and II).[27] Here we have the common image of the lady who turns a deaf ear to the singer's entreaties; we are in the same world as that of Sachsendorf and (the somewhat atypical example from) Winterstetten, without there even being a reference to dance. But the Neidhart singer does not stop with the second strophe, by the third the peasants come bursting in, and before long we find singing and dancing, posturing and brawling.[28] Elsewhere, in a similarly constructed Neidhart song, we hear the complaint that

> Diu wil mit beiden ôren niht gehœren, swaz ich singe.
>   kunde ich sanfte rûnen, daz vernæme sî mir gar. (BN 40 II 1–2)

(She does not wish to hear with both ears [either ear] any of what I sing. If I knew how to whisper softly of love she would gladly listen to me.)

The topic of the singer versus the whisperer of sweet nothings is a fascinating one, but it has little to do with this study.[29] In yet another song, we have a harsh revocation of the stance of the courtly lover, but one which does not completely leave the courtly ambiance; the singer/persona is heaping calumny on his wanton former love, remarking at the end of the second strophe

> do ichs alrest erkande, dô was sî sô tugentrîche
> daz ich ir mîniu liedelîn ze dienste gerne sanc. (BN 55 II 11–12)

(When I first became acquainted with her she was so full of virtue [accomplishments] that I gladly sang my little strophes to serve her.)

---

[27] My entire study is, of course, a sketch, but this holds especially true for my remarks about Neidhart, Tannhäuser, and Winterstetten; if I had incorporated the rich literature on songs in the style of Neidhart, the study would have profited, but I could not have kept within the space restraints set out for it. My comments, therefore, are to be understood as preliminary and decidedly incomplete.

[28] In BN 52 II 1–4, the topic of the lady turning a deaf ear is melded with that of the peasant rival. In KLD 59 Leich IV 93–96 we have a 'courtly' treatment of the topic in what more and more becomes a depiction of a peasant dance scene.

[29] See, for example, BN 46 VI (which also, in isolation, only betrays in its last line that it is not a courtly song — in all these cases, the nature of the melody may have belied the apparent courtliness of the subject matter). Winterstetten's fifth *leich* is, as far as the content is concerned, a pure love lament in the courtly tradition (for a "musical" reference to singing, see KLD 59 Leich 47–49). See also L/K WvdV 63, 26–27. In a study that appeared after the completion of my remarks, Eva Willms presents a provocative sketch of the likely performance situation of minnesongs that would add an investigation of the theme of singing versus whispering: *Liebesleid und Sangeslust: Untersuchungen zur deutschen Liebeslyrik des späten 12. und frühen 13. Jahrhunderts* (Munich: Artemis, 1990), pp. 35–46.

The most vigorous and prolific use of song in and for dancing can also be seen, of course, in Neidhart's songs. His dances are stylized as peasant dances, but they clearly often mirror courtly ones, as can be seen from the regrettably excessive consequences of dancing in a courtly manner on a brash young peasant, who, because he is dancing "im werde" *(with dignity)* became "üppic" *(haughty)* and "hôchgemuot" *(high-spirited)* (BN 44 IV 6–10); the latter quality is negative by association with the first, and because the person in question is not, on the surface, a courtier — though Neidhart may be clothing his courtiers in peasant garb. A very similar description of the dance and its effects (cast in dactyls) can be found in a song by Burkhart von Hohenfels that has been characterized, somewhat against the evidence of its context, as preeminently courtly, a characterization Ann Harding, in an excellent brief discussion of the passage, rejects categorically *(Dancing Terms*, 51–52). Nevertheless, though Burkhart von Hohenfels explicitly sets his dance indoors, as Neidhart does the dances in his Winter songs, and gives it bucolic overtones, it clearly echoes courtly dances and courtly values, as well. He creates an apposite expression to the coalescence of opposing ideals that underlies, for example, Walther's strophe 19, 29 when he depicts a dance both stately and tense (just as appearances at court are marked both by *anschouwen* 'respectful contemplation' and *dringen* 'ostentatiously jostling for position'); when the pipes grow silent, their place can be taken by song, and the dance, with its abrupt movements, can continue (KLD 6 I 2).[30]

When Neidhart has his persona state:

> In kan allen liuten nû ze tanze niht gesingen
> als wîlent dô der guote wille mich ze sange jagt. (BN 53, IVa 1–2)

(I now cannot sing for the dance for all the people as formerly when good will drove me to song.)

he is referring to a convention of the dance (albeit negatively) that goes beyond his song, the singer accompanying the dance (the convention probably lies behind Walther's 19, 29, as well).[31] Another convention is

---

[30] For a discussion of the overreaching theme of oppositions, see Peter Frenzel, "Contrary Forces and Patterns of Antagonism in Minnesang," in *Court and Poet*, ed. Glyn S. Burgess et al., ARCA, 5 (Liverpool: Cairns, 1981), pp. 141–54. See also the brief but meaty comments on this song in Hugo Kuhn, *Minnesangs Wende*, Hermaea, 1 (Tübingen: Niemeyer, 1952), pp. 35–36.

[31] See also, for example, VCB 168, 1, 4–6; BN 34 IV, 10; BSM XXIV 3, 30; SKvW 2, 135–36; ST XI 1, 5; KLD 58 XLVI 1, 1–6; KLD 59 Leich IV 165–66. See also Siegfried Beyschlag's comments, *Die Lieder Neidharts* (= BN), pp. 533–34. Walther's (or a defender of Walther's) L/K WvdV 18, 1 may have a reference to this custom — obliterated by unconscionable editing — in lines 2–3 according to C, though there are other possible explanations: see Edith Herrmann and Horst Wenzel, "'Her Wicman

that the dancers, especially the girls, sing to the dance, either separately or in chorus, as in von Stamhein's

> dar nâch huop sich des meien ein vil michel tanz.
> den sanc in Bêle vor und manig ir gespil. (KLD 55 I 11, 6–7)[32]

(Afterwards arose during May a great dance. Belle and many of her playmates sang it before them.)

It is part of the genre, apparently, for the singer/persona to invite all the dancers to join in the song — perhaps primarily at the choruses, which need not all have been transmitted, since they were doubtless often like the one in Duke Johann von Brabant's song:

> diu eine sanc für, diu ander sanc nâ:
> harba lori fâ, harba harba lori fâ, harba lori fâ.
> (HMS I p. 15; II 1, 7–8)[33]

(One of the girls sang before, the other sang afterwards: harba lori fa [etc.].)

As it happens, this song is a pastourelle, not explicitly a dance song; not all instances of girls' (or men's) singing relate to their accompanying a dance.[34]

Some invitations for others to sing one's song or songs imply that it was a common practice, either because one employed a *joglar* to perform one's songs, or because one expected others to learn one's songs and sing them themselves.[35] The first situation is thematized, in a burlesque manner, by

---

ist der êre / Her Volcnant habt irs ere': Zu Walther von der Vogelweide (L 18, 1)," *Euphorion* 65 (1971): 1–20.

[32] This song is also transmitted under Neidhart's name in c. Other mentions of a girl or girls (and men) singing for the dance include BN 34 IV 10; BN 61 II 6–7; BN 87 I 9–10 (with manuscript B); KLD 59 Leich IV 161–64.

[33] On the European tradition of such refrains, see Olive Sayce, "Carmina Burana 180 and the *mandaliet* Refrain," *Oxford German Studies* 2 (1967): 1–12. Invitations to sing along include KLD 58 XLVI 1, 1–6; KLD 59 Leich III 95–98, 111; Leich IV 177, 185, 193; ST III 114–17; BSM XXVII 24, 9–10.

[34] Other mentions of girls' (or other men's) singing, where it is not clear that a dance is involved, include BN 40 II 11; BN 41 II 6; KLD 55 1, 5–10; 9, 7–10; 10, 1–7; KLD 59 Lied IV 1, 9–11 (Winterstetten's 'non-courtly' song as, literally, a *Gassenhauer* 'popular song sung by the lower classes'), 5, 1–8; BSM XI 2, 5–7; BSM XXVII 52, 115–17.

[35] See, for a discussion of Meister Rumelant's "singerlin," Wachinger, *Sängerkrieg*, pp. 179–81. Rubin's comment that he wishes another luck with his song (i.e., the one being sung) represents another aspect of this topic (KLD 47 XXI 2, 5–6); see also

the Taler, who creates a comic situation out of a difficulty in finding a *joglar* (BSM IV 3,1, 4–6, 8–11). The second situation is thematized in a song by Rudolf von Rotenburg that he took over virtually intact from an earlier one (transmitted in several versions) by Walther (HMiM pp. 254–55). Interestingly enough, the messenger is supposed to deliver a copy of the song to the lady's hands (as is commonly suggested); only if no proper messenger can be found should a thousand voices sing the song to the lady. Franz Viktor Spechtler is doubtless correct when he characterizes such messenger scenes as a stylization of the distance between the suitor and his lady.[36] We certainly cannot draw definite conclusions about performance practice from them. On the other hand, such fictions would probably not have been created if it never occurred that songs were sung, and in some cases were meant to be sung, by others.

Another fiction, in a "Schwanklied" by Neidhart, presents us with the only "realistic" depiction of a singer as a performer we have from the thirteenth century. In this strophe, of course, the thirst the singer feels has erotic overtones, as does its quenching, so even here appearances can deceive (BN 82 IV). Another such strophe, by Winterstetten, has an old woman disparaging the singer's art for being too popular with the wrong people and insufficiently courtly (KLD 59 Lied IV 1). Yet another strophe, variously attributed to Walther and to Meister Rumelant, which Lachmann included only by incipit among the "unechte Lieder" of Walther's, gives us the only realistic description from this period of making instrumental music, in this case a description even more thorough than that in the *Carmina Burana* of what transpires when one plays a whistle, although the realism is in the service of an allegorization — a series of strophes relate various crafts and (related) natural phenomena to a religious meaning, here to the crucified Christ's saying he thirsted and its significance (HMS I p. 267; 2, 1–12).

Just as in Winterstetten's pastoral song, where the "tamber" *(drum)* and the "gîge" *(fiddle)*, as well as "harpfen" *(harps)* and "rotten" *(psalteries)* are mentioned (KLD 59 Lied XXIV 1, 7–8), the dance song since Neidhart has commonly contained references to musical instruments and their employment. Whenever Neidhart mentions instruments or playing instruments to make a characterization, he portrays the musicians using them as unskilled; they are his oafish peasant figures.[37] Tannhäuser, on the other hand,

---

Liechtenstein's KLD 58 XLVI 1, 1,6.

[36] "Die Stilisierung der Distanz: Zur Rolle des Boten bis Walther und bei Ulrich von Liechtenstein," in *Peripherie und Zentrum*, ed. Gerlinde Weiss and Klaus Zelewitz (Salzburg: Bergland, 1971), pp. 178–96.

[37] See BN 25 II 6–10; 27 III 5–6; 46 IV 1–3; 61 II 1–2, 5–7; 81 II 9–10; III 1–3; 87 I 9–11 (singing and dancing according to manuscript B), II 4, VI 1–3 (in C, this song is attributed to Göli).

depicts playing musical instruments in a positive manner; both he and Winterstetten apparently decided that an appropriate ending to a dance leich was to have the fiddler break a string.[38] Rather than characterizing these passages further, I should like to discuss briefly two strophes from a song that only I, apparently, think has a description of playing a musical instrument, Walther's "Owê hovelîchez singen" (HMiM 64, 31 C).[39]

The "ungefüege dœne" *(clumsy [boorish] tunes [sounds])* of the first strophe, although they could be songs, are just as likely to be ungainly, awkward noises that imperil the status of courtly song, making it loathsome even in the eyes of God. The worthiness of courtly song suffers from the influx of boorishness. None of this seems to make much sense if we assume, as most scholars have over the years and many still do, that the uncouth sounds are in fact the songs of Neidhart. To be sure, one could say that Dame Boorishness has won out if Neidhart's bucolic songs displace courtly ones, but this notion, though it could be deduced from the first three lines, does not fit the fourth, the final line of the *Aufgesang*, nor the first three of the *Abgesang*. The next strophe is neutral in this respect, since it merely expresses the wish that someone would restore worthiness. The third strophe, however, clearly refers to uncouth practitioners of song (as does the fourth), not to one singer whose themes are uncouth. My suggestion, based on the *Abgesang*, the last four lines, of the third strophe, is that Walther here is attacking the use of the *organistrum* or *symphonia*, the *Drehleier* or hurdy-gurdy, to accompany courtly songs. With its rosined wheel turning like a millwheel to cause a melody string and one or more drones to sound, with its cumbersome stopping with the use of keys or screws, and with its harsh tonality, it fits the description closely; the drones would ensure, if the mechanical stops did not, that the wheel had "so mange unwîse" *(so many discordant melodies)*. To be sure, the final line of this strophe utilizes a proverb that one cannot harp to the mill, because one's music will not be heard. And it is true that Neidhart uses the same proverb, though in a totally different sense and context (BN 52 II 1–4). But by citing the proverb, Walther is simply reiterating the previously made point that proper music has been debased by uncouth noises. When I wrote on this topic some two decades ago, I posited that the main thrust of the song was Walther's rejection of an innovation in accompaniment, though he might have intended some political undertone as well. I would suggest now that his attack on the hurdy-gurdy was merely a pretext, i.e., the ostensible object of his ire, and that the song has an overt political message now disguised to us (or to me, at least). Since the hurdy-gurdy in Walther's time was primarily

---

[38] See ST I 91–92; III 112–17, 126–29; IV 119–22, 141–44; V 116–27 (all *leichs*). KLD 59 Leich II 121–26, Leich IV 193–94.

[39] "Walther's 'Owe hovelichez singen': A Re-examination," in *Saga og språk*, ed. John Weinstock (Austin: Pemberton, 1972), pp. 273–86.

used in churches, its choice as an emblem of boorishness may relate to the one or the other struggle Walther's patrons had with the Papal factions of the Church, struggles we can see abundantly reflected in Walther's political songs. Be that as it may, the accusation of boorishness would not in and of itself necessarily signal that Neidhart's peasants had entered the field, since Walther was always quick to impugn the courtliness of his opponents and assert his own.[40]

In conclusion I can reiterate, in a summary informed by the observations made in this sketch, a revision of my initial hypotheses as theses. The singers, whatever their status (which ranged from the relatively exalted one of Ulrich von Winterstetten to the doubtless marginal one of Vegeviur), were surely responding to the lack of musical sophistication among their audiences when they refrained, in general, from all too arcane musical terminology; where it did appear, it was in a learned context in which erudition was the point of the song. It was never a popular topic. For many of the singers, melody was merely a medium for a message, and the message was what they focused on, even in their introspective songs. A concern with status can be seen in many of the singers, and some probably avoided explicit references to their making music for fear that confusion with outcast entertainers could arise, though obviously Winterstetten, who had nothing to fear, did not. Nor did Neidhart or Tannhäuser, although their status was surely less secure. Walther, here as elsewhere, is a special case. Precisely those singers who delighted in displaying their knowledge of the *artes* also found it attractive to depict *usus*, so my final hypothesis does not hold up. In the dance leichs and songs, and to a lesser extent in pastoral sketches, making music is a central theme, one that deserves more thorough study.

Editions Cited

BN = Siegfried Beyschlag, ed. *Die Lieder Neidharts: Der Textbestand der Pergament-Handschriften und die Melodien.* Darmstadt: Wissenschaftliche Buchgesellschaft, 1975.

BS = Heinrich Peter Brodt. *Meister Sigeher.* Germanistische Abhandlungen, no. 42. Breslau: Marcus, 1908.

BSM = Karl Bartsch. *Die Schweizer Minnesänger.* Frauenfeld: 1886. Rpt. Frauenfeld: Huber, 1964. Note the exemplary revision of this edition by Max Schiendorfer: *Die Schweizer Minnesänger.* Tübingen: Niemeyer, 1990, which appeared after the completion of my study.

HMS = Friedrich Heinrich von der Hagen. *Minnesinger.* 4 vols. Leipzig: Barth, 1838.

---

[40] Walther has a more overt reference to making music in a political song (with two strophes = 284 and 285 C, transposed in L/K WvdV 80, 27 and 80, 35), also with a reference to courtly status (specifically 80, 32–34, the conclusion of the song).

HMiM = Hubert Heinen, ed. *Mutabilität im Minnesang: Mehrfach überlieferte Lieder des 12. und frühen 13. Jahrhunderts.* Göppinger Arbeiten zur Germanistik, no. 515. Göppingen: Kümmerle, 1989.

H/W N = Moriz Haupt and Edmund Wießner, eds. *Neidharts Lieder.* 2nd ed. Leipzig 1923. Rpt., ed. Ingrid Bennewitz-Behr, Ulrich Müller and Franz Viktor Spechtler. Stuttgart: Hirzel, 1986.

KLD = Carl von Kraus (and Hugo Kuhn), eds. *Deutsche Liederdichter des 13. Jahrhunderts: I. Texte. II. Kommentar.* Tübingen: Niemeyer, 1952 and 1958.

L/K WvdV = Karl Lachmann, Carl von Kraus and Hugo Kuhn, eds. *Die Gedichte Walthers von der Vogelweide.* 13th ed. Berlin: de Gruyter, 1965.

MFvS = Achim Masser, ed. *Die Sprüche Friedrichs von Sonnenburg.* Altdeutsche Textbibliothek, no. 86. Tübingen: Niemeyer, 1979.

M/T MF = Hugo Moser and Helmut Tervooren, eds. *Des Minnesangs Frühling.* 38th ed. Stuttgart: Hirzel, 1988.

OM = Georg Objartel, ed. *Der Meißner der Jenaer Handschrift: Untersuchungen, Ausgabe, Kommentar.* Philologische Studien und Quellen, no. 85. Berlin: Schmidt, 1977.

SF = Karl Stackmann and Karl Bertau, eds. *Frauenlob (Heinrich von Meissen). Leichs, Sangsprüche, Lieder.* 2 vols. Göttingen: Vandenhoeck & Ruprecht, 1981.

SKvW = Edward Schröder, ed. *Kleinere Dichtungen Konrads von Würzburg: III. Die Klage der Kunst. Leiche Lieder und Sprüche.* 2nd ed. Berlin: Weidmann, 1959.

SM = Philipp Strauch, ed. *Der Marner.* Quellen und Forschungen, no. 14. Straßburg: Trübner, 1876.

ST = Johannes Siebert. *Der Dichter Tannhäuser: Leben — Gedichte — Sage.* Halle: Niemeyer, 1934.

T/S WvR = Wesley Thomas and Barbara Garvey Seagrave. *The Songs of the Minnesinger, Prince Wizlaw von Rügen.* University of North Carolina Studies in Germanic Languages and Literature, no. 59. Chapel Hill: Univ. of North Carolina Press, 1967.

VCB = Benedikt Konrad Vollmann, ed. *Carmina Burana.* Bibliothek des Mittelalters, no. 13. Frankfurt: Deutscher Klassiker Verlag, 1987.

WS = Burghart Wachinger. *Sängerkrieg. Untersuchungen zur Spruchdichtung des 13. Jahrhunderts.* Münchener Texte und Untersuchungen, no. 42. Munich: Beck, 1973.

Baroque

German *Tanzlieder* at the Turn of the Seventeenth Century: The Texted Galliard

DIANNE M. MCMULLEN

"TANZEN UND SPRINGEN, SINGEN und klingen."[1] Thus begins a song by the well-known late sixteenth- and early seventeenth-century German composer Hans Leo Hassler. Most people today associate Renaissance and Baroque dancing with instrumental music, but, as Hassler suggests, dancing was also accompanied by vocal music during these eras. This little-studied repertoire,[2] in particular the texted galliard, is the focus of this essay.

In the texted galliard three arts merge in one genre. The composer of an instrumental galliard had to be concerned with merely two arts, music and dance. The composer of a texted galliard, on the other hand, also had to reckon with the rhythms and accents of words and with the lengths of poetic lines. This study examines the texted galliard from three points of view: 1) the accents of words, music, and dance; 2) the phrasings of words, music, and dance; and 3) the musical textures. Among other things, it will be seen how the texted galliard contributed to the development of the poetic art in Germany.

By way of introduction, one might look briefly at the importance of dance in German *art* music of the seventeenth and eighteenth centuries. It is a common experience among musicians that many German Baroque composers seem to have relied heavily upon dance for their rhythms and phrases. The opening of Schütz's motet "Herr, unser Herrscher" from his *Symphoniae Sacrae* of 1647[3] is like a corrente. A gigue rhythm pervades several movements of Buxtehude's cantata "O fröhliche Stunden, o herrliche Zeit."[4] The opening chorus of Bach's "Bleib bei uns" (BWV 6) takes the

---

[1] Hans Leo Hassler, *Lustgarten Neuer Teutscher Gesäng* (1601), vol. 9 of *Sämtliche Werke*, ed. C. R. Crosby (Wiesbaden: Breitkopf und Härtel, 1968), p. 43.

[2] Two publications that do give some attention to late sixteenth- and early seventeenth-century texted dances are Bertrun Delli, "Pavane und Galliarde" (Ph.D. diss., Berlin, 1957) and Walther Vetter, *Das Frühdeutsche Lied* (Westfalen: Verlag Lechte Emsdetten, 1928).

[3] Heinrich Schütz, *Symphoniae Sacrae II*, edited by Werner Bittinger, vol. 15 of *Neue Ausgabe sämtlicher Werke* (Kassel: Bärenreiter, 1964), p. 20.

[4] Dietrich Buxtehude, *Sacred Works for Four Voices and Instruments, Part 2*, ed. Kerala J. Snyder, vol. 9 of *The Collected Works* (New York: The Broude Trust, 1987), p. 155.

form of a sarabande.[5] These compositions borrow rhythms and phrasings from the dances of the corrente, gigue, and sarabande and use them in a way that projects the text. They were not, however, accompanied by dancing, as the texted galliard was.

Dancing to a texted piece is probably as ancient as human civilization itself. For the Greeks, the relationship among the arts of music, poetry, and dance was so close that they used one word for all three, *mousike*, meaning "art of the Muses." In Germany, the oldest extant dance songs come from the thirteenth century, although from much older church records which condemn certain pieces, one can trace the genre in Germanic lands at least to the beginning of Christianity.[6]

The dance of the galliard probably originated in northern Italy. Boiardo's epic *Orlando innamorato* from about 1490 contains the first mention of this dance. The earliest extant pieces that are labeled galliards follow almost forty years later, in Attaingnant's Parisian prints of 1529.[7] The first Italian and English examples of the genre come from the 1540s.[8] In Germany the oldest extant galliards were published in 1552 by Hans Gerle.[9] All of these pieces are instrumental. German-texted galliards first appeared a little later in the century, in the 1590s.

The galliard is a product of the Renaissance, a period when dance played an important role in the social lives of people from all classes. Princes and dukes in Germany would be sure to provide music for their guests to perform the galliard and other dances at festive occasions. Patricians and other citizens from the upper classes danced galliards in the *Tanzhalle*, a building found in almost every city and town by the end of the sixteenth century, usually attached to the *Rathaus*.[10] The working classes, too, celebrated holidays, weddings, and other occasions by dancing the galliard in the streets, in their homes, in taverns, and in the fields.[11] One famous

---

[5] Johann Sebastian Bach, *Kantaten zum 2. und 3. Ostertag*, vol. 10 of *Neue Ausgabe sämtlicher Werke* (Kassel: Bärenreiter, 1955), p. 45.

[6] Franz M. Böhme, *Geschichte des Tanzes in Deutschland*, 2 vols. (Leipzig: Breitkopf und Härtel, 1886), 1:229.

[7] Pierre Attaingnant, *Dixhuit basses dances* (1529/30) and *Six gaillardes et six pavanes ... à quatre parties* (1529/30).

[8] Antonio Rotta, *Intabolatura de lauto* (1546), Guilio Abondante, *Intabolature ... sopra el lauto* (1546), and the keyboard manuscript in the British Museum, Roy. App. 58 (c. 1540). See *The New Grove Dictionary of Music and Musicians*, s.v. "Galliard."

[9] Hans Gerle, *Eyn Neues sehr künstlichs Lautenbuch* (1552). See *Die Musik in Geschichte und Gegenwart*, s.v. "Galliarde."

[10] Böhme, *Geschichte des Tanzes in Deutschland*, 1:71, 82.

[11] Emil Reicke, *Geschichte der Reichsstadt Nürnberg* (Nuremberg: Verlag der Joh. Phil. Raw'schen Verlagsbuchhandlung, 1896), pp. 952ff. and Böhme, *Geschichte des Tanzes in Deutschland*, 1:82ff.

English lady who enjoyed the galliard was Queen Elizabeth. It is said that she danced six or seven galliards as part of her morning exercises even at the age of fifty-six.[12]

The question of precisely when and where German-*texted* galliards were performed remains largely a matter for speculation, although one performance is documented in the chronicles of Dresden. In 1615, Johann Georg I marked the occasion of his fifth son's baptism with an elaborate procession during which skits were performed. In one skit, a sea goddess sat on the back of a whale, singing and playing the lute. At the appropriate moment in her song a boy dressed as a Moor stepped out of the whale's mouth and danced a galliard, accompanied by the sea goddess's song.[13]

Texted galliards were undoubtedly sung on other occasions at German courts, for some of the sources contain dedications to noblemen and royalty.[14] According to Thomas Morley and Michael Praetorius,[15] the Italians danced and sang galliards and saltarellos, galliard-like pieces, at their masquerades. In Germany, perhaps some of the Italian-influenced courts had similar customs. There is evidence that texted galliards were favored by a wide audience. On the dedicatory page of his 1611 publication Erasmus Widmann claimed that people from both the upper and the lower classes had expressed an interest in his collection of pieces, which includes one texted gagliarda and several other dance songs.[16] On the title pages of his 1593 and 1594 collections Nikolaus Rost gave a general suggestion for the use of the texted galliards: "Bei allerhandt Ehrlichen Geselschafften / Gastereien und anderm Wohlleben zur Frewde ganz bequem."[17]

Based on publications, the texted galliard had a short life in Germany, only about thirty years. The first German-texted galliard appeared in 1593 in Rost's *XXX. Newer lieblicher Galliardt, mit schönen lustigen Texten*. The last song labeled a galliard is found in Johann Schultz's *Musicalischer Lüstgarte* of 1622. This span could be extended if one were to include publications with songs labeled "Nachtanz" or "Proportio" (triple-meter

---

[12] Louis Horst, *Pre-Classic Dance Forms* (New York: The Dance Observer, 1937), p. 24.

[13] Irmgard Becker-Glauch, *Die Bedeutung der Musik für die Dresdener Hoffeste* (Kassel: Bärenreiter, 1951), p. 66.

[14] Nikolaus Rost, *XXX. Newer lieblicher Galliardt, mit schönen lustigen Texten* (Erfurt, 1593); Erasmus Widmann, *Musicalisch Kurtzweil* (Nuremberg, 1611); and Johannes Schultz, *Musicalischer Lustgarte* (Lüneburg, 1622).

[15] Thomas Morley, *A Plain and Easy Introduction to Practical Music* (1597), ed. R. Alec Harman (New York: W. W. Norton, 1973), p. 297; Michael Praetorius, *Syntagma musicum III* (1619; facsimile rpt., Kassel: Bärenreiter, 1958), p. 28.

[16] Erasmus Widmann, *Musicalisch Kurtzweil* (Nuremberg, 1611).

[17] Nikolaus Rost, *XXX. Newer lieblicher Galliardt* (Erfurt, 1593) and *Der Ander Theil Newer lieblicher Galliardt* (Erfurt, 1594).

dances often based on a duple-meter dance).[18] However, such works are excluded from consideration in this article because a Nachtanz or a Proportio is not necessarily a galliard. It might be a saltarello, tourdion, currant, or some other type of triple-meter dance. Often the musical differences among these dance types are too few to state conclusively that a certain Nachtanz or Proportio is one dance type and not another.[19] All of the pieces examined in this essay are labeled as galliards in the original print. Appendix I contains a preliminary listing of late sixteenth- and early seventeenth-century collections with German-texted galliards.[20]

The brief life of the texted galliard contrasts with that of the instrumental galliard. The latter flourished in Germany for about 120 years, from the 1550s through the 1670s, although there were fewer and fewer publications of instrumental galliards during the last forty years of its existence.[21]

In spite of the texted galliard's short life, a number of composers contributed to its repertoire. A few of their names will be familiar to lovers of early seventeenth-century music. These include Hans Leo Hassler (1562 until 1612), Christoph Demantius (1567 until 1643), and Valentin Haussmann (1565–70 until c. 1614). Lesser-known composers of German-texted galliards include Nikolaus Rost (c. 1542 until 1622), Johannes Schultz (1582 until 1653), and Erasmus Widmann (1572 until 1634).

The galliard is a dance for a couple[22] or a solo dancer. When the galliard is danced by a couple, typically the man dances a galliard variation first while the woman stands quietly to one side or performs a simple walking step. In the next passage of music the man stands to one side while the woman dances a galliard variation. Generally, the man's variation includes more vigorous leaps than the woman's, allowing him to show off his athletic skill.

The galliard is most often in triple meter,[23] notated with six minims to one tactus, as illustrated in Example 1. There are hundreds of dance

---

[18] Ernst Hermann Meyer observed galliard-like rhythms in a song from the eighteenth century, "Der hat vergeben sein ewig Leben," found in the *Augsburger Tafelkonfekt* from 1733. See *Die Musik in Geschichte und Gegenwart*, s.v. "Galliarde."

[19] See Julia Sutton's introduction to Fabritio Caroso's *Nobiltà di Dame* (1600) (Oxford: Oxford Univ. Press, 1986), p. 42ff.

[20] Delli writes that G. Voigtländer and H. Albert also composed texted galliards, but I found no examples. See Delli, "Pavane and Galliard," 156n. See also Kurt Fischer, "Gabriel Voigtländer," *Sammelbände der Internationalen Musikgesellschaft* 12 (1910–11): 17–93.

[21] *Die Musik in Geschichte und Gegenwart*, s.v. "Galliarde."

[22] The roles of the man and woman differ from one treatise to the next. For a summary, see Mabel Dolmetsch, *Dances of England and France* (1949; rpt. ed., New York: Da Capo Press, 1975), pp. 102 and 107.

[23] Galliards in duple meter do exist. See Fabritio Caroso, *Nobiltà di Dame* (1600), trans. Julia Sutton (New York: Oxford Univ. Press, 1986), p. 198.

patterns for the galliard. One of the most basic patterns consists of five steps or five changes of weight. Known as the *cinque pas*, this pattern is executed over six minims. The *cinque pas* itself exists in many variants; a description of one of the common variants follows.[24] On the first four beats the dancer hops, alternately kicking one foot in front of the other. On the fifth beat of music he jumps into the air, landing on the ground again on the sixth beat. The jump on beat five is called the *saut majeur*, while the landing is known as the posture. Together, beats five and six are known as the cadence. Sometimes a tassel was hung and the dancer aimed to touch it with one foot as he jumped into the air. Illustrations of this may be found in Cesare Negri's 1602 treatise, available in facsimile.[25] Thoinot Arbeau, the author of a late sixteenth-century dance treatise, was of the opinion that the landing should be graceful, with one foot touching the ground slightly before the sixth beat and the other landing on the beat. He criticized those who landed with both feet at the same time on beat six remarking that it sounded like a sack of corn being dumped on the ground.[26]

Begun on the left foot, the *cinque pas* is then repeated starting with the right foot. This entire pattern, the *cinque pas* begun on the left foot plus its repetition starting on the right foot, takes four measures of music, as seen from Example 1.

The same four-measure dance pattern can be repeated over and over until the conclusion of the piece. Usually, however, the dancer includes variations, sometimes quite extensive, on the basic steps. A simple variant during the first four steps is to cross one leg alternately in front of the other instead of kicking forward. One might embellish the jump on beat five by moving the feet back and forth quickly while in the air. A dancer can also delay the leap on beat five until the eleventh or seventeenth beat of music.

Thorough discussion about dancing the Renaissance galliard lies outside the realm of this essay; however, those interested in the topic may refer to six dance treatises of the period. These are listed in Appendix II. Two treatises are by Frenchmen and the other four by Italians. Unfortunately, there are no extant German dance treatises from the Renaissance. Four of the treatises, those by Arbeau, Caroso, de Lauze, and Negri, are available in facsimile and in English translation. Lupi's and Lutij's treatises are not yet available in modern print. Among all of these treatises, Lupi's treatise contains the most extensive discussion about the galliard, according to modern dance scholars.[27]

---

[24] Thoinot Arbeau, *Orchésography* (1589), trans. Mary Stewart Evans, with a new introduction and notes by Julia Sutton (New York: Dover, 1967), p. 100.

[25] Cesare Negri, *Le Gratie d'Amore* (Milan, 1602. Facsimile rpt., New York: Broude Brothers, 1969), pp. 64, 66, and 68.

[26] Thoinot Arbeau, *Orchésography*, p. 89.

[27] See Julia Sutton's introduction to Caroso, *Nobiltà di Dame*, p. 41.

Renaissance dance, like Renaissance music, was largely an improvisatory art. The treatises show us examples of galliard steps, but they are meant to serve only as suggestions. Arbeau mentions this and also hints at the evolving nature of the dance. He writes: "There are an infinity of varieties, which you will obtain and learn from those of your own generation."[28] In this essay, reference will be made occasionally to possible dance steps for specific musical excerpts. Some of these steps are taken from the treatises and are documented as such. Other steps are based on speculation after discussing the possibilities with experts in Renaissance dancing. In some cases, nothing is said about dance steps. Reconstructing Renaissance dances is often complicated by ambiguities in the treatises. It is to be hoped that the current interest in historical dance will yield information that will increase our understanding.

Accent Patterns

Dances with fixed step patterns, by their very nature, require clear accents from the music. The dancer of a galliard needs to hear strong beats from the music in order to begin the *cinque pas* at the correct moment. Like most dances, the music of the galliard has some rhythmic patterns that are found in many galliards. Three common galliard rhythms demonstrate how musical, textual, and dance accents can coexist happily.

One common musical rhythm in galliards consists of alternating semibreves and minims, as found at the opening of "Freu dich nun" by Demantius (Example 2). (Semibreves are transcribed as whole-notes and minims as half-notes.) In this excerpt the musical rhythm and the poetic meter, which is trochaic, are well-suited to one another. The dancer can execute the *cinque pas* in its simplest forms.

A second musical rhythm common to galliards is syncopation, an example of which is found later in the same piece by Demantius at the words "weiche alle Traurigkeit" (Example 3). Once again, the poetic meter is trochaic. The accents of the words are supported by the music through syncopation.

A third common musical rhythm in galliards is hemiola. Hemiola is a reorganization of two large groups of three beats each into three large groups of two beats each. The poetic meter best suited to hemiola as it appears in texted galliards is trochaic. A passage from Haussmann's "Viel Tugendsame" offers one illustration (Example 4). To perform this passage with continuous emphasis on the downbeat would be to ignore the textual accent and the musical hemiola.

The dancer can choose one from among many patterns when dancing a hemiola. Arbeau gives several possibilities. In one step pattern the dancer starts the measure by crossing his right foot in front of his left. At the start

---

[28] Arbeau, *Orchésography*, trans. Mary Stewart Evans, p. 107.

of the second large beat he crosses it behind his left foot. During the third and final large beat he executes the *saut majeur* and the posture. However, the dancer can choose to ignore the hemiola and simply perform a common *cinque pas* pattern instead.[29] This would create a counterpoint between the dance and music.

The common denominator in Examples 2, 3, and 4 is trochaic meter. This poetic meter, with its strong initial accent, is a good match for the strong downbeat in the galliard.

A fourth common musical rhythm for the galliard illustrates a case where musical and poetic accents are not aligned. This rhythm, which consists of three minims to a measure, is found in Example 5. The natural choice for this musical rhythm, if it is to be set syllabically, is dactylic meter. However, dactylic meter was rarely used by German poets of the 1590s and early 1600s. Not until the 1640s and 1650s, at the urging of writers such as August Buchner, did German poets use dactylic meter with any frequency. This was nearly a half a century after the first publication of German-texted galliards and two decades after the last one appeared in print.

If dactylic meter was a rarity in German poetry at the turn of the seventeenth century, what sorts of poetic meter are to be found in texted galliards with three minims to a measure? Most frequently, it is iambic. The opening of Rost's "O höchster Schatz" (Example 6) offers an illustration. Here the first measure has three minims and one can see how the composer forces the opening of the iambic line into a dactyl.

$$- \quad x \quad - \quad x \qquad \qquad x \quad - \quad - \quad x$$
"O höchster Schatz" becomes "O höchster Schatz."

After the initial measure both text and music move in trochees.

Dactylic meter was not totally neglected. In spite of Martin Opitz's objections to the use of the meter, early seventeenth-century German poets frequently inserted dactyls into their iambic and trochaic texts. In the middle of a largely iambic text by Demantius, "Ach das ich doch gnug aussprechen kund," one finds the amphibrachic phrase: "ein wunderschön, weibliches Bild" (Example 7). This text is perfectly matched with one of the common galliard rhythms.

In a recent article entitled "Dance Music and the Origins of the Dactylic Meter,"[30] Gary C. Thomas traces some of the influence that early seventeenth-century dance music had on the development of dactylic meter. Pieces such as Rost's "O höchster Schatz," published in 1593, and Deman-

---

[29] Conversation with Julia Sutton in March, 1989.

[30] Gary C. Thomas, "Dance Music and the Origins of the Dactylic Meter," *Daphnis* 16 (1987): 107–46.

tius's "Ach das ich doch gnug aussprechen kund," published in 1601, should be placed near the beginning stages of this development.

The composer-poets[31] of texted galliards were not, of course, solely responsible for the introduction of dactylic meter into German poetry, but they certainly made an early contribution. The galliard rhythm consisting of three minims to the tactus compelled poets to break new ground in the 1590s and early 1600s. Their experience must have been similar to that of Johann Rist, a German composer who lived from 1607 until 1667. In the 1642 volume of his *Himlische Lieder* Rist wrote: "I remember what happened many years ago with this kind of verse. For example, when a gay saraband ... came into my hands and I was asked to write words to its jolly tune, it turned out that what I produced was in dactylic, although until then I had never seen nor heard of a line in this meter."[32]

Scanning a poem from the sixteenth or seventeenth centuries is sometimes problematic, because the placement of accents is not always obvious. Some of Demantius's texts contain ambiguous accentual patterns, and he seems to have taken advantage of this fact. A portion of Demantius's "Annelein, Annelein" (Example 8) offers an illustration. In isolation, the words "wie dirs gefällt" might be scanned in at least two ways. Without the elision, the phrase is obviously amphibrachic: "wie dir es gefällt." With the elision one might hear it in iambic meter ("wie dirs gefällt") or, if one is swayed by the phrase that precedes it, one might hear it in dactylic meter ("freundlich und milt, wie dirs gefällt").

```
   –  x  –  –  x                   –   x  –   x
   wie dir es gefällt (amphibrachic)   wie dirs gefällt (iambic)


   x  –  –  x  x  –  –  x
   freundlich und milt, wie dirs gefällt (dactylic)
```

The rhyme enhances a dactylic feeling here. The rhythm of the rest of the text also supports the dactylic interpretation.

Demantius uses both accentual patterns. In Example 9, taken from the tenor line, the phrase is set as a dactyl. Example 10, from the bassus, is more complicated. If the singer renders this section with strong accents on the downbeat, the text will be accented incorrectly and one would accuse Demantius of poor text setting. On the other hand, if the singer were to stress the iambic accents of the phrase, the result would be a hemiola,

---

[31] Among the eight publications known to contain texted galliards (listed in Appendix I), none specifies a poet. At the present time one must assume that the composers wrote most of the texts.

[32] Johann Rist, *Himlische Lieder* (1642). Quoted from R. Hinton Thomas, *Poetry and Song in the German Baroque* (Oxford: Clarendon, 1963), p. 71.

creating an interesting cross-rhythm with the tenor.[33] The altus and quintus also have hemiolas, while the discant emphasizes the downbeat along with the tenor.

Phrasing

As shown earlier, the basic galliard step takes four measures of music to perform. This is often reflected in the music and poetry. One instance may be found in the opening of Rost's "O höchster Schatz" (Example 6). For this piece, which has four-bar phrases throughout, the dancer might perform one variant of the *cinque pas* after the other.

Phrases with an odd number of measures are more interesting. Demantius seemed especially fond of these. Take, for instance, the third and final section of his "Kans möglich sein" (Example 11). Here the musical and textual phrasing consists of three-bar phrases, one after another, for a total of twelve measures or four phrases. Negri provides the dancer with step patterns for phrases with odd numbers of measures,[34] and a dancer can choose to follow one of these. However, since this section of Demantius's song totals twelve measures, a multiple of four, the dancer can perform three variants of the common *cinque pas*. The dancer might choose to do this intentionally, or it might happen by default if a dancer does not anticipate the three-bar phrasing in the song. The dancer's three phrases of four measures each thus form a counterpoint against the singer's four phrases of three measures each.

The subtlety of such counterpoints among the arts must have been a source of delight for the composer of the piece, for the dancer, and for the audience. There is no written choreography from the seventeenth century for this piece, and so we can only guess what the dancer of that time might have done based on our general knowledge of the dance. Perhaps specialists in Renaissance dance might further enlighten us on this topic, as they continue their studies of the treatises.

---

[33] Cross-rhythms of this type are often found in the instrumental galliard, as well as in the saltarello, the galliard's older cousin. For some clearly-marked examples, see the instrumental saltarellos in *Sixteenth-Century Italian Dances*, ed. Joel Newman (University Park: The Pennsylvania State Univ., 1966).

[34] Cesare Negri, *Le Gratie d'Amore* (Milan, 1602. Facsimile rpt., New York: Broude Brothers, 1969), p. 93ff. See also Julia Sutton's articles entitled "Galliard" and "Cesare Negri" in the forthcoming *International Encyclopedia of Dance* to be published by the Univ. of California Press. I am grateful to Dr. Sutton for sending me copies of these articles before they appeared in print.

Musical Textures

Homophony pervades many German-texted galliards. See the opening of Rost's "O höchster Schatz" in Example 12. The simple texture and musical rhythms, along with the straightforward four-bar phrasing, would seem to make such pieces accessible to beginning galliard dancers. The piece contains no complications that might confuse them.

At the opposite extreme is a piece by Demantius. The texture of the middle section of his "Freu dich nun mein Herzelein" is polyphonic. Example 13 contains the discant, quintus, and bassus. Starting at the fourth measure in the excerpt, each voice has the same musical motive, a rising scalar figure that encompasses a fifth, but each singer begins the motive on a different beat in the measure. In performance the bassus accents the first beat, the quintus the second beat, and the discant the third beat. The musical accentuation is supported by the text underlay.

Complicating matters, the remaining two voices, altus and tenor, have still other accent patterns (Example 14). The tenor has two hemiolas. The altus follows no consistent pattern of musical and textual accent. The singer of this part may choose to follow the textual accent with good effect. The musical result when all five parts sound together is joyous, one that suits the meaning of the words well.

Most of the texted galliards by Haussmann, Hassler, Widmann, and Schultz have relatively simple musical textures. Occasionally, the parts are animated by some polyphony, but rarely do their pieces approach the textural complexity found in Demantius's music. Demantius himself recognized that his texted galliards were fancier than most when he labeled them "artige Galliarden."[35]

Conclusions

The German-texted galliard was a multifaceted genre. Music, poetry, and dance unite to create a variety of styles. The excerpts from Rost's, Haussmann's, and Demantius's music illustrate some of the extremes in accent patterns, phrase lengths, and musical textures that are to be found within this genre, during its brief existence of just three decades. In general, Demantius, one of the best-known composers among the group, was more experimental than other composers.

The texted galliard was progressive, because it contributed toward the eventual acceptance by German poets of dactylic meter. More work needs to be done before one can determine the extent of the genre's contribution in this area. One might begin with the influence of Paul Kauffmann's

---

[35] Christoph Demantius, *Sieben und siebentzig, neue ausserlesene, liebliche, zierliche, polnischer und teutscher Art, Täntze, mit und ohne Texten* (Nuremberg: Conrad Bauer, 1601), notation preceding piece LVIII.

publications. Kauffmann (1568 until 1632), who directed a publishing firm in Nuremberg from 1594 until 1617,[36] took a special interest in *Tanzlieder*. Three of the eight publications listed in Appendix I come from his presses. Furthermore, in prefaces to their collections containing galliard-like pieces with texts, Valentin Haussmann and Hans Christoph Haiden state that Kauffmann had urged them to publish their pieces.[37] It is worth noting that Kauffmann's shop was in the same town that a few years later became home to the *Pegnesischer Blumenorden* and other poetic societies that experimented with dactylic meter beginning in the 1640s.

A comparison between texted galliards and instrumental ones would be a worthwhile study,[38] useful especially to performers of instrumental galliards. The phrasings and articulations that are made obvious in *Tanzlieder* by the text may help in the interpretation of some instrumental dances.

Another area worth more investigation is the relationship between the German-texted galliard and the Italian balletto, its obvious predecessor.[39] In the 1570s and 1580s, before the first German-texted galliard appeared, Monteverdi, Gastoldi, Vecchi, and others were writing songs to accompany the dance. These balletti, which contain gagliarda sections, were known to German composers. In fact, Haussmann had many of them printed in Germany with translations.[40] Further research will help to determine which elements of the texted galliard the Germans borrowed from the Italians as the balletto crossed northward over the Alps and which elements stemmed from German traditions.

---

[36] *The New Grove Dictionary of Music and Musicians*, s.v. "Kauffmann, Paul."

[37] Valentin Haussmann, *Neue artige und liebliche Täntze, zum theil mit Texten* (Nuremberg: Paul Kauffmann, 1599); Hans Christoph Haiden, *Postiglion der Lieb* (Nuremberg: Paul Kauffmann, 1614).

[38] For some observations on this topic, see Delli, *Pavane und Galliarde*, p. 129ff.

[39] Walther Dürr and Rudolf Velten have addressed some aspects of this topic. See Walther Dürr, "Die italienische Canzonette und das deutsche Lied im Ausgang des XVI. Jahrhunderts," in *Studi in onore di Lorenzo Bianchi* (Bologna, 1960), pp. 71–102, and Rudolf Velten, *Das ältere deutsche Gesellschaftslied unter dem Einfluss der italienischen Musik* (Heidelberg: Carl Winter, 1914), p. 123ff.

[40] A list of Haussmann's translations is attached to the article on Haussmann found in *The New Grove Dictionary of Music and Musicians*.

Appendix I:

A Preliminary List of Collections that contain German-texted Galliards (in chronological order)

Rost(hius), Nikolaus. *XXX. Newer lieblicher Galliardt, mit schönen lustigen Texten.* Erfurt: Georg Baumann, 1593.

Rost(hius), Nikolaus. *Der Ander Theil Newer lieblicher Galliardt: Mit schönen lustigen Texten.* Erfurt: Georg Baumann, 1594.

Demantius, Johannes Christoph. *Sieben und siebentzig, neue ausserlesene, liebliche, zierliche, polnischer und teutscher Art, Täntze, mit und ohne Texten, zu 4. und 5. Stimmen, neben andern künstlichen Galliarden, mit fünff Stimmen.* Nuremberg: Conrad Bauer (Katharina Dietrich), 1601.

Hassler, Hans Leo. *Lustgarten Neuer Teutscher Gesäng, Balletti, Galliarden und Intraden, mit 4.5.6. und 8. Stimmen.* Nuremberg: Paul Kauffmann, 1601.

Haussmann, Valentin. *Neue fünffstimmige Paduane und Galliarde, auff Instrumenten, fürnehmlich auff Fiolen lieblich zugebrauchen.* Nuremberg: Paul Kauffmann, 1604.

Widmann, Erasmus. *Musicalisch Kurtzweil Neuer Teutscher mit sehr frölichen und kurtzweiligen Texten gestellte Gesänglein, Täntz und Curranten sampt denen hievor zu unterschiedlichen malen aussgegangenen dreyen Theylen zu singen und auff allerley Musicalischen Instrumenten zu gebrauchen mit fünff und vier Stimmen.* Nuremberg: Abraham Wagenmann, 1611.

Haussmann, Valentin, and Hans Leo Hassler. *Venusgarten: Oder neue lustige liebliche Täntz teutscher und polnischer Art, auch Galliarden und Intraden mit 4. 5. 6. Stimmen mit und ohne Text.* Nuremberg: Paul Kauffmann, 1615.

Schultz, Johannes. *Musicalischer Lüstgarte, Darinnen Neun unnd Funfftzig Schone Newe Moteten, Madrigalien, Fugen, Phantasien, Cantzonen, Paduanen, Intraden, Galliard, Passametz, Täntze, etc. Mit Lateinischen und Teutschen Geist- und Weltlichen schönen Texten so woll auff allen Musicalischen Instrumenten, Alss Menschlicher Stimme, Artig und lieblich zu Musiciren. Mit 2.3.4.5.6.7.8. Stimmen componiret.* Lüneburg: Autor (Andrea Michaelsen), 1622.

Appendix II:

Late Renaissance Dance Treatises

Arbeau, Thoinot (pseud. for Jehan Tabourot). *Orchésography*. Langres, [1588], 1589; rpt. with expanded title, 1596. Facsimile rpt. of 1596, Geneva: Minkoff, 1972. Trans. into English by Cyril W. Beaumont, 1925. Rpt. Brooklyn, New York: Dance Horizons, 1948. Rpt., with corrections, a new introduction, and notes by Julia Sutton. New York: Dover, 1967.

Caroso, Fabritio. *Nobiltà di Dame*. Venice, 1600. 1605. Facsimile rpt., Bologna: Forni, 1970. Trans. into English by Julia Sutton. New York: Oxford Univ. Press, 1986.

De Lauze, Francois. *Apologie de la Danse*. 1623. Facsimile rpt., Geneva: Minkoff, 1977. Trans. into English by Joan Wildeblood. London: Frederick Muller, 1952.

Lupi, Livio. *Mutanze di gagliarda, tordiglione, passo e mezzo, canari e passaggi*. Palermo, 1600. A second edition, revised and enlarged appeared with the title *Libro di gagliarda, tordiglione ...* in 1607.

Lutij, Prospero. *Opera bellissima nella quale si contengono molto partite, et passeggi di gagliarda*. Perugia, 1587, 1589.

Negri, Cesare. *Le Gratie d'Amore*. Milan, 1602. Reissued as *Nuove inventione di balli*. Milan, 1604. Facsimile rpts. of 1602 edition. New York: Broude Brothers, 1969 and Bologna: Forni, 1969. Trans. into English by Gustavia Yvonne Kendall. Ph.D. diss., Stanford University, 1985.

Musical Examples

Example 1. A "basic" galliard pattern.

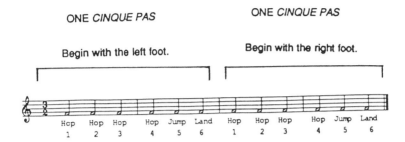

Example 2. A common musical rhythm in galliards: alternating semibreves and minims. Demantius, "Freu dich nun," mm. 1–4. Discant only.

Example 3. A second common musical rhythm in galliards: syncopation. Demantius, "Freu dich nun," mm. 9–10. Discant only.

Example 4. A third common musical rhythm in galliards: hemiola. Haussmann, "Viel Tugendsame," mm. 9–12. Discant only.

Example 5. A fourth common musical rhythm in galliards: three minims to a measure.

Example 6. Iambic meter set to three minims in a measure. Rost, "O höchster Schatz," mm. 1–4. Discant only.

Example 7. Amphibrachic meter set to three minims in a measure. Demantius, "Ach das ich doch gnug aussprechen kund," mm. 15–18. Discant only.

Example 8. Extensive use of dactylic meter in a piece printed in 1601. A portion of the first stanza from Demantius's "Annelein, Annelein" (lines 4–6).

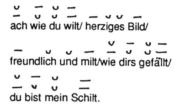

Example 9. Dactylic setting of "wie dirs gefällt" from Demantius's "Annelein," mm. 13–14. Tenor only.

Example 10. Iambic setting of "wie dirs gefällt" from Demantius's "Annelein," mm. 12–14. Bassus only.

Example 11. Phrasing with odd numbers of measures. Demantius, "Kans möglich sein," mm. 19–30. Discant only.

Example 12. Homophonic texture. Rost, "O höchster Schatz," mm. 1–4. All voice parts.

Example 13. Polyphonic texture. Demantius, "Freu dich nun," mm. 9–16. Discant, quintus, and bassus.

Example 14. Polyphonic texture. Demantius, "Freu dich nun," mm. 9–16. All voice parts.

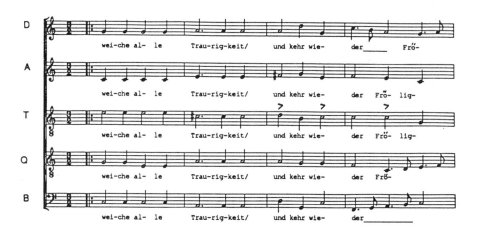

Libretti without Scores:
Problems in the Study of Early German Opera

JUDITH P. AIKIN

IN 1627, THIRTY YEARS after the creation of the first opera in Italy —
Ottavio Rinuccini's *Dafne*, set to music by Jacopo Peri[1] — Martin Opitz
recreated the Italian libretto in German verse, and Heinrich Schütz set this
German *Daphne* to music. Although the text was published for the festive
occasion and reprinted in Opitz's later collection of his *Weltliche Poemata*,
the score by Heinrich Schütz does not survive.[2] Their joint endeavor was
followed in quick succession by a series of operatic productions: Daniel
Czepko's *Pierie* of around 1629, perhaps set to music by Apelles von
Löwenstern — but the score is lost;[3] August Buchner's *Orpheus und
Euridice* of 1638, probably set to music by Heinrich Schütz — but the score
is lost;[4] Martin Opitz's *Judith* of 1635, perhaps never set to music in its
entirety — only its choruses and few imbedded songs, set to music by
Apelles von Löwenstern, survive.[5] Simon Dach wrote two opera libretti,

[1] Libretto published in Angelo Solerti, *Gli Albori del Melodramma* (Milan, 1904; rpt.
Hildesheim: Georg Olms, 1969), 2:74–99. A fine discussion of the process which resulted
in the first opera is that by Barbara Russano Hanning, *Of Poetry and Music's Power:
Humanism and the Creation of Opera*, Studies in Musicology, no. 13 (Ann Arbor: UMI,
1980).

[2] Martin Opitz, *Dafne*, 1627; also published in his *Weltliche Poemata* (1644); rpt. ed. Erich
Trunz, Deutsche Neudrucke, Barock, no. 2 (Tübingen: Niemeyer, 1967), pp. 103–28. On
Opitz's *Dafne*, see especially Anton Mayer, "Zu Opitz' Dafne," *Euphorion* 18 (1911):
754–60. On Heinrich Schütz, see especially Hans Joachim Moser, *Heinrich Schütz: Sein
Leben und Werk*, 2nd ed. (Kassel: Bärenreiter, 1954). A recent collection assembles basic
essays and articles on the composer: *Heinrich Schütz in seiner Zeit*, ed. Walter Blanken-
burg, Wege der Forschung, no. 614 (Darmstadt: Wissenschaftliche Buchgesellschaft, 1985).

[3] Vratislav, 1636; also in Daniel Czepko, *Weltliche Dichtungen*, ed. Werner Milch (1932;
rpt. Darmstadt: Wissenschaftliche Buchgesellschaft, 1963). On this opera, see Mara Wade,
"The Reception of Opitz's *Judith* during the Baroque," *Daphnis* 16 (1987): 147–65. On
Matthäus Apelles von Löwenstern (Matthäus Appelt), see the article in *Musik in Geschichte
und Gegenwart* (Kassel: Bärenreiter, 1949–86), vol. 8, cols. 1117–20.

[4] Never published in the seventeenth century, it appeared for the first time in an article
by H[ofmann] v[on] F[allersleben], "August Buchner," *Weimarisches Jahrbuch für
deutsche Sprache, Litteratur und Kunst* 2 (1855): 13–38.

[5] Martin Opitz, *Judith*, in his *Geistliche Poemata* (1638), rpt. ed. Erich Trunz (Tübingen:
Niemeyer, 1966), pp. 86–120. On this opera, see Anton Mayer, "Quelle und Entstehung
von Opitzens Judith," *Euphorion* 20 (1913): 39–53. On the version set in part to music by
Apelles von Löwenstern, with textual expansion by Andreas Tscherning, see Mara Wade,
"Reception," 153–54.

Cleomedes in 1635 and *Sorbuisa* in 1644, both with music composed by Heinrich Albert — of which only a few arias survive.[6] Georg Greflinger penned a lyric tragedy, *Ferrando-Dorinde*, in 1644; the composer is unknown and the music does not survive.[7] In fact, no musical score survives in its entirety for any of the dramatic or semidramatic festival pieces set to music by Heinrich Schütz or his students for the court in Dresden — including a number of *Sing-Ballette* by the poet David Schirmer — or for other courts to which Schütz had ties: the other Saxon courts, Wolfenbüttel, Copenhagen.[8]

The strophic songs and strophic arias of von Löwenstern and Heinrich Albert are, in fact, the sole surviving music for German opera up to the year 1644; and with only two exceptions, musical settings of German-language operas before 1697 are extant today solely in a few collections of selected arias and songs. There are no surviving scores which include musical settings for recitative or ariose passages for the hundreds of extant German-language libretti that are usually the only record we have of performances of drama set to music at the dozens of Middle German and North German courts.

The first exception is Georg Philipp Harsdörffer's *Seelewig* of 1644, the music for which, composed by Sigmund Theophil Staden, survives in the

---

[6] Published in 1680 and 1696 in the only seventeenth-century collections of Dach's works (aside from his texts published with Heinrich Albert's music), *Cleomedes* and *Sorbuisa* are available in a modern edition, Simon Dach, *Gedichte*, ed. Walther Ziesemer, Schriften der Königsberger Gelehrten Gesellschaft, no. 5 (Halle: Max Niemeyer, 1937), 2:281–310 and 311–18, respectively. *Cleomedes*, not published until 1680, was performed only once, in 1635, on the event of the visit of King Vladislaus IV of Poland to Königsberg. It has been termed "dieses dramatische Festspiel" (by Ziesemer, in his notes to the edition, 2:390), but was apparently set to music in its entirety. *Sorbuisa*, written in 1644 to honor the anniversary of the founding of the university, was published already in that year in its surviving truncated form (synopses of the action in place of the recitative dialogue). It received new performances and republication for university celebrations also in 1645 and 1656. These (and other) works of Dach are also widely available today in a facsimile edition of the collection of 1696: Simon Dach, *Poetische Werke* (Königsberg: Boyen, 1696; rpt. Hildesheim: Olms, 1970). The music to the surviving arias was published in Albert's *Arien oder Melodeien*, which has been republished as Heinrich Albert, *Arien*, ed. Eduard Bernoulli and Hans Joachim Moser with an introduction by Hermann Kretzschmar, Denkmäler deutscher Tonkunst, nos. 12–13 (Wiesbaden: Breitkopf & Härtel, 1903–1904; rpt. Graz: Akademisch, 1958). The two choruses, both from *Cleomedes*, appear in Part IV (No. 10, pp. 125–29) and Part VI (No. 10, p. 186).

[7] Georg Greflinger, *Ferrando-Dorinde, zweyer Hochverliebtgewesenen Personen erbärmliches Ende* (Frankfurt am Main, 1644); excerpts appended to anon., *Poetisches Lust-Gärtlein* (Danzig: Hünefeld, 1645), Faber du Faur Yale Collection, no. 358.

[8] The texts to David Schirmer's Dresden *Sing-Ballette* are contained in his *Poetische Rauten-Gepüsch* (Dresden: Löffler, 1663). Schütz was *Kapellmeister* in absentia in Wolfenbüttel; he was involved with the wedding festivities in Copenhagen in 1634. See Mara Wade, "Heinrich Schütz and the 'Store Bilager' in Copenhagen (1634)," *Schütz Jahrbuch* 11 (1989): 32–52.

published version to be found in volume 4 of Harsdörffer's *Frauenzimmer Gesprächspiele*, published that same year.[9] The music to *Seelewig*, however, consists entirely of *Lieder*, even for dialogue portions (as has been amply demonstrated by musicologists),[10] and thus the exception essentially proves the rule: only *Lieder* survive from the period of early German opera. Musical settings for recitative were apparently discarded and were never considered worthy of publication. The second exception, an *Apollo und Dafne* opera of 1671 for the court in Dresden, written by the Italians Bontempi and Peranda, but with a German libretto, may still exist today in manuscript in Dresden, but I have not as yet gotten access to it and do not even know if it survived the Second World War. The only published portions of this score are arias, not recitative.[11]

For the period before 1669, then, study of German-language opera, aside from *Lied*-forms, is limited to analysis of surviving texts and to making assumptions based on surviving Italian opera scores from the first half of the seventeenth century or on surviving non-dramatic German vocal music. The latter source, of course, also consists almost entirely of *Lieder*, many of them polyphonic rather than the monody which dominated Italian opera libretti of the time.

As I have tried to show elsewhere, in my article on the development of madrigalic versification, the differences between the German language and the Italian of the operatic repertoire Germans took as their model were so massive that the process of absorbing the new art form and transforming it into a German one was extremely slow. Some of the chief obstacles standing in the way of taking over Italian accomplishments directly include the most basic differences between the two languages: in Italian versification, the vowels have duration, while in German they have accent; in Italian it is the vowels which take time to sing, while in German it is the consonants and consonant groupings (many of which are in themselves impediments to song, like the "tzt" combination in "jetzt," for example); in Italian, elision of words ending and beginning with vowels is common, but few German

---

[9] Georg Philipp Harsdörffer, *Frauenzimmer Gesprächspiele*, IV. Theil (1644), rpt. ed. Irmgard Böttcher, Deutsche Neudrucke Reihe Barock, no. 16 (Tübingen: Max Niemeyer, 1968), new pagination pp. 76–209. The score begins on p. 533 of the same volume. A nineteenth-century realization exists: Robert Eitner, "*Seelewig*, das älteste, bekannte Singspiel von Harsdörffer und S. G. Staden, 1644," *Monatshefte für Musikgeschichte* 13 (1881): 53–147.

[10] Peter Keller, *Die Oper Seelewig von Sigmund Theophil Staden und Georg Philipp Harsdörffer*, Publikationen der schweizerischen Musikforschenden Gesellschaft, Series II, no. 29 (Bern: Paul Haupt, 1977), passim; Ludwig Schiedermair, *Die deutsche Oper: Grundzüge ihres Werdens und Wesens* (Bonn: Dümmler, 1940), p. 25.

[11] The opera is mentioned in Renate Brockpähler, *Handbuch zur Geschichte der Barockoper in Deutschland* (Emsdetten: Lechte, 1964), p. 135. See also Richard Engländer, "Zur Frage der Dafne (1671) von G. A. Bontempi und M. G. Peranda," *Acta Musicologica* 13, i–iv (1941): 59ff.

words begin with vowels, and nearly all final vowels in German are the unaccented *schwa* or "uh" sound — not a good candidate for elision, at least as implemented in Italian; in Italian, almost all words are polysyllabic and end in an unaccented or short syllable, while in German there is a large number of monosyllabic words, so that there are nearly as many possibilities of ending a line or phrase with an accented syllable or a single-syllable word as there are ending it with an unaccented syllable. Then there are the very great differences in syntactically-based stress: German word order not only uses first and final position in a clause for emphasis, but also typically suspends significant verbs until the end. The probability that German and Italian texts could utilize the same musical setting was thus poor; certainly Heinrich Schütz, although greatly influenced by his Italian teacher and model, Gabrielli, created a new style in vocal music when he turned to setting his native tongue.

The great southern courts, Vienna and Munich, and eventually Dresden further north, abandoned the German language and produced operas in Italian only. But in various other Saxon courts (notably Weißenfels, Halle, and Weimar), in Silesia, in Rudolstadt, and in Wolfenbüttel, attempts to create German recitative and aria styles continued. The development of poetic forms appropriate for these two kinds of opera music can be traced in the gradual improvements in versification and in the increasingly natural speech in the recitatives[12] and arias of the published libretti.

The most promising source both of a basis for comparison of Italian- and German-language operas of the time, and of a reconstruction of what German-language opera must have sounded like, would be a contemporary singing translation. Very few survive, however, and none from the earliest period in the development of German opera. Indeed, it is probable that the attempt was seldom made. Opitz and Buchner may well have tried to create singing translations of famous early Italian operas in their *Dafne* and *Orpheus und Euridice*, only to give up in despair, given the immense difficulties. The result is, in neither case, a singing translation, for both use not only very different verse forms, but even a differing number of lines for a particular speech — that is, when they choose to follow the format of their Italian original at all.[13] But since evidence indicates that the impetus for

---

[12] As I have attempted to do on a small scale in my article "Creating a Language for German Opera: The Struggle to Adapt Madrigal Versification in Seventeenth-Century Germany," *DVjs* 62 (1988): 266–89. I am currently expanding my investigation to more operas and to aria forms in a book-length study to be titled *A Language for German Opera: The Development of Verse Forms for Recitative and Aria in Seventeenth-Century Germany*.

[13] While it is clear that Opitz's *Dafne* is based on Rinuccini's, the source of Buchner's *Orpheus und Euridice* is less obvious. Mara Wade, "The Reception of Opitz's *Judith* during the Baroque," *Daphnis* 16 (1987): 165, n. 55, states that Buchner's libretto was based on Striggio's *La favola d'Orfeo*, in the version of 1609 set by Monteverdi, but I feel that, aside from verbal reminiscences in many of the solo speeches, the treatment of the story more

both operas came from the composer, Heinrich Schütz, himself,[14] it is more likely that the two poets assumed from the beginning that new music would in any case be provided, thus eliminating the need to attempt to follow the metrical patterns of the Italian originals. Composers in the seventeenth century were, after all, so eager to provide settings for opera texts that there are numerous instances, in Italy and in Germany, of a single libretto receiving a new, up-to-date score by a different composer for each revival.[15] For this reason, it is easy to understand the apparent lack of any interest in creating a singing translation of the sort sought after today, in our own age of adulation for the scores created by musical geniuses. Thus adaptation, rather than translation, was the rule when recreating an Italian opera for performance in German. And this potential source of material for an informed reconstruction of German opera of the period before 1670 is thus almost entirely absent.

There were German translations of Italian libretti for many of the operas performed in Vienna, Munich, and Dresden, but these were generally prose translations — or even narrative paraphrases — with verse used only for the arias. The function of such translations was apparently not unlike that of the dual-language libretti read before a performance by many an opera-goer today. And in almost all cases, even the arias would not lend themselves to being sung with the original music, but were only versified in order to differentiate these reflective solos from the dramatic dialogue in which they are imbedded.

A case in point is the translation by the Nürnberg author Johann Gabriel Meyer in 1672 of the most famous Italian-language opera in the German-speaking world at that time, Francesco Sbarra's *Il Pomo d'oro*, the festive grand opera, with music by important Venetian composer Marc Antonio Cesti, designed for performance in 1668 in honor of the marriage of Holy Roman Emperor Leopold I to his Hapsburg cousin Margaretha, heiress of

closely resembles that in Rinucinni's *L'Euridice* of 1600. Buchner's second act is parallel to the suspense-building technique in Rinuccini's second scene, and Buchner's versification seems more imitative of Rinuccini's less regular line-lengths. The two Italian libretti have been reprinted in Hanning, *Of Poetry and Music's Power*, pp. 270–96 and 305–29.

[14] Anton Mayer, "Quelle und Entstehung von Opitzens Judith," *Euphorion* 20 (1913): 50–51, publishes letters which help to illuminate the relationship between Opitz and Schütz, and, peripherally, Schütz and Buchner. That Schütz was interested in mounting another opera in the 1630s is shown in his letter to a Saxon courtier, Friedrich Lepzelter, of 1633, published in Heinrich Schütz, *Gesammelte Briefe und Schriften*, ed. Erich H. Müller (Regensburg: Bosse, 1931), pp. 125–26.

[15] Rinuccini's *Dafne* was set by Jacopo Peri, Giulio Caccini, and Jacopo Corsi in 1597 and by Marco da Galiano in 1608; Rinuccini's *Euridice* was set to music in its entirety by both Caccini and Peri in 1600. German instances include Lucas von Bostel's *Der hochmütige, gestürtze und wieder erhobene Crösus*, set to music in 1684 by Johann Philipp Förtsch and in 1711 by Reinhard Keiser. See Brockpähler, *Handbuch*, pp. 201–6.

Spain and its rich possessions in the New World.[16] The performance in
Vienna, delayed by several events, apparently occurred in 1668, but the
libretto had already been published and distributed throughout Europe in
an honorific edition of 1667. Performance of the opera probably took place
only once — in spite of the claims of several slightly later chroniclers[17] —
due not only to its honorific, occasion-oriented character, but also to its
scale: the opera, totalling seven or eight hours in length, was performed
over a two-day period, and cost a veritable fortune to mount. But the event
was so lavish, the honorific edition so opulently printed and illustrated, and
the text so extraordinary that the fame of *Il Pomo d'oro* was assured. The
opera is mentioned in eyewitness accounts and in chronicles of the period
with awe, in poetical treatises with approbation.[18] The musical score,
preserved only in partial manuscripts in Vienna and Modena,[19] was not
similarly disseminated, and I have found no evidence of any arias becoming
popular or joining published collections. In other words, it was the text, as
disseminated in the honorific editions of 1667 and 1668, which spread the
fame of the opera across Europe.

Clearly, the Italian libretto was indecipherable to most German readers,
and even those with the requisite smattering of the Italian of diplomacy or
trade would miss the wit and other subtleties. For those who wanted a
German version, one answer was Meyer's translation, published under the
title *Der guldene Apfel / Schauspiel / Behalten in Wien / auf das höchstherr-
lichst-gesegnete / Vermählungs-Fest: Dero Römisch. Käiserl. und Königlichen
Majestäten LEOPOLDS und MARGARETae / aufgesetzt von Francesco Sbarra,*

---

[16] *Il Pomo d'oro Festa teatrale Rappresentata in Vienna per l'augustissime Nozze delle
sacre cesaree e reali maestá di Leopoldo e Margherita componimento di Francesco
Sbarra* (Vienna: Matteo Cosmerovio, Stampatore della Corte, 1667 and 1668). On this
opera, see the introduction by Guido Adler to his edition of the work: Marc Antonio Cesti,
Il Pomo d'oro: Bühnenfestspiel, Denkmäler der Tonkunst in Österreich, vol. 6 (Vienna:
Artaria, 1896), pp. v–xxvi; Egon Wellesz, "Ein Bühnenfestspiel aus dem Siebzehnten
Jahrhundert," *Die Musik* 52 (1914): 191–217; H. Seifert, "Die Festlichkeiten zur ersten
Hochzeit Kaiser Leopolds I.," *Österreichische Musikzeitschrift* 29 (1974): 6–16; and Carl
B. Schmidt, "Antonio Cesti's Il Pomo d'oro: A Reexamination of a Famous Habsburg Court
Spectacle," *Journal of the American Musicological Society* 29 (1976): 381–412.

[17] Gottlieb Eucharius Rinck, in the second edition of his biography of Leopold, *Leopolds
des Grossen Römischen Kaysers Wunderwürdiges Leben und Thaten* of 1713, claims that
the opera was performed three times a week for a year in 1667–68. See Adler, p. vii.

[18] E.g., the chronicle of Rinck; Sigmund von Birken admires its artistry and poses it as a
model in his *Teutsche Rede- Bind- und Dicht-Kunst* (Nuremberg: Riegel, 1679; rpt. 1973),
p. 325.

[19] The Vienna score is available in Adler's edition, Cesti, *Il Pomo d'oro,* Denkmäler der
Tonkunst in Österreich, vols. 6 and 9 (containing music for Acts I, II, and IV); the missing
Acts III and V have been reconstructed on the basis of music found in Modena in Antonio
Cesti, *Il Pomo d'oro, Music for Acts III and V from Modena, Bibliotheca Estense, ms. mus.
E. 120,* ed. Carl B. Schmidt (Madison: A-R Editions, 1982).

Röm. Käis. Majest. Raht. Anjetzo aber aus dem Italienischen übersetzt.[20] Meyer's text, primarily a prose rendition with occasional verse passages, fills one volume, while the second volume of the set contains the engravings from the original Italian editions.

A quick glance at the verse portions — reflecting arias and ariose passages — in Meyer's translation reveals that even these didn't constitute a singing translation, for he does not attempt to imitate the verse-form of his original. The delightful comic aria of Charon, the boatman who ferries the dead across the river Styx into Hades — for a price — is a case in point. The Italian is a two-strophe da capo aria with varying, primarily short line lengths and an interestingly varied rhyme scheme, as the first strophe shows:

E così	Does thus
Sfacendato	nothing get done
Tutto il dì?	all day long?
Vagabondo et otioso	Idle and bored,
A riposo	ready for bed,
Devo star?	must I be?
Non hò pur un sol denar	I haven't earned a single coin
In tutt'hoggi guadagnato;	all day today.
E così	Does thus
Sfacendato	nothing get done
Tutto il dì?[21]	all day long?

But Meyer's translation nearly negates the da capo form and forces the whole into eight lines with a regular four-beat trochaic meter and two rhyme schemes traditional in German (ABAB followed by CCAA), as his first strophe can demonstrate:

So muss' ich im Müssiggang	Must I spend in idleness
Diesen gantzen Tag zubringen!	the entire day?
Wie ist mir die Zeit so lang!	How slowly time passes!
Ich hab durch das Ruderschwingen	I haven't earned a penny
Keinen Pfennig heut erworben.	today with my rudder.
Lieber wär ich längst gestorben.	I'd rather have died long ago.
O verfluchter Müssiggang /	O cursed idleness,
Wie ist mir die Zeit so lang![22]	How slowly time passes!

---

[20] Nuremberg: Felßecker, 1672; rpt. ed. Margret Dietrich (Vienna, 1965). The preface is signed by "Joh. Gab. Meyer."

[21] Cesti, *Il Pomo d'oro*, ed. Guido Adler, vol. 9, p. 33 (Act II, scene vi).

[22] Meyer, *Der guldene Apfel*, unpaginated (Act II, scene vi).

Meyer's lack of poetic talent aside, it is clear that this strophic verse rendering is not intended as a singing translation, and thus his translation has nothing to offer towards the solution of our problem of German-language libretti without scores. The rest of his versified passages similarly ignore the verse form of their originals.

However, Meyer's translation was not the only German-language translation of *Il Pomo d'oro*, and the other to have survived — this one by a major poet and dramatist, Caspar Stieler — while also not intended as a singing translation in its entirety, can certainly be used as if it were in a few passages where the translator has rather exactly transformed the Italian verse of his original into German. And his other versification in this text, which all imitates but does not exactly reproduce the metric and other structures of the original, can also help us to understand in a general way how a German opera of this period might have sounded.

Caspar Stieler's translation of *Il Pomo d'oro*, which he titled *Der Göldene Apfel / Freudenspiel / vorgestellet in Wien / auf das höchstansehnliche Beylager/ Ihrer Keyserl. und Königl. / Maiest.*[en] */ Leopolds und / Margarethen / aufgesetzt / von Frantz Sparra. / Keyserl. M.*[t] *Rath.*,[23] is preserved in a single manuscript presentation copy in what was once the ducal library in Weimar.[24] According to information on the title page, Stieler translated the famous libretto at the behest of his employer and patron, Duke Johann Ernst of Saxony-Weimar, in 1669. There is no indication of the intended use for his translation, nor is there any indication that he had access to the score or any part of it. I have in the past maintained my belief that it was intended for performance utilizing some of Cesti's aria settings,[25] but today I am not so sure. Nevertheless, several of Stieler's aria translations can easily be sung to Cesti's music, and thus it is now possible to hear how German-language arias, at least, might have sounded if set to the Italian or Italianate music that was then the fashion.

One such aria is the song of Charon the boatman, already examined above in the Italian original and in the regular *Lied* version by Meyer. Stieler has exactly copied the use of an odd number of lines, the differing line lengths, the meter, and the rhyme scheme of the Italian original in his German version:

[23] The author identifies himself only with his pen name in the Fruchtbringende Gesellschaft, "der Spahte."

[24] Ms. Q580. Scholar Conrad Höfer made a handwritten copy in the early part of this century which still exists in Coburg (Ms. 104). I have made typescript copies and have plans to publish an edition.

[25] In my book, *Scaramutza in Germany: The Dramatic Works of Caspar Stieler* (University Park, PA: Penn. State Press, 1989), p. 110.

Soll denn nicht
werden heute
ichts verricht?
Jähnend steh' ich und halb schlaffend,
nichts nicht schaffend,
ohn Verdinst,
nicht ein heller ist gewinst,
Dieser tag bringt schlechte Beute.
Soll denn nicht
werden heute
ichts verricht?[26]

Shall then
nothing get done
today at all?
Yawning I stand, half asleep.
Doing nothing,
out of work,
not a Heller earned:
this day brings little booty.
Shall then
nothing get done
today at all?

The three-line da capo segment is intact, with its odd, nearly orphaned rhyme word "heute" echoed in the final line of the five-line "body" of the aria — "Beute." Even the internal rhymes, slant rhymes, and assonances — so easy to do in Italian — find felicitous imitation here. The rhythms of the German fit the Italian closely enough that it is possible to sing Stieler's text to Cesti's score, as in this sample: [27]

---

[26] Stieler, *Der göldene Apfel*, p. 118 (Act II, scene vi).

[27] In this version, both for this example and the following one, the basso continuo line has been reconstructed by Philip Blackburn, Ph.D. candidate in Composition and Graduate Assistant in the School of Music at the University of Iowa, where he is also conductor of the Lynceus Consort, from the realization done in the late nineteenth century by Guido Adler in his edition, Marc Antonio Cesti, *Il Pomo d'oro, Bühnenfestspiel*, Denkmäler der Tonkunst in Österreich, vols. 6 and 9 (Vienna: Artaria & Co., 1896–97). Mr. Blackburn also furnished the transcriptions for this published version. Indispensable in my work on this project was my Undergraduate Scholar Assistant, Donna S. Parsons (a Piano and Voice Major in the School of Music, she also is completing a minor in German), who helped me determine what German passages might be singable to the original music, challenged my hypothesis and at times dashed my hopes, and managed and coordinated the creation of the revised score and its performance recorded on tapes in my possession. My thanks are also due to Dean Philip G. Hubbard and the Office of Academic Affairs of the University of Iowa which provided the financial support of my Scholar Assistant and to the Graduate College, which paid for the other expert assistance received for this project.

A serious aria, too, has a Stieler text which fits Cesti's music. In Act II, scene viii, the eager Paris sings a martial aria as he and his companions set off on their journey to seize Helen of Troy. Stieler's translation fits the format exactly enough that it can also be sung to Cesti's musical setting, for here, too, line length, meter, rhyme scheme, and phrase endings coincide. The first verse of this four-strophe aria offers the opportunity to reconstruct the style of a serious aria:

Ready
and waiting
to head out to sea,
soon
to depart
for Sparta,
soon
to depart
for Sparta.

I have found at least three other arias for which Stieler's translation rather exactly imitates the verse form of his original.[28]

Thus in these arias which Stieler has translated from the Italian into exactly the same structure in German, we can "hear" German opera of the middle of the second half of the seventeenth century, both comic and serious, as never before. Stieler, master translator and poet that he is, even manages to find equivalents for the manipulations of sounds and to place crucial words so that they can be sung to the same notes as in the original.

---

[28] III, v (the Italian has an extra unaccented syllable at the end of some lines); III, x; and V, i.

The sheer difficulty he faced and the virtuosity of his solutions will be recognized by anyone who has ever tried to provide a singing translation for a song or aria. That the task is well nigh impossible in recitative, with its looser rhythms which echo natural speech, should be clear.

Yet Stieler's recitative verses in his translation of *Il Pomo d'oro* (and in other operatic works of his) are indeed a singable German equivalent to the Italian recitative, which, with music composed specifically for it, could — and probably did — provide a successful German-language recitative text for the dialogue portions of opera which resembled natural speech — parlando style, "speaking in tones."[29] Stieler's experiments with recitative, not those of Opitz, Buchner, Harsdörffer, or Schirmer, formed the foundation for the flowering of the Hamburg opera, and particularly for the rendition of comic recitative. One example of this new German verse form for recitative from Stieler's translation of *Il Pomo d'oro* will serve to characterize its requisites — the comic interchange of the fool, Momo, with the highly fallible Olympic deities as they pass around a bottomless goblet of wine:

Apollo.	Zu deinem Ruhm, O Großer Jupiter,
	sey dieser Güldne becher leer.
	Dir, bruder Mars gehört er nun
	der Durst mir ist gestillet.
	Drum sey er bald gefüllet.
Mars.	Auf dein verewigt Wohlergehen
	soll Vater, ihn Neptun,
	mein Vetter, bald in händen sehen.
	Die Brust
	schöpft Lust
	wenn Mund und Geist mit Wein
	begoßen seyn.
Momo.	Der Waßer Gott, soll der auch trinken Wein?
	Das muß nicht seyn.

(I, iv)[30]

Apollo.	To your fame, O great Jupiter,
	may this glass be emptied!
	Your turn now, Brother Mars,
	I've drunk my fill.
	May the glass quickly fill again.

[29] Terminology common in definitions of recitative, deriving from the earliest Italian purveyors and theorists of *dramma per musica*.

[30] It is interesting to note that the Italian original for this particular passage is not irregular, free-form recitative, but aria, with several isostrophic units including internal repetition. Stieler here ignores the regularity.

Mars.   To your eternal well-being,
        father [Jupiter]; now comes the turn
        of Neptune, my cousin.
        The heart
        feels good
        when mouth and spirit
        overflow with wine.
Momo.   [Neptune], the god of water, should he drink wine?
        That must not be.

Although Stieler elsewhere in *Il Pomo d'oro* also uses trochaic or dactylic meter for recitative,[31] such free-form iambic verse as we see here is the standard recitative form which he will bequeath to the Hamburg opera.[32] In this new recitative verse form, the meter is uniformly iambic, lines range from one to five beats in length, and the rhymes are scattered, even across the boundary of a new speaker (although there is a tendency to end comic speeches with a pair of rhyming lines, usually of different length). Each line (and thus each rhyme) coincides with natural phrasing in speech, and will be set in any musical score as musical phrases, possibly — as in the arias discussed above — with a rest in between. Needless to say, such free-form verse, which resists all the traditional sorts of regularizing except for meter without obliterating the sense that it is poetry, was new to German verse-making. So new that Martin Opitz and his followers until the time of Stieler did not — indeed, probably could not[33] — produce a truly singable recitative text. The sole exception — the only poet who, previous to Stieler, produced a continuous free-form iambic dialogue libretto — was Simon

---

[31] In fact, the following segment of this scene is trochaic.

[32] Christian Friedrich Hunold (Menantes) declared iambic the rule for madrigalic verse (recitative) in his *Die allerneueste Art / Zur Reinen und Galanten Poesie zu gelangen* (Hamburg: Brandt, 1735), p. 232.

[33] As a letter from Heinrich Schütz to Caspar Ziegler, published in the latter's slim volume of instructions on how to write madrigalic verse (recitative) in 1653, would seem to show. See Caspar Ziegler, *Von den Madrigalen*, ed. Dorothea Glodny-Wiercinski, Ars Poetica, no. 12 (Frankfurt am Main: Athenäum, 1971), pp. 26–27. The letter, which Ziegler uses in lieu of the more traditional laudatory poems by famous well-wishers to recommend his book to his reader, contains a justification for the need of such a book at this relatively late date and may even imply that Schütz's own expressed dissatisfaction with the current state of affairs had led to the writing and publishing of this volume. Schütz had, of course, contributed scores for a number of operas and *Sing-Ballette* before this date; one can only conclude that he found the recitative portions of the libretti inadequate for the needs of a composer.

Dach of Königsberg,[34] with whom Stieler studied during his sojourn at the university there in the 1650s.[35]

Libretti without scores will remain a major obstacle to any effort to reconstruct German-language opera of the seventeenth century, yet these libretti can still tell us a great deal. Aria style can be studied on the basis of surviving arias, *Lieder*, choruses, and Harsdörffer's *Seelewig* in its entirety, as well as using the few singing translations of Stieler and others from Italian operas for which the scores have survived. Using such material as a basis for comparison, we can make surmises about those arias, *Lieder*, and choruses for which no music survives. The common features are versification and poetic structure. Similarly, listening to Italian recitative of the period from such surviving scores as Cesti's *Il Pomo d'oro* can offer insight into German usage as well, even though we lack any German recitative excerpts complete with music and any singing translation of recitative passages. Stieler's equivalents in *Der goldene Apfel* and his other works[36] can show us the way, just as they probably did the librettists of the Hamburg opera,[37] which made its triumphal entry into the history of German-language opera in 1679,[38] only a decade after Stieler presented his verse translation of what could well be called the grandest grand opera of them all.

---

[34] See note 6, above.

[35] On this period in Stieler's life, see Herbert Zeman, *Kaspar Stieler: Versuch einer Monographie*, Diss. Vienna, 1965, pp. 23–31. I consider it likely that Stieler saw, or even participated in the revival performance of *Sorbuisa* in 1656 on the anniversary of the founding of the university. Influence of Dach and his poetry upon Stieler's lyric poetry has been demonstrated by Albert Köster, *Der Dichter der Geharnschten Venus: Eine litterarhistorische Untersuchung* (Marburg: Elwert, 1897), p. 71.

[36] Including madrigalic songs and madrigals in his *Die Geharnschte Venus* (Hamburg: Guht, 1660), recitative passages in the *Zwischenspiele* of several of his Rudolstadt plays of 1665–67 and the entire text of one of them, *Die Wittekinden* (Jena: Neuenhahn, 1666), plus the pastoral verse drama which is probably an opera libretto, *Melissa*, of 1668. See my treatment of these works in the context of the development of the early German opera in my *Scaramutza in Germany*, Chapter 7, "Caspar Stieler and the German 'Singspiel,'" pp. 105–41.

[37] I believe that one of the earliest, and certainly one of the best early Hamburg operas is a Stieler adaptation of a prose play by Christian Weise. The libretto in question is *Floretto* (1683). See my treatment in *Scaramutza in Germany*, pp. 80–91 and 110–14.

[38] On the Hamburg opera, see especially Hellmut Christian Wolff, *Die Barockoper in Hamburg (1678–1738)* (Wolfenbüttel: Möseler, 1957).

Musical Rhetoric and Politics in the Early German Lied

GARY C. THOMAS

THE THREE SHORT DECADES between roughly 1630 and 1660 encompass the emergence and brief flowering of the so-called baroque song in Germany — the first chapter, as it were, in the history of the modern Lied, the more intimate moments in that protracted and ongoing love-affair between music and the German language. Like the new poetry being written in the wake of Martin Opitz's *Buch von der deutschen Poeterey*, the music for this new type of solo song was fashioned out of both old and new elements. From its modest beginnings in Nauwach's *Teutsche Villanellen* in 1627 to its culmination some few years later in the collections of Heinrich Albert, Adam Krieger, Constantin Christian Dedekind, and others, the new solo Kunstlied represented a convergence of musical styles, both German and non-German. No genre held as tenaciously to old models or was as susceptible to trendy influence from new ones as the Lied and the musical practices found here constitute something of an arena — a *Schauplatz*, to use the baroque term — of different, often competing, and not rarely antagonistic formal impulses. But "formal impulses" don't exist in a cultural vacuum, "styles" don't lead autonomous lives of their own. And meaning in music is never simply a question of notes on a printed page. A good deal of the early development of the Lied, for example, is played out against the devastating backdrop of the Thirty Years' War — also a *Schauplatz* of competing forces, German and non-German, and a powerful and haunting presence in literary discourses of the period. Like all other modes of human expression, music, too, is a discourse, consisting in any given instance of a set of signifying practices which are at once rhetorical, grounded in social and historical reality, and therefore always in some sense ideological. It is in fact in the baroque period, for the first time since the Greeks (indeed inspired by their thoughts on the subject), that the nature of music as a signifying system is first theorized in a way that we would recognize as modern. My purpose here is threefold: to sketch the emergence of such musical-rhetorical connections, to examine some of the musical signifying codes found in the early German Lied, and, finally, to suggest some of the ways in which this genre constitutes a site of negotiation of competing cultural and ideological meanings. I will take as a case study the *Aelbianische Musen-Lust* of Constantin Christian Dedekind, published in Dresden in

1657, the largest self-contained collection and one of the richest sources of the entire period.[1]

The new solo song as we encounter it in the collections of the 1650s is shaped by numerous and geographically varied influences: the French chanson and psalm setting, often by way of the Dutch; the Italian frottola, villanella, and new solo madrigal; native German forms such as the Kirchenlied and Volkslied; and finally the ubiquitous dance-songs found everywhere, from Spain to Poland and Naples to London.[2] While it is possible to tease out the strands of these complicated interrelationships, such is not my intention here. I will speak instead of the two fundamentally different kinds of musical impulse which are to be found in these various sources, taking as my point of departure the generic distinction made by Christoph Bernhard in his short treatise *Von der Singe-Kunst, oder Manier* published around 1660, namely the division between *musica choralis* and *musica figuralis*.

The first, *musica choralis*, refers not specifically to polyphonic music for a chorus, but rather to the simple, homophonic-syllabic (one syllable to one note) kinds of musical setting which are textually and musically organized into self-contained and repeatable strophes. The determining principle of this kind of music is suggested by the two key words "choralis" and "strophe," both of which have their origin in the dance. The signal importance for the strophic lied of impulses originating in dance music, especially the physical involvement of the human body, was first elaborated by Walter Wiora in his 1971 study, *Das deutsche Lied: Zur Geschichte und Ästhetik einer musikalischen Gattung*. On the relation of strophe, chorus, and dance to the Lied he writes:

> Das griechische Wort "strophe" bedeutet Wendung und zwar besonders die "Tanzwendung des Chors in der Orchestra und das der jeweiligen Wendung entsprechende, zum Tanz vorgetragene Chorlied." Ursprünglich war Strophe somit kein spezifisch literarischer oder spezifisch musikalischer Terminus, sondern das Wort meinte eine Bewegungsgestalt aus Wort, Ton und Tanz. Auch die Begriffe "Vers" und Vers "fuß" haben ihren Ursprung in der Bewegung nicht nur der Stimme, sondern zugleich des Körpers. Diese Einheit lebt bis heute im Tanzliede fort und wirkt in den anderen Arten des Strophenliedes nach: im Tanz der Stimme, in pulsierendem Taktrhythmus, in unausgeprägten Mitbewegungen.... Viele Anschauungen über das Strophenlied sind darum unzureichend, weil sie den Anteil der

---

[1] Dedekind's collection is now available in a facsimile reprint, with introduction, bibliography, and transcriptions of selected songs in modern notation, in the series *Nachdrucke deutscher Literatur des 17. Jahrhunderts*, vol. 47, ed. Gary C. Thomas (Bern: Peter Lang, 1991).

[2] John H. Baron, "Foreign Influences on the German Secular Solo Continuo Lied of the Mid-Seventeenth Century" (Ph.D. diss., Brandeis University, 1967).

Körperbewegung an seinem Ursprung oder, anders gesagt, die ursprüng-
liche Einheit des leibseelischen Vorganges nicht berücksichtigen.[3]

As in the dance, the principal structural feature of the strophic lied is that
of orderly recurrence: recurrence of the original strophic shape and, within
the strophe, recurrence of musical and textual phrase groupings, or periods
and, finally, the underlying stability and order provided by a steady
recurrent rhythmic pulse. Whether we find it in the Italian frottola, French
chanson, in the old German Kirchenlied, or the new solo Kunstlied, such
music is based virtually without exception on regular metric and rhythmic
schemata, all of which have their origins in the dance. Several of these
genres were understood to be danced as well as sung and played from the
beginning, hence the common indication *per sonare, cantare e ballare,* or
zum klingen, singen und tanzen. Whatever their origins, however, the
musical-textual relationship of *musica choralis* served essentially the same
purpose: to be simple, memorable, easily grasped, clearly articulated, and
— what is of no little importance — singable by ordinary people.

At the other extreme from the orderly impulses of the dance or Lied, and
in opposition to them, Bernhard places the conventions of *musica figuralis.*
Here he is thinking primarily of those tendencies of Italian solo singing
invented in the late sixteenth-century humanistic circles of the Florentine
Camerata and developed in the new dramatic genres of solo madrigal,
cantata, and opera, principally by Claudio Monteverdi. The most prominent
feature of this so-called "madrigalism" was a voice line shaped not by the
orderly periodicity of a given dance-strophic model, but rather in complete
emancipation from it; that is, a solo line which moved freely above its
accompanying basso continuo in a wide range of melodic and rhythmic
gestures and which employed a new musical vocabulary based on verbal
meanings rather than numerical relationships: based, that is, on rhetoric, the
art of persuasion. If the strophic-dance model aimed at predictable regularity
and a clean simplicity in the word-tone relationship, the new music — the
Nuove Musiche as it was called — sought a freer, more expansive as well as
expressive relationship. Moreover, the new Italian solo song was far from

---

[3] Walter Wiora, *Das deutsche Lied: Zur Geschichte und Ästhetik einer musikalischen
Gattung* (Wolfenbüttel & Zurich: Möseler Verlag, 1971), p. 23; "The Greek word 'strophe'
means turn, specifically the moment when the chorus turns to dance in the orchestra, as
well as the choral songs which accompanied such dances. Thus, originally, strophe was
not a specifically literary or specifically musical term, but referred rather to a form of
movement consisting of word, tone, and dance. Even the concepts of 'verse' and verse
'foot' trace their origin to the movement not only of the voice but also of the body. This
unity survives to the present day in the dance song and is still felt in other effects of
strophic song: in the dance of the voice, in the pulsating rhythm of the measure, as well
as in other more subtle kinds of accompanying movement.... Many reflections on the
strophic lied falter precisely because they fail to take into account the participation of the
body in its origins, or, put differently, in the original unity of the physical process itself."

universally singable: on the contrary, its vocal demands required individual performers of some accomplishment, if not considerable technical virtuosity.

What was being pursued by the gentlemen of the Florentine Camerata and later by Monteverdi and others far exceeds the array of technical devices of *musica figuralis* to embrace a wholly new conception of what music is and is capable of doing. It in fact amounted to nothing short of a revolutionary agenda, one carried out in the sphere of theory as well as practice. The axis of this revolution turned on the shifting relationship of music to words. Theoretical concern for this is evident as early as the mid-sixteenth century, particularly in the emerging distinction between two kinds of music, the "mathematical" on the one hand, and the "poetic" on the other.[4] In Coclicus' treatise *Musica Reservata* of 1552, for example, the two are distinguished in this way: "mathematical" specified composition according to the strict rules of number and proportion associated with Renaissance polyphony and counterpoint — the kind of music perfected by, for example, Dufay and Binchois. The epithet "poetic" was applied to composers who, like Coclicus' teacher Josquin des Prez, were concerned that music express the meaning and feeling of the words. Familiarity with the concept in Germany is evidenced, for example, by Hermann Finck's *Practica Musica* (Wittenberg, 1556), in which the modern or "poetic" composers are described as those who "devote more care to the sweetness of the euphony and are diligent and careful in fitting the text so that it agrees with the notes placed above it and so that these notes express in the best possible way the meaning of the discourse and the various affections."[5] The idea that music should be involved in semantics — verbal meaning — and with the expression of emotions lies at the core the Humanist program for the *musicus poeticus.* The art of music, or at least a very significant branch of it, was thus moving away from the Quadrivium, where for centuries it had consorted with mathematics and astronomy, and into the Trivium and the company of logic, grammar and, most importantly, rhetoric.

At the turn of the seventeenth century a further generation of musicians pitted itself against the old polyphonists with a much more audacious program and the enthusiasm as well as defensiveness of a true avant-garde. One of the major features of this program was precisely the emancipation of the solo line from the community of polyphonic voices. This solo line was to be put at the complete disposal of the text, usually a highly dramatic narrative poem. The distinction between the two styles is in fact now so sharply drawn that two terms separately identified them: the *prima prattica,* meant the old music — which was by no means abandoned — and the *seconda prattica,* referred to the new, and was variously labeled as the

---

[4] Gerard LeCoat, *The Rhetoric of the Arts, 1550–1650* (Bern: Herbert Lang, 1975), p. 19.

[5] Quoted from LeCoat, *Rhetoric*, p. 19. Original: Hermann Finck, *Practica musica* (Wittenberg: E. Rhaw, 1556). Facsimile ed., Bologna: Forni, 1969, fo. 2 S.

"modern," the "luxuriant " and, perhaps most significantly, the "representational" style, or *stile rappresentativo*. It is here in the *seconda prattica* that we can clearly observe the appropriation of music as a rhetorical discourse: it not only adopted the aims of rhetoric, to persuade, to teach, and to move, but it also set about developing musical equivalents to the wealth of technical devices available to the rhetorician.

The key figure in this movement, and its most articulate spokesperson, was Monteverdi himself. In the preface to his fifth book of madrigals of 1605, in which he responded to the allegation that he composed his music haphazardly, Monteverdi makes it clear that music is not only to accommodate the word but is to be absolutely subservient to it. He insisted that he did not compose his music haphazardly, but rather in accordance with the demands of the words, which he intended to make the master rather than the servant of the music. And in the foreword to his *Madrigali guerrieri ed amorosi* of 1638 he makes plain that in the new program, composers, like rhetoricians, must have at their disposal techniques enabling them to express the entire range of human affections; in other words, a complete pathology:[6]

> Havendo io considerato le nostre passioni od affettioni del animo essere tre le principali, cioè ira, temperanza et umiltà o supplicatione, come bene gli migliori filosofi affermano, anzi la natura stessa de la voce nostra in ritrovarsi alta, bassa et mezzana, et come l'arte musica lo notifica chiaramente in questi tre termini di concitato, molle et temperato, né avendo in tutte le compositioni de passati compositori potuto ritrovare esempio del concitato genere, ma ben sí del molle et temperato; genere però descritto da Platone nel terzo *De rethorica*[7] con queste parole: "Suscipe harmoniam illam quae ut decet imitatur euntis in proelium, voce, atque accente," et sapendo che gli contrarii sono quelli che movono grandemente l'animo nostro ... perciò mi posi con non poco mio studio et fatica per ritrovarlo ...

---

[6] Claudio Monteverdi, *Tutte le Opere*, vol. VIII, ed. G. Francesco Malipiero (Asolo, 1929), p. iii: "I have reflected that the principal passions or affections of our mind are three, namely, anger, moderation, and humility or supplication; so the best philosophers declare, and the very nature of our voice indicates this in having high, low, and middle registers. The art of music also points clearly to these three in its terms 'agitated,' 'soft,' and 'moderate' (*concitato, molle,* and *temperato*). In all the works of former composers I have indeed found examples of the 'soft' and the 'moderate' but never of the 'agitated,' a genus nevertheless described by Plato in the third book of his *Rhetoric* in these words: 'Take a harmony that would fittingly imitate the utterances and the accents of a brave man who is engaged in warfare.' And since I was aware that it is contraries which greatly move our mind ... I have applied myself with no small diligence and toil to rediscover this genus." Trans. from Oliver Strunk, *Source Readings in Music History* (New York: Norton, 1950), p. 413.

[7] The reference is actually to Plato's *Republic*.

But the notion of music as a type of rhetoric appears elsewhere as well; the movement was spreading. The degree to which rhetoric had by the early to mid-seventeenth century become a central category for the music theorist as well as the composer is well documented in the numerous references and comparisons found in Italian, French, German, and English sources. Thus Henry Peacham in the *Compleat Gentleman* (1622):[8]

> Yea, in my opinion no rhetoric more persuadeth or hath greater power over the mind; nay, hath not music her figures, the same with rhetoric? What is a revert but her antistophe? her reports [imitations] but sweet anaphoras? her counterchange of points, anti-metaboles [unexpected opposition in figures]? her passionate airs, but prosopopeias [personification]? with infinite other of the same nature.

Even more definitive is the following prescription found in a theoretical source of major importance, one devoted entirely to music, the *Harmonie Universelle* (1636) by the Frenchman Marin Mersenne. In the opening paragraph on the embellishment of songs Mersenne writes that the "harmonic orator" must know "all that which is relevant to the accents of the passions ... in order to provoke in the listener the desired reaction...." He must "imitate the art of the harangue, using all sorts of figures and harmonic passages, as does the orator.... The art of composing airs, and counterpoint, constitutes a kind of rhetoric."[9]

We can thus identify a rough set of affinities along two lines: with the mathematical composers, the *prima prattica* and Bernhard's *musica choralis*, on the one hand — all practices based in one way or another primarily on numerical relationships — and with the poetic composers, the *seconda prattica* and Bernhard's *musica figuralis* on the other — all focused on music as interpreter and producer of verbal (or verbalizable) meaning. But just as important, and quite apart from the specific agenda of the *seconda prattica* and the virtuoso experiments of the Italians, we see that a new conception of music itself has taken root, of music candidly recognized as a discourse or signifying practice, one which could henceforth be theorized not only or even primarily as an autonomous formal-aesthetic structure unto itself, but as one discursive practice among others.

One of the ways of looking at German Lied of the 1650s, then, is as a site of negotiation between principles of the old strophic dance model and the freer, more adventuresome expressivity of the new music. Some collections, particularly early on, evince great delight in experimenting with the new style rapidly insinuating itself from Italy into the north: Thomas Selle's

---

[8] Henry Peacham, *The Compleat Gentleman* (Oxford: Clarendon, 1906), p. 104. Quoted from Strunk, *Source Readings*, p. 337.

[9] Marin Mersenne, *L'Harmonie universelle*, facsimile ed. (Paris: Centre National de la Recherche Scientifique, 1963), p. 365.

Monophonetica, published 1636 in Hamburg, and Caspar Kittel's *Arien und Kantaten,* published 1638 in Dresden, are cases in point. But the most important center of Italian influence throughout the period was and remained the Saxon court at Dresden, and that because of the singular importance of one figure: Heinrich Schütz. Schütz had of course lived in Italy — he studied with Gabrieli in Venice and had at the very least made the acquaintance of Monteverdi — and he was also responsible for bringing Italian musicians, composers, and singers, including castrati, as well as theater people of all sorts to the court in Dresden where they enjoyed enormous prestige and popularity in aristocratic entertainments. Through Schütz and his star pupil Christoph Bernhard, who had also lived and studied in Italy, the virtuoso vocabulary of the new style became thoroughly familiar in the heart of Germany.

Toward the end of the Thirty Years' War, i.e., in the late 1640s, and at the opposite end of the Elbe, however, an ideological reaction was being mounted against all things foreign, Italian and otherwise. During this long war Germany had been the theatre of belligerent forces of many nationalities and as a consequence had been exposed to a great variety of foreign folk and art music. At the end of hostilities and under the banner of nationalistic reform, the search for German roots and a German national character gained urgency. It is at this point that the simple Lied style, with its echoes of the older Kirchenlied and Volkslied and the values associated with them regained prominence and stature, for example in Hamburg under the direction of Johann Rist, Philipp von Zesen, and their subordinates in the Elbschwanenorden and Deutschgesinnete Genossenschaft, but also in the circle of poets around Heinrich Albert in Königsberg. Rist especially inveighed against the "profane art" of the Italians and the permissive "welsch" culture that engendered it, championing instead the simple and easily singable German Lied. By the same token, efforts to gain acceptance for the freer, non-repeating madrigal strophe or for the bouncy dactylic meter in poetry — efforts encouraged by musicians, including Schütz — also met with considerable resistance.[10]

It is between these two extremes that Constantin Christian Dedekind and his massive collection, the *Aelbianische Musen-Lust,* take their place. Dedekind came to the court of Dresden sometime before 1650 and soon established himself as both poet and composer. His connections with Schütz and the Italian school of singing were extensive, partly through Bernhard, with whom he probably studied and to whom he was eventually related by marriage. The *Aelbianische Musen-Lust,* published in 1657 and reissued in 1665, bears in its prefatory apparatus warm recommendations from both Schütz and Bernhard, whose effusive gratulatory poem arrived at the last minute from Italy.

---

[10] Cf. Gary Thomas, "Dance Music and the Origins of the Dactylic Meter," *Daphnis: Zeitschrift für Mittlere Deutsche Literatur* 16, no. 1–2, (1987): 107–46.

But Dedekind's connections with the north were equally important, and if we can consider Schütz his "Musikvater," we must think of Johann Rist, the Hamburg pastor and head of the Elbschwanenorden, as his "Dichtervater." Dedekind became a member of Rist's literary organization at about the time of the publication of the *Musen-Lust* and evidence suggests that he may have had ties to Philipp von Zesen in Hamburg as well.[11] Dedekind's important collection, situated culturally between the upper and lower Elbe and between these two in many ways antagonistic artistic fields, provides us then with an ideal site to investigate their ideological negotiation.

The first thing we notice about the *Aelbianische Musen-Lust* is the remarkable fastidiousness with which it is organized: from the neat symmetry of the title page woodcut and arrangement of the songs to the compositional practices themselves. The work is divided into four main sections, containing first the *Lieder*, whose one hundred fifty-five pieces make up the bulk of the collection, followed by the *Canzonetten,* of which there are but twenty. The four sections are further subdivided into four groups of ten songs each: three groups of ten songs of a single poet followed in each case by a concluding mixed group of various poets. The fourth and final section is divided into two groups of twenty songs each without further subdivision: twenty songs by Dedekind alone, followed by the final twenty canzonettas, again with texts of various authorship. A motto in the form of a rhymed couplet precedes each song, and each group of ten concludes with what Dedekind dubbed an "Inhaltslied" (content song) which programmatically summarizes the theme or themes around which each set of songs is organized. The collection is also structured chronologically by the generation of the poets represented, starting with Opitz and ending with Dedekind, as well as by their geographical location, a symmetrical arrangement mirrored in the title woodcut. This features a double *Musenberg* consisting of an ancient parnassus, bestrewn with the classical muses headed by Apollo, together with its modern German counterpart, with Opitz reigning supreme.

The work brings not merely various groups of poets from these different German regions together, but also presents a broad spectrum of compositional procedures, from the simplest syllabic settings of the *musica choralis* type to the complexly wrought, hyperexpressive gestures of the *musica figuralis*, found mainly in the canzonettas. Let us now turn to a brief examination of the musical signification in two of the Lieder in the collection. The first is a setting of a poem by Martin Opitz:[12]

---

[11] Cf. Wolfram Steude, "Das wiedergefundene Opus ultimum von Heinrich Schütz: Bemerkungen zur Quelle und zum Werk," *Schütz-Jahrbuch 1982/3* 4–5 (1983): 9–18.

[12] Dedekind, *Aelbianische Musen-Lust*, No. I-a-3 (Opitz source unknown).

Wer sich in dem Mittel hält   (a)
und nicht strebt nach hohen Sachen   (b)
wird nicht leichtlich umgefällt /   (a)
sondern seines Feindes lachen /   (b)
wär er unberühmt im Land /   (c)
ist er ihm doch selbst bekannt.   (c)

Dedekind's composition exemplifies what can be considered some of the fundamental musical-rhetorical impulses of the entire collection. The setting is simple and, like the outward disposition of the collection itself, fastidiously organized:

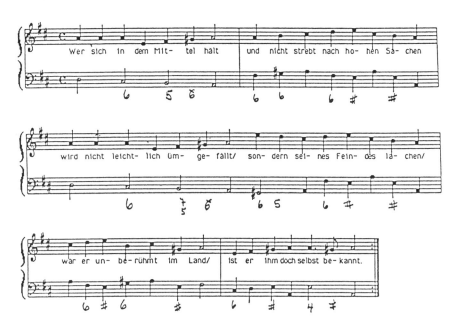

The music virtually mirrors the periodic structure of the strophe, the melody developing in rhythmic-periodic groups, here based loosely on the Allemand dance formula. The a-rhymes are set as rhyming sequences, as are (with slight variation) the b-rhymes. The c-rhymes are also rhythmically almost identical, yielding an almost complete synchronization of musical and textual form. The compositional technique here is deliberately unimposing but in no way unrhetorical, for the subject of this poem, like so many in the collection, is *moderation* (the poem's motto: "Halte Maass in allen Dingen / Das wird dihr kein Nachteil bringen"). The music signifies this with its completely unadventuresome melody which moves cautiously and only as far as the upper and lower E, returning immediately back to A, in other

words back to the note "in der Mitte," which is also the tonal center of the
piece.

The second example is a setting of one of Johann Rist's many poems on
the theme of vanity, "O Eitelkeit! du rechte Pest der Jugend":[13]

O Eitelkeit!	(a)
Du rechte Pest der Jugend	(b)
O schnelle Zeit!	(a)
du Mörderinn der Tugend /	(b)
wie bistu doch /	(c)
ein schwehres Joch!	(c)
den Männschen Kindern auf der Erden /	(d)
denn/ was nur lebt /	(e)
was fleucht und schwebt /	(e)
muß lauter Staub und Asche werden.	(d)

We note in this setting a significant extension of the musical vocabulary in
the service of greater dramatic expression:

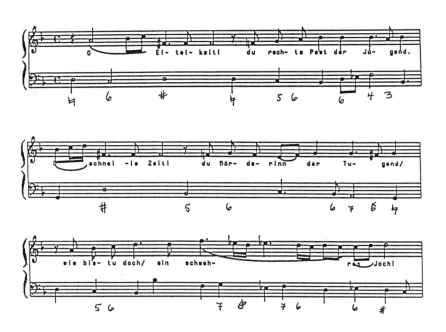

---

[13] Dedekind, *Aelbianische Musen-Lust*, No. II-a-4; from Johann Rist, *Des Edlen Daphnis aus
Cimbrien besungene Florabella* (Hamburg, 1656), No. 71.

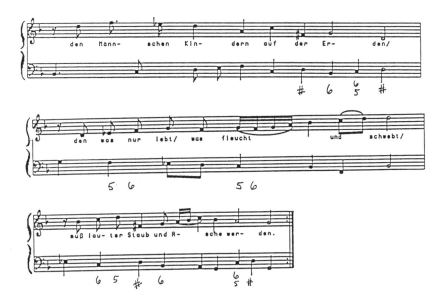

Perhaps Dedekind was tempted by the relatively large number of verses and their varying lengths (10 verses containing from 4 to 10 syllables), both unusual for the Lied, as well as by the presence of the stern rhetorical exclamations: "O Eitelkeit!" "O schnelle Zeit!" and "wie bist du doch ein schwehres Joch!" The opening musical phrase with its drawn out "O" above a virtually motionless basso continuo and containing the rare interval of a diminished fifth, is dramatically isolated by rests; this could well be the opening of a dramatic madrigal in the Italian *stile rappresentativo*. The second phrase however introduces more of a sense of an orderly rhythm and by the time we have arrived at the end of the fourth verse any recitativic tendency has been folded back into an orderly sequence replicating the *abab* rhyme scheme. The next two verses, however, are elided into a single long phrase reaching its expressive climax in a melismatic cadence on "schwehres Joch!," while the following long verse is once again separated by pauses in the music. Built principally on three descending intervals, among them the now motivic diminished fifth from c to f#, this line gently recalls the opening phrase of the song. The next two verses are again elided musically into a single phrase that now recalls, with its painterly ornamentation on "fleucht und schwebt," its previous musical counterpart in verses five and six. The final isolated phrase "muß lauter Staub und Asche werden"

hints at the motivic descending fifth interval (transformed here into a sixth) before returning in resignation to the tonic.

While bearing in mind that the Lied is "Kleinarbeit," a miniature, we can nonetheless see that the musical setting of the Rist poem approaches in its expressive aims and technical means the style of the Italian dramatic recitative. Its unusual and occasionally difficult melodic line would also have required the resources of a fairly accomplished, though not necessarily virtuoso singer. And yet, as a whole, the musical composition betrays a stubborn resistance to Italian madrigalism at the same time that it exploits elements of it, a resistance most plainly marked in its tendency organize itself according to the strict and orderly demands of the strophe.

In the final twenty canzonettas one would have expected much more in the way of hyperexpressive writing. And it is true that the virtuoso rhetorical vocabulary of *musical figuralis* is more abundantly evident here, particularly in the final ten or so numbers which are through-composed. We even encounter occasional tempo and dynamic markings, including — perhaps for the first time in western music — a triple *piano*. Yet if, as in the setting of the Rist poem, Dedekind occasionally approaches the solo madrigal or cantata style in his Lied settings, in the canzonettas he never completely abandons the basic musical scaffolding of the strophic Lied: the same recurrent rhythmical underpinning, albeit more richly varied, is without exception a feature of the canzonettas as well, and most of the texts, even those with through-composed settings, remain thoroughly committed to "German" strophicism.

At issue here is not simply the interface of musical styles, but rather in the larger picture, of different cultural values — values increasingly at odds in a Europe rapidly fragmenting into competing political and cultural factions. The title page of Francis Bacon's *Novum Organum* of 1620 shows a ship in full sail passing through the Columns of Hercules, the *ne plus ultra* of the Old World, to set out on a voyage of discovery.[14] And in his reflections on the baroque style Nietzsche notes the preoccupation of the arts of the period with what he calls "ever new ventures in means and aims."[15] Such images symbolize in many ways the heady, open-ended adventurism of the *Nuove Musiche* and the *seconda prattica*. This music, enterprising of the individual composer as well as performer, and bent on exploring, conquering, controlling, re-presenting, indeed *remaking* the world, is unthinkable apart from the wealthy, early capitalist social class in which it originated. It is hardly fortuitous that in much of the theoretical articulation of this new "baroque" style, whether we look in the fields of music, poetry, or visual art, two notions recur with remarkable consistency: *energeia* (meaning roughly "energy" and referring to the moving or arousal of the

---

[14] John Rupert Martin, *Baroque* (New York: Harper and Row, 1977), p. 66.

[15] Friedrich Nietzsche, *Menschliches, Allzumenschliches, II* (no. 144).

passions) and *enargeia* (meaning to represent or to make visible the world) — forerunners perhaps of Nietzsche's own concepts of the "Apollonian" and "Dionysian." Monteverdi's explorations into the power of music as a rhetorical agent, thematized in his opera *Orfeo,* led him inevitably to texts involving the extremes of human passion, sexuality, sensuality, and violence. His is a thoroughly secularized theatre of human power and desire, and the musical signifying practices situated there constitute an extensive elaboration of the techniques of *energeia* and *enargeia.* External spectacle, internal affect, sensual appeal to the eye and the ear employed for the purpose of "moving our souls through the clashing of the passions" (Monteverdi), "having power over the mind" (Peacham), or "provoking in the listener the desired reaction" (Mersenne): such is the agenda of the baroque rhetoricization of the arts, and of baroque cultural ideology generally. Or in José Maravall's succinct formulation:[16]

> The culture of the baroque is an instrument to achieve effects whose object is to act on human beings and which is designed to ensure that they behave, among themselves and with respect to the society of which they are a part and the power that controls it, in such a manner that the society's capacity for self-preservation is maintained and enhanced.... In sum, the baroque is nothing but a complex of cultural media of a very diverse sort that are assembled and articulated ... so as to succeed practically in directing them and keeping them integrated in the social system.

The German negotiation of this cultural agenda, from Schütz to Bach, is of course quite complex. Generally speaking, the open-ended sensuality and entrepreneurial politics of Italian music are everywhere met with the countervailing forces of control and containment. A typical response is to channel the secular, world- and body-affirming energy of the Italian style into the sphere of the religious. In his book on the painting of the period John Rupert Martin refers to this baroque sleight-of-hand — the process by which the spiritual is given sensual embodiment — rather neutrally as "the secularization of the transcendental."[17] With respect to the German reception of the Italian new music one is tempted to turn the phrase around to read "the transcendentalization of the secular." But even many secular texts, including pastoral love songs, such as those found in Dedekind and many other collections of solo Kunstlieder, are suffused with dour religious moralism, Protestant patriarchalism and misogyny, and, above all, an austere anti-eroticism: there are real and ideologically striking limits to the "Lust" enjoyed by our "Aelbianische Musen."

---

[16] José Antonio Maravall, *Culture of the Baroque: Analysis of a Historical Structure*, trans. Terry Cochran (Minneapolis: Univ. of Minnesota Press, 1986), p. 58.

[17] Martin, *Baroque*, p. 55.

The musical politics of Dedekind's collection are in fact shaped by a conservative, politically reactionary, middle-class agenda aimed at puritanical moderation and sexual repression. Like the outward organization of the collection itself, the compositional procedures control and restrain the musical vocabulary which simultaneously informs it: dances, in their origins intimately associated with bodily movement and passion, are in many cases slowed down, placed beneath an anti-erotic text, or are inflected by allusion to conventional melodic formulas of the Kirchenlied. Chromaticism and dissonance — important features of the *Nuove Musiche* — when not banished altogether, are quickly resolved into tonal harmony, often by the end of each individual verse. The music of the Lied, bent on policing desire and affirming the order and stability of the German middle-class household, its socio-cultural habitat, is every bit as rhetorical as the coy, sensual lyrics of the madrigal or the extravagant virtuoso displays of the courtly opera. Its rhetorical and political thrust aims at containment and order in opposition to openness and liberation; at continuity and national tradition in the face of cultural rupture and a threatening non-German avant-garde — all in all an early and conservative stance in the first of many musical battles to be waged in the post-baroque West between the forces of Carnival and those of Lent.[18]

---

[18] The metaphor is borrowed from Jacques Attali, *Noise*, trans. Brian Massumi (Minneapolis: Univ. of Minnesota Press, 1987).

Enlightenment

Bach and the Literary Scene in Eighteenth-Century Leipzig*

HANS JOACHIM KREUTZER

THE MUSIC OF JOHANN Sebastian Bach is, to an unusually large extent, determined by language. This applies not only to Bach's textual compositions, but naturally also to his choral arrangements for the organ. Above and beyond that, it has even been suggested that the structure of his instrumental works could have been determined by the rules of linguistic expression and logic as propounded in rhetorical theory. Although this hypothesis may not be verified, it nevertheless stresses the special importance of language for Bach's musical structure — a factor which was first recognized by the Bach-reception in this century.

The fundamental importance of pictorial expression for Bach's selection of themes was first discovered by Albert Schweitzer. This pictorial expression is beyond doubt determined by language, independent even of any detailed analogies between musical and rhetorical structures. Yet, Bach's significant repercussions today seem to stem almost exclusively from his music. By comparison, the texts which Bach set to music have almost been forgotten. They have always appeared, and not only to us today, much more antiquated than his compositions, so that even a literary-historical expert in the modern day and age often requires explanatory remarks for many passages.

When attempting to grasp how decisions were made by a composer who consumed, as it were, large quantities of literature, we are in fact trying to comprehend the historical interplay of various art forms. Such attempts are bound to encounter certain obstacles, one of the most common of which is the often wishful assumption that works of equal artistic merit originate at approximately the same time. We instinctively cherish the thought of a genius searching for his congenial counterpart in the supposition of a parallel development between literature and music, whereas incongruencies and compromises present great stumbling blocks. Critics feel secure as long as Goethe's poems are set to music by Schubert, but become uneasy when asked to explain how it is that Schubert's settings of works by Mayrhofer are every bit as good as his vocal arrangements of the harp-player in *Wilhelm Meister*.

Reflections on Johann Sebastian Bach's involvement with the literature of his time can lead one into a deep quagmire. In the past twenty years, literary experts have written a great deal and talked even more about trivial literature, showing particular interest in forms borrowed from poetical

---

* For an expanded version of this essay in German, see the *Bach-Jahrbuch* (1991).

literature. But "functional literature" — a more neutral and encompassing term — continues to be shunned by experts. Only opera librettos have received a certain amount of attention. We must therefore be cautious when we attempt to pursue our main inquiry, namely, what types of literature did Bach find most attractive? Did he at all proceed according to criteria of personal taste or opinion? Was he always in a position to choose?

A book on the literary history of Leipzig would contain the names of the most eminent German writers of the eighteenth century. From approximately 1720 to 1740, literature in the German-speaking world was reformed under the dominating influence of Johann Christoph Gottsched. Likewise, the early publications of Lessing and Klopstock, then students in Leipzig, occurred during Bach's later years. Yet these anacreontical and sentimental works seem to have made little impression on the composer.

Bach's literary partners, however, do not receive an amount of appreciation in literary histories — if they receive any notice at all — which would correspond to Bach's exceptional importance in the history of music. The low assessment of these authors by literary experts would astonish most musicologists. The only widely acknowledged author used by Bach is possibly Christian Friedrich Hunold-Menantes. His importance, however, lies mainly in the history of the novel. Specialists in the early periods of German literary historiography may be familiar with the name Erdmann Neumeister.[1] The text-writer most employed by Bach, Christian Friedrich Henrici, alias Picander, is only mentioned in footnotes. He has yet to receive the special attention he deserves in the history of German comedy. In 1970 another important author of Bachian cantata was discovered: Georg Christian Lehms.[2] His compendium of 620 German and other European woman authors, compiled 270 years ago, could even be viewed as an early example of research into the role of women in literature. His aim was to counter the prejudice

> daß ein Frauenzimmer so wenig tüchtig zum Studieren / als ein verächtlicher Zaun-König in die Sonne zu sehen ... gleich als wenn dieses edle und vortreffliche Geschlecht nur mit den blinden Maulwürffen im Finstern

---

[1] Erdmann Neumeister, *De poetis germanicis hujus seculi praecipuis dissertatio compendiaria* (Halle, 1695), ed. Franz Heiduk with Günter Merwald (Bern and Munich: Francke, 1978). Cf. Helmut K. Krause, "Die unverbotne Lust: Erdmann Neumeister und die Galante Poesie," *Daphnis* 9 (1980): 133–61. Also, by the same author, "Erdmann Neumeister und die Kantatentexte Johann Sebastian Bachs," *Bach-Jahrbuch* (1986): 7–31.

[2] Elisabeth Noack, "Georg Christian Lehms, ein Textdichter Johann Sebastian Bachs," *Bach-Jahrbuch* (1970): 7–18.

herumkriechen / und sich seines ihm von Gott so wohl / als den Männern verliehenen Verstandes nicht bedienen dürffte.[3]

It is interesting to note that one encounters this topic again when viewing Bach's intimate social circles in Leipzig. Bach spent more than a quarter of a century, i.e., more than half of his productive years as an artist, in this focal center of German literary life. For this reason, I would like to concentrate on a few special aspects concerning Bach's role in the literary scene in Leipzig. I will proceed as follows: 1) What was the intellectual setting like into which Bach entered in 1723? Previously conductor at a princely court, he had now accepted the position of city musical director as well as choirmaster and instructor at the St. Thomas school; 2) What conceptions of textual sources did Bach already possess? What exactly was his notion of a cantata?; 3) I shall take a closer look at three authors in Leipzig who worked for Bach, beginning with Christiane Mariane von Ziegler, then Picander, and finally Gottsched; 4) Lastly, since the term "literature" has purposefully been used here rather broadly: what can we learn from the opinions of Bach's contemporaries concerning his works? Can these opinions help determine Bach's historical significance?

I

In 1723, when Bach moved from Köthen to Leipzig, he exchanged the world of courtly culture for the world of scholarship and bourgeois urban life. He was well aware of the contrast. This can be seen from a frequently cited comment made in 1730 by Bach, who by this time was once again looking for a change of environment, in a letter written on 28 October to Erdmann, a former schoolmate: "Ob es mir nun zwar anfänglich gar nicht anständig seyn wolte, aus einem Capellmeister ein Cantor zu werden...."[4] Although this could have meant a step out of the Baroque world into the world of the Enlightenment, one finds neither there nor anywhere else indications that Bach was a supporter of such progressive tendencies. His move to the city was motivated mainly by his desire for more far-reaching

---

[3] "that a young woman is as little suited to studying as a despicable wren is to looking at the sun ... just as though this noble and excellent sex should be allowed only to creep around in the dark with blind moles and not make use of the power of understanding bestowed by God on them as well as on men." [Editor's note: This translation and all subsequent ones from the main body of this essay are by James M. McGlathery.] Georg Christian Lehms, *Teutschlands Galante Poetinnen: Mit ihren sinnreichen und netten Proben; Nebst einem Anhang Ausländischer Dames / So sich gleichfalls durch Schöne Poesien Bey der curieusen Welt bekannt gemacht, und einer Vorrede. Daß das weibliche Geschlecht so geschickt zum Studieren / als das Männliche / ausgefertiget* (Frankfurt am Main, 1715), Preface b 1 recto and verso (rpt. Leipzig: Zentralantiquariat der DDR, 1973).

[4] "Whether, to be sure, it might not be proper for me at the start to turn myself from a Capellmeister into a cantor"; *Bach-Dokumente*, I/23:67.

career opportunities. In this connection, it should be mentioned that the term "courtly-artist" has recently been discovered and historically defined by art historians — this could be of benefit to Bach researchers too.[5]

Bach's decision shows great self-confidence. In spite of the fact that he had mainly held positions in small cities and courtly residences, by the age of thirty-eight his artistic development was almost completely defined. The position of chief musical director, as expressed in modern terminology, required not just talent, but also immense energy and organizational skill. It is difficult to say whether or not Bach was aware of the awkward situation he would get involved in by accepting the position in Leipzig. This simultaneous dependency on two institutions was to prove impossible to maintain for a longer period of time. His position as director of music for the city council could by no means be reconciled with his teaching duties at the St. Thomas School. He must have knowingly accepted certain risks. For instance, in his contract he accepted the conditions forbidding him to compose as he had done in the past, and certainly wanted to in the future — namely, in an "operatic style" — this expression well defines the composition style of his cantatas and passions as viewed in the eyes of Bach's contemporaries. Yet in 1723, no one could predict that he would only devote little more than half a dozen years to the production of church music. It was the nineteenth century's hero-worshipping of artists which first endowed Bach with the guise of arch-cantor. From 1729 onwards, Bach devoted himself to organizing professional musical activities in the civic community. In 1740 he entered into a sort of voluntary "semi-retirement," as Christoph Wolff put it. From then on he devoted himself solely to matters which were important to him personally rather than professionally.[6] In other words, this means that Bach's association with literature in Leipzig only lasted a short space of time.

In the eighteenth century, Leipzig was possibly the most important commercial center in the German empire. The city's closest rival, Hamburg, also had its own theater, but had no university. Zurich, on the other hand, had neither. Through a student named Telemann, the opera in Leipzig had gained a high reputation which lasted until the 1720s. After the closing of this establishment in 1729, Bach rounded up its student musicians to found the Collegium musicum. Leipzig was an impressive sight towards the end of the seventeenth century; the allusion to Paris made by Goethe in the "Auerbach's Keller" scene of *Faust* was meant to be taken seriously. The city's self-esteem was enhanced by various types of industry and trade fairs,

---

[5] Cf. Martin Warnke, *Hofkünstler: Zur Vorgeschichte des modernen Künstlers* (Cologne: DuMont, 1985).

[6] Christoph Wolff, "Probleme und Neuansätze der Bach-Biographik," in *Bachforschung und Bachinterpretation heute: Wissenschaftler und Praktiker im Dialog: Bericht über das Bach-Symposium 1978 der Philipps-Universität Marburg*, ed. Reinhold Brinkmann (Kassel, Basel, and London: Bärenreiter, 1981), pp. 21–31.

as well as by its role as capital of the book-trade. A bourgeois literature in the exact sense of the word, however, did not emerge in Leipzig. Literature was produced mainly by two groups with differing intentions, professors on the one hand, and students on the other.

The university in Leipzig was not held in especially high esteem. Its inflated self-image was disproportionate to its importance. In later years, approximately from the 1740s onwards, the university must have made a rather antiquated impression on the students. One wonders if Goethe could have written the university satire in *Faust* had his father sent him to one of the more modern universities of the time, for instance to Halle, not to mention Göttingen.

Leipzig was not a university preferred by wealthy students. Its location in a large city, capital of the book-trade, was of great importance to poorer students, for this offered numerous possibilities for earning extra money. The highly gifted Henrici, for example, quickly switched to Leipzig from the purely regional university at Wittenberg.

The literature created by students is today considered as belonging to the realm of real poetry, with certain striking highlights, such as the contrariness of Christian Reuter, or Johann Christian Günther's mockery of tradition. The scholarly literary productions of the professors were written mainly in Latin, that is to say, in the European *lingua franca*. Only the nobility among the student body was able to pursue public activities. It is difficult to define the intellectual climate or any dominant literary taste for the short period during which Bach needed texts for his position in Leipzig, partially due to the meager help offered us in this respect by literary historians. They normally offer no information as to what types of reading material were available at a certain period, or in other words, what was printed, reprinted, and bought. We must take into account an overlapping of late Baroque and early Enlightenment literature during Bach's first years in Leipzig, which also means that when studying Bach we once again find ourselves confronted with the contrast between the old and the new.

Our lack of information in this area can be exemplified by the so-called Neukirch Collection, the most well-known and comprehensive anthology series of the early eighteenth century. The first volume was printed in 1695. It documented the climax in the development of the literary style of the so-called Silesian school of authors. Since Gottsched, this type of writing had been dismissed as "bombastic." During the compilation of the seventh and last volume, the series fell into the hands of Gottsched's followers. Yet all volumes in the collection continued to be published up until the 1740s and 1750s.[7] Due to this simultaneous existence of various stages of literary development, the historical shift in literary tastes became apparent to a

---

[7] Angelo George de Capua and Ernst Alfred Philippson, eds., *Benjamin Neukirchs Anthologie*, Neudrucke deutscher Literaturwerke, n.s. 1 (Tübingen: Niemeyer, 1961), pp. vii–xvii.

contemporary readership only after a closer look at the series, if at all. Confronted with this heterogeneous body of texts, published simultaneously, yet representing divergent literary trends, an active composer had to make a host of selective decisions, not an easy task, indeed, given the huge mass of popular religious literature with its lack of individual profile.

II

What did Bach consider to be a cantata? At the beginning of his employment in Leipzig, he already had a set notion of what one should expect from an "ecclesiastical concert"; this term is historically appropriate for what we call a cantata. A crucial moment in Bach's development occurred in 1714. This is the year in which he adopted the Neumeister Technique, that is, recitatives and arias became essential components of his cantatas, as well as of his larger compositions, such as oratorios and passion music. The biblical text was retained from the older style of cantata based on the motet model, as were the free choir and choral arrangements. This leads to a seemingly endless number of possible variations. It would be almost impossible to find an adequate generic term to define the structure of cantata arrangements.

However, our understanding of the "form" or "structure" of a cantata is not tenable from a historical point of view. A cantata is not a work in itself. It is a functional component of a larger event.

We view Bach's cantatas as works of art with indeterminate religious undertones. The large majority of them, in fact, were intended as functional elements in the religious service in Leipzig. The central focus and most important part of the service was a sermon lasting at least an hour. According to Arnold Schering, it softened and wearied the hearts of the listeners, making them receptive to the meaning of the particular religious occasion.[8] The sermon was introduced and concluded either with a two-part cantata, or two separate cantatas. The latter must have occurred frequently, as shown by calculations based on figures contained in the composer's obituary record, which testify to the original existence of five almost complete annual cycles of cantatas.

Bach could therefore not, at least not in the first instance, base his decisions concerning literary texts on artistic criteria or even less on personal literary taste. He was to a large extent bound by the annual church calendar, Bible-readings and their related sermon topics, and especially the theological and personal considerations of particular clergymen. The term "functional literature" takes on the trite dimension of a handicraft, when one considers the incredible time restrictions under which most of the cantatas were composed. Artistic originality was not demanded of the text-writer, but

---

[8] Arnold Schering, *Musikgeschichte Leipzigs*, vol. 2: *Von 1650 bis 1723* (Leipzig: Kistner & Siegel, 1926), p. 12.

rather adroitness and the ability to adapt his text to various purposes. Originality would possibly only have interfered with the creative process.

The separate elements of a cantata do not have a definite schematical relationship to each other. Strictly speaking, a cantata has no structure. A Bachian "ecclesiastical concert" should best be viewed as a methodological concept. A cantata represents an event which takes place on various levels, or better still, between various speakers. Fundamentally, this event reflects the dialogue between preacher and congregation, between proclamation and reception of the sermon. A cantata is in itself a reflection of the church service in which it is performed. The dialogue form mirrors the reception of the sermon by each individual member in particular as well as by the congregation as a whole. Misunderstandings concerning the relationship between a cantata or oratorio and an opera, and thus also a drama, were brought about by none other than Erdmann Neumeister, the inventor of the modern cantata:

> Soll ichs kürzlich aussprechen, so siehet eine Cantata nicht anders aus, als ein Stück aus einer Opera, von Stylo Recitativo und Arien zusammenge-setzt.[9]

Indeed, a Neumeister cantata with its alternating recitatives and arias resembles a detached segment of an opera. In reality, however, there is a well-defined difference between an opera and a cantata. A cantata can be completely independent of any sort of "plot." It represents solely the multiple reactions of the contemplative soul to the sermon. In this respect, incidentally, it corresponds to the drama of German sentimentalism, exemplified in its purest form by Klopstock. In Bach's indispensable chorales, we once again encounter the spiritually "contemplative" individual, this time in the particular situation of a congregation. He evidently urged his text-writers at times to use chorales. On those occasions when his textual source did not allow for chorales, as was the case in Henrici's *St. Matthew's Passion*, Bach added them himself. It is the chorales in Bach's cantatas which give them their historical profile; they are a radical manifestation of the Reformation. For that reason, they cannot be performed in different surroundings without suffering a considerable loss of meaning.

III

Bach set to music a series of nine consecutive cantatas by Christiane Mariane von Ziegler, from May 22 ("Ihr werdet weinen und heulen") to May

---

[9] "If I am to express it briefly, a cantata does not look any different than a piece from an opera put together from the *stilo recitativo* and arias"; quoted in Ferdinand Zander, *Die Dichter der Kantatentexte Johann Sebastian Bachs: Untersuchungen zu ihrer Bestimmung* (Cologne: Kleikamp, 1967), pp. 11f.

27, 1745 ("Es ist ein trotzig und verzagt Ding"). Mariane von Ziegler often testified her love for and practice of music, for example in the preface to her first anthology, *Versuch in gebundener Schreib-Art* (An Attempt at Writing in Verse), in 1728.[10] There she tells of the personal visits made to her by virtuosi traveling through Leipzig.[11] The text of one cantata, entitled "Zu einer Garten-Music" (For a Concert in the Park), describes the actual performance of one of Leipzig's open-air concerts so popular among patrician families.[12] Had Bach lived half a century later, in Mozart's time, one can imagine that he might have also set such a text to music; but there exist no Bachian settings of texts without a specific aim or external demand. In this respect, he was an "occasional composer," if one may apply to him this contemporary term of literary criticism. Mme Ziegler acknowledged the receipt of one composition with the following poem entitled "Antwort-Schreiben" (Letter of Reply):

> Du weist, daß mich nichts mehr als die Music kan laben,
> Denn dieses Element ernehret Seel und Geist.
> Es kan mir in der That kein größrer Dienst geschehen,
> Als wenn ich, wie du selbst davon kanst Zeuge seyn,
> Vom lieben Noten-Volck mich soll umringet sehen,
> Ich räumte, gieng es an, ihm alle Zimmer ein.[13]

Occasional poetry of this type is a historical rarity in the history of literary genres: for Mme Ziegler herself determines the occasion which she embellishes with her poetry. As the daughter of the former city mayor, Romanus, she belonged to one of the leading families in Leipzig. She was an extremely intelligent person of great inner strength and independence, which she proved time and time again during the course of her complicated life. She refused to write poetry upon order, and of course accepted no money for her texts. Her works are thus not "genuine" occasional poetry as

---

[10] (Leipzig, 1728), fol.) ( ) (4 verso.

[11] "Ich halte diesemnach die so genannten Herrn Virtuosen, die mir zum öfftern bey ihren Hierseyn u. Durchreisen die Ehre ihres Zuspruchs gönnen, so werth, daß ich vor aller Welt rühmen muß, von ihnen öffters so viel Klugheit erblickt zu haben, und noch zu erblicken, die ich bei manchen Spanischen Sauer-Töpfen so leicht nicht angetroffen habe ..." (accordingly I so highly value these so-called master virtuosos who often, while visiting here or passing through, grant me the honor of their encouragement, that I must tell all the world that I have often seen more intelligence in them, and continue to see it, than I have not so easily found among many peevish Spaniards); ibid., fol.) ( ) (5 recto.

[12] Christiane Mariane von Ziegler, *Versuch in Gebundener Schreib-Art Anderer und letzter Theil* (Leipzig, 1729), pp. 291–301.

[13] "You know that nothing can refresh me more than music. / For this element nourishes the soul and the spirit. / Indeed, no greater service can be done for me / Than when, as you yourself can witness, I / See myself surrounded by dear musicians, / I would, were it possible, give up all my rooms to them"; *Versuch* (1728), p. 148.

common at the time. One would have had a better appreciation for her writings half a century later under the auspices of Goethe.

Her nine cantatas, set to music by Bach in 1725, were published in 1728. Her printed texts have been criticized on the authority of Bach: he is said to have undertaken significant revisions. This is, from the viewpoint of textual criticism, a dubious assumption, as one continues to compare the cantata text with the published version. Yet we have absolutely no idea as to what versions Bach had received three years earlier. In 1729, Mme Ziegler published a complete annual series of cantatas, excluding, with a reference to her anthology of the previous year, those nine poems composed for Sundays and holidays. One may safely assume that Bach could have maintained a fruitful working relationship with this text-writer for some time to come. It was, for her, an unfortunate coincidence that Bach at this point began to work on a permanent basis with Picander. She herself seems to have entertained some doubts as to whether her texts lent themselves to being set to music, and nota bene to church music. At any rate, she expressed these doubts to a certain degree in the foreword to her second anthology:

> Denn diejenigen Künstler und Meister, so mit Musicalischer Übersetzung und harmonischen lebhafften Ausdruck dergleichen poetischen Wercke beschäfftiget seynd, werden mir vermuthlich die darbey verspührte Länge vor einen grossen Fehler auslegen.[14]

This led her to the practical suggestion that one could either divide up the finished compositions to be played in two halves before the sermon and during the communion, or separate the texts into two annual installments; the most important thing would continue to be the right sermon on the right Sunday. This, of course, assumes a certain flexibility in the work's external form which, however, is well suited to the formal structure of a cantata.

The existence of a female author was, at that time, something new and a topic of discussion, as can be seen in the very carefully formulated personal comments made by Mme Ziegler. Her most concise expression of the problem offers at the same time a portrayal of her attitude towards life, as well as her personal intellectual style. Differentiating between the two sexes is simply a matter of convention, she writes:

> weil, wenn das Frauenzimmer studierete, es auch das Mannsvolck alsdenn im schreiben leicht übertreffen könte, indem ein ungelehrter Mann eben so schlecht zu schreiben scheinet, als ein der gleichen Frauenzimmer, und

---

[14] "For those artists and masters such as are occupied with the musical translation and lively harmonic expression of that sort of poetic work presumably will explain the tediousness experienced there as a great blunder"; *Versuch ... Anderer und letzter Theil* (1729), fol.) (4 verso.

also wohl der Grund von einer guten Schrifft [also einem guten Stil] die
Gelehrsamkeit in der Sprach-Kunst ohnfehlbar seyn muß [und eben nichts
Geschlechtsspezifisches].[15]

Nevertheless, Mme Ziegler officially gave up writing in an ostentatious
manner a year later. She announced her decision in the preface to her
second volume of poetry, which then ends with a poem consisting of 16
verses, entitled "Abschied an die Poesie" (Farewell to Poetry). The muses
simply prefer men:

> Ihr werdt es doch nicht übelnehmen, [redet sie die Musen an]
> Wenn ich, wiewohl gantz leiß und still,
> Um euren Chor nicht zu beschämen,
> Euch was ins Oehrgen sagen will:
> Nicht wahr? Ihr seid gesteht es immer,
> Dem Männer-Volck weit mehr geneigt,
> Und holder, als dem Frauenzimmer,
> Wie die Erfahrung täglich zeigt.

Powerless against such odds, she continues with unmistakable disdain:

> Der Vorzug ist sehr groß zu nennen,
> Hört nur der Männer Flöten an,
> Ihr selber müst es mir bekennen,
> Daß man nichts netters hören kan.
> Was Zeigen sie vor Kunst? vor Griffe?
> Sie sind an Geist und Feuer reich,
> Und wenn man sich zu todte pfieffe,
> So spielt man ihnen doch nicht gleich.[16]

This was written as Bach began a new series of cantatas, his so-called
Picander annual series. Naturally, however, Mme Ziegler did continue to

---

[15] "because, if young women studied they could then easily best the men-folk in writing,
since an uneducated man writes just as badly as an uneducated woman, and therefore the
reason for writing well [i.e., the reason for a good style] must be, certainly, knowledge of
the art of language [and precisely not anything peculiar to the one sex or the other]";
Preface, *Versuch* (1728), fol.) (8 verso.

[16] "You will not take it amiss now, will you, [she addresses the Muses] / If I, although
most softly and quietly, / In order not to put your choir to shame, / Want to whisper
something to you: / Is it not true? You are, go ahead and admit it, / Much more favorably
inclined to men-folk / And more devoted, than to women, / As experience daily teaches";
"The advantage must be called very great, / If one only listens to the men's fluting, / You
yourselves would have to confess it to me, / That one cannot hear anything nicer. / What
art they display? What technique? / They are rich in spirit and fire, / And if one piped
oneself to death, / One still would not play equally to them." *Versuch ..., Anderer Theil*
(1729), pp. 438–43.

write and publish, but from then on under the influence of Gottsched. One cannot precisely define Mariane von Ziegler's role in her contemporary society as a woman poet. Her counterpart, at any rate, was Luise Adelgunde Gottsched, who tried her hand at poetical writings possessing a scholarly fundament. In her own words, she languished away in an intellectual gallery. This patrician amateur Mme Ziegler was concerned with poetry and nothing else. The roles of these two women were mutually exclusive.

A female poet could also become the object of satire. This was aimed, however, not so much at Mme Ziegler as at a type of author like Luise Adelgunde Gottsched. She had just married the leading figure of scholarly language and literature in 1735, and her first comedy, "Pietism in a Whalebone Dress," was published in 1736. In the same year, Johann Sigismund Scholze-Sperontes published his anthology of songs entitled "The Singing Muse of the River Pleisse," containing the delightful murky, "You Beauties, Take my Advice and Study," which ends as follows:

> Continuirt drey Jahr,
> Denn könnt ihr promoviren,
> Und andere dociren.
> O schöne Musen-Schaar,
> Continuirt drey Jahr.
> Ich sterbe vor Vergnügen,
> Wenn ihr an statt der Wiegen,
> Euch den Catheder wehlt,
> Statt Kinder Bücher zelt,
> Ich küst euch Rock und Hände,
> Wenn man euch Doctor nennte,
> Drum Schönste fangt doch an,
> Kommt zur Gelehrten Bahn.[17]

This song quite possibly originated in the Bach family, from one of the two older sons, or even indirectly from their father. No doubt, this will become clear later on from the new *Bach Compendium*, I am sure. The beginning of the song is identical with the headmotif of a short composition for piano in E-flat major, contained in the second "Music Booklet for Anna Magdalena Bach" from the year 1725.

Henrici-Picander is overshadowed historically by those two prominent figures in Leipzig of the Enlightenment period, namely Bach and Gottsched.

---

[17] "Continue on for three years, / Then you can get your degree / And teach others. / Oh beautiful band of Muses, / Continue for three years. / I shall die of delight / When instead of choosing cradles / You choose the lectern, / Counting books instead of children, / I would kiss your skirts and hands, / If they called you Doctor, / Therefore, beautiful lady, go ahead and begin, / Come choose the career of scholar"; quoted in Jürgen Stenzel, ed., *Gedichte 1700–1770: Nach den Erstdrucken in zeitlicher Folge*, Epochen der deutschen Lyrik, no. 5 (Munich: Deutscher Taschenbuch Verlag, 1969), p. 143.

All three began their careers in Leipzig at the same time, although Bach was at a different stage than the other two, who were fifteen years junior to him. Picander received his first position in 1727. Even though Gottsched had been teaching at the university since 1724, he did not become a full professor until 1734. Gottsched and Picander attacked each other polemically for years in various publications. They occasionally competed against one another for promotion during the years of their social climb. In 1726, the city council in Leipzig even had the writings of the two confiscated altogether. There can be no doubt as to Bach's high assessment of Picander's abilities; he is highly praised on the title page of the autographical score for the *St. Matthew's Passion*. Philologists have shown absolutely no interest in him. Karl Goedeke's short characterization of Picander is enigmatic for us today: "Er hatte das Unglück, seiner Plattheit durch rohe Schlüpfrigkeit aufhelfen zu wollen. Elender Nachahmer Günthers."[18]

Picander was one of those intellectual social outsiders who sought refuge in a large university city. He sold his eminent talent of verse-writing almost as if it were a handicraft. Carmina were often used to celebrate special events in everyone's life and made them stand out against the doldrums of daily routine. One could compare this with the work of a tailor who sews garments for festive occasions — the Latin word *textus* means a woven fabric (or textile). Picander led an extremely demanding professional life: "Es ist mir wie einem Postillon gegangen; ich habe offt bey Nacht und Nebel den Pegasum satteln müssen, wenn mir auch nicht der allergeringste poetische Stern geschienen."[19] Funeral poems were difficult for him. He wrote fifty-six of them compared to 436 wedding poems. From a total of 650 poems, there are only about two dozen for which the specific occasion cannot be determined. Picander so successfully furnished Saxony, Lausitz, and Thuringia with poems that he was able to rise above the misery of a private tutor's existence. This type of poet was known as a "congratulator." Intellectuals sharing the same social status were non-certified doctors, private tutors, and proof readers. The academically qualified authors dismissed these competitors with terms such as "starving-poets," or "tattered-poets." Gottsched made a futile attempt to ridicule them publicly, by announcing the following project on 29 September 1727 in his weekly journal *Der Biedermann* (The Upstanding Citizen):

> eine vollständige Sammlung aller der Gedichte heraus zu geben, die seit 1700 in Leipzig von Jahr zu Jahr, auf alle Hochzeiten, Geburts- und Nahmens-Feste, Neujahrs-Tage, Doctor- und Magister-Promotionen und Leich-Begängnisse, theils gedruckt worden, theils noch in MS. verbor-

---

[18] Karl Goedeke, *Grundriß zur Geschichte der deutschen Dichtung*, 2nd ed., III (Dresden: Ehlermann, 1887), p. 352.

[19] Quoted in Christian Friedrich Henrici, *Picanders Ernst-Schertzhaffte und Satyrische Gedichte: Erster Theil, Andere Auflage*, 2nd ed. (Leipzig, 1732), fol.): (3 recto/verso.

genliegen. [Der Verleger erbittet] sonderlich der so genannten Herrn Gratulanten artige [d.h. kunstgemäße] Schrifften, von welchen er seiner Sammlung eine besondere Zierde verspricht.[20]

Gottsched was mistaken, Picander took care of the matter himself. He collected his works (which, incidentally, would have otherwise been lost today) in four splendid volumes, printed in 1727, 1729, 1732, and 1737. Each volume was reprinted as many as two to four times. In 1751 another volume was added, followed by two volumes of his selected works in the same year, then a third volume in 1768, the year in which Goethe left the Leipzig university.

In 1740, Picander was offered a special position in the bureau of taxation. Nothing characterizes his role as an author better than the fact that at that point he almost entirely gave up writing. All that he had become he owed to his writing, as is signified by his adopted name. The name was actually inspired by a hunting accident: Henrici shot and wounded a farmer in 1722 while aiming at a magpie (a "pica" in Latin). As can be seen from Picander's works, he had a precise sense for the symbolic meaning of emblems. Joachim Camerarius shows in his collection of emblems a magpie with a laurel-wreath in its beak flying to its nest, a symbol of independence: everything I am, I have earned myself, is the interpretation of this emblem. To be sure, all of this presupposes the conscious awareness of a basic social threat. Picander dedicated his first volume of poems to "good fortune." In the second edition, he replaced "good fortune" with the name of its personal ambassador: the minister of state Graf Brühl. The idea of *fortuna prospera* and *fortuna adversa* who continuously rotate mankind's wheel of fortune — this image had previously captivated Petrarca and his contemporaries — was still widely known in the eighteenth century. The "rock of good fortune," a sphere seemingly unattached to the cube on which it stands, can still be seen near Goethe's summer house in the Park at Weimar. Goethe had had it erected in 1777.

The preoccupation with Henrici's poems should not lead us to forget his three "German Plays," published together in 1726 and most likely never performed.[21] They stand completely outside of the comedy's traditional

---

[20] "to edit a complete collection of all the poems — that in part were printed, in part still lie hidden in manuscripts — which since 1700 were devoted year-by-year to all wedding, birthday, and saint's day celebrations, New Year's, doctor's and master's degree conferrals, and burials. [The publisher solicits] especially from those so honored artful [i.e., artistic] writings from which he anticipates a particular ornamentation for his collection"; facsimile printing of the original edition (Leipzig, 1727–29), ed. with afterword and commentary by Wolfgang Martens, Deutsche Neudrucke, Reihe Texte des 18. Jahrhunderts (Stuttgart: Metzler, 1975), p. 88.

[21] Christian Friedrich Henrici, *Picanders Teutsche Schau-Spiele, bestehend in dem Academischen Schlendrian Ertzt-Säuffer und der Weiber-Probe: Zur Erbauung und Ergötzung des Gemüths entworfen. Auf Kosten des Autoris* (Berlin, Frankfurt, and

historical development. "The Academical Bum," the "Incorrigible Drunkard," and the "Wives' Test" are plays firmly anchored in their time. There exist no comparable literary works offering such an extensive portrayal of eighteenth-century society in Leipzig. Picander, it is true, exercised a brand of critical realism; that is to say, he deliberately chose those elements of the society which lent themselves to satirical depiction: for instance a student whose non-academical pursuits lead his father to the grave; or the escapades of a good-for-nothing wife. His pieces scarcely display uniform plots bound together by well motivated events; yet the juxtaposition of individual scenes is carefully devised, the underlying stylistic principle being the correlation of grotesquely clashing situations.

Picander's prose is surpassed by his poetry due to his gift of linguistic style and expression. The greatest merit of Henrici's poetry, hardly noticed by today's reader, lies in his exceptional command of prosody. He manipulated the elements of language with a correctness which would have done credit to any author during Goethe's time. He obviously knew which consonants could be sung, so that they could be used at the beginning of a verse, and which syllables for the same reason should be placed at accentuated positions in a verse. There was nothing for Bach to improve on. Picander made a point of writing in correct High German. It was one of Gottsched's followers named Adelung who was basically responsible for creating the myth that Saxony was Germany's linguistic Tuscany. In actual fact, the High German of the period was by no means identical with the Saxonian dialect. Wieland contributed some amusing comments on the topic as late as 1782 in an essay entitled "Concerning the Question: What is High German?" Picander, however, already fully mastered the German propagated by Gottsched and his supporters in their "Deutsche Gesellschaft" (German Society). A look at Gottsched's "Trauerode" (Funeral Ode) and then at the words changed in Bach's score shows that Gottsched's language was considerably older than Henrici's — who knows, perhaps it was ironically Picander who actually refined Gottsched's dialect forms and solecisms.

Picander's stylistic capabilities are revealed even more clearly in his secular texts, as they allow for more freedom of expression. He loved to begin with images of movement, and therefore chose a more rapid, dactylic meter; particularly suitable in this regard are descriptions of distinct weather conditions or the course of daily activities. He can thus freely evoke scenic imagery. A special feature of Picander's works is his practice of depicting in each aria a complete situation in itself. Within the text as a whole, however, he quickly and characteristically alternated these situations, so as to create a certain inner rhythm as a subtle stimulus for the composer.

Particularly conspicuous for today's reader are the numerous erotic innuendos in Picander's poems, which Karl Goedeke found so scandalous.

Hamburg, 1726).

Reading just a few of them can be rather amusing. I will give you a harmless example, addressed to a newly married couple:

> Geht hin, und spielt in euerm Bettgen,
> Ein concertirendes Duettgen,
> Halt den Accord gesegnet aus;
> Und wenn ihr also fortgefahren,
> So werde nach drey Viertel-Jahren
> Ein angenehmes Trio draus![22]

If, however, one reads a hundred samples of such literature, it becomes boring, just as sexual allusions always do in large quantities. This sheds some light on the contempt for congratulators. Picander, however, rarely repeated the same joke. Moreover, suggestive remarks of this kind occurred more frequently in the smaller cities, such as Zittau, Guben, or Annaberg, rather than in Leipzig; and more often among the middle and lower classes than in the families of aldermen or professors or even the nobility. Obscenities are characteristic of this genre. They were a matter of course for anyone ordering a wedding-carmen and in no way reflected on the author as a person. He just delivered the texts as requested. None of Bach's textwriters supplied him with such tailor-made poems of comparable quality.

Gottsched could not have managed this for the simple reason that he lacked the specific talent. He would not have wanted to do it anyway. His and Bach's opinions of the relationship between art and society were so different as to be almost contradictory. In his early years in Leipzig, Bach seems to have established contact with the city's leading families. In 1725 he composed a wedding-cantata for the daughter of Johann Burchard Mencke, one of the greatest minds of the university. Since Mencke was Gottsched's mentor, Bach and Gottsched were brought together for the first time at the performance of the cantata, "Auf! Süß entzückende Gewalt." The composition has been lost. The text must have impressed Gottsched; he printed it in 1730 in his *Critische Dichtkunst* (Criticism of Poetical Methods), the early German Enlightenment's leading book of literary theory. The cantata is a series of three-part recitatives and arias, concluding with a chorus; it corresponded outwardly to both Gottsched's and Bach's concept of a cantata.

The next artistic meeting of the two, centering around the "Funeral Ode," was completely different, almost disastrous. The ordering of the composition did not go smoothly, as Bach had no permission to take part in ceremonies at the university. Such problems could be dispelled, however, if the contract orderer were of nobility. As it happened Karl von Kirchbach,

---

[22] "Go on in, and play in your little bed, / A concerted little duet, / And sustain the chord blessedly; / And if you continue on that way / Then after three-quarters of a year / A pleasant trio will come of it!"; ibid., p. 394.

the contractor, was also a member of the "Deutsche Gesellschaft" (German Society), of which Gottsched was the senior member.

Bach decidedly altered Gottsched's ode. The nine uniform verses written by the latter were changed by Bach into ten choruses, arias, and recitatives of extremely varied lengths, as if he had cut up the text into irregular pieces with a pair of scissors. One can't help but think Bach wanted to demonstrate emphatically, especially to the learned poet, which artistic form was suitable for a courtly occasion. He prepared an opening chorus stylizing a French overture rhythm, to which he added a considerable amount of onomato-poetical effects, such as in "Verstummt! verstummt ihr holden Saiten" and again at the passage, "Der Glocken bebendes Getön." The subjective captivation of each individual was animated through minute, almost imperceptible alterations in the text's vocabulary. It was made known publicly that Bach had composed in Italian style.[23]

For Gottsched, anything Italian was automatically antiquated; he associated the word with overly pretentious art. His life was dedicated to opposing late Baroque poetry, namely that of Hofmannswaldau, and including incidentally, that of Lehms, who had furnished Bach with at least eight cantatas between 1725 and 1726. Gottsched could hardly object to the structural reorganization of his ode. For Bach's composition corresponded exactly to Gottsched's description of an Italian cantata in his book *Critische Dichtkunst*. Anything Italian, however, was too ornate; and it was from this point of view that Gottsched soon attacked Bach as a composer. Approximately a year later he criticized the genre of the opera in his journal *Der Biedermann*.

He concluded with a ranking of the three most important composers of the time: Telemann, Händel, and Bach, whereby Telemann was proclaimed as indisputably the greatest. His grounds are irrefutable from the viewpoint of the historical development of style, and are also completely convincing in their defense of more recent trends:

> Sonderlich höre ich von dem ob gedachten Hrn. Telemann rühmen, daß er sich nach dem Geschmacke aller Liebhaber zu richten weiß…. Er vermeidet alle ausschweifende Schwierigkeiten, die nur Meistern gefallen könnten, und ziehet die lieblichen Abwechselungen der Thöne allezeit den weitgesuchten vor, ob sie gleich künstlicher seyn möchten. Und was ist vernünftiger als dieses? Denn da die Music zum Vergnügen des Menschen dienen soll; so muß ja ein Künstler eine grösseres Lob verdienen, wenn er bey seinen Zuhörern eine lächelnde Mine, und vergnügte Stellung wircket; als

---

[23] *Bach-Dokumente*, II/232:175.

wenn er bloß eine ängstliche Verwunderung, und lauter in Falten gezogene Angesichter verursachet hätte.[24]

Despite this, Gottsched had in theory nothing against music. In his *Critische Dichtkunst*, he derives poetry from music. Cantatas are, immediately following odes, the second item discussed in the genre section of the first edition of this great textbook. In accordance with his support of music lovers as quoted above, he later on disputed the contentions of Neumeister and Hunold-Menantes that a thorough knowledge of music is required for writing texts intended to be set to music. Indeed, he certainly promoted music, albeit in moderation. That is enough, however, to ruin music. The opinion that music should not disturb logical reasoning is the foundation of his heated criticism of word repetitions and coloraturas on single syllables. I quote him once again: "Singing is simply the pleasant reading or articulating of a verse, in correspondence with the verse's nature and content."[25]

That may sound peculiar in connection with Bach, or, more accurately, in contrast to him. It was exactly Gottsched's unshakable adherence to the imitation of nature which Bach's compositions did not follow. It has been a historically recurring notion that music should be a devoted servant to poetry. The statement regarding singing as slightly enhanced speech is also consistent with Goethe's attitude towards musicalization; Zelter complied with it as well. But poor Franz Schubert in Vienna, who had set sixteen of Goethe's poems to music, including "Erlkönig," "Gretchen am Spinnrade," and "Heidenröslein," probably never understood why his compositions were returned from Weimar without comment.

Gottsched, the patron of music amateurs, was definitely no musical expert. This he acknowledged on one occasion with almost charming awkwardness. In 1732, he sent piano music to his fiancée, Miss Kulmus, in Danzig. He chose the best music available in Leipzig at that time, namely a newly published composition by Bach. Judging by the date, it must have been the partitas of Bach's opus no. 1. The gift was not a success. Today, since Bach's works have established themselves for more than a century as standard pieces practiced in piano lessons, the partitas can even be managed

---

[24] "Especially I hear it said of the above-mentioned Herr Telemann that he knows how to adjust to the taste of all music lovers.... He avoids all extravagant difficulties that could only please master musicians, and ever prefers the pleasant modulation of notes to more distant ones, although the latter might be the most artistic. And what is more rational than this? For since music is supposed to provide pleasure to mankind, then an artist, after all, has to earn greater praise if he occasions in his audience a smile and a delighted attitude than if he only causes anxious amazement and nothing but wrinkled eyebrows"; *Der Biedermann, Zweyter Theil Darinnen gleichfalls Fünfzig wöchentliche Blätter enthalten sind* (Leipzig, 1729), p. 140 (cf. fn. 20).

[25] *Critische Dichtkunst*, 4th ed. (1751); rpt. Darmstadt: Wissenschaftliche Buchgesellschaft, 1962, p. 725.

by some amateurs. Then, however, his works were exclusively for virtuosi. And that applies all the more so to the contemporary attitude regarding piano instruction for women. Johann Ludwig Krebs, recommended by Bach in 1736 as piano instructor for Mrs. Gottsched, was once explicitly said to have also written a few "simple tidbits" for women. That was a completely separate genre. As for Miss Kulmus, she may well have possessed a certain degree of expert knowledge of music. She replied very tactfully to the musical gift from her fiancé:

> Die überschickten Stücke zum Clavier von Bach, und von Weyrauch zur Laute, sind ebenso schwer als sie schön sind. Wenn ich sie zehnmal gespielet habe, scheine ich mir immer noch eine Anfängerin darinnen. Von diesen beyden großen Meistern gefällt mir alles besser als ihre Capricen; diese sind unergründlich schwer.[26]

Bach's partitas contain only a single caprice, in C minor. If she was referring to that, then one must admit that she selected with connoisseurship the most technically difficult piece of the entire collection.

There are no indications of any sort of open quarrel between Gottsched and Bach. The two could not, however, have shared the same political views. Gottsched was a proponent of radical Enlightenment principles in language, literature, theater, philosophy, and education. Bach, on the other hand, was never committed to the Enlightenment. He just wanted to — or had to — compose. He had moved to the city only because the princely court no longer offered a favorable opportunity for composing. Upon encountering obstacles in the city, he took great pains to secure help from the Electoral court in Dresden by seeking the title of Court Composer.

IV

The stylistic contrasts between Bach and Gottsched did not become vividly apparent until relatively late in the so-called Scheibe-Birnbaum dispute, about which I should like to conclude with a brief discussion. One should by no means attempt to understand this dispute from the viewpoint of the persons involved. Polemics as a literary genre was taken more lightly during the Enlightenment. One did not immediately view a written disputation as a personal insult, as we do today. In any case, Bach and Gottsched were still able to collaborate on the ovation cantata, "Willkommen! Ihr herrschenden Götter der Erden!" (Welcome, Ye Ruling Gods of the Earth), at the climax of their quarrel, during Easter of 1738. If one takes a

---

[26] "The pieces for the clavichord by Bach, and by Weyrauch for the lute, that you sent over are just as difficult as they are beautiful. After I have played them ten times over I still seem to myself a beginner with them. From these two masters I like everything better than their capriccios; these are unfathomably difficult"; *Bach-Dokumente*, II/309.

closer look at Gottsched's last collaboration with Bach — or, more accurately, the testimony of the last collaboration we possess today — then it becomes apparent that Gottsched adopted exactly that which one could learn from Picander in this field — it is impossible to deny that Gottsched occasionally rhymed "invita Minerva."

The dispute between Scheibe and Birnbaum occurred at the peak of Gottsched's influence, and at a time when his popularity was already beginning to wane as a result of opposition among his close associates. None of the following generations of students, some of which were greatly influential in the development of German literature, established close contact with Gottsched; neither the Schlegels, nor Klopstock's friends, the "Bremer Beyträger" (The Bremen Contributors), nor Klopstock himself or Lessing.

The dispute over Bach was induced by a fictitious report from a correspondent, published by Scheibe in his journal *Critischer Musicus* (The Critical Musician) in 1737.[27] First, the music director of the university, Görner, is accurately portrayed as the blunderer he was, followed by somewhat reserved praise for Bach. The reservations concerned principles of musical aesthetics; the passage is actually an unnecessary digression. Of special importance, leaving aside the main points of dispute, is the person who defended Bach, Johann Abraham Birnbaum. Tracing this man's historical importance as a scholar would be a worthy endeavor. Birnbaum was a fascinating scholarly personality of great independence, both outwardly and inwardly. He was, incidentally, also one of the most important intellectuals involved in the early history of the copyright.[28] From the linguistic angle of conceptual precision and level of argumentation, his remarks concerning the composer are among the best we have from Bach's contemporaries.

The dispute revolved around three main topics: 1) A comparison of Bach and Lohenstein, 2) the criticism that pomposity and excessive intricacy predominate in Bach's compositions, 3) the demand that compositions should be more natural. The word "Lohenstein" signifies more than just a historical category. It was often claimed that Bach's style corresponded more to those of previous decades than to the style of the 1740s. The three topics are related. The name "Lohenstein" sums up in a word the terms pomposity and intricacy. Pomposity refers basically to the incompatibility of the embellishments used for the occasion being celebrated; in literature, the

---

[27] *Critischer Musicus*, 6. Stück, 14 May 1737, Neue, vermehrte und verbesserte Auflage (Leipzig, 1745), p. 54 (rpt. Hildesheim: Olms, 1970).

[28] Cf. Johann Abraham Birnbaum, *Eines Aufrichtigen Patrioten Unpartheyische Gedancken über einige Quellen und Wirckungen des Verfalls der ietzigen Buch-Handlung, Worinnen insonderheit Die Betrügereyen der Bücher-Pränumerationen entdeckt, Und zugleich erwiesen wird, Daß der unbefugte Nachdruck unprivilegirter Bücher ein allen Rechten zuwiderlauffender Diebstahl sey* (Schweinfurth, 1733).

term is most often applied to exaggerated imagery. Intricacy signifies constructions which are excessively sophisticated. This was the framework of an entire aesthetic philosophy, and one standing in direct contrast to the standards of the past.

The criticism of intricacy is explained by Scheibe as follows. Intricacy occurs when there is no dominant voice. A leading voice must be distinguishable at all times. This amounts to the dominance of melody over harmony; and indirectly to the dominance of text over composition, thereby touching upon the third topic of dispute: naturalness. Scheibe associated naturalness with simplicity. Birnbaum was not basically against the principle of the imitation of nature; he denied, however, the equation of naturalness with simplicity. Birnbaum was in favor of more autonomy in art and in the employment of artistic methods. At this same time, the Swiss literary theoreticians established the right of artistic fantasy, as especially manifested in imagery. Bach was still living as Klopstock's poetry began to appear, in which Gottsched saw nothing but a mass of intrepid images and barely comprehensible sentence structures, causing him to fear the recurrence of a bygone age. Birnbaum's arguments were in no way historically apologetic. The reference to "Lohenstein" had already become ambivalent by this time. The basis for future aesthetic conflicts was already contained in the Scheibe-Birnbaum dispute.

The historical reception of music proceeds differently from that of literature. Even after Bach's cantatas were elevated to the status of works of art, one continued to view the texts as casual poetry. An exact historical analysis of the texts reveals Bach's music in its historical significance.

A short epilogue. All statements concerning Bach and his texts are based on dubious premises: for we are only able to name the authors of one-third of the texts he set to music. The repeated claims that Bach wrote some of the texts himself are understandable, although the arguments are contradictory, attributing to him both texts which are amateurish and those which are outstanding. I doubt that Bach was included among the literati in the sense of the time, that is to say, as a man adept in the formulation of texts, and I believe this can be proved. His predecessor in Leipzig, Kuhnau, was the last in the line of great scholarly choirmasters. He was a certified notary public, whose talent as a novelist should certainly not be disregarded. — Determining the authors of anonymous texts was a popular course topic at German universities during the first years following World War II. This activity, however, was jokingly but inaccurately described as being like a "parlor game." Nevertheless, working together with experts in theology and historical science, literary historians could perhaps demonstrate their abilities on Bach's texts.

Bach's Leipzig as a Training Ground for Actors, Musicians, and Singers

GLORIA FLAHERTY

THE FATE OF THE German-speaking lands has long been inextricably tied to geography. Those who have read some history know that. And, so do those of us who have been mysteriously engulfed on the *Autobahn* by swarms of screaming European families who tried to start driving north or south or east or west as soon as the local schools let out for the summer. Germany quite literally lies at the crossroads of Europe. The geographical point where all those roads intersected in the pre-*Autobahn* days fell in Saxony. The city that flourished on that point was Leipzig. The name, by the way, is also indicative of the central or middle European orientation. It derives "entweder von dem slawischen Wort '*lipa*' (= Linde, also etwa Lindenort) oder von dem Namen eines sorbischen Stammesältesten."[1]

By the opening decades of the eighteenth century, Leipzig had well established itself as a commercial center. The trade fairs it hosted — at Easter, Michaelmas, and New Year's — began with salt, learned to include furs from Russia or Russo-America, and then quickly expanded to other international commodities. Johann Wolfgang von Goethe's remembrance of his initial reactions when he went to study there in 1765 underscored both its commercialism and its international flavor:

> Als ich in Leipzig ankam, war es gerade Messzeit, woraus mir ein besonders Vergnügen entsprang: denn ich sah hier die Fortsetzung eines vaterländischen Zustandes vor mir, bekannte Waren und Verkäufer, nur an anderen Plätzen und in einer anderen Folge. Ich durchstrich den Markt und die Buden mit vielem Anteil, besonders aber zogen meine Aufmerksamkeit an sich, in ihren seltsamen Kleidern, jene Bewohner der östlichen Gegenden, die Polen und Russen, vor allem aber die Griechen, deren ansehnlichen Gestalten und würdigen Kleidungen ich gar oft zu Gefallen ging.[2]

---

[1] *Die Musik in Geschichte und Gegenwart* (Kassel, Basel, London, New York, 1960), vol. 8, col. 540. "… either from the Slavic word 'lipa' (=Lime tree, that is, place near the lime trees) or from the name of a Sorb elder." Unless otherwise noted, I am responsible for the renderings into English.

[2] *Goethes Werke*, ed. Erich Trunz et al., 14 vols. (Hamburg: Christian Wegner, 1961–64), vol. 9: *Aus meinem Leben, Dichtung und Wahrheit*, Part 2, Bk. 6, pp. 244–45. "When I arrived in Leipzig, I was especially pleased to see that the fair was in progress, for here I beheld a continuation of home conditions at Frankfurt; the same wares and salesmen, only in different places and in another order. I roamed through the markets and booths with great interest, but my attention was especially drawn to the strangely clad inhabitants of the eastern regions, the Poles, Russians, and above all the Greeks, whom I often returned

Publishing houses also found Leipzig congenial since the city fathers were somewhat less strict than those of other municipalities when it came to matters of censorship, licensing, and legitimizing. As a result, publishing became big business, at least big enough to surpass both London and Paris.[3] The economic climate was so healthy that other industries were attracted to Leipzig as well. Among them were the manufacture of scientific equipment and also musical instruments. A great deal of entrepreneurial cross-pollination went on, so that mutually advantageous inventions were made. Among them, were certain technological changes that better facilitated the printing of music.[4]

The great wealth that was accruing in Leipzig led to a boom market in real estate. The avid construction of new dwellings in the first half of the eighteenth century produced what has been called the bourgeois baroque style of architecture. In the eyes of the young Goethe, there were "die mir ungeheuer scheinenden Gebäude, die, nach zwei Strassen ihr Gesicht wendend, in grossen, himmelhoch umbauten Hofräumen eine bürgerliche Welt umfassend, grossen Burgen, ja Halbstädten ähnlich sind."[5] Goethe repeatedly came back to the conspicuous consumption of domestic space on the part of the Leipzig burghers, singling out especially the Breitkopf family of music publishing fame and fortune.[6]

The real estate market also allowed for some shady deals that did not go unpunished. When, for example, Franz Conrad Romanus was named mayor by August der Starke, he decided he needed a splendid house in which to fulfill his political duties. He hired himself an architect, namely Johann Gregor Fuchs, and had the house built. The problem was that Romanus did not have enough liquid assets. He solved that problem by forging municipal debt papers so as to raise the money to pay for the construction costs. He got caught. After being incarcerated for forty-one years — no plea-bargaining or parole in those days — he died in prison in 1746.

The citizenry of Leipzig preferred mayors who earned their money legally, if not honestly. They were solid burghers with middle class economic

---

to see for the sake of their stately figures and dignified costumes," trans. Robert R. Heitner, *From My Life Poetry and Truth: Parts One to Three*, ed. Thomas P. Saine and Jeffrey L. Sammons (New York: Suhrkamp, 1987), p. 187.

[3] *The Encyclopaedia Britannica: A Dictionary of Arts, Sciences, Literature and General Information*, s.v. Leipzig, vol. 16, 11th ed. (Cambridge: Cambridge Univ. Press, 1911), p. 401.

[4] *Musik in Geschichte und Gegenwart*, s.v. Leipzig, vol. 8, col. 559.

[5] Hamburger Ausgabe, vol. 9: *Dichtung und Wahrheit*, Part 2, Bk. 6, p. 245. "Yet I felt an affinity toward some buildings that seemed enormous to me: with facades on two streets and large courtyards that enclosed a whole world of civic life within their towering walls, they were like large castles, nay, little cities," trans. Heitner, p. 188.

[6] Ibid., p. 325.

aspirations, orthodox religious beliefs, and conservative political values. Although they were living in a boom-town, they felt they had more style, class, and culture than the people living in those swampy eastern frontier towns, like Berlin. They themselves were not only highly literate, but they valued literacy in general and recommended instruction for all newly arrived immigrants. The Leipzigers went so far as to support their belief with hard money, funding a city library as early as 1677. They read in the library; then they exchanged ideas in the coffeehouses. Such public places became an urban institution in the early eighteenth century. Among the most famous was Zum Kaffeebaum, which was established in 1717 by Joseph Lehmann, the Royal-Polish Court Chocolatier.

Leipzig perceived itself as "Klein Paris" (little Paris) and had its boosters promulgate that kind of reputation. Its citizens had more than enough cash to pay for instruction in the French language, in French gallantry, repartee, badinage, fencing, acting, and singing. They even supported a number of dancing masters to guide them through the intricacies of French dance. In sum, they readily indulged themselves in that game of out-Frenching the French, without, however, forgetting their place at what I have called the crossroads of Europe. Leipzig may seem to have been a conservative reflection of a foreign culture, yet it was progressive enough to defend its Germanic identity and Germanic law by precedent. It wanted to prove that Saxony, or Germany, was as great as France. In order to do so, it supported different kinds of organizations to encourage indigenous cultural patriotism. One of them, the Deutschübende poetische Gesellschaft, even grew to have wide ranging international influence.

Another went on to gain mythic significance. That was Auerbach's establishment with its inn, its courtyard or mall, and its wine-cellar. Students resided at the inn, as did the customers of the merchants who plied their wares in the courtyard. All of them, plus an occasional professor or two, sought refreshment in the cellar. According to carefully preserved local legend, it had been visited in 1526 by that German peasant's son who became one of the biggest celebrities on the university lecture circuit. Doctor Faustus was said to be the kind of professor who enlivened ancient history by actually conjuring up Helen of Troy for an eyewitness account of the Trojan war. Two frescoes were painted on the walls of Auerbach's cellar to commemorate the one-hundredth anniversary of that visit. While the one shows Faustus at a table with students drinking and making music, the other shows him riding away astride a wine-cask. Goethe, who had a friend renting a room at the inn, frequented this very wine-cellar during his student years. By the way, when he immortalized it in the first part of *Faust*, he did not have the students playing musical instruments. Instead, he had some debauched failures sing obscene songs that disgusted Faust.

Leipzig became one of the most important training grounds for performers in the early eighteenth century precisely because of its strong sense of municipal identity, social pretensions, multifarious cultural demands, educational aspirations, and, not to be underestimated, its wealth. The twenty some odd thousand burghers who lived there were willing to pay for various kinds of theater and music. And the six or seven hundred students enrolled at local institutions of learning earned spending money, or free tickets, or just experience, by joining with those whose livelihood it was to perform in public.

There were many vehicles through which to learn firsthand about performing. I shall begin with the five theatrical ones that eventually in the course of the eighteenth century merged into the German popular stage tradition — the English style, the *commedia dell'arte*, the marionettes, the medicine shows, and the opera. Then I shall discuss two major academic forms of drama before turning at the end of the essay to evidence about musical training.

Itinerant troupes of players wandered in and out, suiting their performances to the particular crowds of the day. Some of those players were runaways, juvenile delinquents, or university dropouts. Many were sincerely stagestruck. Their training often derived from the style of the *Englische Komödianten* (English Comedians), who had arrived in the German lands during the late sixteenth century via Denmark, or the north-south road. They brought the repertory of Elizabethan drama, albeit at first wildly altered to have impact on audiences who understood no English. Action counted for more at the box office than did poetic declamation, consequently these actors simplified texts as well as plots and developed naturalistic non-verbal means of communication. They not only relied on exaggerated facial expressions and hand gestures, but they also ranted and raved, fenced and fainted. Their acrobatics were especially popular, as were their jigs and songs. Although their carts carried few scenic effects, they always managed to get some swine blood and a bladder or two in order to perform the death scene vividly on stage. Abusing children, raping women, and molesting the elderly were usually among the expectations of the audiences, so the actors had no compunctions about portraying such activities in full public view. Such unrestrained violence, sexuality, and exhibitionism were often lauded. Clowns supplied as much comic relief as their colleagues would allow. The two British writers with whom the Germans primarily identified this kind of play were Marlowe and Shakespeare.

Other wandering troupes had taken the road from the south. The players of the *commedia dell'arte* were equally successful with their theatrical improvisations. They used scenarios that derived from the three most important events in human life — being hatched, matched, and dispatched. They read widely, availing themselves of what the best European writers had produced. They also used those texts to hone their wits and their rhetorical skills. Their memories were well-trained, sharp, and fantastically adaptable. Their energy was boundless and their talent genuinely great, in spite of the fact that their antics were often earthy, if not downright obscene. They were true masters and mistresses of pantomime and dance. Masks and costumes were among the other non-verbal means of communication they used with great sophistication to create the personality of a character, like the Dottore, the Capitano, and Pantalone, the Venetian merchant. The stereotyped characters who played out the scenarios remained Italian until this kind of theatrical performance merged into the mainstream of popular German theater. Eventually Arlecchino coalesced with other "zanies" or clown figures to become the notorious Hanswurst.

Improvised comedy of this sort appealed to the playful instincts of aristocrats and burghers alike. Among the leading financial backers were the Saxon-Polish sovereigns. At one time, one of them even promised to underwrite a troupe consisting of two hundred players. Although destined to be successful, the venture failed because of the manager's indiscretion in making love to the sovereign's favorite mistress. Needless to say, he got caught and was sentenced to twenty years.

Another form of theater that provided experience for aspiring performers was that of the marionettes and puppets. Their operators created a make-believe world that appealed directly to the imagination. In doing so, they stole from the repertories of other theaters, used the stolen goods in order to make up their own scenarios, and then freely improvised dialogue on the spot. They usually parodied or ridiculed works that were well-known to local audiences. The occult remained of interest to everyone, so plays about spirits and devils became sensationally popular. They were so popular, as a matter of fact, that the devil had to be married off so he could propagate his species and provide the stage with his offspring. Goethe fondly reports in *Dichtung und Wahrheit* about his own childhood fascination with such plays, especially when they were about selling one's soul to the devil, as did Doctor Faustus, the renowned professor, magician, and lover of Helen of Troy.

The shows put on by the medicine men and mountebanks who succeeded Faust in the eighteenth century cannot be overlooked, for they also contributed mightily to the development of theatrical techniques. The main one had to do with working an audience. Such performers instinctively knew how to divert attention so that their actual activity would not be noticed. Consequently they were masters of ventriloquism and legerdemain. Rhetorical *savoir faire* and glibness enabled them to extemporize at will, construct reality as they wished, and escape potentially embarrassing situations. Sometimes such theatrical techniques were adapted by rambunctious students who sought to finagle their way out of pecuniary and other difficulties. Christian Reuter, who prepared some cantatas, also wrote several plays to satirize his Leipzig landlady as the notorious Frau Schlampampe. He became as well-known for the on-going legal proceedings that resulted as for the plays.

Operatic performances had begun in Leipzig in the middle of the seventeenth century, and they became so popular by the 1690s that they were regularly mounted during the trade fairs. As a commercial operation

— with some royal subvention — the officially established Leipzig opera house was in trouble more often than not, often due to those real-estate speculators. Nevertheless, the opera did rise to prominence in the early years of the eighteenth century to the credit of many young, ambitious singers, musicians, and composers from the city's schools and academies for whom it then served as a kind of professional *Pflanzschule* (preparatory school). Lack of leadership and financial problems might have led to the dissolution of the standing opera company in 1720, but it did not bring an end to operatic opportunities in Leipzig. In addition to concert performances of musical dramas by the *Collegium Musicum*, there were productions by Italian troupes.[7]

The decidedly negative reaction that Leipzig teachers and professors had to all such displays would serve to indicate that those multi-talented young people were simply learning too much too fast. Somehow performing in public in an ensemble involved factors that went beyond the enlightened rationally explicable and intellectually conquerable syllabus. There was something excitingly ineffable about successful performances of make-believe. They were downright magical and sometimes even blatantly sexual. When the German opera in Leipzig closed its doors, the youngsters who had partaken of its magic simply went out to other cities and courts, all the while spreading the magic.[8]

There was no magic and precious little fun in academic theater, to which I should now like to turn. Such theater, if it can even be called that, was governed by schoolmasters and professors, honest, decent, law-abiding folk who mostly only wanted to do their jobs so as to get tenure or collect their paychecks. A few of them, however, were ambitious enough to hope to purge the world of all those irrational things, like play and song and music and fun. For them, rhetoric and logic loomed most important. The high school teacher of many Leipzig university students, Christian Weise, stands out among those enlightened types. His theatrical interests surfaced during his childhood and swam free during his years of theological study in Leipzig. He earned his master's degree, gained faculty status, and then dared to express interest in Shakespeare. As a result, he was denied tenure. He subsequently bounced around from position to position, finally landing at the bottom of the alphabet, in a place called Zittau, where he founded a school theater with the expressly didactic purpose of teaching his pupils the last two of the traditional five rhetorical steps, namely memory and delivery. He supplied a sum total of sixty-one plays, each of which, of course, presented a clear-cut moral lesson.

---

[7] Renate Brockpähler, *Handbuch zur Geschichte der Barockoper in Deutschland*, Die Schaubühne: Quellen und Forschungen zur Theatergeschichte, 62 (Emsdetten, Westphalia: Lechte, 1964), pp. 254–55.

[8] Brockpähler, p. 254.

Despite Weise's decidedly rhetorical bent, he, at least, tried to build bridges to living theater. He more than once blinked an eye at the textbook definition of pure genres. Occasionally he included music, singing, and dancing. He even went so far as to produce a few farces and ballets. His comic figure, Pickelhäring, was a composite from the clown tradition, who was made to serve the overall didactic purpose by supplying simultaneous humorous commentary on the dramatic action. Weise also countered the standard rules by encouraging his one hundred and fifty charges to recite verse naturally and to be well enough in command of the text to extemporize if necessary. His inclusion of stage directions was yet another infraction of the rules. The text was not to be so adulterated but rather to consist solely of the poetry to be declaimed. In many instances, he compounded his sin by using prose.

Schoolmasters like Weise also regulated the way in which pupils delivered their lines. This tendency had been evolving since the sixteenth century when some sought specific rules not only for facial expression and deportment but also for the hands and their individual fingers. Chirology was the language of the hands or fingers, and chironomy was the art of expressive hand movement. In 1644, an Englishman, John Bulwer, published a two-volume summation of the one hundred and twenty possible positions.

Fritz Lang (1654–1725), a Jesuit aware of such research and well-versed in rhetoric, produced his rule-book on acting in 1727.[9] He did so because he thought that acting possessed a magical power capable of moving the human soul. Needless to say, he wanted it to be moved in the correct direction, that is, towards God and not towards the devil. His aim was to prevent pupils from getting carried away with their assigned role, or from becoming possessed by a spirit not their own. They had to be made to realize that play-acting was just not reality and that its main objective was instruction.[10]

Lang insisted that gesture, intonation, and movement be harmonized. In addition to chapters on the voice, there are those giving prescriptions for the soles of the feet, the knees, the hips, the arms, the elbows, and the hands. He was especially concerned with bashful schoolboys who awkwardly kept their hands in their pockets or behind their backs. Although he wished to disabuse them of that, he did not want them thrashing around agitatedly when portraying great passion, or covering their faces when it came to fear or shame. He urged them always to pay attention to their fellow players and ignore the spectators. Lang's innumerable prescriptions were accompanied

---

[9] *Abhandlung über die Schauspielkunst*, ed. and trans. Alexander Rudin (Bern and Munich: Francke, 1975).

[10] I have taken up this subject in "The Dangers of the New Sensibilities in Eighteenth-Century German Acting," *Theatre Research International* 8 (1983): 95–109.

by detailed illustrations. There has even been some speculation about their resemblance to baroque figures in the librettos of courtly operas.

The academician who became most famous for his indefatigable attempts to purge German theater of everything I have talked about thus far was Johann Christoph Gottsched. He was anti-Shakespeare, anti-Marlowe, anti-Faust, anti-improvisation, anti-puppet, anti-street-theater, anti-opera, anti-dance, and anti-music. He had begun his university career with studies of theology and philosophy in Königsberg, Prussia, receiving the master's degree in 1723. When he learned of his sovereign's desire to conscript extraordinarily tall fellows, such as he, he decided to become a draft dodger, seeking asylum in Saxony. Gottsched evaded the border police as well as the conscription officers and arrived in Leipzig in 1724.

Once safely ensconced, he began to ingratiate himself with leading members of the intellectual community. He was a smooth operator. Even Johann Ulrich König, who had survived the vicissitudes of Saxon political life to become influential with the Dresden court, believed him long enough to help him obtain a tenure-track professorship. As soon as Gottsched was assured of tenure, however, the friendship began to deteriorate.[11] Gottsched was even so bold as to mount a campaign to abolish from the very face of this planet all traces of opera, which happened to be König's favorite art form and also his major source of income. Another target of professorial wrath was Christian Friedrich Henrici, the popular writer of cantata-texts composed by Bach and of relatively successful comedies for the indigenous public stage. In addition to holding his plays up to rules never intended to be observed, Gottsched subjected him to personal as well as professional vilification.

In 1728, Gottsched described opera as "ein ungereimter Mischmasch von Poesie und Musik, wo der Dichter und Komponist einander Gewalt tun, und sich überaus viel Mühe geben ein sehr elendes Werk zu Stande zu bringen."[12] Opera failed to follow French rules, so it could not be classified as either tragedy or comedy, which meant it did not belong in the canon of

---

[11] For information on the German university system in the eighteenth century, see Friedrich Paulsen, *Geschichte des gelehrten Unterrichts auf den deutschen Schulen und Universitäten vom Ausgang des Mittelalters bis zur Gegenwart, Mit besonderer Rücksicht auf den klassischen Unterricht*, 3rd enl. ed., ed. Rudolf Lehmann, 2 vols. (Leipzig: Veit, 1919–21), 1:552–53; and also, Charles E. McClelland, *State, Society, and University in Germany, 1700–1914* (Cambridge: Cambridge University Press, 1980), p. 28.

[12] *Der Biedermann* (1728), *Gesammelte Schriften*, ed. Eugen Reichel (Berlin: Gottsched Verlag, 1903), 3:219. "a nonsensical hotchpotch of poetry and music where the poet and the composer violate each other and take exceedingly great pains to bring about a very miserable work," trans. Gloria Flaherty, *Opera in the Development of German Critical Thought* (Princeton: Princeton University Press, 1978), p. 95.

legitimate art forms.[13] Furthermore, its voluptuousness, its indecorous content, and the questionable character of its performers made it a dangerously seductive form of entertainment as well as a stupid one.[14]

Gottsched's subsequent writings against opera are filled with even more vitriolic rhetoric. In one, he called it "das ungereimteste Werck, so der menschliche Verstand jemahls erfunden."[15] In another, he made comparisons to the barbaric music of the Janissaries.[16] Gottsched was actually a German patriot, who wanted to raise the cultural level of his countrymen so that they could compete successfully with the French. He did not want Leipzig to be merely a "little Paris." He wanted it to be Leipzig. However, rather than admit to historical or social differences between the two countries, he unquestioningly embraced the Franco-Roman Neo-Classical code, and he sought to impose, if not superimpose, it on the Germans. No one capable of rational thought, he wrote at one point, would ever challenge that code. The students who needed grades from Herr Professor Gottsched certainly did not. And, even those who were not in his courses only saw fit to publish their objections across a safe border in Bremen in *Neue Beiträge zum Vergnügen des Verstandes und Witzes*. Some of them, like Johann Elias Schlegel and his brother, Johann Adolph Schlegel, absorbed enough from the Leipzig scene to go on to become relatively powerful critical theorists in their own right. They had learned not only about drama, but also about the dangers involved in inventing a literary establishment that sought control over all aspects of creative expression, especially the public varieties.

Surprisingly, Gottsched found an ally among the practitioners of living theater in Leipzig. Friederike Karoline Weissenborn had been one of those middle-class, paternally abused female adolescents who happily succumbed to the enticements of a disgruntled university student just to get away from home. Johann Neuber dropped out for the sake of a theatrical troupe, and she joined him. As a result of their partnership, she entered the history books as Caroline Neuber or "die Neuberin."

---

[13] In this matter, Gottsched followed senior Leipzig colleagues, like Johann Burkhard Menke, whose writings not only poked fun at scholarly vanity, but also staunchly upheld the Franco-Roman Neoclassical Code with all its prescriptions for the arts.

[14] Throughout his career, Gottsched's research habits were impeccable. Despite his great aversion to opera, for example, he listed the titles of all the ones produced in Leipzig in his *Nöthiger Vorrath zur Geschichte der deutschen Dramatischen Dichtkunst*, 2 vols. (Leipzig, 1757 and 1765), 1:269–72, 274–75, 286–87, 297, 308–9, 311, 322–23, 326, 328–32.

[15] *Versuch einer Critischen Dichtkunst* (Leipzig, 1730), p. 604. "... the most nonsensical work the human mind ever invented," trans. Flaherty, *Opera in the Development*, p. 95.

[16] *Beyträge zur Critischen Historie der deutschen Sprache, Poesie und Beredsamkeit*, III, 12 (1735), p. 614. I give full attention to Gottsched's anti-opera campaign in *Opera in the Development*, pp. 93–101.

After forming their own troupe in 1727, the Neubers managed to acquire the prestigious title of "Royal Polish and Electoral Saxon Court Comedians," which meant they would have no difficulties obtaining the needed licenses to play the Leipzig fairs. Professor Gottsched agreed to supply scripts by translating the acknowledged classic French dramas or by imitating them. The most famous was Gottsched's own *Der sterbende Cato* (1731).[17]

The Neubers' part of the agreement had to do with improving the quality of performance by relinquishing all forms of improvisation, music, slapstick, buffoonery, or whatever might constitute the fun factor, and also by having planned rehearsals. Those rehearsals, in addition to their firm insistence that lines actually be memorized did, indeed, serve to revolutionize German theatrical practices. Caroline Neuber also insisted upon structuring the free time of her troupers. Such was to be spent with productive duties. The males were to paint scenery and make handbills, while the females were to do women's work, like sew costumes or mend them. Caroline Neuber, who hoped to raise the lowly civil status of her troupers, monitored their sex lives as well. Any couple that seemed to be getting too intimate she forced into a legal relationship. Many an unsuccessful marriage was blamed on her.

All such reform ideas were very well-intentioned. The burghers of Leipzig, however, voted with their feet. They simply did not attend the performances of the Neuber troupe. Face to face with the equivalent of bankruptcy, Caroline Neuber realized that recognition from academicians, like Gottsched, could not offset a downtrend in box-office receipts. As a result, she dumped her recently acquired Francophile ideals in order to cut her losses. She might have mounted a production banning Hanswurst in early 1737, but, by late 1738, she just had to exonerate him and welcome him back home. She did the same with that legendary figure so very closely tied with Leipzig's home-grown traditions, Doctor Faustus. Caroline Neuber saw to the mounting of a play entitled *Das ruchlose Leben und erschreck-liche Ende des weltbekannten Ertzzauberers Dr. Johann Faust.*[18] Not only was it not French, but it also had lots of make-believe, machines, and music, in addition to much else from the Germanic tradition. It was a breathtaking success.

In 1739, Caroline Neuber officially broke with Gottsched. She thereupon tried to regain her fame by going to St. Petersburg. She failed, and, when she returned to Leipzig in 1741, she found others ensconced in her theater. Her career was on the wane. She no longer had promise or clout. Neverthe-less, she continued to recognize raw, unformed theatrical talent, mounting,

---

[17] Its mixture of elements from works on the subject by Joseph Addison and Deschamps exemplifies yet again Gottsched's adaptability to exigency, "Nachwort," *Sterbender Cato*, ed. Horst Steinmetz (Stuttgart: Reclam, 1964), p. 137.

[18] For information in English, see Philip Mason Palmer and Robert Pattison More, *The Sources of the Faust Tradition from Simon Magus to Lessing* (1936; rpt. New York: Haskell House, 1965), p. 247.

for example, Gotthold Ephraim Lessing's early play about a conceited young scholar.[19] The last ten years of Caroline Neuber's life were spent drifting. When she was on the verge of death in 1760, she was evicted from the inn in which she had sought refuge. The owners did not want their establishment tainted with the illegitimacy of a person involved with theater. Had it not been for a loyal peasant, her corpse would not have been put to rest in a plain wooden box in consecrated ground. He happened to be a sly peasant who knew how to bypass deviously the establishment and its rules.[20] In 1776, some young men with a strong sense of German pride saw to the construction of a monument in her honor.

Christian Felix Weisse applauded that monument. As a stagestruck Leipzig student, he had done translations and odd jobs for the Neubers in order to earn free tickets to their performances. They taught him a great deal about theater and also about Leipzig audiences. He applied those lessons in 1752, when he adapted Charles Coffey's *The Devil to Pay, or The Wives Metamorphosed*. To the great horror of Gottsched, this operetta — with irregularities in form, English origins, and distracting music — became an overnight sensation. Gottsched's attempts to have it suppressed only served to increase its popularity, for the entire city of Leipzig became intensely involved. Weisse epitomized their Germanic identity; consequently, the Leipzig burghers rose to his defense against Gottsched. They had already had enough of the Franco-Roman Neo-Classical code, not to mention the French.[21]

Music was important to the Leipzigers, not only when it came to theater but also when it came to political banquets, marriage ceremonies, funerals, memorial services, academic convocations, and so on. In addition to the usual private lessons and apprenticeships, there were many institutions providing formal musical instruction in the city. Training in vocal and instrumental music was available at the renowned Thomasschule. And, due to the sustained efforts of another man of the Enlightenment who studied both with Bach and with Gottsched, Lorenz Christoph Mizler von Kolof, music was being rehabilitated to its full dignity as something worthy of study

---

[19] The importance of gaining practical lessons from someone directly involved in living theater was, on the other hand, recognized by Lessing, who wrote the following in the preface to his play: "Mit so vielen Verbesserungen unterdessen, als ich nur immer hatte anbringen können, kam mein 'Junger Gelehrte' in die Hände der Frau *Neuberin*. Auch ihr Urteil verlangte ich; aber anstatt des Urteils erwies sie mir die Ehre, die sie sonst einem angehenden Komödienschreiber nicht leicht zu erweisen pflegte; sie liess ihn aufführen." *Lessings Werke*, ed. Kurt Wölfel, 3 vols. (Frankfurt am Main: Insel, 1967), 1:631.

[20] Günther Schöne, *Tausend Jahre deutsches Theater, 914–1914* (Munich: Prestel, 1962), pp. 111–12.

[21] Some of the numerous pamphlets printed during this campaign were made available in the appendix to Jakob Minor, *Christian Felix Weisse und seine Beziehungen zur deutschen Litteratur des achtzehnten Jahrhunderts* (Innsbruck: Wagner, 1880).

as a university discipline. The journal he began, *Neu-Eröffnete Musikalische Bibliothek, oder Gründliche Nachricht nebst unpartheyischen Urtheil von musikalischen Schriften und Büchern*, together with the Societät der musicalischen Wissenschaften, made Leipzig into a center for research into musical theory and history in the late 1730s. The basic books — reference and theory as well as how-to — would have been long available because of the active publishing industry and also because of the library facilities.

Basic training in the performing arts, however, involves more than books and book-learning. There is a myriad of components. Pinpointing and documenting those components in music, as in any other art, for that matter, is always very difficult since eyewitness accounts, diaries, memoirs, and the like are by definition interpretations or justifications of experiential perceptions and reactions made after the fact. When those perceptions are themselves about intangibles, the matter becomes almost impossible. That being the case, I should like to rely on the medium most often touted to be less strange and more accessible than fact, namely fiction. Music has often been the subject of fiction. In German literature, musicians and their training have figured importantly since the very beginning because of close ties to cultural developments. The earliest are often a combination of deity-musician-warrior, often with explicit connection to the demonic or superhuman sphere.[22] Nor has that combination been overlooked in more modern times.[23]

The best seventeenth-century example, a novel that would certainly have been known in a book-publishing city like Leipzig, was Hans Jakob Christoffel von Grimmelshausen's *Der Abentheuerliche Simplicissimus Teutsch* (1669). It tells about the adventures of an innocent simpleton during the time of the Thirty Years' War. This particular war orphan, who is swept along by the historical currents, is self-taught in just about everything, including music. The kind of music he plays or sings reflects his spiritual disposition, or lack thereof, and serves to show how he moves from primordial ignorance through the decadent world of material delights to genuine salvation. His first instrument is the bagpipe, which he masters only after a series of abortive attempts. As his constant companion, it responds almost humanly to the vagaries of wartime when both are attacked by cuirassiers: "als wann sie alle Welt zu Barmherzigkeit bewegen hätte wollen:

---

[22] George C. Schoolfield, *The Figure of the Musician in German Literature*, University of North Carolina Studies in Germanic Languages and Literatures, 19 (Chapel Hill: Univ. of North Carolina Press, 1956; rpt. New York: AMS Press, 1966), p. 1.

[23] For treatment of that specific subject, see my article, "The Performing Artist as the Shaman of Higher Civilization," *Modern Language Notes* 103, no. 3 (April 1988): 519–39.

aber es halff nichts / wiewol sie den letzten Athem nicht sparete / mein Ungefäll zu beklagen."[24]

After many intervening adventures, martial and marauding, as well as musical, the hero, Simplicissimus, arrives in the world-capital of decadence, Paris. There he meets up with some courtiers who introduce him to the king's master of ceremonies. That gentleman is so very impressed by him that he requests "ein Teutsch Liedlein in meine Laute."[25] Simplicissimus then comments in his first-person narrative: "ich folgte gern / weil ich eben in Laun war / wie dann die Musici gemeiniglich seltzsame Grillenfänger sind / beflisse mich derhalben das beste Geschirr zu machen / und contentirte demnach die Anwesende so wol / dass der Ceremonien-Meister sagte: Es wäre immer Schad / dass ich nit die Frantzösische Sprach könte."[26] That master of ceremonies wanted him for a new opera.

Simplicissimus's great native intelligence and inherent musical talent allowed him to overcome his deficiency in linguistic sophistication. He gets the part and explains how he managed: "die Melodeyen der unterschiedlichen Lieder / so ich zu singen hatte / schlug ich gleich perfect auff dem Instrument / weil ich das Tabulatur-buch vor mir hatte / empfieng demnach die Frantzösische Lieder / solche auswendig / und die Aussprach recht zu lernen / welche mir zugleich verteutscht wurden / damit ich mich mit den Geberden darnach richten könte; Solches kam mich gar nicht schwer an / also dass ichs eher konte / als sichs jemand versahe."[27]

All who hear him at rehearsal are convinced that he is not only a born Frenchman but also a re-born Orpheus. His description of his brilliant performance is quite amusing. It evokes a mood of good fun, until he reaches the scene where Orpheus is supposed to realize that Euridice is irretrievably lost. Then, it becomes quite mysterious. Grimmelshausen, the author, has his hero describe it thusly:

---

[24] Ed. Rolf Tarot (Tübingen: Max Niemeyer, 1967), Bk. 1, chap. 3, p. 16. "... as it would move all the world to pity: which availed nought, though it spared not its last breath in the bewailing of my sad fate," trans. A. T. S. Goodrick, *The Adventurous Simplicissimus, Being the Description of the Life of a Strange Vagabond Melchior Sternfels von Fuchshaim* (Lincoln: University of Nebraska Press, 1962), p. 7.

[25] Ed. Tarot, p. 297. "... a German song sung to the lute," trans. Goodrick, p. 244.

[26] Ed. Tarot, p. 297. "This I did willingly, being in the mood (for commonly musicians be whimsical people), and so busied myself to play my best, and did so please the company that the Master of the Ceremonies said 'twas great pity I could not speak French," trans. Goodrick, p. 244.

[27] Ed. Tarot, pp. 297–98. "The tunes of the songs I had to sing I could play at once perfectly upon the lute: for I had the notes before me: and thereafter I received the French words, to learn them by heart and likewise to pronounce them, all which were interpreted for me in German, that I might use the actions fitted to the songs. All this was easy enough to me, and I was ready before any could have expected it," trans. Goodrick, p. 245.

Da ich aber meine Euridice ohnversehends verlohr / bildet ich mir die
gröste Gefahr ein / darein je ein Mensch gerathen könte / und wurde davon
so bleich / als ob mir ohnmächtig werden wollen / dann weil ich damals
allein auff der Schaubühne war / und alle Spectatores auff mich sahen /
beflisse ich mich meiner Sachen desto eyferiger / und bekam die Ehr darvon
/ dass ich am besten agirt hätte. Nachgehends setzte ich mich auff einen
Felsen / und fieng an den Verlust meiner Liebsten mit erbärmlichen Worten
und einer traurigen Melodey zu beklagen / und alle Creaturen umb
Mitleiden anzuruffen / darauff stellten sich allerhand zahme und wilde Thier
/ Berg / Bäum und dergleichen bey mir ein / also dass es in Warheit ein
Ansehen hatte / als ob alles mit Zauberey über-natürlicher Weis wäre
zugericht worden.[28]

In contrast to Grimmelshausen's born musician who is capable of
teaching himself almost everything, there are the musicians who are
depicted by Wolfgang Caspar Printz, whose writings — some of which were
familiar to Bach — were often published with Leipzig houses.[29] Printz
might have known infinitely more about music than Grimmelshausen, but
he could not match him in narrative technique and sheer literary artistry.
Nevertheless, the three musician novels that Printz published, *Musicus
Vexatus* (1690), *Musicus Magnanimus* (1691), and *Musicus Curiosus* (1691)
are all more than worthy of passing attention. Printz staunchly defended the
dignity of music, claiming that it was one of the original liberal arts. And,
when it seemed advisable, he insisted on its mathematical connection. He
hoped to reform the public image of the musician and elevate music once
again to a profession. He strove to get rid of the unwanted element.

The first novel, *Musicus Vexatus*, explains how the hero as a seven-year-
old found a fiddle and began playing with it. His middle-class father, who is
very worried that he will become a beer-fiddler, forbids him to continue. His
mother intercedes when he is caught disobediently playing his fiddle in
secret. She convinces her husband that studying music would be less
harmful than hanging out with other little boys who preferred to break the
neighbors' windows. Since the boy was otherwise obedient and industrious,
the father bought him a violin and allowed him to do odd jobs for local
musicians, eventually apprenticing himself to one of them.

---

[28] Ed. Tarot, p. 299. "But when I again lost my Eurydice all unexpectedly I did fancy to
myself the greatest danger wherein a man could find himself, and thereupon became so
pale as if I would faint away: for inasmuch as I was then alone upon the stage and all
spectators looked on me, I played my part the more carefully and got therefrom the praise
of having acted the best. Thereafter I set me on a rock and began to deplore the loss of
my bride with piteous words and a most mournful melody, and to summon all creatures
to weep with me: upon that, all manner of wild beasts and tame, mountains, trees and the
like flocked round me, so that in truth it seemed as if 'twere all so done in unnatural
fashion by enchantment," trans. Goodrick, p. 246.

[29] *Musik in Geschichte und Gegenwart*, vol. 1, col. 1021.

As his father had predicted, the musician brutally exploited him without providing for him or teaching him very much. In addition to changing and washing the baby's diapers, the son had to empty the chamber pots. When he became thoroughly nauseated by such duties, the musician claimed that drinking tobacco juice and smoking a pipe would help. As a result, his problems worsened. Eventually, however, he learned to develop strategies for survival.

His musical training consisted primarily of boxes on the ear, blows, and beatings: "Denn mein Lehr-Herr war ungedultig und verdriesslich / und gedachte die Kunst seinen Jungen mit lauter Schlägen einzubringen."[30] Drawing blood was considered the only punishment for failure, and, in the course of his apprenticeship, twenty bows were broken in whacking him, and five violins were destroyed in banging him on the head. After about six years, he was freed from such misery to become a journeyman (p. 70). His disappointment was enormous when he learned there were so many uncultured, coarse aristocrats who had as their court musicians nothing but beer-fiddlers, pipers, and organ-grinders (p. 80). He himself refused to allow himself to be called a *Spielmann*, a player, because of his honestly obtained musical knowledge: "Ich bin kein Spiel-Mann: ein Bier-Fiedler ist ein Spiel-Mann. Ich aber habe meine Kunst redlich gelernet."[31] Despite all the punishment he had endured, he was tremendously proud of his profession, defending it against all comers (p. 98).

The hero of Printz's second novel, *Musicus Magnanimus*, is equally proud of his profession, the difference being that he spent his apprenticeship with an impeccably honest teacher who never beat him and never required menial chores of him. He makes his colleagues jealous just by reminiscing. This all serves as a backdrop for discussing certain pressing issues. One considers, "ob auch ein guter Christ dissweilen einen Tantz thun möchte?"[32] The conclusion is that dancing is generally beneficial to human health because it creates good moods, stimulates appetite, aids digestion, and, moreover, the sweat it generates purges the body of deleterious elements. Another issue is legitimacy, which is thought to be wielded by the

---

[30] *Musicus Vexatus, oder Der wohlgeplagte / doch noch nicht verzagte sondern jederzeit lustige Musicus Instrumentalis, In einer anmuthigen Geschicht vor Augen gestellet von Cotala, dem Kunst-Pfeiffer Gesellen,* in *Ausgewählte Werke,* ed. Helmut K. Krause, 2 vols. (Berlin and New York: Walter de Gruyter, 1974, 1979), I: 48. Page references given in the text refer to this edition. "For my teacher was impatient and annoyed and proposed to inculcate the art into his boys with nothing but blows."

[31] Ed. Krause, p. 89. "I am no mere player. A beer fiddler is a player. I, on the other hand, learned my art honestly."

[32] *Musicus Magnanimus Oder Pancalus, Der Grossmüthige Musikant / In Einer überaus lustigen / anmuthigen / und mit schönen Moralien gezierten Geschicht vorgestellet von Mimnermo, des Pancali guten Freund,* ed. Krause, I: 152. "... whether a good Christian could ever do a dance?"

enemies of music in order to deny them their livelihood and keep them disenfranchised (p. 217). They are made to be confused with the *Spielmann*, the player. He differs, however, from an honorable musician because he is given to severe emotional fluctuations and fits of frenzy that can become senseless raving. The music he makes in his enthusiastic state is not only artistically but also socially tainted, as one sees from the burgher who considers a serenade by *Spielleute*, players or entertainers, an insult to his honor.

The third novel by Printz, *Musicus Curiosus*, picks up the thread of defending music as an honorable profession that requires study in addition to talent. Its hero explains that his boyhood curiosity was so great that he wanted to learn everything. He took art lessons as well as music lessons, all the while devouring books on diverse subjects. His experimentation with certain magic tricks was relatively harmless, but the fireworks he managed to put together started a potentially dangerous conflagration.[33]

At age eighteen, the precocious young man decided that he wanted to pursue a career in music. A requisite, in his opinion, was study at the university, where he could learn musical theory and poetics (p. 406). He also intended to do enough jurisprudence to avoid ever needing a lawyer. His father considered the plan sensible and had him named a journeyman. For three years, the young man studied assiduously at the university, supporting himself by giving lessons. Then he realized he must go out and see the world. One of his first confrontations is with beer-fiddlers; it ends well because he had learned to think like a lawyer when necessary. The attempt at litigation is turned into a multi-act comedy by the cantor, "Praecedenz-Streit der Kunst-Pfeiffer und Spiel-Leute / In einer Spann-funckel-neuen Comoedie vorgestellet."[34] The authorities decide in the end that while there is room for both in the world, the *Spielleute* belong only "in denen öffentlichen Schanck- und Bier-Häusern / Dorff-Kirmessen / Lobe-Tanzen und Bauer-Hochzeiten / um ein Billiges Tranck-Geld / aufzu-warten."[35] The hero thereupon joins the army, serves for a while, is honorably discharged in Italy, and, after experiencing carnival in Venice, he matriculates at the university in Bologna, where he comes in contact with many musicians and opera singers. The novel concludes with his investiga-

---

[33] *Musicus Curiosus, Oder Battalus, Der Vorwitzige Musicant / In Einer sehr lustigen / anmuthigen / unertichteten / und mit schönen Moralien durchspickten Geschichte vorgestellet von Mimnermo, des Battali guten Freunde*, ed. Krause, 1:396.

[34] Ed. Krause, p. 427. "Precedence Dispute of the Pipers and Players Presented in a Sparkling New Comedy."

[35] Ed. Krause, p. 468. "... in those public tap rooms and beer houses, village church festivals, dances and peasant weddings in order to beg for a reasonable tip."

tion of the human imagination and its inscrutable workings: "Was thut die Einbildung nicht?"[36] He has become part of a medicine man's show.

Interestingly enough, medical and musical quackery are also brought together in the vigorously patriotic novel *Der Musicalische Quack-Salber* (1700). It was written by the student of Christian Weise who was Bach's predecessor at the Thomasschule. Johann Kuhnau, yet another of those cantors whose talents not only bridged music and literature, but also encompassed ancient languages, mathematics, and jurisprudence.[37] It satirized the German predilection for things foreign, especially musical training. Italy, the narrator states, has its ignoramuses, just as Germany has its masters.[38]

After having pursued music in Italy for about a year, the novel's hero was unable to land a job, so he returned to Germany. He italianized his name, his speech, and his bearing in order to make himself attractive to potential German employers. He is all style without substance, for he has learned precious little about music. Instead of being the virtuoso that he claims, he is a quack, a swindler. However, he is absolutely brilliant at public relations and at creating his own self-image. He misses no opportunity to promote his own cause. Calling himself the "maestro incomparabile di musica," and the "Hochberühmter Italiänischer Musico und unvergleichlicher Virtuoso," he floats rumors, plants letters, fakes fan mail, and has messengers paging him throughout the city.[39] He insists he has mastered all instruments, as any world-class composer should have. And, he passes off his grotesque gestures and bizarre gyrations as inherent in the very latest style of playing. He claims that one of his performances was so great that the audience was inspired to dance. But he objected and would not allow it because he did not want to be taken for a lowly *Spielmann* or player. He explained, "dass ich vor keinen Spielmann, der zum Tanzen fiedelte, wollte gehalten seyn, so blieben sie sitzen."[40]

---

[36] Ed. Krause, p. 525. "What isn't the imagination capable of?"

[37] Percy M. Young, *The Bachs 1500–1850* (London: J. M. Dent, 1970), pp. 131, 134. Johann Hermann Schein, for example, was the Thomascantor who was of crucial importance for poets like Paul Fleming. Another musician-novelist whose early training was gotten in Leipzig was Johann Beer. He wrote *Teutsche Winter-Nächte* (1682) and *Kurtzweilige Sommer-Tage* (1683) in addition to advocating specific rights for professional musicians.

[38] Ed. Kurt Benndorf, *Deutsche Litteraturdenkmale des 18. und 19. Jahrhunderts*, No. 83–88, N.S. No. 33–38 (Berlin, 1900; rpt. Nendeln, Liechtenstein: Kraus, 1968), p. 8. Page numbers given in the text refer to this edition.

[39] Ed. Benndorf, p. 34. also, pp. 60–61. "Highly Famous Italian Musician and Incomparable Virtuoso."

[40] Ed. Benndorf, p. 48. "… that I did not want to be taken for a player who fiddles at dances, as a result of which they remained seated."

This hero instinctively understands about human psychology, so he zeroes in on people's basic insecurity, all the while flattering their great musical sensitivity. He is an artful dodger when it comes to the critics. And, he has the provincial German musicians so intimidated with his purported international scope that it takes them some time to muster up enough courage to begin asking questions. Little by little, they try to put him to the test. When his performance elicits howls of laughter from the real musicians, he sets a new strategy into operation (pp. 64, 74). He avoids them by quick thinking, by side-stepping, and even by claiming that a street gang mugged him and cut up his hands (pp. 53–54). Finally realizing that he is an impostor, the musicians taunt him into one after another amusing trap until he loses all face and has to skip town (p. 95).

Without relinquishing a drop of arrogance, he continues his campaign in other cities. He gives music lessons, teaches composition, plays Orpheus and other roles in the opera, and generally earns his keep by bilking the ignorant. When once showing off for a prospective girlfriend, he gets so totally carried away with his performance that she cannot get him to snap out of it until she give him "was vom Opium."[41] Using drugs as a cure-all was something that performing artists of the late seventeenth and early eighteenth century readily did. It simply belonged to their milieu.

The hero's luck, however, begins to diminish and eventually all his victims converge upon him at the same time and demand retribution. When things cannot possibly get any worse, a theology student has compassion for him. That student takes him along to a preacher in the country, who manages to modify his behavior and make him more modest. Since he is an intelligent young man with a lot of book-learning, the preacher arranges a position for him under the ducal capellmeister.

The young man does a complete about-face. He reforms his lifestyle, discovers true musical aptitude, and assiduously follows the directions of his teachers. The capellmeister gets him a salaried job; he becomes wealthy; he marries the girl of his dreams; and he spends the rest of his life as a genuine virtuoso.

I should like to conclude with the fiftieth of the precepts Kuhnau gave his hero because it is so very important for training and can be applied to actors and singers as well as musicians:

> Wenn die Bauren sehen, dass sie der Quacksalber betrogen hat, und ihnen zerriebene Ziegel-Steine vor Zahn-Pulver oder sonsten dergleichen vor was Guts verkauffet hat; So kommen sie ihm nicht wieder, ja sie tragen ihn allenthalben aus, und schmeissen ihm noch dazu die Haut voll, wenn sie seiner habhafft werden können. Dergleichen Tractamentes kan sich gleichfalls unser ungeschickter und betrüglicher Musicante versehen:

---

[41] Benndorf, p. 223. "… some opium."

Sobald die Scholaren ihm recht in die Karte werden gegucket, und seine Ignoranz gemercket haben, werden sie ihn nicht alleine bald abdancken, und noch andere neben sich ihm abwendig machen, sondern auch, wofern es nur sonst in ihren Kräfften stehet, zur Danckbarkeit vor die Lehre, ihm noch eine gute Hocke Schläge nachtragen, oder er wird doch sonst auff andere Weise von ihnen geschimpffet werden.[42]

---

[42] Ed. Benndorf, p. 254. "When the peasants see that the medical quack has deceived them and has sold them pulverized bricks as tooth powder or something else of that nature, they do not come to him ever again. Indeed, if possible, they throw him out and also beat the hide off him if they can just get hold of him. The same treatment can likewise be performed on our incapable and deceptive musician. As soon as the scholars have correctly discovered his designs and noticed his ignorance, they will not only quickly fire him and blackball him, but they will also, as far as it stands in their power, out of gratitude for the lesson, add a good number of blows or he will be otherwise disgraced by them in different ways."

Speculum Ludi: The Aesthetics of Performance in Song

MARGARET MAHONY STOLJAR

ART IS ONE OF the ways we know about the world. We look at the world within the medium of art as we do through science and mathematics, law and logic. In a sense, the act of knowing itself mimics art, for it seems that to know is to represent in the mind. The mind provides us with an inner spectacle within which we move, bringing order to that which we are told by the senses. Such an ordered spectacle is what we call reality. And the principle of its ordering distinguishes art from other things.

If we are to get a hold on the world in art we must be able to perceive the particular coherence that the art work in question lays before us; we must be able to grasp its meaning. But the question of meaning in music is more puzzling and elusive than in the other arts. Music seems to bear little relation to reality, since it is non-conceptual. The most austere view maintains that it neither represents nor expresses anything: music has meaning only in its patterning of sound. Yet unlike other art forms it cannot be realized without at least one active participant. An explanation of the nature of meaning in music must take account of the fact that as a social activity it undoubtedly has a functional relationship with reality.

Consider the different ways the arts are experienced over time. Painting and sculpture, once completed, remain the same while their materials have not decayed; architecture and ornament can outlive their makers and users by thousands of years. If we set aside for the present the more uncompromising accounts of reading as performance and admit the validity of the written or printed text, it will be true to say that poetry and prose narrative continue to exist in the absence of any reader. The case of literary drama is more complex. It is a two-stage genre consisting firstly of written text and then of performance; its two stages are discontinuous in that a written text can serve as the complete work in the form of literature.

In this respect drama differs essentially from music and dance, although these are customarily also two-stage forms. Even when they exist as written notation in the first place, they still require performance. As performance arts, music and dance cannot properly be said to take place while no one is engaged in them. The survival of a written score or other notation does not invalidate this claim, since any such text is not sufficient in itself. Although it may be in one sense complete, notation constitutes only the pre-performance phase or directions for the implementation of the art form. If the conventions of performance are lost or imperfectly recorded, as for the music and dance of antiquity, it can scarcely be claimed that these arts are known at all.

Because it is a performance art, music exists within a social framework. As a social fact it is bound to something external to itself and cannot otherwise come to be. An explanation of meaning in music therefore needs to be aware of its context in a given community. As philosophers of art continue, however reluctantly, to concede, historical circumstance penetrates the substance of art.[1] Beyond this, however, there remains another dimension of meaning which is more elusive. It is this which obstinately suggests to those who make and listen to music that it intrinsically has something to say about reality. In seeking to explain this connection we shall be obliged to question the kinds of inferences that are made about the way all the arts may relate to the world.

Since antiquity, philosophers have seen music as one of the mimetic arts, believing it to produce models or images of the natural world by imitation or through mathematical analogy. The *Affektenlehre* of the eighteenth century conceived it as a different kind of mimetic system which could emulate psychological states. In our time post-analytic theory has challenged the idea of meaning itself, and with it assumptions about signification in all texts. Not least in the philosophy of music, claims for representation or expression have been undermined by radical critiques such as Nelson Goodman's theory of reference in the arts. Like the different kinds of verbal and visual discourse, music is construed within this argument as a symbolic system having its own internally coherent structure. If we accept this view we no longer seek to ask how music depicts or expresses reality. We speak instead about worldmaking, how a world is organized and articulated in musical discourse. The positions suggested by Goodman in *Languages of Art* and elsewhere provide a new basis for an aesthetics of performance.[2]

As a symbolic system music must refer to something outside itself. To discover how it refers is to go some way towards an answer to the question of meaning in music. Let us agree that except in rare uses of onomatopoeic imitation such as the simulation of bird song, a composer does not set out literally to denote or depict the extrinsic world. How, then, does music refer to it other than in these few instances? The answer I am proposing is in effect the converse of the idea that music symbolizes reality by denotation or depiction. It does not represent the physical characteristics of the natural world or the sense data we receive from these, nor does it express psychological states. The relation between music and reality runs the other way.

---

[1] Arthur C. Danto, *The Philosophical Disenfranchisement of Art* (New York: Columbia Univ. Press, 1986), p. xi; also *The Transfiguration of the Commonplace: A Philosophy of Art* (Cambridge: Harvard Univ. Press, 1981), pp. 36, 39, 64.

[2] Nelson Goodman, *Languages of Art: An Approach to the Theory of Symbols* (Indianapolis and New York: Bobbs-Merrill, 1968); *Ways of Worldmaking* (Hassocks: Harvester Press, 1978); *Of Mind and Other Matters* (Cambridge: Harvard Univ. Press, 1984).

Like other non-denotative arts such as abstract painting or some kinds of dance, music refers to the world by selecting and ordering some of its features. It does not denote or represent the individual or the society which produces it, but exemplifies aspects of these through possessing them in its structures. Music is able to do this in that the technical and stylistic character of a composition is projected by the conventions of performance that obtain at the time it is written. Any music exemplifies the type of performance that is envisaged by the composer for its realization; exemplification, in this special sense, is the way the music refers to the moment of its production.

The title of this essay encapsulates a line of enquiry which turns away from music as document towards music as performance. *Orbis terrarum est speculum ludi*, runs the mysterious saying quoted by Borges from the seventeenth-century lexicographer Du Cange, the world is the mirror of the game.[3] The world made in music mirrors the playing of it, an ordered activity which, like a game, proceeds according to a set of agreed conventions. Within this world we can discern something of the *ludus* that brought it into being: what its rules and etiquette were like, what kind of people the performers were, how and where they played. The music's symbolic world refers to the kind of playing which gave rise to its creation, the assumptions that shaped its first performance.

The presence of extrinsic reality in music, the "realism" of the musical text, is not a function of imitation. Rather it derives from the way the text is structured.[4] The features of the text are marked by the conventions of performance that participate in its shaping. These may derive from the social function served by the music, whether as religious ritual, public or private entertainment or ceremony. They may concern the amateur or professional status of the players, the physical conditions of performing and the state of the instruments used. The demands of particular kinds of instrumentation or of the presumed level of competence of the players produce specific and recognizable features in works composed contemporaneously. In these respects the music refers literally to performance practice through exemplification.

The type of literal exemplification in which reference is made to social and material conditions of performance relates to extrinsic factors which are antecedent to the actual playing. A different dimension of reference obtains where intrinsic conventions are concerned. These all-pervasive determinants of musical discourse comprise the mutually comprehensible stylistic practices adopted in private or public performance within a particular culture. Matters of style like formal or informal diction, delimited or spontaneous expressive modes or the balance between melody, rhythm, and

---

[3] Jorge Luis Borges, "The Sect of the Phoenix," in *Labyrinths* (Harmondsworth: Penguin, 1981), p. 133.

[4] Cf. Goodman, *Languages of Art*, p. 232.

harmony are established over time as conventions within which performance takes place. They are referred to metaphorically in the musical text, which provides examples of the understood style through possessing them.[5]

Literal and metaphorical reference to performance practice constitutes the ordering principle that inhabits any musical composition. To understand the structure of reference in a musical text is to open up its symbolic terrain. Given that performance is symbolized in a musical text, it follows that knowledge of the expectations and the practices referred to there will constitute not only a sociology of musical history but also the basis for its aesthetics. Questions about meaning in music can begin with an examination of the conventions of performance which are responsible for its particular coherence.

The aesthetics of performance I wish to propose holds good for any kind of musical text, whether vocal or instrumental or both. It asserts the necessary intervention of reality into music at the moment of production through the composer's exemplification of the known conditions of performance. While it may be less immediately possible to document this process for music that exists only within an oral tradition, the principle of performance informing composition will still hold. For modern European art-song, where a written and then published verbal and musical text is the norm, such documentation can usually be assembled with little difficulty. My paradigm for analysis of the aesthetics of performance will be the German pre-classical keyboard song, or what I have called *Sturm und Drang* song.[6]

The art-song of the 1770s and 1780s takes on a definable stylistic character by virtue of the coincidence of a number of social and generic factors, but primarily as a result of its derivation from the lyric of the *Sturm und Drang*. Composers trained in the North German Protestant towns and courts find in the diction and forms of the poetry of Klopstock, Bürger, Claudius, the *Göttinger Hain*, and their contemporaries an impetus which leads to the creation of a new musical language for song. At the same time changing performance practice is shaped by the cultural expectations of the age of sentiment, which include the expression of individual feeling in all the arts. This aesthetic, technological, and social conjuncture is precipitated especially in the domestic art forms of the period, among them the solo song at the keyboard. The increasing popularity of the new style sets up a continuing momentum so that the demand for expressiveness, for instance, is in turn reinforced. There is a continuous interlocking process of composition and reception which has its fulcrum at the culmination of musical production, that is to say, at the moment of first performance.

[5] Ibid., p. 85.

[6] Margaret Mahony Stoljar, *Poetry and Song in Late Eighteenth Century Germany: A Study in the Musical Sturm und Drang* (Dover, NH: Croom Helm, 1985).

Before examining the historical case in greater detail, we can illuminate this model of the musical process by a comparison with the production of literary texts. Recent exploration of the nature of writing and reading has emphasized the idea that the writer always has a reader in mind. The making of a text takes on the character of a dialogue with an implied reader to whom the text is addressed; what is written becomes a discourse, language designed for another person to understand.[7] The notion of dialogue is strengthened by the contemporaneity of writer and implied reader. A text is normally written in the expectation that it will reach an audience within the same social environment as the writer. The implied reader therefore assumes familiar contours for the writer, she is present during the writing and answers silently, as it were, to his questions and suggestions.

Given the communicative function of verbal language, it is not difficult to understand why this sense of dialogue can seem so immediate for the writer, and why, in analyzing a literary text, it often appears patent that this is the way the discourse is structured, as a special instance of *parole* presupposing a jointly known *langue*. It is when we begin to look for a similar structuring of musical texts that a difficulty arises. Is it possible to speak of a dialogic relationship between composer and listener such as exists between writer and reader? In claiming music as a symbolic system with discernible networks of reference, we may also be able to posit a dialogic relationship of this kind.

The social process of music, like that of literature, rests on an implicit connection between the author and the recipient of the text. A composer sets out to write a work which he expects or hopes will be accepted and understood by audiences in his own time and within his own society. For this to happen listeners need to be competent to understand the kind of musical language being employed, not necessarily in its technical aspects but because they are sufficiently familiar with the conventions and experiences of the music of their culture. What this means is that the composer writes for a listener who is ready to hear and understand, whose response is presupposed as the music is offered. Even where a work is consciously or defiantly innovative, the implied listener is one who will be able to recognize this fact and to engage with its novelty.

In the course of this process a dialogue between composer and listener is set up which is analogous to that between writer and reader, but there is an additional speaker in the exchange who has no counterpart in literature. It is the performance which speaks the musical text so that the listener can hear and understand; performance is necessary for the realization of the text

---

[7] Wolfgang Iser, *The Implied Reader: Patterns of Communication in Prose Fiction from Bunyan to Beckett* (Baltimore: Johns Hopkins Univ. Press, 1974); *The Act of Reading: A Theory of Aesthetic Response* (Baltimore: Johns Hopkins Univ. Press, 1978). Cf. M. M. Bakhtin, "Discourse in the Novel," in Michael Holquist, ed., *The Dialogic Imagination* (Austin: Univ. of Texas Press, 1981), pp. 259–422.

in auditory form and so for the music to exist in its completed stage. (For the present argument we may disregard those rare instances of a trained person's reading a score to "hear" the music silently in the head. This is equivalent to the individual activity of reading a literary text, silently or otherwise, which has rightly been identified as a kind of performance. The construction of a text through reading, a notion which is related to but not identical with that of the implied reader, cannot be said to have equal validity as a social fact as the performance of music.)[8] In our perception of the coherence of a literary text we can distinguish the active function of the implied reader in structuring it. For music we need to consider the historical role of the implied performer or, more properly, of the implied performance which shapes the musical text.

The feature of *Sturm und Drang* song that is most immediately significant for its specific stylistic character is its appropriation by amateur performers. The composers who were attracted to the new poetry were among the educated readers who demonstrate the rapidly increasing literacy of the last third of the eighteenth century in Germany. In making settings for the lyric of their contemporaries they offered their own generation material which allowed them to extend their participation in the artistic life of the age. Musical literacy, like the wider kind, was a mark of the educated and leisured class which was taking shape as a new bourgeoisie, especially in the Protestant communities of the North German states. The sons and significantly also the daughters of the clergymen, university teachers, and officials who constituted this class understood, welcomed, and propagated the new forms of art that were beginning to take on unmistakably bourgeois character.

A result of more widespread musical literacy is that for this generation the distinction between performer and listener, professional player and competent musical amateur, becomes less fundamental. This is especially so in respect of small scale musical forms like solo vocal and instrumental works. The German keyboard songs of the 1770s and 1780s were designed for the domestic use of performers who were also listeners; their roles were interchangeable. Here the social history of a musical form intersects with its generic development, as the demands of amateurs playing and singing in the domestic circle are projected into the structures of both melody and accompaniment.

In the performance of the keyboard song of the period, a number of changes are symptomatic of the comprehensive evolution of the form, as it moves from the established conventions of the baroque age towards the flowering of the classical and Romantic lied. The two dimensions of melody and accompaniment both illustrate this evolution, and both may be shown to possess features that refer to performance practice in complementary

---

[8] Cf. Stanley Fish, *Is There a Text in This Class?: The Authority of Interpretive Communities* (Cambridge: Harvard Univ. Press, 1980).

ways. In regard to the vocal line, the participation in music-making of significant numbers of untrained singers meant that the forms are simplified in comparison with the continuo lied of the mid-century and earlier. There is an unassuming range, comfortable for the untrained voice, the diction is artless and ornamentation is absent or rare. The easily-learnt *Strophenlied* is most common although through-composition is not unknown. These streamlining characteristics demonstrate what is meant by literal exemplification of performance practice. There is metaphorical reference also in these same features in that many composers sought to create a new popular tone in song-writing. Some, like J. A. P. Schulz and J. F. Reichardt explained in the prefaces to their collections that this style was explicitly meant to make their music accessible to a wide public. The *Volkston* possessed by many of these songs refers metaphorically to the democratic aspirations that are typical of the *Sturm und Drang*.

In terms of execution, stylistic conventions shaped the vocal dimension of the solo song in that an expressive singing tone was prized above all else. A significant innovation is the use of frequent dynamic marks, both in the interests of greater expressivity as well as to help the less accomplished singer, who could not be expected to be fully competent in matters of musical taste and judgment. As well, manuals and other musical publications of the period universally stress the desirability of *cantabile* playing for all instruments, so that an expressive voice was understood to be essential for the performance of the new song. The desire for maximum expressivity in singing was met by the use of poetic texts which are themselves transparently expressive of feeling. An example is the lyric of Claudius, one of the most frequently set poets of the age, which uses an artless language free of rococo conceits. Straightforward and eloquent execution was sought in song, so that feeling might be articulated as freely as possible. In these ways the *Sturm und Drang* song employs metaphorical reference in its possession of the features most cherished by the age of sentiment.

While a history of singing must rely on contemporary pedagogical or aesthetic writing to provide documentary sources, apart from the indications provided on original scores or printed music, more information can be found with regard to instrumental playing. In the accompaniment to the keyboard song, the most important evolutionary changes of these years are the passing of the figured bass and the slower replacement of the harpsichord and the clavichord by the fortepiano or hammerclavier. Both reforms bring with them enhanced possibilities for the non-professional musician in performance. Their impact upon the diction of the song at the keyboard further illustrates the kind of musical reference to the extrinsic world that we have described as literal exemplification. Written-out accompaniments and the use of emphatic and flexible dynamic contrasts refer to the change from professional to amateur performance and the popularity of the fortepiano.

As anyone who has attempted it knows, playing an accompaniment from a figured bass is an exacting and expert task at any level beyond the most mechanical. Eighteenth-century manuals like the second part of Carl Philipp Emanuel Bach's *Versuch über die wahre Art das Clavier zu spielen* (1762; Essay on the True Art of Playing Keyboard Instruments) ostensibly provide instruction for the novice, but in truth supply a compendium of the most skilled contemporary practice. The appearance, around the seventh and eighth decades of the century, of written-out accompaniments both in the instrumental sonata and in solo song is an indication that a different kind of performer is envisaged. The accompaniments in these works are fully rendered, allowing the amateur to read and learn them without difficulty and obviating the need for the practiced accomplishment demanded by playing from a figured bass. The level of skill required is modest, for they are often no more than the simplest Alberti bass. Readily intelligible harmonic progressions are articulated whereas the traditional style expected the continuo to generate more elaborate contrapuntal patterns.

While the professional continuo player had most often been a conductor and composer as well, as C. P. E. Bach and his brothers were, the player who required accompaniments to be written out was different. He and frequently now she, was one whose skills were more modest and whose experience was limited. Bach's own practice illustrates the distinction made at that time between the professional and the enthusiast. His six sets of keyboard pieces designed for *Kenner und Liebhaber* ("for connoisseurs and amateurs") show that the latter could be expected to demonstrate not inconsiderable musical facility, but in the eyes of the professional they were still in need of guidance in matters of style like dynamics and ornamentation. The musical content of these works could satisfy the *Kenner*, the expert, but technically they were pitched at a level attainable by the competent amateur.

This player typifies the reader of contemporary poetry who also becomes the performer, and in the perspective of social history therefore the creator, of a new musical form in the *Sturm und Drang* song. The lyric was disseminated by means of its inclusion in literary journals like the *Göttinger Musenalmanach* and occasionally in small collections. The journals themselves commissioned composers such as Reichardt and Schulz to write settings for some of the new poetry, which were printed as companion pieces at first publication. Like the lyric, the song was designed to be learnt and performed in a domestic setting, played by the same reader who would enjoy the poetry. Evidence for the domestic performance of these songs is amply found in novels of the period, in genre painting, in the stage directions of contemporary plays and in correspondence.

An occasional poem makes fond mention of the speaker's instrument, usually the *Clavier*, with its silver tones. This most often means the clavichord, but nonetheless the advent of the fortepiano is the second major aspect of performance practice that can be discerned within the text of

Sturm und Drang song. The introduction of new or modified instruments was rapid during the decades of the *Sturm und Drang*, especially those which were in domestic use. Accompanying instruments like the guitar and the harp were improved in ways which enhanced both robustness and flexibility; the violin and the flute finally triumphed over their more complex and diffident cousins of the viol and recorder families. But it is in the use of keyboard instruments that these changes illustrate most strikingly how performance assumptions may be read in the music.

In the first place the fortepiano offered dynamic range and sustaining power which were beyond the capabilities of the other domestic keyboard instruments. It also provided an expressive flexibility superior to that of the brilliant but uncompromising harpsichord. The clavichord, still the household favorite of the age of sentiment, could scarcely be heard beyond the distance of a few paces, and its singing tone and capacity for vibrato seemed little enough to sacrifice for the spectacular effects of the fortepiano. The new instrument also had the virtues of a sturdier construction and an action that allowed for thicker strings, meaning less fragile tuning and less need for renewal of its parts. All in all, it seemed the perfect domestic instrument, being a piece of furniture as well, as the classic nineteenth-century interior came to testify.

The keyboard sonatas and fantasias of C. P. E. Bach are among the earliest works that demand the dynamic range of the fortepiano. It is not surprising that the most adventurous of the new song composers are his stylistic pupils. The young Beethoven's teacher in Bonn, Christian Gottlob Neefe, produced agitated melodic lines and flamboyant dynamics in his settings of Klopstock, for instance, which demonstrate the most literal version of *Sturm und Drang* in song. The voice part is often turbulent, while the keyboard uses suddenly alternating *forte* and *piano* in the accompanying chords. Marked dynamic contrasts and rapidly changed timbres are only possible on a keyboard instrument like the fortepiano. Although it was still not extensively found in Germany during the 1770s except in the possession of professionals or aristocratic patrons, its capabilities were known and its use was foreshadowed in the keyboard writing of the day. The other domestic keyboard instruments, including the organ, were not entirely superseded until early in the nineteenth century, and in rural areas much later. But those composers like C. P. E. Bach, Neefe, and Beethoven, whose temper was progressive and who gave the lead to their contemporaries, rejoiced in the wide percussive range of the keyboard with hammers. In song as much as in the keyboard or instrumental sonata, the new dimensions of performance structured the forms of both melody and accompaniment in unmistakable ways.

The symbolic construction of reality in music may be analyzed in the same way whether we are considering purely instrumental or vocal music, or the latter with and without accompaniment. Art-song nevertheless provides us with a model of some complexity, since its performance entails the presentation of a literary as well as a musical text. It involves not just a two-stage art, but something like a five-stage one, if we place the composer at the end of the process of literary reception but at the beginning of that of musical production. The sequence begins with the literary process of author — text (poem) — reader, then continues with composer-as-reader — text (song) — listener. This is the schema that underlies the system of reference which this essay has proposed, where performance practice provides the dynamic for the structuring of the musical text of the song.

It remains to consider the difference which the use of a verbal text makes to the meaning of music. It is true that the purely musical dimension of song displays features of its own which it shares with non-vocal forms of the same period. These are the features which exemplify contemporary performance practice and which may not always refer to the verbal text. However, the words chosen function as a preliminary partial notation, as a script for the composer. As well as supplying semantic and aesthetic substance, the poem shapes the musical discourse by providing vocalic and rhythmical patterns to be either replicated or employed obliquely. A verbal text is contained within the composite song text in a kind of quotation.[9]

Since the literary text that is used for song is taken over ready-made, so to speak, its construction *as song* is not governed by the same dialogic relationship between writer and reader or listener that exists in texts meant for reading or speaking. While the original poem may possess qualities such as simplicity and expressiveness, the song text it becomes is *pointing* to these qualities and their effectiveness for song rather than possessing them directly.[10] Nonetheless music which incorporates literary texts retains a high level of semantic validity in its verbal mode. The introduction of realistic material in the literary dimension of such music, such as the use of colloquial or bourgeois speech in late eighteenth-century opera or song, is the first step in the strictly musical reference to reality that rests on performance. This material is a literary symbolization of the extrinsic world that is itself quoted in the verbal mode of the song text, the sung words. In the musical mode of that text the same material constitutes some of the features to which the music metaphorically refers. Poem, melody, and accompaniment together construct a symbolic world in which the extrinsic is organized and articulated through exemplification. This kind of multiple reference can be found in *Sturm und Drang* song.

The age of sentiment displays the ideological character of the late Enlightenment at the moment when its focus has moved to a new valuation of feeling. This changed emphasis complements rather than moves against the pursuit of rationality which had been dominant, in the sense that both are evidence of the recognition of personal experience as paramount. The

[9] Cf. Goodman, *Of Mind and Other Matters*, p. 58.

[10] Danto, *Transfiguration of the Commonplace*, p. 37.

cultivation of the individual mind is apparent across the spectrum of aesthetic theory and the arts, where it is signalled by the emergence of bourgeois subject matter and a retreat from classicist convention. We have noted the extent to which *cantabile* playing and the expressiveness of the voice part is prized in *Sturm und Drang* song. In a longer perspective, the emergence of dominant melody is central to the transition from counterpoint to the accompanied single voice which characterizes classical and Romantic forms in both vocal and instrumental writing. It attests at the same time to the late eighteenth century's drive for spontaneous articulation of individual experience.

The movement towards a new language that is apparent in the emancipation of melody is matched throughout this period by wider cultural changes, so that "modern" elements begin to appear in German belles-lettres as well as in the arts. Both these spheres exhibit a growing sense of cultural nationalism, confronting the classicist and French traditions, and are receptive to the expression of democratic aspirations. An expansion of their social function is evidenced by the wider participation of women as writers, readers, and musicians. In sum, the passing of the *ancien régime* is heralded culturally by the great movement of *embourgeoisement* that is discernible to a greater or lesser degree in all the arts.

The idea of expressivity permeates the aesthetics as well as all the developing art forms of the period. In seeking to explain how the new song brought expressivity into its own structures, we need to distinguish carefully between ways of symbolization. Recall that we have not espoused the view that the music itself literally has feelings to express or that it expresses those of the poet or the composer. Nonetheless it cannot be denied that then as now the songs of the *Sturm und Drang* seem to the listener at the very least to bear some relation to, or even directly to characterize, the desire for expressivity that is a hallmark of the age. Again, we need to trace the music's reference to the world in the reverse direction.

In German poetry, the phenomenon of *embourgeoisement* appeared in the lyric of the *Sturm und Drang* in short, quasi-spontaneous forms devoted to personal feeling. An unadorned language was created that contrasts markedly with formal rococo style. Throughout the decade of the 1770s a new, expressive diction was established, so that it is possible to speak of a paradigmatic change in the language of poetry. It soon became apparent that the song versions which accompanied the new lyric from its earliest publication were taking possession of this language in their own musical diction. While quoting the words of the new poetry, *Sturm und Drang* song also created settings which allowed for this possession. Two kinds of reference are at work here. The first, verbal quotation, is a literal reference through the demonstration of innovative poetic language; the second, the creation of new kinds of melody and accompaniment, refers metaphorically to the emotional content of the poetry and, more generally, to the value placed universally on the expression of individual feeling.

We have seen that certain formal and structural elements of the song text, such as melodic freedom or strongly and rapidly contrasting dynamics, refer literally to the instruments newly available, in particular the fortepiano. In another way these elements, whether they belong to the vocal or instrumental mode of the text, refer metaphorically to the emotional range sought; they express this range and refer to it by exemplification. In this sense the emotion or feeling is possessed symbolically by the music. The contemporary expectation that performance could and ought to possess such emotional range shaped the forms and the structures of keyboard song accordingly.

Sturm und Drang composers wrote for a different public from that of the generation before them. Where the continuo lied had presupposed professional or equivalent competence, the keyboard song of the 1770s and 1780s, significantly known as the *Gesellschaftslied*, shows a divergent character in that it belongs to the moment of the amateur performer. The aesthetics of *Sturm und Drang* song rest on a dialogue between composer and listener who is, for the short period under consideration, usually also the performer. Men and women, themselves readers of the new poetry as were the composers who made the settings, appropriated the songs which had been written with their own performance practice in mind. The innovations of the 1770s and 1780s such as written-out accompaniments of modest difficulty, together with an extended dynamic range and flexibility, speak of the new musical literacy of the age and its embrace of instruments particularly suited to it.

In shaping the expectations of composer, performer, and listener, the lifeworld leaves its mark upon the structures of the music which is produced within a particular culture, here that of the nascent German middle class. By the end of the century, with the advent of the public concert and the arrival of a new kind of virtuoso player, the solo song found itself enjoying an expanded social context which enabled it to move once more into the realm of professional music-making. The age of the nineteenth-century concert lied had arrived.

The argument presented here goes some way towards answering an enduring question. Why does art insistently seem to have meaning beyond the patterning of sound, shape, or language? The answer has to do with the substantive link between art and reality which resists all attempts to do away with it. If meaning resides in the coherence of a musical text as it may do more patently in a verbal or pictorial one, then it does so by virtue of the symbolic system of which that text is an exemplar. Within this system a network of reference establishes a relationship between music and reality. The location of the source of this network in performance practice aligns the question of meaning with the production rather than the reception of the musical text.

This approach differs from those presupposed by either of the two extreme views of meaning in art and other texts: one which asserts the necessity of a single correct interpretation and another which maintains that all readings have equal validity. A hermeneutics of music would seek to discover the true interpretation of an extrinsic meaning embodied in a work by the conscious or unconscious action of the composer. This method examines the process of production but assumes that there is a privileged key to interpretation situated beyond the text, in biographical context, for example. Deconstructive approaches would assert the freedom of the listener to hear and respond to a meaning construed spontaneously. The exclusive emphasis on reception adopted in this case means that historicity and social function can be overlooked. Neither of these solutions provides an explanation for the stubborn suggestion inherent in art that there is both a conditioned and an unconditioned dimension to its meaning.

For music, the succeeding frameworks of symbolization rest as for the other arts on changing historical circumstance. But meaning is not located outside the symbolization awaiting recognition by the discovery of a correct set of codes. Meaning is that structure of the symbolic system which endows it with coherence and whereby it refers to extrinsic reality. In this sense, an image of the real world can be said to be present in the musical text itself; it is understood by those who perform and listen, who *read* the musical text. If the symbolic order the system possesses is to be construed as its meaning, the reality it refers to cannot be disregarded. The task of the historian of music is to illuminate this order synchronically by elucidating those circumstances which have informed its making.

In the process of composition the world of the music is created through the mirroring of performance. This mirroring informs the substance more truly than that, in another more limited sense, each single performance is an image or a projection of the score. Our metaphor, *speculum ludi*, like its grammar, is dialectical. It is therefore particularly apt to capture the idea of music in its symbolic relation to reality. The world of music, its spaces, its perspectives, and its paths, refers to the playing of it in a continuous process of shaping and re-shaping. It is a process that is alive both before and after the production of the musical text. The circumstances of the playing contribute to musical history in a more immediate way than those that belong to biography or to the evolution of genre. Performance is that Other to which music intrinsically refers. Not only does it give the text a voice, it is the essential intelligence that allows its voicing.

On Goethe's *Tonlehre*

John Neubauer

The little "schemata" of Goethe's *Tonlehre* has been republished recently in volume 9 of the Hanser (or "Münchener") Ausgabe of Goethe's works under the rubric *physics*. As editor of the text, I accepted the choice somewhat reluctantly, and only because I saw no sensible solution for placing it anywhere else. But my pragmatic decision forces me to justify by way of introduction why Goethe's piece on physics should be discussed in the context of German literature and music, which rightly focuses on literary texts, musical scores, and their combination.

I

The *Tonlehre* was written in the summer of 1810, after the conclusion of the *Farbenlehre*, during one of Goethe's yearly sojourns in the Bohemian spas. Its immediate occasion was a rereading of Ernst Florens Friedrich Chladni's book *Die Akustik* (1802) and longer discussions with Zelter, who visited Goethe in Teplitz.

Goethe was fond of drawing up schematas, and since so many of his jottings survived, it may be asked why we should give particular attention to it, especially if you, like myself, get irritated by the habit of some Goethe scholars to look with wide-eyed reverence at every scrap of paper the great man ever graced with his handwriting — not to speak of those that he dictated to his secretaries.

Now Goethe himself declared on 19 June 1805 to Zelter he knew about music more through reflection than through pleasure ("mehr durch Nachdenken als durch Genuß") and when he prepared for publication his correspondence with Zelter twenty-four years later he rephrased his remark in another letter to Zelter on 17 May 1829, by writing that the *Tonlehre* afforded him a strange view into a region "in welcher ich nicht einmal genießen, geschweige genießend denken sollte" (in which I should not even take pleasure, let alone think pleasurably).

The remarks of 1805 and 1829 seem to declare Goethe's emotional as well as intellectual incompetence in matters of music. This engaging readiness to self-deprecation has contributed to the emergence of a stereotype according to which Goethe was an *Augen-* not an *Ohrenmensch*, a visual person with little sense for music. If we add to his a second commonplace, namely that he had a strong aversion to abstract theorizing, we may indeed wonder whether his brief theoretical schema on the theory of music is worth our attention.

That Goethe valorized *Anschauung*, that he gave priority to vision over hearing and ocular image over tonal or verbal structures, may be evident if we compare the sheer size of the *Farbenlehre* to the *Tonlehre*, which is just a skeleton. Yet excessive emphasis on the visual in Goethe's thought tends to overlook — as I have shown in a recent article on morphological poetics — the importance of language in his theory and poetic practice. Twentieth-century theories of a Goethe-based morphological science and morphological poetics seem to me both dangerous and illegitimate offsprings of Goethe's thinking.

How important a role language played in Goethe's thinking may be readily seen if we turn from the visual arts to music, and note that he regarded the song as the exemplary form of music. Now the song constitutes a symbiotic union of music with language that cannot be readily duplicated in combinations of language with sculpture or painting. Furthermore, Goethe steadfastly insisted that language had to play the leading role in this union. Language-dominated music assumed such a normative role in his thinking that it often became the barrier to his music-appreciation, for instance in recognizing the genius of Schubert, who did not always follow the strophic structure of the poems he set to music. At times, however, as in the case of Bach's instrumental music, Goethe could overcome his limiting theoretical commitment.

If we turn to the second commonplace, namely that Goethe disliked abstract theorizing, we should not rush to agree with Mephisto, who claims: "Grau, teurer Freund, ist alle Theorie / Und grün des Lebens goldner Baum" (*Faust*, ll. 2038–39).[1] Let us remember that his longest work is the *Farbenlehre* — a work that Albrecht Schöne justly characterized recently as *Goethes Farbentheologie* — and that Goethe himself remarked in the *Vorwort* to that work that every attentive glance into the world is already laden with theory. His self-depreciatory remarks notwithstanding Goethe passionately and intelligently concerned himself with music theory throughout his life. Though the *Tonlehre* is brief, it emerged from a lengthy series of reflections and Goethe often returned to it after its formulation in 1810. Surrounding the *Tonlehre*, there are a great many comments and statements on music theory in Goethe's correspondence.

As early as 1791, Goethe proposed to Johann Friedrich Reichardt, his musical advisor in those years, that they collaborate on a treatise on acoustics. The plan fell through, but Goethe's interest in the subject was periodically rekindled during the following decades, in connection with his work on color theory, or external impulses such as his acquaintance with the physicist Chladni. In 1808 there followed an important exchange of letters with Zelter on the question whether the major and minor scales had equal

---

[1] "Gray, my dear friend, is every theory, / And green alone life's golden tree" (trans. Walter Kaufmann).

status, but music had to be put aside once more in order to complete the work on color theory.

II

Evidently, however, the writing of the *Farbenlehre* prepared the ground for the *Tonlehre*, not only by providing some principles of organization and nomenclature, but also by forcing Goethe to reflect on the analogies and differences between vision and hearing. His point of departure in this was a critical remark he made as early as 1799 in his commentary on Diderot's *Essai sur la peinture*, to the effect that color and sound were not analogous. In the fifth section in didactic part of the *Farbenlehre* this principle is restated but softened by the recognition that although the phenomena are different the underlying laws of polarity are similar:

> Vergleichen lassen sich Farbe und Ton unter einander auf keine Weise; aber beide lassen sich auf eine höhere Formel beziehen, aus einer höhern Formel beide, jedoch jedes für sich, ableiten.... Beide sind allgemeine elementare Wirkungen nach dem allgemeinen Gesetz des Trennens und Zusammenstrebens, des Auf- und Abschwankens, des Hin- und Wieder-wägens wirkend, doch nach ganz verschiedenen Seiten, auf verschiedene Weise, auf verschiedene Zwischenelemente, für verschiedene Sinne. (Section 748)[2]

Goethe regarded the fusion of science and art in music theory to be so fascinating that he thought the time had come to attempt a *Tonlehre*, at the risk of "die für uns gewordene positive, auf seltsamen empirischen, zufälligen, mathematischen, ästhetischen, genialischen Wegen entsprungene Musik zu Gunsten einer physikalischen Behandlung zu zerstören und in ihre ersten physischen Elemente aufzulösen" (Section 750).[3]

Goethe treats sound in rubrics that correspond to the categories of physiological, physical, and chemical in the *Farbenlehre*. The corresponding three acoustic dimensions are labeled in the *Tonlehre* as "Organisch (subjektiv)," "Mechanisch (gemischt)," and "Mathematisch (objektiv)." Organic (subjective) refers to the domain of human *sound-perception* and

---

[2] "Color and sound are in no way comparable; but both of them can be related to a higher formula, they can be deduced, each in its own way, from a higher formula.... Both are elementary general effects that follow the general law of separating and striving to unify, of swinging up and down, of swaying back and forth — both in completely different directions, in different manners, upon different intermediaries, for different senses" (except as otherwise indicated, the translations in the body of the text and in the notes are by the author).

[3] "even if the physical analysis threatened to destroy and to dissolve into its physical elements that positive music which was invented for us in strange empirical, accidental, mathematical, aesthetic, and inspired ways."

sound-production, mechanical (mixed) to mechanical modes of sound-production, and mathematical (objective) to inherent qualities of sound. Like the *Farbenlehre*, the *Tonlehre* concludes with questions of application, the most important of which pertains to the artistic use of sounds.

A few words of qualification before I proceed. I have indiscriminately used color and visual, as if they referred to the same domain. This may be correct if one followed Newton, for whom white light was just another, albeit compounded color. But Goethe did not accept the theory that white was composed of all the colors of the rainbow. He conceived of the colors as resulting from the interaction of two more fundamental entities, namely light and darkness. From his perspective, a *Farbenlehre* was a part of a more fundamental *Lichtlehre*, which, to be sure, he never considered writing.

Now the *Tonlehre* is also a part of a larger domain of study, but the demarcation is characteristically different. As Goethe says in the introduction, the realm of the audible (*das Hörbare*) is limitless; and he immediately eliminates from the endless sea of sound all non-musical sounds (such as *Geräusch*, *Schall*, and *Sprache*). Hence his *Tonlehre* actually becomes a study of "musical sound" (*das* musikalisch *Hörbare*), for which there is no exact counterpart in the realm of color. The colors in nature or colors used for non-artistic purposes are not intrinsically different from or differently organized than painterly colors. I shall want to come back to Goethe's crucial, and in my opinion quite questionable distinction between musical and non-musical sound, but at this point I merely note that the Enlightenment and the *Goethezeit* universally shared his belief in this distinction.

I shall skip the rest of the introductory part that concerns itself with the construction of scales, and note only two of Goethe's remarks: 1) the octave is for him identical with the base-note of the scale; hence teaching the octave via the scale is a "self-reunification" (*Selbstwiederfinden*). The term is, of course theoretically and ideologically loaded, for musical scales thereby become a particular case of the *Urphänomen* of dividing and reuniting. 2) Artistic creativity can "comfortably" or "easily" (*bequem*) synthesize the organic, mechanical, and mathematical dimensions, which analytical, scientific representations tend to keep apart.

If we turn now to the main body of the schema, I wish to call attention to the following fundamental priorities implied by Goethe's distinction. Generally speaking, it would seem most logical to start by distinguishing between sound-production and perception, and to go on from there to discuss the various ways and means of each. But Goethe starts by distinguishing between organic and inorganic bodies, and goes on from there to examine how each of these produces and registers musical sounds. (Parenthetically I note that the scheme is, of course, incomplete since inorganic sound-recording was not yet invented.)

The reason for Goethe's choice is obvious: he gave highest priority to the question whether a musical sound was produced by a lifeless, mechanical instrument or by an organic body. Furthermore, since he makes only one, marginal remark about sounds produced by animals ("Zugabe von den Stimmen der Tiere, besonders der Vögel"; addition concerning the sound of animals, especially birds), his discussion of organic musical sounds is actually restricted to the voice. It is somewhat of a moot point whether this implies that he would regard birds' whistle non-musical. In any case, the categories organic and inorganic, human and mechanical, are of unequal value, for mechanically produced sounds are mere surrogates of the voice. They are below it ("sie stehen unter derselben") although they can be raised if they are used with technical skill to express emotions ("gefühlte und geistreiche Behandlung").

Goethe's treatment of musical sound in relationship to the human body is richer than his discussion of instrumental sound, for it distinguishes between sound-production, sound-perception by the ear (called *Akustik*) and total bodily response to sound, called *Rhythmik*. Let me postpone the discussion of his statements on sound-production and comment now only on his notion of sound-registration, which constitutes another contrast to the *Farbenlehre*. There you will find in the introduction the memorable lines:

Wär' nicht das Auge sonnenhaft,
Wie könnten wir das Licht erblicken?
Lebt' nicht in uns des Gottes eigne Kraft,
Wie könnt' uns Göttliches entzücken?[4]

Indeed, one of the most important achievements of the *Farbenlehre* was to show that the eye does not passively register color but co-produces perception and may even become autonomously productive, for instance in the case of the so-called after-images.

Coming from this notion of color-perception, Goethe is first quite hesitant to attribute similar creative power to the ear. Noting its sensitivity and "seeming passivity," he remarks that hearing is a dull, partial sense compared to vision ("Gegen das Auge betrachtet, ist das Hören ein stummer Sinn. — Nur ein Teil eines Sinnes"). But he immediately qualifies this: "Dem Ohr müssen wir jedoch, als einem hohen organischen Wesen, Gegen-wirkung und Forderung zuschreiben; wodurch der Sinn ganz allein fähig wird, das ihm von außen Gebrachte aufzunehmen und zu fassen. Doch ist bei dem Ohr die Leitung noch immer besonders zu betrachten, welche durchaus erregend und produktiv wirkt. Die Produktivität der Stimme wird dadurch geweckt, angeregt, erhöht und vermannigfältigt."[5] The following,

---

[4] "If the eye were not sunny, / How could we perceive light? / If God's own power did not dwell in us, / How could the divine delight us?"

[5] "But being a higher organ, the ear must be assigned a counterforce and demand, by means of which it can register and grasp by itself what is brought to it from outside. Yet in the case of the ear we must still give special attention to the channel of mediation,

last sentence on the ear provides then the link to bodily rhythm, which Goethe regards as a manifestation of a kind of universal pendulum movement. The ear has therefore an active role in musical perception, which includes a "feedback" on the voice and a mediation of sound to the body as a whole.

The third, mathematical-mechanical section restates Goethe's ideas on the natural foundations of music and the status of the major and minor chords, which were the subject of his exchange with Zelter in 1808, and were subsequently discussed between Goethe and Schlosser in 1815 and once between Zelter and Goethe in 1826–31. I shall refrain from repeating what I have said in my book on *The Emancipation of Language* about these debates.[6] Their historical background is to be found in the arguments between Rameau on the one hand and Rousseau, Diderot, and d'Alembert on the other. This time I am concerned with Goethe's idea of the human voice rather than with his notion of polarity in music, and I wish to draw the line from him forward rather than backward.

III

Reactions to the *Tonlehre* have predictably fallen into three categories: 1) discussions that place it within the context of Goethe's other writings, 2) critical treatments by musicologists, and 3) attempts by some musicologists to show that Goethe has important things to say about issues in contemporary music aesthetics. Instead of attempting a full survey of the *Tonlehre* reception I shall select a few representative positions in order to develop my own conclusion, namely that Goethe's ideas on music cannot and should not be used as a foundation of a contemporary theory of music, but they are eminently suited to discuss music because they raise fundamental issues. We may use Goethe's historically distant views to clarify our own ideas.

Let us start with the most ambitious and the most flawed approach, that of Ernst-Jürgen Dreyer, which attempts nothing less than a radically comprehensive unorthodox theory of music based on principles in Goethe's *Tonlehre*.[7] Its failure is due in part to the boldness of the claim, in part to Dreyer's inimitably obscure style.

---

which functions quite stimulatingly and productively. The productivity of the voice is thereby awakened, stimulated, heightened, and multiplied."

[6] John Neubauer, *The Emancipation of Music from Language: Departure from Mimesis in Eighteenth-Century Aesthetics* (New Haven: Yale Univ. Press, 1986).

[7] Ernst-Jürgen Dreyer, *Versuch, eine Morphologie der Musik zu begründen: Mit einer Einleitung über Goethes Tonlehre* (Bonn: Bouvier, 1976), and his "Musikgeschichte in Nuce: Goethes dritte grundsätzliche Äußerung zur Natur der Musik," *Jahrbuch des Freien Deutschen Hochstifts* (1979): 170–98.

As I understand it, Dreyer wants to use the *Tonlehre* against all those who claim that music originated from natural sounds and natural laws. His targets include the following passages from Behn and Kirby:

> Die Geschichte der Musik beginnt bei den Lauten der Natur, dem Rauschen des Meeres, dem Brausen und Pfeifen des Sturmes, dem rhythmischen Klopfen des Regens, dem Gebrüll der Raubtiere und dem Zwitschern der Vögel, sie alle waren dem Menschen Lehrmeister und Führer zur höchsten aller Künste.[8]

> Unter glücklichen Umständen ergab die Bogensehne, wenn sie in voller Spannung gezupft wurde, einen Ton mit einer Anzahl von Obertönen, besonders 4 bis 9, die der Buschmann durch die Resonanz seiner Mundhöhle, deren Volumen er dem Zweck entsprechend veränderte, verstärken konnte.[9]

According to Dreyer, the flaw in these and similar approaches is that they start with nature: "[der Fehler liegt] in der Einigkeit darin, die Musik als zunächst 'auf die Natur beschränkt' festzusetzen, und den Menschen als von ihr und ihrem Gesetz ausgesperrt zu denken."[10] The answer to such theories is to be found in Goethe's statement: "Der Gesang ist völlig productiv an sich," for, as Dreyer writes, "mit solchem Satz ist denn auch das Wagnis eines nicht aufzulösenden Widerspruchs eingegangen. Denn definiert die Musik, die sich in ihm gebiert, die Hervorbringung der Stimme als Gesang, so definiert zugleich der Gesang erst das Hervorgebrachte als Musik, und als solche von sämtlichen anderen Hervorbringungen der Stimme, als dem Ruf, dem Gelächter, dem Sprechen, Schreien etc. qualitativ verschieden."[11]

---

[8] "The history of music begins with the sounds of nature: the rushing of the sea, the raging and whistling of the storm, the rhythmic patter of the rain, the roaring of the predatory animals, and the twitter of the birds. All of these were man's teachers and leaders in the highest of the arts"; Friedrich Behn, *Musikleben im Altertum und frühen Mittelalter* (Stuttgart: Hiersemann, 1954), p. 1.

[9] "Under fortunate conditions, when plucked under full tension, the bowstring would emit a tone with a number of overtones, especially the fourth and the ninth, which the Bushman could amplify by correspondingly changing the volume of his oral cavity"; Percival R. Kirby, "Buschmann- und Hottentottenmusik," in *Die Musik in Geschichte und Gegenwart*, 17 vols. (Kassel: Bärenreiter, 1949), II, cols. 502–11, here col. 502.

[10] "[the mistake lies] in the agreement to define music as originally 'limited to nature' and considering mankind as excluded from her and her law"; Dreyer, *Versuch*, p. 17.

[11] "Singing is completely productive in itself"; "such a sentence incorporates the venture of an unresolvable contradiction. For if music, born in song, defines the vocal production as song, so too, simultaneously, it is song that defines the production as music, and, as such, is qualitatively different from all other products of the voice, like the call, laughter, speech, shouting, etc."; ibid., p. 23.

The upshot of this is that nature has silent laws, which man displays through the singing voice. Dreyer's theory postulates some kind of teleology in nature that stands in preestablished harmony with the human potential. It may be justly objected that Dreyer's theory is based on too many metaphysical assumptions — assumptions that Goethe himself would have hardly granted.

Let me turn therefore to another line of interpretation, taken up by Hans Joachim Moser and others, who read the *Tonlehre* as a manifesto of the autonomy of the singing voice. Moser sums up the significance of the *Tonlehre* as "man is the measure of all things, including music" (67), and he believes that color theory has proven the general principle:

> Die Zeit ist gottlob vorbei, da man seine Farbenlehre als dilettantisches Spielzeug des "Dichters" besserwissend beiseite schob; man hat längst begriffen, daß dies Buch neben der auf Newton und Helmholtz gegründeten physikalischen und physiologischen eine psychologische Optik darstellt, die als solche wissenschaftliche Geltung beanspruchen darf. Genau so wäre es ... mit der voll ausgeführten Tonlehre gegangen; und es wäre heilsam, wenn unsere heutigen Musiktheoretiker ... seinen Hauptgedanken in sich aufnehmen wollten, ... daß die Musik als ein Reich der Urphänomene nicht der arithmetischen Begründungen bedarf, sondern *sui generis et juris* in und für sich selbst besteht.[12]

I had to quote at length because Moser's point of departure, namely that man is the measure in music, clashes with the final statement that music is an *Urphänomen. Urphänomene* are not to be understood anthropomorphically!

Did Goethe believe that man was the measure in music? Considering that he regarded musical sound as superior to all other ones, the suggestion seems unobjectionable, especially if placed within the context of Goethe's *Altersphilosophie.* Yet if we remember that in his essay *Der Versuch als Vermittler* Goethe recommended the greatest abnegation in studying nature, if we remember that his greatest objection to the Newtonian method was its arrogance vis-à-vis nature, if we remember the unfortunate consequences of Eduard's coercive treatment of nature in *Die Wahlverwandtschaften,* and finally if we remember how strenuously he objected to the Fichtean egotism of some romantics, then "man is the measure of all things" will hardly be a

---

[12] "Gone, thank God, are the times when, with a sense of knowing better, his color theory was pushed aside as a dilettantish toy of the 'poet'; for some time it has been understood that this book represents, next to the physical and physiological optics founded by Newton and Helmholtz, a psychological optics, and as such can lay claim to full scientific validity. The same would have happened ... with the 'Tonlehre,' had it been completed fully, and it would be salutary if our contemporary musicologists ... had adopted its main idea, ... that music, as a domain of primal phenomena, needs no mathematical foundation but exists in and by itself *sui generis et juris*"; Hans Joachim Moser, *Goethe und die Musik* (Leipzig: Peters, 1949), p. 67.

fitting summary of Goethe's philosophy. Beyond the ecstatic years of *Sturm und Drang*, he consistently cautioned us to be modest in using human power, and he showed a Spinozistic humility with respect to nature. If his warning against human hubris does not become explicit in his *Tonlehre*, this is very likely due to the fact that in his mind a "nature-centered" music was associated with mathematical, and hence Newtonian science — which was for him, of course, the epitome of human arrogance. In the absence of this association he would have very likely taken a less anthropomorphic view of music and a more liberal approach to the sounds of nature.

In the last decade of our twentieth century the anthropomorphism of Goethe's music theory seems more problematic than it appeared to Moser, who published his book in 1949, for the two-hundredth anniversary of Goethe's birth. Celebrating Goethe's celebration of the human voice implied then, immediately after the barbarism of national socialism, a reaffirmation of humanism. The same associations, at the same time, inform Thomas Mann's *Doktor Faustus*, where the narrator Serenus Zeitblom describes the imitation of instruments by the human voice as a form of barbarism.

The humanistic valorizing of the voice over instruments has a long history that extends all the way back to Plato, and both Goethe and Thomas Mann are indebted to this tradition. But we may ask whether this tradition had a substantial foundation and was not merely a convention. Let us not forget that the *Tonlehre* and many of Goethe's forerunners sharply separated not only voice and instruments, the organic and the inorganic realms, but also the singing and speaking voices, which almost always meant a degrading of speaking and rational discourse. Was Thomas Mann's Settembrini not right when he warned, early enough, that degrading the humanistic medium of speech is the easiest way to slip into barbarism?

The mixing of singing and speaking — as practiced by Schoenberg and Berg in the *Sprechstimme* and anticipated already in a piece called *Pygmalion* by the greatest defender of humanism in music, Jean-Jacques Rousseau — is not intrinsically anti-humanist, and may, in fact, be used for expressive purposes. Just a few years after the 1949 Goethe celebration the Italian composer Luciano Berio started to experiment with songs that open up the musical register of the voice in an even more radical manner. In these songs entitled *Sequenza* the voice runs the gamut of singing, speaking, sighing, crying, moaning, and a lot more. Anybody who heard them in a good performance will agree that they are deeply moving and lacking anything one would rashly call "barbaric."

There are, of course, profound tendencies in our postmodernist culture that run counter to the maxim that man is the measure of all things. Witness the "nouveau roman," structuralist and semiotic thought, Foucault's concept of history, or, to come back to music, John Cage's Taoist notion of emancipating sounds from the tyranny of human consciousness. Traditional humanists as well as marxists like Adorno and his followers are inclined to label such phenomena anti-humanist. Would Goethe have done so? My guess is that he would not have liked John Cage's music, nor the accompanying theories. Yet I cannot help thinking that he would have responded, perhaps deeply resonated, to the humanism in Cage's words:

> Impose nothing. Live and let live. Permit each person, as well as each sound, to be the center of creation.

Nineteenth Century

E. T. A. Hoffmann's Language about Music[*]

HELMUT GÖBEL

WHAT ATTRACTS ME TO E. T. A. Hoffmann, fascinates me, and causes me to turn my thoughts to him are the tensions inherent in his works as well as in his life, and which take shape there. It seems to me that present in these tensions are analogies to those that must be endured by people who concern themselves with literature or music, who have to survive seminar papers and examinations, or even have to relate to legal questions as a result of serving on committees — people who then once again hear Hoffmann's magnificent "Miserere." This essay is concerned with the tensions in Hoffmann's language about music.

Throughout his life Hoffmann was driven by a certain longing. The goal of this longing is not always clearly discernible. What occasionally is clearer, though, is the aim of this longing to leave behind unfulfilling heavy burdens of everyday life. In his multifaceted works, various promising means for responding to this basic motivation are named, circumscribed, and employed. Nature, in a pure sense, and music, including the music of human beings created by compositional geniuses, appear to set in motion the desired longing most lastingly and thoroughly, even to fulfill it for a few moments. This occurs in such a way that feeling seems to give hearers of music to understand that these moments have changed everyday reality or liberated them from it, and would transport them to a place which Hoffmann — like Wackenroder, Tieck, and Jean Paul — named and poetically described with words referring to a particular "country" (*Land*) or "realm" (*Reich*). Relatively much has been written lately concerning this romantically colored metaphysical conception of music. While I cannot go into detail about these studies here, I wish nonetheless to stress that in my essay I see coming together observations by Klaus-Dieter Dobat, John Neubauer, and Carl Dahlhaus,[1] insights for which I am most grateful and with the aid of which I am attempting, both cautiously and daringly, to think further on the matter.

---

[*] The English translation of the German original is by James M. McGlathery with assistance from Ellen Gerdeman-Klein.

[1] Cf. Klaus-Dieter Dobat, *Musik als romantische Illusion: Eine Untersuchung zur Bedeutung der Musikvorstellung E. T. A. Hoffmanns für sein literarisches Werk* (Tübingen: Niemeyer, 1984); John Neubauer, "Die Sprache des Unaussprechlichen: Hoffmanns Rezension von Beethovens 5. Symphonie," in Alain Montandon, ed., *E. T. A. Hoffmann et la Musique,* Actes du Colloque International de Clermont-Ferrand (Bern, Frankfurt am Main: Lang, 1987), pp. 25ff.; Carl Dahlhaus, "E. T. A. Hoffmanns Beethoven-Kritik und die Ästhetik des Erhabenen," *Archiv für Musikwissenschaft* 38, no. 2 (1981): 79ff.

My subject is called "language *about* music" (*Sprache zur Musik*); with this "about" I wish to indicate especially that with Hoffmann, language and music are separate. Radically carrying forward certain ways of thinking already present in the eighteenth century and beginning of the nineteenth, instrumental music in its lack of referentiality, compared with language, enjoyed a rise in estimation as being as absolute, as that which is poetic purely and simply. I wish to turn my attention to those parts of Hoffmann's literary works in which the beginnings of this view are indicated in a particular way, namely his reviews of instrumental music. In these, he attempts to express himself through language in such a way that he can appropriately convey to his readers a sense of the achievement in the various pieces of music. In particular, I wish to describe the type of language in the interpretive passages especially, and to discuss which traditions play a role there.

The first text that I would like to investigate regarding several details is Hoffmann's review, written in 1811, of Louis Spohr's first symphony in E-flat major.[2] Without wishing, as a literary scholar, to elaborate on the matter, the charm of this review resides also in the fact that a few years earlier Hoffmann himself had composed a symphony in E-flat major that was possibly of similar character in the first three of four movements. He does not mention this fact in his review, yet he is speaking here surely as not only as a reviewer and experienced musical connoisseur, but also as one who has tried and failed in competition with the achievements of Viennese classicism that still radiated then in the background. Using the Spohr review as my starting point, I shall draw for comparison on several passages in Hoffmann's famous review of Beethoven. The method employed is chiefly that of stylistic analysis. On the basis of the resultant findings, though, I will venture to speculate at the end of the essay about questions which thereby pose themselves for intellectual and literary historians.

Beginning with the critique of Beethoven's Fifth Symphony, almost all of Hoffmann's music reviews are organized in three parts, thus also that of Spohr's E-flat Major Symphony. The introduction emphasizes the greater worth of instrumental music, as derived from the great Viennese triumvirate Haydn, Mozart, and Beethoven. The long main section is devoted chiefly to description and analysis of the work under review; following the description one finds here also beginnings of an interpretation that point to the norms established in the introduction. The conclusion largely consists of thoughts about the performance of the work or the quality of the published edition. The division into three parts is accompanied by hardly any differences in style between the parts as such, but that sort of difference does undoubtedly exist between the analytical passages on the one hand and the interpretive

---

[2] Cf. E. T. A. Hoffmann, *Schriften zur Musik: Aufsätze und Rezensionen*, rev. ed., ed. Friedrich Schnapp (Darmstadt: Wissenschaftliche Buchgesellschaft, 1978), pp. 75ff. All further page references to this edition are given in parentheses in the text.

and evaluative ones on the other. Precisely this difference is what I would like to try to demonstrate.

First, though, an important observation regarding Hoffmann's entire reviewing procedure. He considers his music criticism the result of an intensive study of a particular work of music that he has *heard* and the notes of which he can survey precisely, a process he calls *reading* music. In this sense, his object of study is the imagined result of a potentially ideal performance; conclusions based on such hearing of the music combine in the analysis with those from reading the notes. For this reason, he has examples from the score printed in his reviews. Of the fifteen printed pages in the Spohr review, about four are taken up with these examples. Printing the examples indicates that his language about music, being only supplementary, needs to be augmented by a corresponding optical presentation of the notes. Syntactically, the examples from the score are connected to the written language chiefly in two ways: 1) they follow a colon in order to support the preceding observations or in order to base the argument on the notes, which have been only briefly described in an introductory way, or 2) short examples from the score are syntactically embedded in the verbal presentation, as happens five times in the Spohr review. Thus, it is said for example that the brass and woodwinds form a fundamental chord or intone a "theme" in a "figure," which then appears in the illustration from the score. In the continuation of the sentence then, a relative pronoun refers both to the verbally reproduced word "figure" or "theme" as well as to the graphic reproduction in the musical notation. In this way, connoisseurs are supposed to be able to reenact the presentation for themselves. This undoubtedly represents a most intimate juxtaposition of language and music. The examples, as a rule, characterize musical details on the level of description, in which musical terminology predominates. To be sure, next to the words "Figur," "Akkord," and the names of instruments stand such concepts as "character," "secondary idea," and "main idea" that verbally approximate the chief aim of the presentation, namely to grasp the trend (*Tendenz*) of a work, or part of it, as well as its spirit (*Geist*).

With this procedure has begun a hardly noticeable transition from the level of description to that of interpretation and evaluation. This change in the character of the discourse is the most typical feature of all in Hoffmann's language and music. The element of process in music is the focus of attention. Metaphors grown pale from overuse, but — waiting to be revived — become stylistically relevant for interpreting these musical passages and are combined with formulaic images. In the use of the verbs "führen" and "zurückführen" there are for example various possibilities. "Nachdem der Satz wieder in B-dur zurückgekehrt ist ..." (After the movement has returned again to B-flat major, p. 80); a sentence such as this remains totally lacking in images. Contrasting with this type of sentence is the following form, for example: "Jetzt tritt das Tutti ... wieder in As-moll ein, dieselbe enharmonische Verwechslung [As moll, gis mit dem Sextenakkord] und auch wieder die acht Septimenakkorde führen ganz gemächlich den Zuhörer in das bekannte Land zurück" (Now the tutti returns to A-flat minor again, the same enharmonic substitution [A-flat minor, G-sharp with the sixth chord] and also again the eight seventh chords lead the listener quite gradually back to familiar territory; p. 81). The formulation "back to familiar territory" has something generally metaphorical about it; it belongs to a Hoffmannian storehouse of ready phrases with dynamic and antithetical character. With this arsenal, things in a modulation familiar and foreign, sudden and gradual are named and evaluated.

Hoffmann finds in Spohr's first symphony only very few of those things that in the famous Beethoven review constitute a metaphysical point of reference, using the familiar formulations which, for example, "tear" the listener "along to that miraculous spiritual realm of boundlessness" ("in das wundervolle Geisterreich des Unendlichen fortreißt"; p. 37). Nonetheless, these phrases are just as present in the interpretive and evaluative parts of the review, and are developed sometimes more clearly, sometimes in an almost unnoticeable, metaphorical way, not infrequently by insertion of a catachresis. The reviewer is not happy with a modulation; he attempts to support his judgment with an image: "dann verwischt aber auch die bequeme, verbrauchte Rückkehr aus der fremden Sphäre in die bekannte Heimat ganz den beabsichtigten Eindruck. Es ist ein glänzendes Meteor, das sich in wäßrichten Nebel auflöst" (but then the comfortable, overworked return from the foreign sphere to the familiar homeland completely erases the intended impression. It is a shining meteor that dissolves in watery haze; p. 80). With the rather emphatically loaded opposition of "foreign sphere" and "familiar homeland," a Romantic journey is indicated, to be sure nothing more than indicated. The sententious succeeding comment about the meteor evokes a completely different world of imagery and yet, in the context of Hoffmann's œuvre, does not appear accidental. In that sentence is contained the realm of images and symbols for light and darkness as well as, potentially, energies that — expanded — can appear in others of his writings.

To the images that recur in a certain stereotypical way belong the metaphors concerning the meaning of the verb *fließen* (to flow). Hoffmann uses that verb very frequently in the portrayal of the continuation of a twin formula — of the sort he loved — like "melodious and flowing" (p. 77) or in adjective-noun combinations like "fließendste Melodien" (flowingest melodies, p. 82). In speaking of the flowing of a melody, however, only a moderate musical mode is described; more important for Hoffmann, because in music its effect is much richer, is an "Auf– und Dahinbrausen" (roaring up and away) that more than once evokes from him images like the following simile: "Das erst ruhig und sanft gehaltene Thema gleicht einem friedlichen Bach, der, so wie er weiter durch das Gebirge rinnt, immer höher und höher anschwellend, zum reißenden Waldstrome wird!" (The theme, kept at first quiet and gentle, resembles a peaceful brook that, swelling ever higher as it runs on through the mountains, becomes a rapid forest stream!; p. 78). Immediately afterwards, we hear again of a "gently maintained theme" (ibid.). These images are sometimes metaphors, sometimes similes that can be expanded to extended images. In this sort of verbal illustrativeness, a *tertium comparationis* for the music is always supplied. The language thus behaves as though the music self-evidently contains this reference to the object of comparison. We are dealing here with Romantic "as if" evocations. As conventional as these comparisons may be, they convey something like seminal images that make possible for Hoffmann a stylistic development of the simplest sort appropriate to the basic aesthetic and artistic ideas at which he is aiming.

Such metaphorical images are thus usually contained in the introductory assertions in Hoffmann's music reviews. In the critique of Spohr, the important orienting sentences are as follows:

Ungeachtet des Bestrebens nach dem starken, kräftigen Ausdruck, welches nicht selten hervorbricht, hält sich [die Sinfonie] mehr in den Schranken des Charakters von ruhiger Würde, den schon die gewählten Themen in sich tragen und der dem Genius der Komposition mehr zuzusagen scheint, als das wilde Feuer, welches in Mozartschen und Beethovenschen Symphonien wie ein Strom dahinbraust. Schon deshalb sind die Themata mehr angenehme Melodien, als bedeutungsvolle Gedanken, tief in das Gemüt des Zuhörers eindringend, welches bei jenen Komponisten, und auch bei Haydn, so sehr der Fall ist. (p. 76)

(Despite the striving for a strong, forceful expression that not infrequently manifests itself, the symphony remains more within bounds characterized by quiet dignity, which are already contained in the selected themes and which seem to agree better with the genius of the piece than does the wild fire that roars like a torrent through the symphonies of Mozart and Beethoven. For this reason alone, the themes are pleasant melodies rather than thoughts laden with meaning that penetrate deeply into the soul of the listener, as is so very much the case with those composers, as with Haydn, too.)

A "wild fire" that "roars through like a torrent" — once again we are dealing with an image that approaches catachresis.

Right at the start Hoffmann thus concludes that since Spohr is more concerned with "quiet dignity" he also lacks what distinguishes Beethoven and Mozart, that which is called here "fire" and "roaring." When in the more thorough discussion the talk then is of the qualities of brightness and energy, this imagery, as a result of the introductory interpretation, proves negative as Spohr is compared to the two great Viennese composers.

As John Neubauer has remarked,[3] Hoffmann's language in his music criticism is not characterized by stylistic elements that imitate the music. Nor does one observe any emotional outpourings with the typical characteristics of the language of the earlier Storm and Stress period, that is, no interjections, no specially contrived inversions, no sentence fragments. Clearly, the syntax is characterized by complete, rounded sentences (being understood in a traditional grammatical way, considering the linguists' uncertainty as to what constitutes a sentence).

Hoffmann's images place less value on a specific picturesque vividness than on an effective element to be produced for the reader, with reference to the music, through energized and optical stimulations. Stereotypical expressions and catachreses are employed, not synesthesia. The catachresis here is not to be evaluated negatively as a stylistic lapse, that is to say — using Jean Paul's phrase — "without punishment for catachresis" ("ohne Katachresen-Strafe").[4] Yet the liberties taken by Jean Paul are perhaps not as broad as Hoffmann's. "'Die Melodien der Sphärenmusik der Dichtkunst glänzen und brennen durch die Welt,' das werd' ich nie wagen, außer hier, wo ich ein geschmackloses Beispiel zu erfinden gehabt" ("The melodies of the music of the spheres of poetic art shine and burn throughout the world," I would never dare to write except here where I needed to invent a tasteless example). Thus Jean Paul wrote in the fourteenth "Program" of his *Vorschule der Ästhetik*, where then the following sentence example is so to speak just barely still within the limits of the allowable: "Das Leben ist ein Regenbogen des Scheins, eine Komödienprobe, ein fliegender Sommer voll mouches volantes, anfangs ein feuriges Meteor, dann ein wässeriges" (Life is a rainbow of appearances, the rehearsal of a comedy, a fleeting summer of mouches volantes, at the start a fiery meteor, then a watery one). We are dealing here with examples in which the repulsiveness of the catachresis is removed through bringing together several sensory perceptions in a single effect ("*einer* Wirkung"), the catachresis therefore is created for effect and with regard to the spirit of the work ("auf den Geist des Werkes") — that "spirit" which for Jean Paul, too, justifies greater license with catachresis.[5]

Still further images can be added to those already mentioned. Thus, occasionally a musical treatment is rendered vivid with an image from the experiential realm of eating and drinking (e.g., p. 85 in the Spohr critique) or a musical piece as a whole will be compared with another art form, such as theater or architecture: masterful edifices ("meisterhafte Gebäude") are raised up on solid ground (p. 89), or a passage in a finale or overture is criticized because it tires the listener ("den Zuhörer ermüdet") "... wie im

---

[3] Neubauer, p. 31.

[4] Jean Paul Friedrich Richter, *Vorschule der Ästhetik*, in his *Werke*, ed. Norbert Miller, vol. 9 (Munich: Hanser, 1975), p. 296.

[5] Ibid., p. 297.

Schauspiel lange Reden, die sich der Entwicklung des Knotens nachschleppen, das Interesse des Zuhörers für die Darstellung vernichten" (as long speeches in a play that drag along behind the development of the dramatic complication destroy the audience's interest in the presentation; ibid.). Along with the frequently employed images, there is a certain predilection for illustrative images concerning effects, images that have in common ready comprehensibility and simplicity.

I suspect that this sort of language relates to music the same way that Hoffmann wished to understand that of the stage scenery in relation to a drama or opera. "Nichts ist lächerlicher," one reads in his *Seltsame Leiden eines Theaterdirektors* (Curious Sufferings of a Theater Director), "als den Zuschauer dahin bringen zu wollen, daß er ohne seinerseits etwas Fantasie zu bedürfen, an die gemahlten Palläste, Bäume und Felsen ob ihrer unziemlichen Größe *wirklich glaube* ... " (Nothing is more laughable than to try to get the audience *really to believe* in the painted palaces, trees, and rocks despite their inappropriate size without the audience having to exercise a little imagination ... ; p. 503). In 1816 Hoffmann put a similar comment into the mouth of a character in his "Brief über die Tonkunst in Berlin" (Letter about the Musical Arts in Berlin) regarding *Die Zauberflöte*: "Jede Dekoration müsse rein-fantastisch sein, weil sonst die aus der Natur herausgetretenen Personen durchaus fremdartig und phantastisch in natürlicher Umgebung erschienen; mithin könnten mit Nutzen — rote — himmelblaue — Bäume stattfinden" (every stage decoration has to be purely fantastic because otherwise the characters who have stepped outside of nature will appear entirely foreign and fantastic in a natural setting; therefore it could be useful to have red or sky-blue trees; pp. 305f.). I quote these comments on the tension between the play and the scenery in order to point to an analogy between a staging possibility that anticipates modern techniques and the relation of music to language. Along with the descriptive level, the interpretive and evaluative language about music, which is mostly metaphorical in a stereotypical way, is supposed primarily to stimulate the fantasy in listening to music, or at least to pave the way for this stimulation. For that reason, therefore, we find only brief hints at images, seminal images without purpose of their own, but functioning to serve the process of musical reception to produce emphatic or quiet connotations stimulating the imagination! A formulaic and stereotypical stage-scenic language is indeed a common characteristic of some German Romantics. Alewyn pointed this out in the case of Eichendorff, and Adorno rather simultaneously perceived in Eichendorff's style a quality of "stage-propness" (the "Requisitenhafte der Sprachelemente").[6]

---

[6] Cf. Richard Alewyn, "Eichendorffs Symbolismus," in his *Probleme und Gestalten: Essays* (Frankfurt am Main: Insel, 1974), p. 236, and Theodor Adorno, "Zum Gedächtnis Eichendorffs" in his *Noten zur Literatur I* (Frankfurt am Main: Suhrkamp, 1958), p. 129.

I would like to enlarge this perception of Hoffmann's stage-scenic language by pointing to a noteworthy peculiarity of his. It concerns the way he uses the words "deep" (*tief*) and "high" (*hoch*). "Deep" or "depth" occurs about a dozen times in the review of Beethoven's Fifth Symphony. Here "deep" is the place in the soul where music has its effect (p. 34); the spirit realm has "depth" (p. 35), and is at the same time a quality of Beethoven's (p. 36); the night is "deep" a number of times; further, there is a "deep penetration into art" or "deep study of art" (pp. 37 and 43); finally, there is talk of "deep presence of mind" (der "tiefen Besonnenheit," p. 50). In almost all the syntactical units in which this "deep" appears it is joined more or less immediately by "high" or there is talk of "upwards" (*hinaus*) or of "above" (*oben*). Thus, for example, Beethoven's "depth" is connected with his "high degree of fantasy" (p. 36), or in the "depths of the spirit realm" clouds fly by (pp. 35f.). In the review of Beethoven's Piano Trios, one finds the following sentence elements in virtual juxtaposition: in "der höchsten Einfachheit regt der tiefe Genius seine kräftigsten Schwingen," and "Aber es gehört auch eine seltene Tiefe des Geistes, ein hoher Genius dazu ..." (in "the highest simplicity the deep [i.e., profound] genius lifts his most mighty pinions"; and "But for that it requires, too, a rare depth of spirit, the height of genius"; p. 156). Thus, in the one case, "deep genius" then "high genius," first "deep presence of mind" then "height of awareness" (e.g., p. 37). The attributes "high" and "deep" thus are interchangeable, as if they had the double meaning of Latin *altus*. They do not contain any vividness, they are stereotypical and connote evaluative intensity. It is therefore not surprising to find "deep" and "intimate" (*innig*) together. To sharpen the point, one could interpret the situation presented as follows: the analytical part of Hoffmann's language about music is concerned with describing acoustical aspects, the interpretive and evaluative parts with the musical works' non-acoustical modes of being, to borrow these categories from Roman Ingarden.[7] My observations about the language thus deal almost exclusively with this non-acoustical share of the music's effect and its assessment.

Compared with Hoffmann's famous reviews of Beethoven's instrumental music, with their emotion-filled passages — Carl Dahlhaus called them "dithyrambic"[8] — the critique of Spohr's orchestral piece turns out to be more moderate, which seems perfectly appropriate to the review's subject. And although the central categories "presence of mind" (*Besonnenheit*) and "enthusiasm" are missing, together with the phrases about being transported to the "realm of the monstrous and the infinite" as well as the "enraptured visionary" ("entzückte Geisterseher") to whom, among many other effects,

---

[7] Cf. Carl Dahlhaus and M. Zimmermann, eds., *Musik — zur Sprache gebracht: Musikästhetische Texte aus drei Jahrhunderten*, dtv, 4421 (Munich: Deutscher Taschenbuchverlag, 1984), pp. 446ff.

[8] Dahlhaus, "E. T. A. Hoffmanns Beethoven-Kritik," p. 81, in analogy to certain odes.

the "pain of boundless longing" is granted — although these assertions and images so central for the discussion of Beethoven's music are lacking, nonetheless a similar concept of music is indicated in most of the images that are used critically. It is not denied, to be sure, that the Spohr symphony possesses beauty and dignity, but it lacks the greatness and sublimity which transcends dignity so as to produce the rending of the emotions, the deep penetration into the "realm of the infinite."

If in comparing Haydn to Spohr there is talk of "enveloping with rays," in Beethoven's case these are "glowing rays" that "shoot" through "this realm's deep night" (p. 36). The simple "rays" that "envelope" here, the "glowing rays" there express a greater intensity in that instance. In this manner, Hoffmann varies his phrases and stereotypes rather precisely and appropriately according to the degree of the effect described. A precise system of phrasing is basic here, like that which Helmut Müller worked out for the presentation of conflicts in Hoffmann.[9]

All in all, with these metaphoric elements Hoffmann places himself in the tradition of both sentimental and enthusiastic speech. A survival from the mid-eighteenth century period of sentimentality (*Empfindsamkeit*) is the piling up, with a certain inwardness, of effects that refer to the soul. The tradition of enthusiasm appears in the combined effects of images of motion, of flying high and falling, of the pinions or wings of genius, of images of light and shadow. In Plato's *Phaedrus*, for example, part of this storehouse of images is used for the metaphysical soaring of the inspired soul, which is there quite specific. Here there is also prefigured the dualism of the everyday world and a higher realm separated from it, in which the evaluative difference in perspective already appears, as it does in Hoffmann: the inspired soul is "scolded probably by people as being confused, but that he is inspired, they fail to notice."[10]

It would be worth further study to see whether right up to the degrees of enthusiasm in Hoffmann, these variable modes of expression do not have their origin in differing positions in the history of enthusiasm. The "noble" quality of enthusiasm found in Shaftesbury and the description Hoffmann chooses once for the designation of a passage in Beethoven's music as having "aristocratic character" lend support to this supposition.[11]

---

[9] Cf. Helmut Müller, *Untersuchungen zum Problem der Formelhaftigkeit bei E. T. A. Hoffmann* (Bern: Haupt, 1964).

[10] Cf. Plato, *Sämtliche Werke 4: Nach der Übersetzung von Friedrich Schleiermacher ...*, Rowohlts Klassiker, 39 (Hamburg: Rowohlt, 1958), p. 30.

[11] Hoffmann calls special attention to this formulation with the phrasing "es sei der Ausdruck erlaubt"; cf. his *Schriften zur Musik*, p. 132. To be sure, Hoffmann several times speaks of "noble character" (ibid., p. 26, as well as in the Spohr critique, p. 78), where "character" means for example "style" or "peculiarity" (*Eigenart*). "Character of the whole" is therefore a phrase that Hoffmann uses relatively often, too. Only rarely do we find the contradiction "characterlessness" (ibid., p. 67); but here it becomes clear that in the word

In referring to Plato, I do not mean to place Hoffmann among the neoplatonists; the point is rather to indicate that his language stands in a very old tradition that it has pressed into service to foster a new direction in the theory of the arts. The derivation of the mid-eighteenth century enthusiasm and the corresponding analogies between the idea of the ode and that of music are thus only links in a long chain.[12] Ultimately, this fact may be quite essentially responsible for Hoffmann's unusually wide influence. It is not the stereotypes and phrases as such, but the stereotypes and phrases of these traditions that gain him broad entry, but which make him susceptible as well to easy appropriation by differing audiences and fashions.

Just as the phrases from this tradition recur, Hoffmann refers repeatedly, too, to the importance of Haydn, Mozart, and Beethoven for the new instrumental music. Hoffmann as music reviewer developed an insight once and for all, and he is intent on achieving recognition of this idea. He adapts the old treasury of elements of enthusiastic speech to describe the inward effect of music. And in its constant repetition over a period of at least five years this language of set phrases and the exaltation of the Viennese triumvirate takes on the quality of a ritual. It is a litany-like formulation which possibly is justified only by metaphorical-enthusiastic speech, in all of its simplicity and stereotypicality. This interpretation of enthusiastic speech in Hoffmann as ritual meshes with the interpretation of the stage-scenicness of his language (his *Kulissensprache*) about music made earlier in this essay. Intensity is the thing, and in this a certain theatrical and illusionary element has a role to play. In the music reviews, the resulting problem of the perspective of the enthusiasm is not present, or only is indicated where Hoffmann comes to speak of difficulties in performance. That is to say, he clearly distinguishes between the ideal review of a work and the performance, in which a tension between genius and craft ("Spanung zwischen Genius und Handwerk") manifests itself, a tension between the Romantics' artistic aims and artistic realization.[13] The performance — music's everyday world, so to speak — more clearly occupies the foreground in the "Letters about Musical Arts in Berlin." But that leads to the areas of poetically narrative language in which the differences in modes of receptivity regarding the performed music plays a more important role in determining the various perspectives. The introduction of the perspective of the figure Johannes Kreisler in the "Kreisleriana" takes as its starting point precisely

---

"character" the matter of evaluation is being addressed. In this we hear no doubt an echo of the valuing of individuality familiar from the period of Storm and Stress.

[12] See the studies referred to in the first note to this essay.

[13] Cf. Klaus-Dieter Dobat, "Zwischen Genie und Handwerk," in Alain Montandon, ed., *E. T. A. Hoffmann et la Musique*, pp. 239ff.

enthusiasm's relativity and its endangered position, as Dobat has shown.[14] The language of criticism contains only one predisposition to that direction, in the tension between its stereotypical stage-scenicness and the Romantic "as if." On the one hand, the manifest intensity is important, while on the other hand, the insight is also present, too, that language can convey only little of that. With this tension, the language about music attempts to circumscribe the new value of music.

The astounding fact remains, however: with a traditional language composed of stylistic elements tending toward cliché, and thus entirely of a conservative character, Hoffmann — as music historians have repeatedly shown — helped produce a paradigmatic change in music theory and criticism. As a continuation of the studies from Shapiro in 1909 to Müller, Rotermund, Dobat, Neubauer, and Scher, I would like to formulate the following thesis: in his language about music, Hoffmann develops both a scepticism about language and a referential function for language — deriving from that scepticism — that points toward music, fantasy, dream, and magic, and also toward a presentation of the tensions of human emotion in general. If this thesis is correct it could serve ultimately as a basis, too, for explaining Hoffmann's language as a whole.

[14] See the studies referred to in the first note to this essay.

Heinrich Marschner's "Romantische Oper" *Hans Heiling*: A Bridge between Weber and Wagner

ULRICH WEISSTEIN

If musical Romanticism ever recreated *Don Giovanni* in its own terms, it was in *Hans Heiling*.

Volkmar Köhler[1]

Ich finde die Musik recht hübsch und besonders die einzelnen Stücke; aber ein so gänzlicher Mangel an Total-Effekt ist mir noch in keiner Marschnerschen Oper vorgekommen.

Richard Wagner[2]

WRITTEN IN 1827 BY Eduard Devrient, brother of the more widely known Ludwig and of the *primadonna assoluta* of her age, Wilhelmine Schroeder-Devrient, the text of *Hans Heiling* (1833), a "Romantische Oper in drei Akten nebst einem Vorspiele. Nach deutsch-böhmischen Volkssagen" (Romantic Opera in Three Acts and a Prologue, after German-Bohemian Folktales)[3] was first offered to Felix Mendelssohn-Bartholdy who, though obviously intrigued by the subject, ultimately rejected it because, as Devrient reports in his *Recollections*, he felt not only that "supernatural subjects, such as the *Freischütz*, were henceforth exhausted, and the hopes of opera rested upon the working up of subjects from grand historical events,"[4] but also,

---

[1] *Grove's Dictionary of Music and Musicians*, 6th ed., ed. Stanley Sadie (London: Macmillan, 1982), 11:702. The passage is missing in Köhler's near-identical contribution to *Musik in Geschichte und Gegenwart*, ed. Friedrich Blume (Kassel: Bärenreiter, 1959), VIII, columns 1682–88.

[2] "I find the music, especially that of the individual pieces, rather pretty; but in none of Marschner's operas have I encountered such a total lack of overall effect"; *Sämtliche Briefe*, ed. Gertrud Strobel and Werner Wolf (Leipzig: VEB Deutscher Verlag für Musik), I (1967), p. 140. The letter, addressed to Wagner's sister Rosalie, dates from 11 December 1833.

[3] I quote throughout from Devrient's *Dramatische und dramaturgische Schriften* (Leipzig: Weber, 1846), 1:255–322. I have been unable to determine when *Hans Heiling* (extant in a manuscript copy owned by the University of Illinois) was originally published and to what extent the text reproduced in this volume might deviate from the *Erstdruck*.

[4] *My Recollections of Felix Mendelssohn-Bartholdy and His Letters to Me*, trans. Natalia Macfarren (London: Bentley, 1869), p. 41. I had no access to the original German edition of the book.

on more personal grounds, because "he had no sympathy with the leading character" and did not find the verses "to be suggestive," i.e., capable of inspiring him as a composer.[5]

Devrient, who had written his highly eclectic libretto using a variety of legends, most of them etiological (*Ursprungsmythen*), surrounding a strange rock formation in the Eger valley near Karlsbad in Bohemia,[6] subsequently turned to Marschner, whose theatrical successes with *Der Vampyr* (1827) and *Der Templer und die Jüdin* (1829) had caused him to be generally considered the leading German operatic composer of the day. Marschner found the subject, and its treatment, quite congenial, without, however, accepting Devrient's text uncritically — as is shown by their correspondence, only partly preserved, which includes many suggestions for improvements and changes, most of them approved and executed by the playwright.[7]

While, in the present context, it would lead too far to discuss their lively exchange of views, both pragmatic and programmatic, in detail, it might be useful to broach at least some of the issues that throw light on Marschner's views on opera with respect to character presentation and melodramatic structure. Thus, as regards the figure of the protagonist, the composer begs strongly to disagree with the librettist's calculated and, in a strictly dramatic sense, apt because blatantly paradoxical portrayal ("Sie wünschen den Heiling überall kurz, beinahe maulfaul, nichts wiederholend. Was er sagt, sagt er nur gezwungen, da er über sich sich nicht auslässt. Zum Ausbruch seiner Gefühle soll es nirgends kommen")[8] and, as an artist charged with making him convincing in a musical sense by bringing out his *Menschlichkeit* in an empathetic sense, opines:

> Abgesehen davon, dass Ihre strenge Forderung des Obigen die Musik bizarr und gesucht machen muss, kann ich mir auch nicht gut vorstellen, wie die Musik (die Sprache des Gefühls und der Leidenschaft) ein Gefühl unterdrückt ausdrücken soll (von der Monotonie, die in der musikalischen Behandlung dieser Art entsteht, zu schweigen), so ist doch in Ihrer eigenen

---

[5] Ibid., p. 126f.

[6] For details regarding these legends and the use Devrient made of them see pp. 130–36 of A. Dean Palmer's monograph *Heinrich August Marschner, 1795–1861: His Life and Stage Works* (Ann Arbor: UMI Research Press, 1980) and the two pamphlets by Anton Gnirs mentioned in the comprehensive bibliography.

[7] See "Aus Heinrich Marschners produktivster Zeit: Briefe des Komponisten und seines Dichters Eduard Devrient," ed. Edgar Istel, in *Süddeutsche Monatshefte* 7 (1910): 774–820, which supersedes the unreliable and fragmentary publication of the same material in the *Deutsche Rundschau* 19 (1879): 87–106. Unfortunately, Istel was unable to locate the bulk of Devrient's letters to Marschner.

[8] "You want Heiling to be laconic and almost taciturn throughout, never repeating himself. What he says he says reluctantly since he is unwilling to speak about himself. His emotions never show."

Ausführung des Charakters so manche Abnegierung Ihrer mir später zugekommenen Idee darüber zu finden. Sagt er nicht selbst im Vorspiel, "dass
ich auf der blühenden Erde ganz zum Menschen werde"? Diesem Vorsatz,
ganz in die Menschlichkeit einzugehen, sucht er auch möglichst nachzukommen, und wenn er noch, ebenfalls im Vorspiel, sagt: "Fahrt wohl, ihr
trüben, freudenlosen Brüder," so liegt darin ein Gesättigtsein an ihrer
trüben Genossenschaft und der Wille, sich selbst auch ... jener freudlosen,
starren Kälte in der warmen Sonne des Lebens zu entwöhnen.[9]

Perhaps the liveliest debate revolved about the position of the Overture,
which, contrary to hallowed practice, Marschner wished to place (and
insisted on placing) between the lengthy *Vorspiel* and Act One of their three-
act opera. His argument in favor of such a solution is quite persuasive, both
from a theatrical and a dramaturgical point of view:

Meines Erachtens kann [die Ouverture] dem Vorspiel nicht vorangehen,
und lass ich sie nachfolgen, gleichsam dem letzten Chor entströmend (denn
eine Pause zwischen Vorspiel und Ouverture würde ersteres zu einem Akt
unwillkürlich formen), so würde das Publikum aller Orten, obwohl die Idee
und Form neu wäre, wenig darauf achten und den gewöhnlichen Entreakt-
Spektakel verführen, nichts weniger ahnend als das nun erst eigentliche
Beginnen der Oper.... Sie wissen selbst zu gut, dass das Niederfallen des
Vorhanges dem Publikum das Zeichen ist, sich auf diese oder jene Art Luft
zu machen, da ein Teil seiner Schaulust zum Teil schon befriedigt ist und
[es] vor Aufgang des Vorhanges sich nur einer gewissen regungslosen
Spannung hingibt. Ist aber keine Ouverture dazwischen, so wird das
Vorspiel nur ein Aufzug und kann auch als solcher benannt werden.[10]

[9] "Apart from the fact that your strict demand is bound to make the music bizarre and
precious, I cannot imagine how the music, which is the language of feeling and passion,
can express a suppressed feeling (not to mention the monotony which results from that
kind of musical treatment); your own handling of the character partly disagrees with the
views you subsequently broached to me. Doesn't he himself say in the Prologue that 'on
this verdant earth (he) would become altogether human'? He does his very best to attain
this state; and when, still in the Prologue, he bids farewell to his gloomy and sombre
brothers, he shows his dissatisfaction with their company and demonstrates his desire to
wean himself of that numbing cold in the warming sun of life"; letter dated 18 October
1831, as reprinted in "Aus Heinrich Marschners produktivster Zeit...." The passage, taken
from p. 793, is followed by two more pages of pertinent discussion.

[10] "In my opinion, (the Overture) must not precede the Prologue; and if I make it follow
the latter as a natural outgrowth of the final chorus — for a break between Prologue and
Overture would stamp the former as an Act — the audience, unaware of the formal and
conceptual innovation constituted by this technique, would pay little heed and would
make the usual intermission noise, without realizing that the action proper was only now
getting under way. You yourself know quite well that the public takes the falling of the
curtain to be a signal for relaxing since its curiosity has been partly satisfied and it can
thus indulge in a kind of subdued tension. But if no Overture intervenes, the Prologue
becomes a regular Act and might as well be labeled as such; letter dated 8 July 1831. Ibid.,
p. 778. Marschner returns to the subject in a subsequent letter, reproduced ibid., p. 808f.

(Regarding the overture itself, Marschner, repudiating the conventional medley type, strongly defends his unorthodox practice: "Sie ist selbständig, mehr Charaktergemälde, das heisst sie besteht nicht aus verschiedenen Motiven verschiedener Musikstücke der Oper.")[11]

Another structural matter to which the composer calls attention in his letters is the accumulation of tercets — end of the Introduction, #2 and #4 of the score[12] — in Act One, which poses the problem of proper diversification and variety: "Es war nicht leicht, die drei ersten Terzetts auseinanderzuhalten, doch glaub' hab' ich's leidlich getroffen."[13] And concerning the stratification of modes of vocal projection on the scale extending from spoken dialogue at one end to strictly musical numbers at the other, he initially voiced his apprehension about Devrient's excessive use of melodrama, in the sense of "text spoken to instrumental accompaniment": "Gesteh ich vom Melodrama in der Oper kein Freund zu sein, und würde Sie deshalb bitten, die erste Szene des dritten Akts anders zu arrangieren."[14] However, he heartily welcomed its use in the second act (#12, Gertrude's "Melodrama und Lied" "Des Nachts wohl auf der Haide," about which more later).[15]

As a seasoned operatic conductor in the service of the Court of Hannover, Marschner was naturally concerned not only about the register and timbre of the voices of the singers to be employed for the premiere of *Hans Heiling* but also about the length of the piece ("Und endlich glaub' ich, es würde der Wirkung nicht schaden, wenn einige Gesangsstücke, namentlich aber die Dialoge noch etwas kürzer gehalten würden")[16] and the size of the chorus ("Glaub' ich, haben Sie im letzten Akt nicht daran gedacht, dass ausser Berlin und Wien kein so grosser Chor existiert, um die verschiedenen

---

[11] "It is autonomous, a kind of character sketch; that is to say, it is not a medley of various motives drawn from the different pieces of the opera"; letter dated 8 January 1832. Ibid., p. 796.

[12] Throughout, my references are to the orchestral score edited by Gustav F. Kogel (Frankfurt am Main: C. F. Peters, n.d.).

[13] "It wasn't easy to make clear distinctions between the three tercets; but I think I've managed reasonably well"; letter dated 8 January 1832. Ibid., p. 795.

[14] "I confess not to be a friend of melodrama in opera and must, therefore, ask you to rewrite the first scene of Act Three"; letter dated 8 July 1831. The correspondence offers several subsequent references to this topic.

[15] "Wenn ich gegen Melodramen in Opern sprach, so meint' ich nicht damit # 13 (= #12 of the final version), welches Ihnen ganz vortrefflich gelungen ist" (When I speak out against the use of melodrama in opera, I do not include No. 13, in which you succeeded so well); letter dated 21 September 1831. Ibid., p. 791.

[16] "I believe, finally, that it wouldn't be detrimental to the effect if some vocal numbers, and especially the dialogue, were slightly shortened"; letter dated 8 July 1831. Ibid., p. 778.

Chöre von Erdgeistern, Schützen usw. entsprechend besetzen zu können").[17] He also kept the audience in mind and wondered what effect
certain features of Devrient's making would have on it. Thus he observed,
with a twinkle in his eye: "Fürchte ich, werden uns die Zwergenchöre auf
den meisten Theatern zu schaffen machen, denn sind unsere Chordamen
auch Zwerge in der Kunst, so können sie doch dem Auge nicht als solche
erscheinen und Kinderballetts gibt's nicht überall. Ja, wenn das Publikum
Ironie verstände!"[18] And his sense of decorum was offended by the text
which the librettist had furnished for Stephan's "Lied mit Chor" (#16, "Es
wollte vor Zeiten ein Jäger frei'n"; Once upon a time, a huntsman went a-
wooing) — quite apart from the fact that he regarded the piece itself as
superfluous, Stephan's role in the opera being essentially limited to that
presentation in dubious taste:

> Zu dem Liede hab' ich bis jetzt noch keine Lust finden können, und es
> scheint mir, ja es ist mir klar, dass dieses Lied die Handlung nur aufhält.
> Stephan hat durch die ganze Oper weiter nichts zu singen, und dieses Lied
> allein wird die Bassisten nicht bestimmen, den Stephan für eine gute Partie
> zu halten. Überdies aber hat Stephan Reden, die durch den Mund der mir
> bekannten Bassisten nicht in das gehörige Licht treten werden. Wäre es
> denn nicht besser, die Rolle durch einen Schauspieler spielen und das Lied
> lieber ganz weg zu lassen?[19]

(By contrast, Marschner urged Devrient to strengthen the role of Heiling's
mother, the "Königin der Erdgeister," in order to make it more appealing to
the singer to be entrusted with the part.)[20]

---

[17] "You may not have realized that except in Berlin and Vienna there is no choir large
enough to accommodate the various choruses of earth spirits, marksmen, etc."; ibid.

[18] "I'm afraid the dwarf choruses will pose a problem for most theaters; for though our
choral ladies are dwarfs artistically, they do not appear as such to the eye. And children's
dance groups are not to be found in every city. If only the public could savor irony!"; ibid.

[19] "So far I've not been in the mood to compose this song, which I think, nay believe,
merely retards the action. Stephan has nothing else to sing in the entire opera; and by
itself the song will hardly convince the Bass that this is a good role. Stephan, moreover,
is charged with saying things that will not sound right in the mouths of the Basses known
to me. Wouldn't it be preferable to have the part played by an actor and drop the song
altogether?"; letter dated 17 July 1832. Ibid., p. 798. As subsequent letters show,
Marschner, having raised further objections to the text, finally relented and composed the
Lied.

[20] "Auch Nr. 2 (= unnumbered part of the Introduction in the final version [p. 23f.] of the
score), 'Schimmernde Demanten,' ist vollendet, und ich möchte es nicht gern wegwerfen,
was ich aber müsste, wenn Sie auf der neuen Bearbeitung bestünden. In dieser tritt die
Königin weniger hervor, worauf wir der Sängerin wegen merken müssen, die ohnedies
weniger beschäftigt sein wird und deshalb ein wenig schadlos gehalten werden muss" (No.
2 "Shining diamonds," is also finished; and I would hate to discard it, as I would have to
if you insisted on the change. In your version, the Queen is less prominent. We have to

Marschner's critical attitude toward various aspects of Devrient's text notwithstanding, the composer was sufficiently impressed by the libretto to set to work almost immediately; for already on 15 July 1831, he reported: "Übrigens kann ich Ihnen melden, dass ich schon einiges daran gearbeitet habe, womit ich nicht ganz unzufrieden bin."[21] Following the example set by Weber in *Der Freischütz*, he did not — at least initially — compose the individual numbers of the score in order. The Introduction (#1), for instance, was completed, along with the Finale of Act II, in March of 1832 only, and the Finale of Act I was not ready until late June of that year, i.e., after, except for it, the first two acts had achieved final form — as can be gleaned from the dates affixed to most of the numbers in the printed score. He completed the full orchestral score in August, 1832, with the premiere, slightly delayed by the machinations of the Prussian *Generalmusikdirektor* Gasparo Spontini, taking place at the Berlin *Hofoper* in May of the following year, with the composer conducting and the librettist appearing in the title role.

Hans Heiling was a huge success, to be repeated in the major opera houses of the German-speaking lands, including that of Dresden, where Richard Wagner, a by no means uncritical admirer of Marschner, "rescued" it from the shelves of the *Hofoper's* library where, according to him, it had gathered dust.[22] (By Wagner's own admission, his youthful operatic indiscretion, *Die Feen* after Carlo Gozzi's play *La donna serpente*, had been directly inspired by that master.)[23] But within a decade or two the

keep this in mind; for the singer entrusted with the role has fairly little to do, to begin with, and must be compensated for this neglect); letter dated 21 September 1821. Ibid., p. 790.

[21] "I can report to you that I've already done some work on it with which I am not entirely dissatisfied"; *Briefe*, p. 784.

[22] See the letter to Karl Gaillard dated 4 June 1845, in *Sämtliche Briefe*, 2:432. In his later years Wagner spoke rather scathingly of the composer, to whom he owed so much, a typical case of sons renouncing their spiritual fathers. Thus Cosima records her husband as calling Marschner "einen Esel, dem der Sinn für Form völlig abging" (an ass who totally lacked a sense of form; 5 April 1879, with regard to the setting of a passage in *Der Vampyr*) and as stating "wie schön es sei in der Musik, wenn ein Instrument zum anderen sich geselle; man müsse oft sich etwas versagen, um eine Steigerung hervorzubringen; das seien Dinge, von denen Leute wie Marschner und Schumann keine Ahnung hätten" (how beautifully apt it is when in music one instrument joins another. One must sometimes renounce an effect for the sake of a subsequent climax. These are things Marschner and Schumann know nothing about; 7 February 1882). See Cosima's *Tagebücher*, ed. Martin Gregor-Dellin (Munich: Piper, 1976), 3:327, and 4:887. Similar quips are recorded in 3:112, 226, and 344, as well as in 4:777.

[23] See "Eine Mitteilung an meine Freunde ...," in *Gesammelte Schriften*, ed. Julius Kapp (Leipzig: Hesse & Becker, n.d.), 1:80, with the subsequently deleted footnote: "[Marschner], den man sehr mit Unrecht für einen Nachahmer Webers hält" (who is unjustly regarded as an imitator of Weber). The choice of a libretto derived from Gozzi further cements young Wagner's indebtedness to Hoffmann, whose "Der Dichter und der

"Romantische Oper in drei Akten," along with the rest of Marschner's increasingly mediocre contributions to the operatic repertory, faded from public view, one suspects partly, if not largely, on account of Wagner's rising star.

However, together with *Der Vampyr*, *Hans Heiling* was granted a temporary reprieve by Hans Pfitzner, that ardent and untiring champion of German Romantic opera, who conducted it in Strassburg, where he served as chief *Kapellmeister*, and subsequently directed it at the Dresden *Staatsoper* (1923), with Fritz Busch in charge of the musical forces. His pragmatic account of that production,[24] as well as an earlier, comparative treatment of the work,[25] bear witness to his enduring love for and fascination with the piece. But Pfitzner's intervention on Marschner's behalf did not amount to a permanent rescue; for as A. Dean Palmer shows in his exhaustive but tedious monograph on the composer, only a handful of stagings of *Hans Heiling*, including two at Oxford, one at Bristol, and a concert performance in Frankfurt, have occurred within recent memory.[26] We are fortunate, therefore, to have available two more or less heavily cut recordings, none of them on a major label. Personally, I have derived much pleasure from listening to the Voce version, in which the orchestra and chorus of Radio Turin are conducted by George Alexander Albrecht, and the well-known baritone Bernd Weikl lends conviction to the vocal portrayal of the title role.[27]

Scholarship, too, has treated Marschner's masterpiece cavalierly; for apart from Volkmar Köhler's comprehensive entries in two basic reference works (see footnote 1), the same author's dissertation,[28] Palmer's doctoral thesis, and the usual run of biographies — none of them of recent vintage — no serious musicological or librettological studies of his oeuvre have seen print, as, incidentally, is also the case with Marschner's contemporary Ludwig Spohr.[29] To be sure, most dictionaries and surveys of the operatic genre

---

Komponist" concludes with a detailed analysis of the Venetian playwright's masterpiece, *Il Corvo*, taken as an exemplary treatment of truly Romantic subject matter.

[24] Hans Pfitzner, "Zu meiner *Heiling*-Inszenierung am Dresdner Staatstheater im März 1923," in *Gesammelte Schriften* (Augsburg: Filser, 1926), 1:109–23.

[25] Pfitzner, "Zur Grundfrage der Operndichtung," ibid., 2:1–74, specifically pp. 29–34.

[26] The information is provided in Appendix V ("Summary of Source Materials: *Hans Heiling*") of Palmer's monograph. See especially the tables on pp. 449–60 of that book.

[27] The two-record album is designated as Voce 45. No recording date is given.

[28] "Heinrich Marschners Bühnenwerke" (Göttingen, 1956).

[29] Aubrey S. Garlington's University of Illinois dissertation "The Concept of the Marvelous in French and German Opera 1770–1840: A Chapter in the History of Opera Esthetics" (1965) is rather superficial, and the relevant chapter (401–16) offers few pertinent insights. I have not consulted Isaac E. Reid's Boston University dissertation (1968) "Some Epic and

acknowledge Marschner's historical contribution; but, by and large, they do so grudgingly and with obvious condescension. Thus, in the one-volume edition of his widely used *Short History of Opera* Donald J. Grout, after noting the family resemblance between Heiling and Wagner's Dutchman — a commonplace in Marschner criticism — makes the following perceptive but, on the whole, unflattering remarks about the opera:

> In the working out of the story as well as in the music much of the trivial is mingled with the serious. The style in general is that of the popular Singspiel with simple tunes in symmetrical patterns, interspersed with spoken dialogue. Echoes of Weber, Italian opera and Meyerbeer's *Robert le Diable* are heard. In some respects the music looks ahead to Wagner: the frequent chromatic passing tones in the melody, especially at cadences; the use of modulating sequences; and occasionally a passage of grimly powerful declamation. Many of the choruses are interesting, and the finales of the first and third acts are well constructed and effective.... Yet on the whole [Marschner's] talent was of second rank, the Biedermeier spirit in music.[30]

In his *Encyclopedia of the Opera*, David Ewen offers an extremely brief and not entirely accurate plot summary ("The setting is the Harz Mountains in the sixteenth century. Hans Heiling [baritone], son of the Queen of the Spirits [soprano], assumes human form. He falls in love with Anna [soprano], but when she learns of his origin she abandons him for Konrad [tenor]. Hans calls on the spirits for revenge. They fail to help him. He sinks into the earth, vowing that never again will any living mortal see him") and concludes his entry with the apodictic statement: "'An jenem Tag,' Hans' aria in Act I, is famous."[31] And Patrick J. Smith's history of the libretto, *The Tenth Muse*, while describing *Hans Heiling* as a work which "well demonstrates the scope of [Marschner's] opera" and characterizing the protagonist as being "neither all good nor all bad," i.e., as a "mixture" who "as a prince and as a non-mortal ... is quick to anger and terrible in his punishment," while "as a man in love he is only human," otherwise limits himself, stereotypically, to the "futuristic" features of that figure: "Wagner studied the character of Heiling and used it in various guises in the *Ring* [sic!] librettos; he also adopted for his Dutchman the aspect of Heiling which demanded

Demonic Baritone Roles in the Operas of Weber and Marschner," a sizeable chunk of which deals with *Hans Heiling*.

[30] New York: Columbia Univ. Press, 1947, p. 370.

[31] New York: Hill & Wang, 1971, p. 295.

absolute obedience to love."[32] In short, with regard to the opera under consideration there exists a need for critical *Wiedergutmachung* as well.

As I was pondering my subject, it dawned on me that, in casting my lot with *Hans Heiling*, I had acted in my own behalf; for it became increasingly clear that this project complemented and, in fact, completed a series of essays, grown into a full-fledged tetralogy, my *Ring*, which began with a still unpublished paper on *Der Freischütz*,[33] was continued with a piece on *Der fliegende Holländer*[34] and capped by an extended though, in the nature of things, speculative treatment of the question "Was ist die Romantische Oper?"[35] in which E. T. A. Hoffmann's double role as author of the poetological dialogue "Der Dichter und der Komponist" and as the composer of the "Zauberoper" *Undine* is duly acknowledged. The present essay should, accordingly, be viewed as part of an ensemble which, in its totality, offers a panoramic view of what I take to be German Romantic opera.

In order to be able to place *Hans Heiling* in its proper historical context, we would do well, perhaps, to rehash some important data: first, as regards birthdates, Hoffmann was born in 1776, Weber, a decade later, in 1786, Marschner in 1795, and Wagner, lagging behind by nearly twenty years, in 1813. Separated by thirty-seven years, this foursome of German composers constitutes the Romantic generation defined, biographically, by its outer limits. As for their crucial works, Hoffmann, who, in the words of Friedrich Blume, was surely the individual, "der den Musikbegriff in der Romantik für Deutschland ... geprägt und ... das romantische musikalische Denken und Empfinden für ein Jahrhundert entscheidend beeinflusst hat,"[36] completed and published his manifesto, "Der Dichter und der Komponist," in 1813 and composed *Undine*, based on a fairy tale by Friedrich de la Motte-Fouqué (who also furnished the libretto) between 1812 and 1814. The opera's premiere took place on 3 August 1816, at the Berlin Königliches Schauspielhaus; but, owing to a number of unfortunate circumstances, including a fire

---

[32] *The Tenth Muse: A Historical Study of the Operatic Libretto* (New York: Knopf, 1970), p. 256.

[33] The paper — entitled "Carl Maria von Weber's *Der Freischütz*: 'Nummernoper' or Gesamtkunstwerk?" — was read at the McMaster University Conference on German Romantic Literature and Music held in 1983. The proceedings are to be published by the American Universities Press.

[34] "Wagner loben ist nicht schwer, Wagner lesen um so mehr: Produktion, Reproduktion und Rezeption in Sentas Ballade im zweiten Akt des *Fliegenden Holländers*," *Jahrbuch Deutsch als Fremdsprache* 13 (1987): 42–64.

[35] *Einheit in der Vielfalt: Festschrift für Peter Lang zum 60. Geburtstag*, ed. Gisela Quast (Bern: Peter Lang, 1988), pp. 568–88.

[36] "who defined the nature of Romantic music for Germany and profoundly influenced Romantic musical thought and feeling for a century"; quoted from the article "Romantik" in *Die Musik in Geschichte und Gegenwart*, II, column 787.

by which the stage-sets and costumes were destroyed, the work was almost entirely lost sight of and, having been "replaced" by Weber's *Freischütz*, whose pivotal role was immediately recognized, has remained impervious to all subsequent attempts to rescue it permanently from oblivion.[37]

As is well known, Weber wrote *Der Freischütz* (with a book by Friedrich Kind, a hack-writer and active member of the Ludwig Tieck circle in Dresden) between 1817 and 1820 and saw it performed in Berlin on June 18 of the following year. (While at work on this opera, he penned *his* version of "Der Dichter und der Komponist" in a section of the "Fragmente eines Romans" to be entitled *Tonkünstlers Leben*, which was published posthumously.) Third in the sequence, *Hans Heiling* was mounted twelve years later, while *Der fliegende Holländer*, the only member of the quartet not to be premiered in the Prussian capital — it was staged in Dresden, with Wagner himself conducting — was written between 1840 and 1841 and first performed on 2 January 1843.[38] Thus, while the German composers who made Romantic opera both their *metier* and their *confession de foi* were born, at fairly equal intervals, in the course of, roughly, four decades, those of their works which exemplify the period style emerged during a slightly shorter time span. However, lest I be misunderstood, it is well to keep in mind that *Der fliegende Holländer*, one of Wagner's three self-styled Romantic operas and, in my view, the apogee of operatic Romanticism in more than one respect,[39] will hardly do as a paragon of that more enduring, because historically neutral, strain of Romanticism "in the abstract" which climaxed, later in the century, with two Buddheo-Christian works: operatically, with Wagner's own "Handlung" *Tristan und Isolde* (completed in 1859 but not performed until six years later) and dramatically with August Strindberg's cinematographic *Dream Play* (written in 1902 and premiered in 1907) — two works in which the essence of that perennial syndrome transpires on a higher because more abstract and, hence, universal level.

II

Having briefly surveyed the territory that is occupied by German Romantic opera, and having assigned Marschner's *Hans Heiling* a tentative place within that ambience, I am now free to turn to the work itself, seen as the manifestation of a common spirit — let us call it the *Zeitgeist* — of

---

[37] Throughout, I have used *Der Freischütz: Texte, Materialien, Kommentare*, ed. Attila Csampai and Dietmar Holland (Hamburg: Rowohlt, 1981).

[38] Throughout, I have used *Der fliegende Holländer: Texte, Materialien, Kommentare*, ed. Attila Csampai and Dietmar Holland (Hamburg: Rowohlt, 1982).

[39] Regarding Wagner's evolving use of the label "Romantic" as applied to the triad *Der fliegende Holländer*, *Tannhäuser*, and *Lohengrin* see p. 581 of my essay "Was ist die Romantische Oper?"

which it partakes and to which it contributes its own nuance. Given the
limitations of space, I shall focus my comments on thematic matters, while
giving short shrift to problems of characterization, which is a pity in so far
as Marschner, building on Devrient, shows himself, throughout, to be a
subtle psychologist. As for structure — what I have called melo-dramaturgy
in other contexts — I should like to make some basic observations with
regard to both the overarching totality of the work and, by way of illustration, to two scenes which I value as the finest examples, in this modified
version of the *Nummernoper*, of the fusion of text and music: the first-act
finale (#7, "Wie hüpft mir vor Freude das Herz in der Brust," where, in
emulation of #3 ("Walzer, Rezitativ und Arie") of *Der Freischütz*, both words
and action are embedded in a waltz-like tune that pervades the scene, and
the "Melodrama und Lied" (#12) after the *Verwandlung* in Act II where, in
the familiar vein of Shakespeare as understood and interpreted by Germany's *Stürmer* and *Dränger*, Anna's mother, Gertrude, anxiously awaiting her
daughter's return, speaks, hums, and chants her "Gothic" folk tune.

Characteristically, the plot of Marschner's opera centers about the
confrontation and interpenetration of the natural with the supernatural
sphere, the latter, as in Hoffmann's *Undine*, taken to symbolize natural —
more specifically: elemental — forces. (It goes without saying that in the
case of *Undine* the dominant element is water, and in that of *Hans Heiling*
earth.) This dialectic, in fact, determines the shape and governs the action
in both instances. In *Hans Heiling*, the supernatural is represented by the
protagonist's mother, the "Königin der Erdgeister," while Heiling himself,
being, literally, a "Zerrissener," participates in both realms, at least until the
final resolution and reconciliation; for as the Queen straightforwardly puts
it,

> So hat der Mutter Wahn sich Dir vererbt, / Der mich noch heut mit bittrer
> Reue quält. / Du weisst es, dass das Leben / Die Liebe eines Menschen Dir
> gegeben, / Dass Du darum, ein unglückselig Doppelwesen, / Zu ew'gem
> Zwiespalt bist erlesen.[40]

Clearly differentiated from this subterranean realm, and dramaturgically
set off from it, is the social domain, which consists of a serious and a comic,
or potentially comic, layer. The center of the serious action, which is
Romantic in the trivial sense, is occupied by Anna, who is wooed first by
Heiling, in whose presence she feels uncomfortable from the start, and then,
more successfully, by Konrad who, as "burggräflicher Leibschütz," is,
professionally, a blend of soldier and hunter. The popular level, on which
fairs (here in honor of St. Florian), hunts (here merely alluded to in

---

[40] "Thus you have inherited your mother's (= my) delusion, which I still bitterly repent.
You know that you owe your life to the love of a human being and that, therefore, you are
doomed always to be divided within yourself"; Devrient, p. 259.

Konrad's abortive *Lied* #10 ["Wohl durch den grünen Wald ..."]) and weddings are enacted, is represented by Niklas and Stephan (the latter, a peasant in Devrient's original text, having been elevated to a smith in Marschner's score) and, as a sort of intermediary, Gertrude. Once the existence of this pattern has been acknowledged, it is natural to view the progress of the action in terms of rhythmic alternation as follows:

The supernatural element (A) clearly prevails in, and provides the sole setting for, the "Vorspiel," which, as we have seen, is anomalously, but for carefully enunciated dramaturgical reasons, *followed*, rather than *preceded*, by the Overture. In the Introduction (#1, Act One), the transition from the supernatural to the natural realm is explicitly thematized ("Heiling steigt aus dem unterirdischen Gange herauf.... Er blickt in den Gang hinab, der sich schliesst"),[41] and social reality asserts itself with the arrival of Gertrude ("Meister Heiling") and her daughter ("Meister Heiling, guten Morgen"). All but forgotten in the remainder of Act One, the spirit world reasserts itself, with a vengeance, in #9 (Act Two), which triggers the *peripetia*; for here the Queen who, at the end of the "Vorspiel," had vowed to do everything in her power to reverse the course on which her son was about to embark, confronts Anna and tells her, in no uncertain terms, who Heiling really is: "Wisse denn, dein Bräutigam ist Geisterfürst der Berge. / Er gehört dem Stamm der Gnomen und Zwerge."[42]

Once Heiling realizes that, as Anna's suitor, he has lost out against his rival, Konrad, who, by burning the magic book, which assured his rule, had renounced his claims to power in the subterranean world, he invokes its spirits (#14, Act Three), whose help in wreaking his revenge he enlists only after vowing to resume his throne. But the evil scheme he and his cohorts have hit upon is subsequently foiled by the Queen (#19, Finale), who persuades him to "come home," thus completing the circle.

Complementing the supernatural action, the "Romantic" one (B) involving Anna, Heiling, and Konrad, unfolds in several stages occupying ##2–4 (Act One: Anna and Heiling), #8 (Act Two: Anna by herself), ##10–11 (Act Two: Anna and Konrad) and #13 (Finale: Act Two: all three participants in the love triangle), while the popular action (C) occupies ##5–7 (Act One) and 15–18 (Act Three) of the opera. The rhythmic curve to which I have previously referred may, accordingly, be illustrated by means of the following graphic scheme:

---

[41] "Heiling ascends through the subterranean passage.... He looks down into the passageway as it closes up"; Score, p. 70, with a slight modification of Devrient, p. 264. Regarding Marschner's final disposition of the transition from the "Vorspiel" to the Introduction, see the fourth paragraph of his letter to Devrient dated "am ersten Ostertage 1832" ("Briefe," p. 797f.)

[42] "Know that your betrothed is the Prince of mountain spirits and belongs to the tribe of gnomes and dwarfs."

Vorspiel		A
Act I	#1	A > B
	##2–4	B
	##5–7	C
Act II	#8	B
	#9	A/B
	##10–13	B (interrupted by #12)
Act III	#14	A/B
	##15–18	C
	#19	A/B/C

That much for the dramatic structure, or dramaturgy proper, of *Hans Heiling* which in some important but not as clearly discernible ways is paralleled by the opera's melo-dramaturgical configuration. I refrain from discussing the strictly musical organization of the piece and Marschner's role as an intermediary, in this respect as well, between Weber and Wagner. (Relevant information can be gleaned from the pertinent passages in Köhler's admirably succinct and penetrating overview in the two reference works listed in footnote 1, and from the painstakingly detailed treatment of "Aspects of Marschner's Style and His Contribution to the History of Opera" in Chapter Seven of Palmer's monograph.) In effect, we can discern three modes corresponding, roughly, to the layering discussed above, B being represented by certain features of *opera seria*, C by the Singspiel elements, and A perhaps by the use of various types of *Melodrama*, a technique which, as Palmer (223) rightly asserts, tends to "create a feeling of foreboding and fear."

As for the first of these three categories, Marschner, employing a serious, or even high serious, tone that would seem to be out of keeping with his less exalted purpose, introduces several arias and ensembles which point in the direction of grand, or in one case grand magic, opera. To demonstrate the truth of my contention I shall briefly discuss one example from each class of what I regard as stylistic flaws. Thus the "Königin der Erdgeister" in *Hans Heiling* seems to have been conceived, more or less consciously, as a clone of Mozart's *Königin der Nacht*, which, judging by the precedent, makes her conciliatory role in the conflict much less plausible. The similarity, at any rate, between one of the Nocturnal Queen's arias from *Die*

Zauberflöte and the *risoluto* passage "Nein, nein, nicht umsonst will ich die Macht besitzen" ("Vorspiel," p. 35 of the orchestral score), especially in the instrumental accompaniment, is "unüberhörbar." — Similarly, the opening portion of the duet between Konrad and Anna ("Ha, dieses Wort gibt erneuertes Leben …," #11, p. 174 of the score) echoes, with a ring that is made false by the humbler context, the famous exchange between Arnold and Mathilde in Act II of Rossini's then recently completed *Guillaume Tell* (1829).

At the other end of the scale, we encounter the distinct profile of the Singspiel with its songs ("Ein sprödes, allerliebstes Kind" [#6], "Wohl durch den grünen Wald" [#10], and "Es wollte vor Zeiten" [#16]) and choruses ("Juchheissa, heut' dürft ihr die Kannen nicht schonen" [#5] and "So wollen wir auf kurze Zeit" [#19a]) entrusted to the folk, and complemented by the rather extensive prose dialogue, maintained largely though not exclusively on its level. In between, and taking the place, as it were, of the two prevalent forms of operatic recitative, *recitativo secco* and *accompagnato*, is the melodrama which, as I have suggested, might well be considered the most characteristic form of vocal utterance in this opera as well as in other of Marschner's works for the musical theater and, perhaps, in German Romantic opera as a whole. Since Palmer (222–27), who lists four instances of the use of this technique in *Hans Heiling* alone, discusses the matter at some length, I can cut the argument short at this point, especially since I will shortly analyze a cogent example of the practice.

A thorough and penetrating study of *Hans Heiling* such as, for obvious reasons, I cannot undertake on this occasion would hardly be complete without a look at its formal structure aimed at determining exactly where between the poles of "Nummernoper" (the classical pattern) and through-composed opera (the Romantic goal, not to be achieved until *Tristan und Isolde*) this particular work is located on the broad operatic spectrum. But even a glance at the distribution of numbers, nineteen in all, in Marschner's score[43] shows that the work in question does not occupy a position halfway between Weber and Wagner; for in comparison with both *Der Freischütz* and *Der fliegende Holländer* it offers relatively few *Verklammerungen* (or bracketings, as I have called them in my critical analyses of these two operas). Indeed, except for the three finales, where such concatenations are, naturally, *de rigueur*, we have only two modest examples (#9, "Ensemble und Arie mit Chor," and #14, "Melodrama, Scene und Arie mit Chor") of this unifying device, while Marschner's famous predecessor as well as his even more famous successor indulge in this practice on a much grander scale that causes their respective enterprises to

---

[43] As the correspondence shows, the numbering was repeatedly changed in the course of Marschner's work on the opera, especially as a result of the composer's decision not to number the subdivisions of the "Vorspiel."

be milestones on the high road leading to the accomplished *Gesamtkunstwerk*.

The fact that in the discussion of any and all aspects of *Hans Heiling*, including those which I have considered in this section of my essay, *Der Freischütz* comes inevitably to mind underscores the need for a detailed analysis of their multifaceted relationship. Marschner himself was fully aware of the problem and was upset by Devrient's having produced a text which raised the specter of imitation or involuntary parody on the younger composer's part. The following quotation from a letter to the librettist shows him hiding his keen sense of *déjà vu* under a mask of humorous banter:

> No. 17 wollen Sie ja ändern und statt des Jägerliedes ein anderes suppliren. Damit bin ich ganz einverstanden. Man muss alle Ähnlichkeit in Situation und Formen vermeiden. Sollten nun die Brautjungfern [19a] nicht auch dazu gehören? Ist auch die Art und Weise, wie sie ausgeführt sind, ganz verschieden und mögen sie auch ganz andere Dinge zu singen haben wie im *Freischütz*, es wird doch Esel und Böswillige genug geben, die eine Kopie oder Ähnlichkeiten finden wollen.[44]

Having provided some clues as to the nature of the macrocosm as which the overall structure of this, and any, true total work of art might be viewed, I now turn briefly to the microcosm of two individual numbers in *Hans Heiling* in order to demonstrate, with the help of these telling examples, Marschner's talent for integrating text and music. I begin with the analysis of #7 (Act Two, Scene Four of Devrient's libretto), the "Melodrama und Lied" assigned to Anna's mother, Gertrude. This scene (pp. 181–86 of the orchestral score), of which, in spite of his general apprehensions about the use of this technique, the composer emphatically stated that he considered it to be "gänzlich gelungen,"[45] conveys, in its sixty *andante sostenuto* measures, a density of atmosphere fully compatible with that which prevails in the opening scene, with its Willow Song, of the final act of Verdi's *Otello*, composed over half a century later.

The esthetic triumph of the scene results from a variety of factors, which combine to produce the intended effect. There is, first, the thematic relevance; for the hard-hearted miser who wants to unearth the buried treasure on the deserted heath ("Ein geiz'ger, hartherz'ger Mann / Den

---

[44] "You wish to change No. 17 and replace the hunter's song with another Lied. That suits me well. One must at all costs avoid thematic and structural similarities. Wouldn't that apply to the bridesmaids' chorus as well; and even though the content of their song and its musical shape are quite different (from the supposed model), there will be fools and maligners who will accuse us of theft"; "Briefe," p. 791.

[45] Ibid.

Schatz zu heben kommt er an / Des Nachts wohl auf der Haide")[46] and is strangled by a skeleton ("Und wie er gräbt, da steigt empor / Ein bleiches Totengeripp: ... Du hörst nicht auf der Armen Not, / Drum würge ich dich jetzt zu Tod")[47] might well be construed as symbolizing Heiling wooing Anna, his "Schatz," to whom he is about to give a *Schatz* as a wedding present — all this in a characteristically vague and twisted sense emanating from the subconscious of a person, the singer, who has reason to be ill at ease about her future son-in-law. Would it be too farfetched to assume that the *Lied*, sung "mechanically" but not without emotional *engagement*, also recreates the scene (#10) concurrently unfolding in the forest?

That much for the dramatic function of the scene, whose melo-dramatic effect results from a combination of skillfully blended instrumental and vocal techniques which give #12 a flavor all its own. As for the orchestration, Marschner here appropriately uses a small ensemble of strings augmented by sparingly used clarinets, bassoons, and horns. But even that sparse *Besetzung* was criticized by the librettist who, in a no longer extant letter, took exception to the composer's usage. Marschner responded to Devrient's critique by noting:

> Von Nr. 12, Melodrama und Lied, weiss ich auch nichts zu sagen als: es war eine verfluchte Aufgabe, und — man muss es vom Theater herab mit Instrumentation hören.
>
> Letztere finden Sie zu stark? ... Denken Sie sich die vorgeschriebenen Instrumente mit Dämpfern, diskret und im Sinne des Ganzen ausgeführt, so kann der Effekt kaum fehlen. Freilich bleibt die Hauptsache der Sängerin und Schauspielerin überlassen, wie denn überall. Indessen, gleichgültig habe ich mir Gertrude in dieser Spannung, in solcher Nacht, bei solchem Aberglauben ... niemals gedacht, ebensowenig, dass der Zuschauer von der Situation oder der Musik nicht mit ergriffen werden soll.
>
> ... Hören Sie es nur erst im Zusammenhange, gut vorgetragen auf der Bühne. Sie werden sich vielleicht noch damit befreunden.[48]

---

[46] "A miserly man with a heart of stone arrives on the heath at night to dig up the treasure"; in the score (p. 184), the phrase "geiz'ger, hartherz'ger Mann" is accompanied by a *pizzicato* in the lower strings.

[47] "And as he digs, a pale skeleton rises up and says: 'Because you don't take pity on the poor, I will strangle you.'"

[48] "About No. 12 (Melodrama and Lied), too, I can only say that it was a very difficult task and that in order to savor the results one must hear the full orchestra play it in the theater. You find the orchestration too thick? Think of the instruments as being muted and played discreetly in the underlying spirit, and you'll find the effect to be striking. To be sure, the principal burden falls on the singer and actress, as is always the case.... However I never intended Gertrude to be calm under such tension, in such a night, and given such superstition, just as I did not intend [two lines missing] that the viewer should not be affected by the action or music. Listen to it in context and well delivered on the stage! Perhaps you will appreciate it then"; letter dated 24 September 1832. "Briefe," p. 805.

Oddly enough, Marschner, in composing the scene, refrained, wisely perhaps, from musically enacting the onomatopoeia called for by his own directions ("Durch die ganze Nummer hört man den Wind sausen, aber nur an den bezeichnenden Stellen stark," score, p. 181); for what we hear as accompaniment to Gertrude's words "und der Wind heult kalt über die Heide" and "Hei, hei, das stürmt ja, als wäre das wilde Heer los" (There's a storm as if all Hell had broken loose) and the stage direction "der Wind rüttelt am Fenster, es fliegt auf" (The wind rattles the window, which bursts open; all on p. 182 of the score] is more a sighing than a whistling or booming sound. Marschner's restraint in this regard — which has a parallel in #2 (p. 87 of the score), where the "dumpfe Donner," to be heard following the destruction of Heiling's magic book, remains inaudible — is praiseworthy in so far as the subdued effect which is thus created enhances the contrast between this intimate scene and the more extroverted ones which precede and follow it.

By all signs the most distinguished feature of #12 is the large variety of vocal means used in alternation and ranging all the way from plain speech ("Wo nur Ännchen bleibt, es ist finstre Nacht" [measure 12 on p. 181]) and melodrama ("Es ist auch kein Sternchen am Himmel" [measure 17 on p. 182]) by way of humming with closed (*con bocca chiusa* [measure 25 on p. 183]) or open ("summend" [measures 28 to 30 on p. 183]) mouth to actual singing (the ballad, instrumentally foreshadowed in measure 21, which begins at the end of measure 30 and concludes, after several melodramatic inserts, in measure 57). In providing unity in so much variety, Marschner reaffirms his genius as an operatic composer of distinctly "Romantic" leanings.

The first Finale (#7; Act One, Scene Nine, of Devrient's libretto; pp. 128–40 of the orchestral score) is more elaborate, comprising over 400 measures; but as the tempo here is a fast *allegro* the entire scene takes up no more than four to five minutes of actual performance time. Since, as is customary with finales, this is an ensemble scene in whose action all major characters are involved, the foreshortening of the conflict that here erupts and calls for a resolution is rather painfully felt and, as Devrient himself noted in a letter that is unaccounted for, causes the whole sequence to be lopsided and psychologically unconvincing. Yet, though conceding this point, Marschner was unwilling to make more than token concessions to his librettist; for, as he told Devrient in his reply to the latter's suggestions, he had already composed the scene and was eager to preserve its musical shape. All one could hope for, he said, was that the actors/singers involved in the production had enough psychological finesse to make their untoward behavior palatable to the audience:

Was die Stelle im ersten Finale "Nein, lasst es vergessen sein" [score, p. 135] und so weiter betrifft, die Sie und eine Partei verwerfen, ein anderer bei Ihnen viel geltender Kritiker aber gut heisst, so bin ich des letzteren

Meinung und lasse sie stehen. Es ist gar nicht zu viel, was Anna ihrem nicht geliebten Bräutigam auf sein patziges, unvergnügliches Wesen erwidert, und es kommt auf die jedesmalige Anna an, sich nicht unliebenswürdig zu machen und den Grundcharakter der Rolle ins rechte Licht zu stellen. Überdies übertüncht solche Stellen grösstenteils die Musik, wodurch jederzeit etwas zu Herbes gemildert wird.[49]

What interests me specifically, however, is the melo-dramaturgical construction of the scene of which the composer prided himself so justly; for here two kinds of music, produced by two different orchestral bodies, are used, both simultaneously (with some fragmentation and distortion) and, more often, consecutively, to give expression to the human conflict which lies at the heart of this Finale and is caused by Anna's desire to join the dance and Heiling's refusal to let her do so. Marschner has divided the tasks assigned to the two instrumental groups in such a way that the "Musik auf der Bühne," as it is called, consists solely of a waltz which persists throughout the entire scene but, from time to time, yields to, or intersects with, the "Musik im Orchester" which correlates with the various psychological and physical confrontations that constitute the *agon* of this dramatic sub-entity. It is ironic and, exactly for that reason, to the point that while Anna, though repeatedly pulled into the other sphere, is irresistibly drawn to the perpetuum mobile-like rhythm of the dance, with which, after she has physically joined it in the company of Konrad and Gertrude, she, in her newly-found *joie de vivre*, is identified, while Heiling, left behind, continues to be haunted by the waltz, which asserts its power by invading his innermost thoughts, thus celebrating its unmitigated triumph.

As for the technical aspects of this doubling of musical forces, Devrient had originally wanted the dance to occur backstage, with the proviso, still found in the orchestral score (p. 128), that in the opera, the band was to march across the stage before "setting up shop" behind it; but Marschner found this solution unsuitable for pragmatic reasons and, anticipating a practice common to twentieth-century Epic Opera (Stravinsky and Brecht), proposed that the dancers and the band be placed, visible to both audience and conductor, at the rear of the stage:

Ich komme nun zur Verteidigung meines Anfangs des Finale und der Abweichung von Ihrer Idee: alles Musizieren auf dem Theater hat seine

---

[49] "As far as the passage in the first *Finale* ('Nein, lasst es vergessen sein') is concerned, which you and several of your friends reject but which a critic highly esteemed by you approves of, I share the latter's view and will return it. I, for one, don't find Anna's response to her beloved fiancé's rude behavior excessive; and it depends on the artist charged with playing the role not to give her the appearance of a hoyden but to bring out the basic nature of her character. Moreover, the offending passages are largely buried under the music, which has a way of softening rough places"; letter dated 7 August 1832. Ibid., p. 801. The letter dated 18 October 1831 (ibid., pp. 792–95) offers a much more detailed analysis of Heiling's character and its musical portrayal.

Schwierigkeiten, besonders hinter der Szene, wenn das Orchester mit hinein spielen soll, was gewöhnlich schlecht zusammenklingt. Die Schwierigkeit wird dadurch noch vermehrt, dass sie erst über die Szene spielend gehen und sich dann erst hinter den Kulissen arrangieren sollen. Das würde die meisten Male verunglücken. — Ich habe mir die Musikanten gleich daseiend gedacht und die Szenerie etwa so: Im Hintergrunde, auf einer Anhöhe, neben dem Wirtshaus eine grosse Tenne, wo die Spielleute musizieren und einzelne Paare tanzen. Dadurch, dass dies alles im Hintergrunde geschieht, wird vorne die Szene nicht gestört; der Dirigent und die Spielleute haben einander im Auge (eine grosse Hauptsache), Konrad und Anna gehen Heiling und dem Publikum nicht verloren, Heiling gewinnt mehr am Spiel und die ganze Szene an Lebendigkeit, und gibt ein nettes Tableau.[50]

If one is to judge by the evidence found in the published score, the composer does not seem to have had his way; for in the *più allegro* section on p. 136 Anna is described as leaving "rasch" with her mother and her future husband, an action lamented by Heiling in the *sempre più agitato* section that follows; but, naturally, each stage director and conductor will have to make his own decision in actual practice.

III

And now to the thematic aspect of *Hans Heiling* seen in relation to that of the other operas which mark the path of German Romanticism. As a preliminary step, I would like to present a synopsis of Marschner's work freely adapted from the outline included in Palmer's monograph (137f.). I do so begging the reader's indulgence; for as often as not operatic plots are trivial and the librettos, taken by themselves, hardly worth bothering about. But, as happens at times with this kind of esthetic *Zwitter*, if the chemistry is right, miracles happen; and *Hans Heiling* may well approach the condition of being at least half a miracle. Here goes, then:

---

[50] "I now proceed to the defense of the beginning of the *Finale* and the departure from your (original) idea. All music-making on stage is difficult, especially if the orchestra is posted behind the scene and is to play simultaneously (with the orchestra in the pit). The difficulty is enhanced by the fact that they first have to traverse the stage, playing, and are only then posted backstage. The manoeuver is likely to fail in most instances. My idea was to have the musicians already present (on stage) and I have envisioned the following setting: in the background, on a hill adjoining the inn, is a large threshing barn, where the musicians play and individual couples dance. Because all this takes place in the background, the action in the foreground is unencumbered and the players can make eye contact with the conductor, which is very important. Konrad and Anna are within sight of Heiling and the audience; Heiling's role, as well as the liveliness of the action, are greatly enhanced; and a nice *tableau* is created"; letter dated 23 September 1832. Ibid., p. 805.

PROLOGUE: A subterranean scene. Gnomes work at mining gold and diamonds. Hans Heiling, the son of the Queen of the Earth Spirits and of a human father, declares that he has fallen in love with a mortal woman, Anna, and is about to forsake his kingdom for life on earth with her. (Anna has been urged by her mother to marry the rich stranger, whom she respects but does not love.) Because Heiling must renounce his throne if he wishes to live above ground, his mother and the spirits which serve her entreat him, vainly, not to leave. When it is evident that he has made up his mind, his mother gives him the Magic Book, without which he would lose his power over the spirits, as well as a precious *Brautschmuck* for Anna.

ACT ONE: Heiling ascends to earth, and the entrance to the subterranean realm closes behind him. He is met by Anna and her mother, Gertrude, and gives a golden chain to Anna who, adorning herself, imagines how she will be envied by her friends. She asks Heiling to accompany her to the village fair in honor of St. Florian; but he refuses. Left alone, Anna opens the Magic Book, which lies on the table, but is terrified when she sees its pages turning, by themselves, at a rapid clip. Heiling, who is upset by her having meddled with the book, pushes her away. She entreats him to destroy the tome, and, after briefly pondering the matter, he obliges her by casting the last vestige of his power into the fire. Anna thanks him but at the same time begins to be distrustful.

The scene changes to the village fair. Heiling has yielded to Anna's demand by agreeing to take her there, on the condition that she will not dance. When they arrive, however, she is greeted by the young men, who want to dance with her. Breaking her word, she consents and dances with Konrad, a soldier whom she has known since childhood and whom she loves without as yet knowing it. Heiling rebukes her sharply; but she ignores him, and he leaves in anger.

ACT TWO: Anna is in the forest, daydreaming. Darkness falls, and the Queen of the Earth Spirits appears with her retinue and reveals to the girl the true origin and nature of her son, urging her to release him. When the spirits have vanished, Konrad appears, and Anna confesses her love for him. He accompanies her home, where Gertrude receives them with open arms. Heiling appears and gives Anna her *Brautschmuck*, by which Gertrude is dazzled but which her daughter rejects. When Heiling asks for an explanation, Anna divulges that she knows his true identity. Bereft of all hope, he decides to leave. Before doing so, however, he stabs Konrad, wounding him only slightly.

ACT THREE: Heiling by himself in a mountain ravine. Having decided to return to the spirit realm, he summons his former subjects to enlist their help in the revenge he plans to take; but they mock him by informing him that Konrad is not dead and that he must swear renewed allegiance to them if they are to acknowledge his sovereignty. Heiling does so, and in their company returns to his mother.

The scene changes to the courtyard of the village church. Konrad has recovered from his wound and is about to marry Anna. Heiling enters to take his revenge. Konrad attacks him, but to no avail since he is invulnerable. The Queen appears and begs her son to forgive and forget. His anger having evaporated, Heiling follows her to his true abode, never to see the light of day again.

One of the most symptomatic and, hence, most frequently encountered thematic nodes within the realm of German Romantic opera is the conflict between human beings and subhuman or supernatural agents, whether Christian, as in *Der Freischütz* and *Der fliegende Holländer*, or pagan, as in *Undine* and *Hans Heiling*, where *Elementargeister*, that is to say spirits inhabiting, and concurrently symbolizing, the elements interact with the known world. Given the latter constellation, two possibilities for action, leading to conflict, arise: either a human being, driven by an impulse beyond his control, descends into the spirit realm, as happens, prototypically, in Hoffmann's novella "Die Bergwerke zu Falun,"[51] or a spirit feels impelled to ascend to the human sphere, as is the case in de la Motte-Fouqué/Hoffmann's *Undine*. Invariably, these figures are divided in themselves, beings who, at great peril, wish to be made whole by embracing one extreme, i.e., either by becoming, through love, entirely human or by altogether escaping from the human condition viewed as being half-angelic and half-bestial.

Seen from this perspective, Heiling offers a very special case, for, though *Geisterfürst* and heir to the subterranean throne currently occupied by his mother, he is, as we have seen, the son of a mortal. This bastardy cogently explains both his split personality — according to the stage directions, he is "schwermütig und verschlossen, von glühend ungestümer Zärtlichkeit. Gemessen im Reden und Benehmen, die Äusserung des Zorns bemeisternd, bis die Wut ihn übermannt"[52] — and the conflicting sets of values which he tries, in vain, to reconcile. (It is never determined, for instance, whether it is man ("der Menschen falsches Geschlecht," 258; the treacherous race of men) or the spirits who are false, although the thrust of the action would seem to lend credence to the belief that the *Elementargeister* may be more trustworthy in so far as they are simple-minded. The material values they

[51] The novella depicts what Novalis called the "geheimnisvolle Weg nach innen" rather than, as in *Hans Heiling*, the "Weg nach oben."

[52] "melancholic and introspective, full of glowing, impetuous tenderness, slow in speech and action, controlling his wrath until it overpowers him"; Devrient, p. 256.

create underground, at any rate, may be used by those dwelling above for both good and evil purposes ("Wonach die Menschen ringen und werben / Zum Nutzen und Schaden, zum Heil und Verderben," 297; what men strive for, doing good or evil, attaining salvation or perdition.)

The serious intention underlying Devrient/Marschner's treatment of the subject is underscored by the fact that while Heiling actually presides over a tribe of dwarfs, gnomes and goblins akin to the Nibelungen, he himself, though a "half-gnome," is shown to be distinctly human in body and mind, an individual of whom it is impossible to believe that he would consort with his subjects in the way that is parodistically, and with an ominous thrust, described in Konrad's *Lied* (#6 of the score), at whose conclusion Heiling abruptly enters so as to dispel that notion:

Doch Freitags schliesst das Gräfelein
Sich fest in seine Kammer ein ...
Sie [his wife] denkt: ei, das ist doch kurios,
Hier ist der Teufel los ...
Da guckt sie einst durchs Schlüsselloch,
Sieht wie ihr Mann, zwei Spannen hoch,
Mit andren Zwergen tanzt.
Mit kurzen Beinen, dickem Kopf,
Springt der Herr Graf, der arme Tropf ...
Schlägt Purzelbäume flink voran,
Ein Kobold war ihr Mann.[53]

This is an unusual twist, as is also the opera's conclusion, which shows Heiling, in contrast to Hoffmann's Elis, to resign himself to his fate ("Es war beschieden, was geschehn"; what happened had been fated) and return to the *Geisterreich* — a solution which, in its conciliatory vein, is more in keeping with the Biedermeier, as embodied in the "Zauberspiele" of Ferdinand Raimund, than with the somber mood of High Romanticism. — Let it be noted, in passing, that, in a peculiar but very specific way, *Hans Heiling* may be regarded as an inverted *Faust*, from which the setting of its first scene ("Das Innere von Heilings Wohnung, finster und angeraucht. Bücher, Phiolen, Schmelztiegel und astronomische Geräte sind an den Wänden und über dem Herde aufgestellt")[54] was clearly derived. The reference is parodistic in so far as the *Erdgeist* (= Heiling) takes the role of Faust; and so does Anna, his "Gretchen," inadvertently, when, sitting in

[53] "Every Friday the little count locks himself up in his chamber. She thinks: that is strange; something is cooking there. Once, looking through the keyhole, she sees her husband, three feet tall, cavorting with other dwarfs. With short legs and a swollen head, the fellow turns somersaults in quick succession. Her husband was a goblin."

[54] "The interior of Heiling's dark, smoke-stained dwelling. Books, phiols, alembics, and astrological instruments are strung on the wall and above the hearth."

Heiling's "Studierstube," she opens the Magic Book ("Ha, welche Zeichen! So glänzend, so schön. / Wie sie nahen und weichen, / Wie ich's nie gesehn! / Wirre Gestalten / Treiben und walten, / Schwellen / Wie Wellen. / Wie sie sich verschlingen, / Mächtig auf mich dringen")[55] and has to be rescued from the ensuing predicament.

Speaking of *Der Freischütz*, we should remember that, in contrast to *Hans Heiling*, the action of Weber's uncontested masterpiece, which is firmly embedded in a Christian context (complete with a hermit representing the Church), might be described as a mixture of Morality and *Schicksalsdrama* — what with ancestral portraits hung on poorly fastened nails! Here the dichotomy of good and evil is clearcut, as God's representative on earth fights with the devil (= Kaspar as Samiel's willing henchman) for the soul of Max, a rather passive Everyman altogether lacking moral fibre. In *Der fliegende Holländer*, the Christian element is just as strong, but the pattern is different and more complex. For the Dutchman, in Satan's clutches and blown about the seas (as Paolo and Francesca, for entirely different reasons, are blown about in the first Circle of Dante's Hell), has become a legendary figure in his own "life time" and finds a self-styled, though perhaps divinely ordained, angel in the person of Senta, who is dramaturgically equivalent to Anna but rendered superior to the latter by her total devotion to the cause of achieving transcendence by *Erlösung* in death brought about, quite literally, through what Kierkegaard calls a qualitative leap.

To take the argument one step further: it is hardly an accident that the principal characters in the three Romantic operas in question which bear the male hero's name in their title are, or can easily be construed to be, of the melancholic, i.e., brooding and introspective Hamletian type. Once again, Hoffmann's Elis Fröbom "leads the pack"; for, as in response to Elis' observation: "Mir ist eure wilde Tollheit zuwider. Was ich hier draussen treibe, geht dich nichts an," his fellow sailor Joens remarks: "Nun, nun, ich weiss es ja, du bist ein Neriker von Geburt, und die sind alle trübe und traurig und haben keine Lust am wackeren Seemannsleben"[56] — prophetic words, as the subsequent development shows.

---

[55] "Ha, what signs! So shiny and beautiful! How they come and go in ways unknown to me. Confused spirits moving about, rising like waves. How they interweave, threatening to engulf me!"; ibid., p. 269. These come very close to being direct quotations from Goethe's drama.

[56] "Your unruly behavior annoys me. What I am doing out here is none of your business.... I know you are a born melancholic — and those are all sad and moody and take no pleasure in a brave sailor's life"; I quote from Hoffmann's *Die Serapionsbrüder* (Munich: Winkler, 1963), p. 190.

Of this melancholic *Trifolium*, Max, being a cardboard figure,[57] is the least philosophically inclined. Observing his premarital state of paralysis, Kaspar, rather than offering a plausible psychological explanation, seeks to persuade him, falsely, that evil forces are at work ("Es hat dir jemand einen Weidmann gesetzt, und den musst du lösen, oder du triffst keine Klaue"),[58] which causes the poor *Jägerbursche* to sulk. By contrast, Heiling, whom Devrient describes as "schwermütig" and "verschlossen" — two tell-tale signs of the prevalence of the black bile (*melancholia*) among his humors — meets the standard requirements in his outward appearance as well: "[Er] ist von bleicher Gesichtsfarbe, dunklem Haar und Bart. Er trägt ganz schwarze Kleider, fein mit Gold gesäumt."[59]

This matches, almost to a *t*, the attributes assigned to the nameless captain of Wagner's ghost ship who, in deep mourning over his lost but, in this case *unfortunately* immortal, soul, disembarks to sing his aria (#2, "Die Frist ist um"; Your time is up). The Holländer, whose salvation is at stake in the opera, suitably wears "schwarze spanische Tracht" (black Spanish garb), that is to say colors which are more appropriate for a nobleman than for the skipper of a boat carrying no matter how rich a cargo. And the portrait which occupies such a prominent place on one wall of the living/spinning room of Daland's home and, partly for that reason, serves as the chief object of Senta's fixation is aptly described as "das Bildnis eines bleichen Mannes mit dunklem Barte in schwarzer spanischer Tracht" (the portrait of a pale man with dark beard in Spanish dress).

So far, so good; but let me suggest, in conclusion to this not altogether unmusical argument, that the condition of *melancholia* so poignantly displayed in German Romantic opera is closely linked to that *taedium vitae* which, rampant in many deep thinkers and dreamers, is a bane to Christianity and could well be characterized as the mental condition of those individuals who, whether for good reasons or not, despair of their *Seelenheil*.[60] But, and here precisely lies the rub, salvation may come to these extraordinary creatures by a different route, that of art, which is equally suspect to the Church. "Art as salvation and as secularized religion" — such would seem to be a typically Romantic motif. Hence the supposition, voiced

---

[57] In his Stuttgart production of the opera which was shown on West German television in the spring of 1982, Achim Feyer anticipated that insight by using a card game as the dominant visual metaphor.

[58] "Somebody has laid a trap for you, from which you must extricate yourself before you can shoot another bird."

[59] "His face is pale, his hair and beard are dark. He is wearing a black costume trimmed in gold"; Devrient, p. 256. Black, the color of coal, and gold, that of precious metals — both mined by the dwarfs and gnomes — offers, as it were, a realistic explanation for this color scheme.

[60] For an elaborate treatment of the phenomenon see Reinhard Kuhn's book *The Demon at Noontide: Ennui in Western Literature* (Princeton: Princeton Univ. Press, 1976).

by Hans Pfitzner, among others, that the introspective hero of musical drama in the age of Romanticism causes many of these works to be *Krypto-Künstleropern* — which is not to say, of course, that their protagonists, though "shadowed o'er with the pale cast of thought" and blessed with esthetic sensibility, are to be viewed as practicing artists; for it would be ludicrous to think of Max as a woodcarver, Heiling as a sculptor, the Dutchman as a "Singer of Songs," and Lohengrin as a composer of symphonies or swan songs.

I mention Lohengrin, whose name has not yet surfaced in this paper, because Pfitzner steadfastly maintains that it is he rather than the Dutchman who must be regarded as Heiling's true "bedfellow." Here is a crucial excerpt from his essay "Zur Grundfrage der Operndichtung":

> Die Parallele ... Heiling und Holländer ist nur komisch. "Das schwarze Wams, die bleiche Mien'." Das ist alles. Soll man wirklich noch erwähnen, dass der Tenor hier wie dort ein Jäger ist, und dass dort die Mutter, hier der Vater gern einen reichen Schwiegersohn haben möchte? — Eher lassen sich direkte Gegensätze finden, soweit sich die beiden Handlungen und Personen überhaupt vergleichen lassen. Heiling will leben, der Holländer sterben. Anna will ohne Heiling möglichst vergnügt leben, Senta mit dem Holländer und für ihn sterben. Der Holländer wird erlöst und befriedigt, Heiling nicht. Dagegen sind Heiling und Lohengrin in der Tat dieselbe Tragödie: die des höher gearteten Menschen, der aus der tiefsten Einsamkeit seiner Natur heraus sich sehnt nach Vereinigung, nach einer menschlichen Liebesheimat, und mit Schmerzen erfahren muss, dass es für ihn dieses nicht gibt. Er muss seine, ihm von einem unerbittlichen Naturgesetz auferlegte Pflicht einsam und fernab von der Menschheit erfüllen. Und wie Lohengrin, gesenkten Hauptes traurig nach dem heiligen Gral zurückkehrt, um von dort aus unbelohnt Liebe und Segen zu spenden, so kehrt Heiling resigniert und blutenden Herzens in sein dunkles Geisterreich zurück, dort herrschend "ewige Gesetze" zu erfüllen. Es ist die Tragödie jedes grossen Künstlers, jedes grossen Menschen.[61]

---

[61] "The parallel between Heiling and the Holländer is humorous at best. 'The black doublet, the pale visage,' that's all. Does one need to mention that both tenors are huntsmen, and that, in one case, the mother, and in the other, the father would like to acquire a rich son-in-law? To the extent that the two plots and characters can be compared at all, it would be easier to find contrasts between them. Heiling wants to live, the Holländer to die. Anna wants to enjoy life without Heiling, whereas Senta wants to die for, and with, the Dutchman. The latter is redeemed and satisfied, but Heiling is not. — Heiling and Lohengrin, on the other hand, are one and the same tragedy — that of a superior being who, being profoundly alone, longs for a union, for security in human love, and who agonizingly discovers that this is impossible for him to achieve. He must perform the duties, imposed on him by an inexorable law of nature, all by himself and in total isolation. And just as Lohengrin, sadly and with lowered head, returns to the Holy Grail in order to dispense, from there, unreciprocated love and blessing, so Heiling, resigned to his fate and with a bleeding heart, returns to the dark spirit realm as its ruler and in order to fulfill the 'eternal law.' This is the tragedy of every great man and artist"; Pfitzner, "Zur Grundfrage der Operndichtung," p. 30.

This was said by one of the last Romantics — such, at any rate, was Thomas Mann's justification for including a chapter on Pfitzner in his polemical *Betrachtungen eines Unpolitischen* (1919) — a man and artist who knew exactly what he was talking about; for as he penned these lines, Pfitzner was mulling over *Palestrina*, an opera in which the problematic of the artist (in this case an important historical figure and, not incidentally, a composer) is thematized, and whose protagonist, following in Heiling's footsteps, ends up by plucking melancholy's finest flower, resignation. (The line of descent could easily be extended to Paul Hindemith's "Künstleroper" *Mathis der Maler* [1935], with which I have dealt in a paper recently delivered at a conference in Houston and soon to be published in the proceedings.)[62] And this is where my story, having taken the form of an analysis of *Hans Heiling* in the larger context of German Romantic opera, ends.

---

[62] "Die letzte Häutung: Two German 'Künstleropern' of the Twentieth Century: Hans Pfitzner's *Palestrina* and Paul Hindemith's *Mathis der Maler*." The proceedings will be published by Fink in Munich.

Vermischte Gedichte

Nikolaus Lenau's "The Bust of Beethoven"[*]

ALBRECHT RIETHMÜLLER

AN ODE WRITTEN ON the occasion of a victory by an aulos virtuoso in ancient Greek competitions might well have attained the status of a world literary classic if Pindar had written it. A modern poem, though, that is not occasioned by the deeds of a musician, but which instead takes as its subject the musician himself, by name — as an artist and person — has a good chance of being insignificant as literature if not indeed a complete blunder. What is meant here is not those rhymes put together to honor anniversaries of the births and deaths of musicians, a tradition in which a certain segment of the musical world takes pleasure, providing that the enthusiasm for these musical heroes is such as to render admirable even the products of the sorriest versifiers. An anthology of poems does not become a work of art just because Johann Sebastian Bach figures in it. More noteworthy are the cases in which poets of rank chose to sing the praises of composers — productive artists like themselves. The question poses itself as to what motivated the poets in these cases, and why so few happy results were achieved. Poems about composers can, if expectations do not deceive, only rarely be the pride even of important authors; and most poets who have become prominent have not even made the attempt at all.

The figure of the first tribune of nineteenth-century music — Ludwig van Beethoven — found considerable literary attention from the beginning, especially in the prosaic form of belles-lettres.[1] In addition, authors of the first rank from Brentano through Grillparzer to Baudelaire — although they hardly dealt with or examined his works — all greatly admired Beethoven in verse,[2] while attention to him as a person as opposed to his music, seems to have declined somewhat among twentieth-century poets. It is

---

[*] English translation by Ellen Gerdeman-Klein and James M. McGlathery. For the German original, see Albrecht Riethmüller, *Gedichte über Musik* (Laaber bei Regensburg: Laaber Verlag) forthcoming.

[1] See Sieghard Brandenburg, "Künstlerroman und Biographie: Zur Entstehung des Beethoven-Mythos im 19. Jahrhundert," in *Beethoven und die Nachwelt: Materialien zur Wirkungsgeschichte Beethovens*, ed. Helmut Loos (Bonn: Beethoven Haus, 1986), pp. 65ff.; and Egon Voss, "Das Beethoven-Bild der Beethoven-Belletristik: Zu einigen Beethoven-Erzählungen des 19. Jahrhunderts," pp. 81ff.; as well as Brigitte Weselmann and H. Schröder, "Beethoven in der Belletristik: Eine Bestandsaufnahme," pp. 95ff. in the above-named anthology.

[2] Specifically "Nachklänge Beethovenscher Musik" by Clemens Brentano; "Beethoven" by Franz Grillparzer; and the poem "La Musique" by Charles Baudelaire from the *Fleurs du mal* which originally was entitled "Beethoven."

entirely uncertain how without some distancing Beethoven could have been portrayed after World War I in a poem that as a poem should have had any lasting poetic value. Wary contemporaries were suspicious of the Titan myth that was indissolubly associated with Beethoven, and only in the wake of the events of 1933 was it perhaps possible to relate this myth again. It seems — if one limits oneself to only the greatest composers of the German-speaking lands — that Bach overtakes Beethoven as the subject of poetry, as a source of poetic inspiration. The same can be seen in the visual arts, to the extent that portrayals of Bach or Beethoven occurred. This reversal of chronology should not come as a surprise: in the nineteenth century Bach and his music had to challenge Beethoven's for recognition, not the other way around. Moreover, the subjects for poems and edification — leaving aside the tributes on personal occasions — were influenced by trends of the times, by the models of compositions and composers available at the given time. The respective view of music — the respective reception of Beethoven or Bach — set the tone. The Titan of the nineteenth century, the strict constructivist of the twentieth: these themes suggest themselves, in representative and exemplary fashion, as models of thought, in any case more so than does using as a basis "just any" composer, however important for music or music history he may be. It is hard to imagine that an excellent poem could be written about Joseph Haydn and his compositional mastery, as a model for what a poet can find interesting about a composer or a piece of music, as can be done with Bach or Beethoven. (It would be certainly worth the attempt, if the poetic maxim is true that anything whatsoever can become the subject of a good poem.) But then it is just as hard to imagine that highly regarded contemporary composers can be exalted in poems of great merit. If not about the generation of Ligeti, Boulez, and Stockhausen, at least poems should have been written about Schönberg, Bartok, and Stravinsky — all by now more than a century old. Can the lack be explained simply by a general timidity about writing poems at all about individuals — just as in the art business one has refrained from erecting statues of famous contemporaries?

I

A full generation younger than Beethoven, Nikolaus Franz Niembsch, nobleman of Strehlenau — known as Nikolaus Lenau (1802–50) — was twenty-five when the composer died. His poem on Beethoven is not among his best-known works, but, considering the topic, it would be remarkable perhaps if it were. Would it be a mark of distinction — at least by today's standards — if a poem about Beethoven were Lenau's most notable poetic achievement? Nevertheless it is not easy to find a better poem devoted to Beethoven; it is perhaps — if one remains aware of the subjectivity of such an interpretation — the most beautiful of them all. It is in any case largely free of embarrassments. That alone distinguishes it from most of the others.

And this needs emphasizing all the more, seeing that Lenau is among the victims of the schoolbook versions of German literary history, which describe him as an unstable character who was no longer able to muster the discipline, orderliness, or strictness possessed by the classicists, but rather dreamed along in half-somnambulistic, half-depressive states as a last remnant of Romanticism, so to speak, never coming down to earth — whereby as everyone can see he maneuvered himself out to the perimeter of the circle of German literary masters. Literary historians must have an interest in lending sharper contours to this horizon filled with prejudice and distortion — reason enough for an outsider to be permitted, while not interfering or intruding, to investigate the poem by itself alone, without placing it in the context of Lenau's works:[3]

Beethovens Büste

[I] Traurig kehrt ich eines Abends
In mein einsam düstres Zimmer,
Überraschend drin entgegen
Blinkte mir ein Freudenschimmer.

[II] Mit dem sichern Blick der Liebe
Hatt ein Freund den Spalt getroffen,
Wo des Unmuts düstre Zelle
Blieb dem Strahl der Freude offen.

[III] Ha! ich fand des Mannes Büste,
Den ich höchst als Meister ehre
Nebst dem schroffen Urgebirge
Und dem grenzenlosen Meere.

[IV] Ein Gewitter in den Alpen,
Stürme auf dem Ozeane
Und das große Herz Beethovens,
Laut im heiligen Orkane,

[V] Sind die Wecker mir des Mutes,
Der das Schicksal wagt zu fodern,
Der den letzten Baum des Edens
Lächelnd sieht zu Asche lodern.

---

[3] Nikolaus Lenau, *Sämtliche Werke und Briefe*, ed. Eduard Castle (Leipzig: Insel, 1910), 1:413–15.

[VI] Kämpfen lern ich ohne Hassen,
Glühend lieben und entsagen,
Und des Todes Wonneschauer,
Wenn Beethovens Lieder klagen;

[VII] Wenn sie jubeln, Leben schmetternd,
Daß die tiefsten Gräber klüften
Und ein dionysisch Taumeln
Rauschet über allen Grüften.

[VIII] Wenn sie zürnen, hör ich rasseln
Menschenwillens heilge Speere,
Und besiegt zum Abgrund, heulend,
Flüchten die Dämonenheere. —

[IX] Sanftes Wogen, holdes Rieseln;
Sind des Weltmeers kühle Wellen
Süß beseelt zu Liebesstimmen?
Wie sie steigen, sinken, schwellen!

[X] Auf der glatten Muscheldiele
Halten Nixen ihren Reigen,
Keime künftger Nachtigallen
Träumen auf Korallenzweigen.

[XI] Horch! noch leiser! dem Naturgeist
Abgelauschte Lieder sind es,
Die er flüstert in das erste
Träumen eines schönen Kindes;

[XII] Die er spielt auf Mondstrahlsaiten,
Ob dem Abgrund ausgespannten,
Deren Rhythmen in der Erdnacht
Starren zu Kristallenkanten;

[XIII] Und nach deren Zaubertakten
Rose läßt die Knospe springen,
Kranich aus des Herbstes Wehmut
Lüftet seine Wanderschwingen. —

[XIV] Ach, Koriolan! vorüber
Ist das Ringen, wilde Pochen,
Plötzlich sinds die letzten Töne,
Dumpf verhallend und gebrochen.

[XV] Wie der Held im schönen Frevel
Überstürmte alle Schranken,
Dann — der tragisch überwundne
Stehn geblieben in Gedanken.

[XVI] Sinnend starrt er in den Boden,
Sein Verhängnis will Genüge;
Fallen muß er, stummes Leiden
Zuckt um seine edlen Züge. —

[XVII] Horch! im Zwiespalt dieser Töne
Klingt der Zeiten Wetterscheide,
Jetzo rauschen sie Versöhnung
Nach der Menschheit Kampf und Leide.

[XVIII] In der Symphonien Rauschen,
Heiligen Gewittergüssen,
Seh ich Zeus auf Wolken nahn
und Christi blutge Stirne küssen;

[XIX] Hört das Herz die große Liebe
Alles in die Arme schließen,
Mit der alten Welt die neue
In die ewige zerfließen.

([I] Sadly I returned one evening to my lonely, gloomy room, and was met by a surprising glimmer of joy.
[II] With love's sure gaze, a friend had found the crevice through which ill humor's gloomy cell remained open to joy's ray.
[III] Ah! I found a bust, of him whom I honor above all others, together with the jagged ancient mountains and the endless sea.
[IV] A blizzard in the Alps, a storm upon the seas, and the great heart of Beethoven, sound in the holy hurricane,
[V] Are the wakers of my courage, which dares to challenge fate, which smilingly watches the last tree of Eden burn blazingly to ash.
[VI] I learn to struggle without hate, to love glowingly, and renounce, and about death's ecstatic thrill, when Beethoven's songs mournfully resound;
[VII] When they rejoice, blaring with life, so that the deepest graves are torn open, and a Dionysian rapture sounds above all the tombs.
[VIII] When they anger, I hear rattling the holy spears of human will, and the howling army of demons fleeing conquered into the abyss.
[IX] Gentle billowing, lovely rippling; are the cool waves of the world's oceans sweetly inspired to words of love? How they soar, sink, swell!

[X] On the smooth bank of shells, nixies perform their round-dance, seeds of nightingales dreaming on twigs of coral.

[XI] Shhh! Still softer! Hear the songs picked up from nature's spirit, which it whispers in the first dreams of a beautiful child;

[XII] Which it plays on strings of moon beams, stretched across the abyss, and whose rhythms in the earth's night, become frozen edges of crystal;

[XIII] And after hearing whose magic measure, the rose lets its bud spring open, the crane awakening from autumn's melancholy spreads its migratory pinions. —

[XIV] O Coriolanus! The struggle, frenzied drumming is over, suddenly only the last tones echo empty and broken.

[XV] How the hero in his beautiful crime stormed across all barriers, then tragically defeated, stood lost in contemplation.

[XVI] Thoughtfully he stares at the ground, his destiny demands fulfillment; fall he must, silent suffering quivering around his noble features. —

[XVII] Listen! in the discord of these tones sounds the weather divide of the times, now they murmur reconciliation after mankind's struggle and suffering.

[XVIII] In the symphonies' thunder, sacred downpours, I see Zeus approach on clouds and kiss Christ's bloody forehead.

[XIX] The heart hears a great love enclose everything in its embrace, the new world flows together with the old into an eternal one.)

All of Lenau's main qualities as a poet are combined here: the energy and the elegance, the movement, the richness of sound and color, in short — the musicality of the language. These qualities are summoned up to produce an image of Beethoven on the occasion of seeing a bust of him. It is obvious, however, that Lenau is aiming not at a likeness or a copy of Beethoven or simply the person portrayed, but on this occasion rather at the phenomenon Beethoven itself. One should not be misled by the fact that busts and heads of the composer were part of the cherished stock of parlors both in Germany and abroad in the late nineteenth century, and in a massive way still are even today. In earlier times one surrounded oneself at home with the heads that the youth today carry around with them in a somewhat different form but nevertheless related function, namely on T-shirts. Lenau perceives Beethoven, to begin with, as a piece of statuarial inventory. It is immediately apparent, however, that at a time when Beethoven's greatness was publicly celebrated with monuments, Lenau chooses the intimate framework of a room, rather in opposition to the monumental. Just as little is said about the size of Beethoven's bust as about the size of the room. It makes little difference whether Lenau had a particular bust of Beethoven in mind — and which one exactly — or whether he even had one at all in front of him or whether he invented the prop himself — from memory or a portrait perhaps. The differences in the likenesses of Beethoven that have survived may indeed be substantial, particularly the differences in the faithfulness of the representations and the quality of the reproductions (for example in the form of busts and engravings),[4] but it is questionable whether the differing interpretations that Beethoven's face thereby received and which are iconographically decipherable had any effect on Lenau's poem. More than in the Beethoven illustrations by visual artists who were often interested primarily in portraiture, Lenau aimed at representing Beethoven's music through and beyond his facial features. Therefore the following discussion can with good conscience ignore the face, which functions here as a mediator between Lenau's language and Beethoven's music, especially because we do not know exactly which model he used and no particular likeness of Beethoven can be determined with certainty from the poem itself: the little that Lenau decidedly expressed about the appearance — in stanzas XV and XVI — can refer to different familiar portrayals of the older Beethoven.

For the poet, busts, which often depict more prominent persons than portraits on the wall, are an attractive prop, even if they are not always used as effectively as by Edgar Allan Poe, who in "The Raven" (1844) describes the melancholy produced by the loss of the beautiful beloved, and has the black bird that flutters into the room find its perch on Athena's white marble head:

> Open here I flung the shutter, when, with many a flirt and flutter,
> In there stepped a stately Raven of the saintly days of yore;
> Not the least obeisance made he; not a minute stopped or stayed he;
> But, with mien of lord or lady, perched above my chamber door —
> Perched upon a bust of Pallas just above my chamber door —
> Perched, and sat, and nothing more.[5]

Although in Lenau's poem the narrator himself enters his (own) room, whereas in Poe's it is the raven who demands admittance, the introductory situation is the same in both — namely the confined space of a room with a bust, the loneliness, the mourning. In what follows, to be sure, the bird on Pallas Athena's head brings bad tidings, whereas in Lenau's poem, the

---

[4] Howard Chandler Robbins Landon, *Beethoven: Sein Leben und Werk in zeitgenössischen Bildern und Texten* (Zurich: "Universal Edition," 1970), illus. on p. 155. This work calls the Beethoven bust and its copies by the sculptor Anton Dietrich (from 1821) "recht genau," but the bronze bust by Franz Klein taken from the death-mask of 1812 "das vielleicht getreueste Abbild von Beethovens Antlitz" (illus. p. 145).

[5] Edgar Allan Poe, *Werke*, trans. Arno Schmidt and Hans Wollschläger, 4 vols. (Olten and Freiburg im Breisgau: Walter, 1966), 4:138. In his *Philosophy of Composition* (1846) in which he reflects about artistic creativity using as his example the creation and poetics of "The Raven," Poe himself spoke of the contrast between the marble and the feathers (p. 544).

Beethoven bust introduced into the room becomes on the contrary a sign of joy and perhaps hope, in so far as its presence gives rise to a wide-ranging panorama that refers to Beethoven all right, but that at the same time reaches far beyond him and addresses the poet's own concerns. Lenau's theme is thus not Beethoven or his music in themselves, but Beethoven in his interaction with the narrator of the poem.

Despite its length, the poem is constructed with very regular meter. The trochaic tetrameter is strictly maintained and arranged in nineteen four-line stanzas in which every second line rhymes with the fourth. This unvaried and monotonous framework necessitates some effort in choosing the words, the relationship between the words, and the stream of thought in order to produce the multifarious and flowing quality which doubtless most distinguishes this finely crafted and well-ordered poem. The exposition — or more exactly, introduction — in the first two stanzas is relatively clear: a dark room by night; a mood depressed by mourning, loneliness, and darkness, without the reasons being given; a return about which it is not said from where and after how long a time. A surprise brightens the darkness and casts a beam of light, at least a glimmer ("Schimmer") of happiness upon the scene. The object of interest and, at the same time, the first dramatic moment — Beethoven's bust — has not been placed in the room by the returning traveler himself, but rather by a third party, a "friend," about whom we learn nothing further. On the one hand, this motivates the surprise; on the other, it introduces a contrast, in so far as the setting up of the bust occurred out of "love," that is, out of a feeling about which we do not know whether the "I" in the poem (at the moment) is fit for or capable of it. Already in the first stanza, with this positive "glimmer of happiness," a key word is provided which will then achieve decisive importance in the poem.

Once the returning traveler's first glance has fallen on the bust, Lenau changes at the beginning of the next stanza (III) from the past into the present tense and steadfastly maintains it throughout the rest of the poem. Stanzas III and IV deal with three (one may add, unattainable) models of man's melancholy (unlikely, that its object is a woman): Beethoven himself, the mountains, and the sea, which are associated with Beethoven. Next to the artistic master steps nature as instructor. Moreover, in the comparison with the finite ancient, primitive mountains ("Urgebirge") and the infinite sea, Beethoven becomes mingled with the elements earth and water, no longer remaining a model for art, but rather becoming so to speak "naturalized" and thereby acquiring the status of an element. The elements awaken and enter into actions inherent in them. To the mountains, specifically the Alps, belongs the thunderous storm; to the sea, specifically the ocean, belongs the raging tempest. With this, air is added as a further element, and in a daring turn of phrase is applied to Beethoven the man, to his heart, which is seen as a "sound in the holy hurricane" ("Laut im heiligen Orkane"). It is noteworthy that the first closer identification of Beethoven made in the poem is not with anything outwardly visible. Although the obligatory capitalization at the beginning of the line could also permit a reading as the adverbial form of the word "laut" (loud), in contrast to "leise" (soft), the possibility can be rejected as foolish: the sound of Beethoven's heart would then have to be greater in volume than that of the holy hurricane. But also, the noun "Laut" as a sound or tone is only understandable in an unspoken, traditional context rooted in animism: the heart as the locus of the soul, which combined with a stream of air, expresses itself through the voice as sound. Speech and that music produced by the human voice are not yet distinguished here, but the first close identification made of Beethoven in Lenau's poem — after his general introduction as "Meister" — is with an acoustical area, with an elementary acoustical phenomenon.

II

Insofar as mountains, the sea, and Beethoven are "Wecker des Mutes" (wakers of courage), as is said at the beginning of stanza V, a new level is added to the "I" in the poem. If the "I" surrenders itself to these forces it becomes more courageous and gains the self-confidence to challenge fate, to stand on its own two feet; without simply longing to return to the sheltered, fateless original state of the Garden of Eden, it can nevertheless assume a positive stance toward the lost paradise. Insofar as courage smilingly watches as paradise is blazingly reduced to ash ("lächelnd sieht zu Asche lodern"), the last and final element, fire, is brought into play. With the emergence of courage, the introductory motif "Freudenschimmer" (glimmer of joy) is continued, but through this budding courage Lenau makes the preceding image of depressive infirmity that much more telling. The mountains, sea, and Beethoven work as antidotes to melancholia. And then — in stanza VI — the didactic result of awakened courage is presented: struggle, love, renunciation, death. Yet this balance sheet of acquired human traits, for which Beethoven's songs are named as the source, do not appear in a wholly positive light. Death's thrills of delight ("Wonneschauer") stand even more in an ambiguous light than does renunciation ("Entsagung"). Beethoven the therapist sets free fantasy worlds that one can less properly than properly call highly romantic.

Let us right from the start answer negatively the question as to how pertinent it would be to examine Beethoven's piano songs and arias as to whether the characteristics cited by Lenau could be connected with the one or the other piece. Let us also consider that it may be a poetic practice (and would also be appropriate in the case of Beethoven) for "Lied" to be a synonym for "Melodie" and be applied possibly also to instrumental works, in any case not necessarily only to one particular genre or form of vocal music, just as well as in the opposite case "Lied" can be a title or designation of a poem that has no musical accompaniment. Getting ahead of the argument, let it be noted as well that the characteristics cited here by Lenau

— like many that follow later in the poem — approximate those elements that, without reference to Lenau's poem, Hans H. Eggebrecht puts forth in his journey through the forest of Beethoven's reception as remaining constant over time.[6] Eggebrecht places in center stage the "Leidensnotwendigkeit" (necessity of suffering), in so far as in view of Beethoven's suffering it is judged as having been necessary for producing art and at the same time art is perceived as the condition for overcoming suffering (his deafness, his fate) through joy, and with an eye toward "freedom" and "utopia." Around this central theme he then gathers further constants of Beethoven's reception derived either from his person or his music, such as "Erlebensmusik" (music of experience), "Wollen" (will), "Ethos" and "Transzendierung" (ethos and transcendence), "Säkularisation" (secularization), "Autorität" (authority), "Inbegriff" (essence), and "Zeitlosigkeit" (timelessness), which can be and have been appropriated by every possible ideology — mostly positively, sometimes negatively. In Lenau's poem, it is not only astounding how many of these constants are present, but also how early they are gathered together here.

The aforementioned characteristics are not those of the songs themselves, but rather qualities of which the "I" of the poem is made capable of perceiving ("lern ich"). Beethoven's songs of mourning ("Klagelieder") that Lenau first introduces are seen from the perspective of their effect, not what they are. Only with the subsequently mentioned songs of jubilation ("Jubellieder") are specific attributes given. To be sure, one must note here that in connection with the strong contrast of content intended between the last line of stanza VI and the following line (with the parallel conditional form "wenn ..."), the entire stanza VII consists only of one incomplete sentence; the missing main clause must be added — if at all — from stanza VI. On the other hand, Lenau's highly developed art of transitions and connections enables the poem to flow smoothly. With the "Jubellieder," unlike the "Klagelieder" before, a therapeutic-pedagogical process is no longer set in motion, but instead the immediate exercise of the power of Beethoven's music is described. It is no longer an analogue of nature and elemental like the phenomenon Beethoven himself, no longer human like the "Klagelieder," but simply superhuman: the rising of the dead in dionysian rapture ("dionysischem Taumel"). Beethoven, or the force of his "(Jubel)-Lieder," transcends even the natural order. The aura of divinity begins to shine forth.

The possibility that Lenau acquired this notion through his feeling about Beethoven's music cannot be excluded. But the creator behind the idea can be found, in the first instance, to be Friedrich Schiller, in whose 1786 poem "An die Freude" (Ode to Joy) we find the same meter as in Lenau's and

---

[6] See Hans Heinrich Eggebrecht, *Zur Geschichte der Beethoven-Rezeption: Beethoven 1970*, Akademie der Wissenschaft und der Literatur, Mainz: Abhandlungen der geistes- und sozialwissenschaftlichen Klasse, 1972, no. 3 (Wiesbaden: F. Steiner, 1972).

where Lenau's images "Gräber klüften" and "Über allen Grüften" have the following formulation:

> Auf des Glaubens Sonnenberge
>   Sieht man ihre [sc. der Wahrheit] Fahnen wehn
> Durch den Riß gesprengter Särge
>   Sie im Chor der Engel stehn.

> (On faith's sunlit mountain
>   We see truth's flags waving
> Through the cracks in ruptured coffins
>   We see truth in the angel chorus.)

And the "dionysisch Taumeln" Lenau finds in Beethoven's "Jubellieder" has its counterpart in Schiller's bacchantic apotheosis of joy:

> Freude sprudelt in Pokalen;
>   In der Traube goldnem Blut
> Trinken Sanftmut Kannibalen,
>   Die Verzweiflung Heldenmut —
> Brüder, fliegt von euren Sitzen,
>   Wenn der volle Römer kreist,
> Laßt den Schaum zum Himmel spritzen:
>   Dieses Glas dem guten Geist!

> (Joy bubbles in the goblets;
>   In the grape's golden blood
> Cannibals imbibe gentleness,
>   Despair drinks in heroic courage —
> Brothers, leap from your seats,
>   When the full goblet makes the rounds,
> Let the foam splash up to heaven:
>   This glass for the good spirit!)

Beethoven passed over this particular part of Schiller's poem in his setting of the Finale of the Ninth Symphony (1826), although decades before in Bonn he had had the intention of setting the entire poem to music.[7] That feat has in the meantime been attempted by dozens of other Lieder composers with more, or (usually) less success — which probably displeased Schiller in his later years, since the popularity that this poem in particular gained caused him to value it less, perhaps out of justifiable self-criticism or

---

[7] Regarding the relationship of Beethoven to Schiller see the essay, "Beethoven and Schiller," in Maynard Solomon, *Beethoven Essays* (Cambridge, Mass.: Harvard Univ. Press, 1988), pp. 205–15.

possibly in a mood of coquetry. (The particular success of a certain work can be a double-edged sword for authors, who may not be bothered by the success itself, but may find unjust reverence given to a single one of their works at the expense of others.) Can we thus assume that Lenau appropriated certain of Schiller's words in order to characterize Beethoven's songs? For a poet it is definitely easier and safer to paraphrase the words and tropes of another poet than to have to capture with words the tones and sounds of a composer. In the case of topoi that have become standard in Beethoven criticism this is a stumbling-block insofar as the claim to authorship becomes precarious: in the last analysis Schiller cannot be fit into Beethovenian criticism, and the deepest essence of Beethoven can hardly be expressed with words Schiller had already written when the young Beethoven was composing his first works, and his image was still not yet that which was soon to become fixed in men's minds for two centuries as "Beethoven" — an image based indeed on works that in his Bonn period it could not have been foreseen that he would ever compose. But it is equally true that since the late Ninth Symphony, the words of Schiller's poem have blended together with the prevailing concept of Beethoven in a remarkable way, whereby a momentous *petitio principii* is involved — probably rather subconscious than tacitly assumed — namely that Beethoven did not set Schiller's ode or hymn but rather identified himself with it.

In the case of Lenau's poem both the more famous parts of the ode which were actually set by Beethoven (with the since well-worn phrases "Alle Menschen werden Brüder" and "Seid umschlungen, Millionen!") play a role — which we will examine more closely — as well as parts (like the dionysian giddiness in stanza VII) which Beethoven chose finally not to use in his Ninth Symphony. Besides, Beethoven did not need Schiller's words at the end of the finale: he was able to express in the music the overflow of joy raised to the level of intoxication without help from the text. He was able to make the bacchanal believable simply through the tones themselves, whereas it is understandable that Schiller later perhaps was no longer so happy about the hard-drinking revelers leaping up from their seats. It was Friedrich Nietzsche with his unshakable faith in the power of absolute music who, in looking back on Schiller's noble, stirring, and lofty ("edle," "schwungvolle," "erhabene") verses, perceived that passage as the only flaw in Beethoven's finale, a flaw one must literally fail to hear[8] while others, among them Richard Wagner, on the contrary, praised the inclusion of the words in the symphony. With reference to the fact that the poetry of the late eighteenth and first half of the nineteenth centuries is full of expressions of this type, the argument for a link between Lenau and Schiller could be refuted as arbitrary or contrived. Yet insofar as we are dealing with a poem

---

[8] See the well-known fragment known as " Über Musik und Wort" in Friedrich Nietzsche, *Sämtliche Werke*, ed. Giorgio Colli and Mazzino Montinari, 15 vols. (Berlin: de Gruyter, 1967–77), 7:366f.

about Beethoven by Lenau and a text by Schiller used by Beethoven for his Ninth Symphony, it is hard to believe that the parallels are mere coincidence: it is simply too obvious that someone who wanted to write about a bust of Beethoven would take a look at Schiller's poem, that he would remember Schiller's verses in order to describe Beethoven's songs. In literary portrayals, especially in poems, it can be taken for granted that just as much attention, at least, will be paid to the figure of Beethoven, his suffering and death, as to his music itself.

After Beethoven's songs of sorrow and jubilation, a third type is touched upon in mention of the stormy ones in stanza VIII, which again leads us back to the man, particularly to his striving. Unlike earlier, battle is no longer being learned, but instead is carried to victory out of anger (not hate), which touches on a further topos — and a particularly obstinate one — among those applied to Beethoven and his music, a topos applied especially to the Fifth Symphony and which is the most famous topos of all. It is indeed hard to imagine that it could be applied to other composers such as Haydn or Mozart. The armies of demons ("Dämonenheere") that are, through man's will, put howlingly to flight — in a kind of secular exorcism — again permit a connection with the end of "An die Freude": "Festen Mut in schwerem Leiden / ... Untergang der Lügenbrut!" (Steady courage amidst hard suffering / ... Death to the pack of liars!)

III

It is no longer these tones but completely different ones that play the key role in the middle part of the poem (stanzas IX–XIII). According to strict symmetry, stanza X would have to be considered the mid-point of the nineteen stanzas, but such a mechanical division is not recognizable here. Beethoven's songs no longer mourn, rejoice, and rage, they are no longer loud, but are — in abrupt contrast — now soft, gentle, and magical. If one will, the songs now sound feminine rather than masculine. Our attention is drawn from the conflagration of worlds ("Weltenbrand") to the world sea ("Weltmeer"). Lenau entices us, or rather Beethoven's songs entice Lenau's poetic narrator, into a fantastic world, a world of nature, that nevertheless like every magical land has something artificial about it. Again Lenau proceeds animistically. Of course, one could be reminded here of the union of love and cosmos in Schiller's poem, or just as well the finale of the Ninth Symphony, but more striking here than the historical prologue is an historical epilogue which stanza IX found in the so-called "Liebestod" at the end of Richard Wagner's *Tristan und Isolde* (1859):

Sanftes Wogen,   Heller schallend,
holdes Rieseln;   mich umwallend,
Sind des Weltmeers   sind es Wellen
kühle Wellen   sanfter Lüfte?

Süß beseelt	Sind es Wogen
zu Liebesstimmen?	wonniger Düfte?
Wie sie steigen,	Wie sie schwellen,
sinken, schwellen!	mich umrauschen,
	soll ich atmen,
(Lenau, stanza IX)	soll ich lauschen?
	…
	In dem wogenden Schwall,
	in dem tönenden Schall,
	in des Weltatems
	webendem All, —
	(R. Wagner, *Tristan und Isolde*)

If one halves the four stresses of Lenau's trochaic lines into two stresses (as above) and compares the still present thought from stanza VI "des Todes Wonneschauer" (of death's delightful thrill) to the two famous lines of the dying Isolde, "unbewußt, — / höchste Lust," (unconscious, — / highest pleasure), then the similarity, including the use of the interrogative (this is Lenau's only formulation of a question in the poem), is even more striking. Assuming that other, even closer, inter-dependencies do not exist as "tertium comparationis,"[9] then we can see in Lenau's Beethoven poem a source of inspiration for Isolde's "Liebestod." This is neither remarkable nor disturbing. Wagner did not hesitate to borrow inspiration precisely for those passages in which words and music were to express something important: the portrayal of the holiest in *Parsifal* — the "Glaubensthema" (theme of faith) and "Gralsmotiv" (motif of the holy grail), as the one immediately follows upon the other in the prelude — are drawn entirely from the supposedly also reviled Felix Mendelssohn, and it offers no cause for irritation that the holy grail, of all things, should be represented with music that is from a Jewish composer.[10] In both cases songs were expressly apostrophized, Beethoven's songs by Lenau, and by Isolde the dead beloved's melody that she imagines she hears: "Höre ich nur / diese Weise, / die so wunder- / voll und leise, / Wonne klagend, / alles sagend" (Do I alone hear / this melody, / that so wonder- / fully and softly, / lamenting bliss, / saying all).

The fantastic "Weltmeer" (world sea) that Lenau, so to speak, murmuringly pours out before us, is further enlivened by stanza X and peopled with fabled creatures (nixies) who perform their round-dance, whether by dancing or singing. Poetry intersects with nature mysticism. The liquid does not spray (as it does in Schiller's attempt to put joyous rapture into words),

---

[9] One could think of Clemens Brentano as a possibility.

[10] For more on this see Albrecht Riethmüller, "Aspekte des musikalisch Erhabenen im 19. Jahrhundert," *Archiv für Musikwissenschaft* 40 (1983): 46.

but rather illuminates the fairy-tale dream world of an underwater kingdom, whose symbolism, including the sexual metaphors, is too obvious to dwell upon. If the poem began in the past tense and changed at the sight of Beethoven's bust into the present, now for the first time the future ("künftge") comes into view. It appears as though the cosmic, damp land of magic is the locus of love, procreation, and birth (rather as though out of the spirit of music): this is what is referred to by the curious "seeds of nightingales dreaming on twigs of coral," and moreover also by Beethoven's whispering of songs into "the first dreams of a beautiful child" (stanza XI) — a variation on the breathing in of life that is as persuasive as it is affected, and at the same time an image of something becoming almost archetypically and unforgettably anchored deep within a young soul; on the other hand, at the beginning of the stanza ("Shh! still softer") Lenau especially retreats to an even softer pianissimo whereby he turns our gaze away from the underwater world.

Beethoven's songs appear in ever new figures of speech. As already in stanzas III and IV, Beethoven himself now becomes his music, his songs become so closely tied to nature that they are presented as music of nature. The phrase "songs picked up from nature's spirit" points, to be sure, in the first instance, to a poetic circumscription of the old topos *ars natura imitatur*, but puts a finer point on it in so far as it is implied that the songs become (like) nature itself. And the "strings of moon- beams" spanning the abyss (stanza XII) recognizably paraphrase the phenomenon of the aeolian harp, paradigm of a thoroughly natural music independent of man. In Lenau's poem, to be sure, in the person of Beethoven a player is at hand who entrusts his songs to this instrument. The aeolian harp thus serves also as Beethoven's lyre. Lenau makes use of the figure of the singer with his lyre in pale light, and considering the rarity of a formulation such as "Mond-strahlsaiten" (strings of moonbeams) is striking. We encounter the word "Sonnenstrahlsaiten" (strings of sunbeams), likewise in cosmic dimensions, in an extensive fragment of verse by the young Friedrich Nietzsche (1863) entitled "Beethovens Tod" (Beethoven's Death), in which the composer's ascension to heaven after death is described thusly:[11]

> Nicht seufzt die Welt, — sie tönt ein Lied
> Auf Sonnenstrahlensaiten,
> Indess der Rose Auge glüht
> und drüber die Wolken gleiten.
>   O du [Beethoven], des Sang der Erd' entquoll,
> Du ew'ger Himmelsfahrer,

---

[11] See Friedrich Nietzsche, *Gesammelte Werke*, ed. Fr. Würzbach (Munich: Musarion, 1894ff.), 20:54. The phrases "Und schaue dich mit lichten Schaaren" and "In weissen Kleidern aufwärts fahren" at the end of this fragment (ibid., p. 55) will be discussed later in this essay.

O du, des Sang zum Himmel schwoll
Nun tönst du reiner, klarer,
Du selbst ein Ton, der süss erklang,
Auf Erden bald verklungen.

(The world sighs not, — she sounds a song / On strings of sunbeams, / While glows the eye of the rose / and glide above it the clouds. / Oh you [Beethoven], the song flowed forth from the earth, / You eternal traveler to heaven, / Oh you, whose song welled up to heaven / Now you resound purer, clearer, / Yourself a tone that sweetly sounded, / On earth soon faded away.)

These gentle verses full of vivid, exquisite objects (among them, the "beautiful child") show Lenau to be most far removed from the cliches of Beethovenian reception. With the beginning of stanza XII, with the "strings of moonbeams," however, the gait of the poem again becomes harder, darker, and harsher. Following upon the spheres of the world sea and spirit of nature, it is now the sphere of earthly night that is associated with Beethoven's songs, in order that their rhythmic side can be imagined now in three different ways (stanzas XII and XIII). To express this, Lenau chooses three differing forms of movement that are separate from the up to now irregular flowings of water: namely first — so to speak ice-cold and in apparent paradox — statics as the absence of movement ("Rhythms ... frozen to edges of crystal"); it is hard to imagine a sharper contrast to the previous waves of the world's ocean that have come alive as voices of love. He then shifts to a form of motion, sudden change ("the rose lets its bud spring open"), followed by a periodic movement ("the crane ... spreads its migratory pinions"). With this side-glance at the elements of a theory of movement, the dream world that occupies the middle part of the poem fades away, or rather the magical worlds vanish that Lenau has created and employed in order to characterize Beethoven's melodies with words in whose earthly and cosmic net the references, in accord with the poetic imagination, are stretched as with that music instrument itself whose strings are supposed to be spread across the abyss. The leading theme remains the boundless effect of the music, proceeding from the positive effect of Beethoven on the poetic "I" and then broadened to its effect on nature, on the supernatural, on all creatures. Lenau wholly vindicates that myth about the singer, concerning whose "metamorphoses in this and that" ("Metamorphosen in dem und dem")[12] Rilke later radically maintained it does not matter whose name they carried — this also applies to Beethoven — since when anyone is singing it is once and for all Orpheus ("ein für alle Male / ists Orpheus, wenn es singt").

---

[12] In the *Sonette an Orpheus*, I, 5.

IV

With the last two images (the rose and the crane) a sudden change announces itself, a new beginning in the poem. If the previous stanzas were characterized rather by the themes of birth, youth, and the future, now in quick succession maturity, self-evident decline, and a reversal of awakened courage ("autumn's sorrow") are implied. Right at the beginning of the concluding part, which includes stanzas XIV to XIX, collapse and tragedy follow; indeed the end, in a nutshell, is already contained here, ("vorüber," is past). In the episode contained in the next three stanzas Lenau turns to the figure of Coriolanus. But which Coriolanus? Is it the historical figure, Shakespeare's Coriolanus, the dramatic persona created by Heinrich Joseph Collin, or Beethoven's overture based on Collin's figure? Is it permissible to equate Coriolanus with Beethoven? This would be a doubtful compliment to Beethoven. In part Lenau uses the Coriolanus legend as he had previously used Schiller's "An die Freude" in order to facilitate the discussion of music by availing himself of the inherited medium of poetry. The misdeed of the shady Roman aristocrat Coriolanus, who out of vain pride raised himself above his people — Lenau speaks of his "beautiful sacrilege" and expresses the excess with the verb "overwhelmed," the only preterit since the beginning of the poem — leads necessarily to death (in a skillful parity of the prepositions, "der tragisch Überwundne," the tragically conquered one). It is not a matter of someone who himself conquers something, but rather someone who, because of his misdeeds, must be conquered, that is, gotten rid of by killing him. Having fled from Rome to the Volsces and been chosen to lead their army, Coriolanus besieged Rome out of revenge because he had been voted out of office there. His wife and mother were able to mollify him and dissuade him from militarily vanquishing Rome with the Volsces. Thereby, however, he signed his own death warrant in that he was subsequently accused of treason by the Volsces and killed.

The Coriolanus episode can be associated with Beethoven in two different ways. First, the allusions to the external details of the person and the facial features (stanzas XV and XVI) remind us of the bust itself, on which no thought had been wasted since the third stanza. Secondly, the Coriolanus episode contains, heaped together, images that have proven to be dominant with regard to Beethoven, above all "suffering" and "conquering" along with expressions like "wrestling" and "frenzied drumming." There is some evidence against mirroring the images of Beethoven and Coriolanus in one another though. As a rule Beethoven was seen as a hero, and to be sure, he appeared in a double regard not always only as a glowing and noble hero, but for one thing also as a tragic hero in view of his very real hearing loss (and all that meant as a difficult fate for a composer), and for another thing as not very heroic in consideration of the thick-setness, indeed plebeianness of his person (including the gossip about his counting out the coffee beans for his housekeeper). Yet neither the motif of the sacrilege, even if described as "beautiful," nor that he must fall ("Fallen muß er") because of guilty involvement can be meaningfully associated with Beethoven. In what way is Beethoven supposed to have committed a sacrilege, whereby is he supposed to have burdened himself with guilt?

The necessary ambiguity of poetry allows us to associate the "hero" (stanza XV) with the *Sinfonia eroica* or to relate the "hero" to Beethoven's "Coriolan Overture." The first possibility leads nowhere because the thought of a (tragic) hero builds too weak a bridge; with the latter possibility the question remains if and to what extent Lenau had the overture in mind, which early on belonged to the best-known among Beethoven's "serious" works,[13] and if Lenau was able to, or wanted to, describe it. This question cannot be answered with certainty. But the "last tones" in stanza XIV may point especially to the conclusion of the overture just as may, too, the reference to a silent anguish convulsing the noble features in stanza XVI. Granted, the words that Lenau uses are too distinct to have been picked up from the music itself; "der tragisch Überwundne / stehn geblieben in Gedanken" (the one who has been tragically defeated / stands lost in contemplation) says more than any musical passage in the overture is capable of saying or actually says, and allows us to think sooner of a poetic deliberation, a pause on Coriolanus's part before he decides his own destiny, before he seals his fate. At the same time, Lenau's words must be seen in the context of the nineteenth century practice of writing about music, particularly in poetry, namely that overtures particularly suited to the purpose were described, in greater or lesser detail, in the same manner as program music. Still today in modern concert guides, one reads such sentences about the "Coriolan Overture" as "Der Held zerbricht an der Vermessenheit seines frevelhaften Wollens. Sein stolzes Thema erlischt todesmatt in den tiefen Streichern" (The hero comes to grief because of the presumptuousness of his sacrilegious striving. His proud theme dies out, mortally exhausted in the low strings)[14] — sentences that belong more properly in a drama guide. An explanation which hopes to do justice to the music would have to suppress as much as possible all that is inaccessible to the music (all the motivating elements) and base itself on that which the music is able to portray (thus neither the sacrilege nor presumption), as Adolf Bernhard Marx did not fail to notice when he tried to explain the Overture in terms of a "Grundelement" (basic element) which he found to

---

[13] See Adolf Bernhard Marx, *Ludwig van Beethoven: Leben und Schaffen*, 2 vols. (1859; Leipzig: A. Schümann, 1902), 2:51.

[14] Hans Renner, *Reclams Konzertführer: Orchestermusik*, 5th ed. (Stuttgart: Reclam, 1961), p. 189.

be "Zorn" (rage).[15] To expect or indeed to ask this of Lenau would be both presumptuous and a senseless anachronism. He needs a transition for the poem; if he is to prepare for the ending, he needs a fermata: with the convulsions of a silent agony he expresses yet another, further form of movement. The convulsiveness means at the same time a perishing; in so far as a "stummes Leiden" (silent anguish) is evident in it, it is also announced that Beethoven's songs, which have sounded, so to speak, throughout most of the poem, now die out, as is prepared for already by the words "last tones" in stanza XIV. This ending is served by the Coriolanus episode of stanzas XIV to XVI, without this coordination being to be carried to the extreme, indeed neither with reference to the musical text of the overture nor to the association of Coriolanus with Beethoven. Associating these two is a bold move, and this is perhaps a weaker passage in the poem. Be that as it may, Lenau expressly deals only with Coriolanus's death and not with Beethoven's, which Nietzsche then took as the subject of his above-mentioned poem on Beethoven.

V

The coda of Lenau's poem, consisting of stanzas XVII to XIX, is characterized by broadening, generalizing, and heightening. The "Horch!" (Listen!) at the beginning of stanza XI that creates a caesura in the middle part, is used here as an introduction in order to focus attention on the poem's decisive statements that follow. Lenau returns neither to the elevatedness of the poem's beginning nor to the phantasmagoria of the magical world in the middle. The reference is now in the first instance still to the person of Coriolanus in the phrase "Zwiespalt dieser Töne" (discord of these tones). Reconciliation and salvation do not proceed from individuals or mankind, but rather are transferred to the postmortal sphere. Even Beethoven's music, too, is rendered heroic not with regard to this life but rather to the beyond. Throughout the entire poem we can sense a tendency to remove from reality the associations as they apply to Beethoven or to his music; and this is thoroughly within the framework of the romantic concept of music as a realm apart from the unfortunate if not indeed seemingly miserable reality of life. In order to describe this discord of tones more fittingly, Lenau introduces the scintillating phrase about the "Zeiten Wetterscheide" (the weather divide of the times) — once again (as in stanza IV) a meteorological image, this time taken from the topographical realm (the Alps as weather divide, for example) and applied to history. Whether "jetzo" (now) embraces both of the previous lines or marks a break does not really matter in the end. The reconciliation effected by Beethoven after struggle and suffering doubtlessly stands in the foreground of the topoi associated with the composer up to today. And in this context we can again call to mind the two

---

[15] Marx, 2:51.

choral verses from "An die Freude" which Beethoven likewise did not set to music:

> Unser Schuldbuch sei vernichtet!
> Ausgesöhnt die ganze Welt!
>
> (Let all our old scores be settled!
> Let the whole world be reconciled!)

Lenau leaves no doubt that the timbre of words in stanzas XVII and XIX is to be transferred into a time sphere "post festum," "post mortem." He employs more than a few dramatic means in order to stage the climax of the poem. In the timbre of the reconciliation he compares Beethoven's symphonies to "heiligen Gewittergüssen" (sacred downpours). One involuntarily thinks back to the "Laut im heiligen Orkane" (sound in the holy hurricane) with which Beethoven's heart was compared in stanza IV (in the same section where, in addition, a storm was mentioned in reference to the Alps), but at the same time one will not want to miss the intensified reminder of the realms of sea and water spread out before us earlier. Aside from the rather unspecific references to "Lieder" (songs), the only further definite music form named is the symphony, if indeed we do not interpret "symphony" here in the broader, more literal sense as accord or harmony, as was often the case in the poetic usage of the time. The acoustical groundwork is thereby laid for the vision ("Seh ich ...") that in accord with musical logic is supposed to produce the culmination at the point of the penultimate. Lenau summons up Zeus who kisses Christ's bloody forehead. Nowhere in the poem "Beethovens Büste" is it said that this vision of reconciliation of gods and religions is applied to Beethoven himself as at once God the father and the son of man, but it is obvious that Beethoven was later deified more and more and associated both with Zeus and with the crucified Son; therefore it is not contrary to the spirit of the poem to imagine it was this same deification of Beethoven that led Lenau to make of this kiss a gift to the whole world.

Already in the "Nachklängen Beethovenscher Musik" (Echoes of Beethoven's Music) by Clemens Brentano (from his middle period between 1803 and 1817) enthusiasm as a traditional model of artistic achievement was seized upon and appropriated for application to Beethoven, whereby the simile which he uses ("dem Gott gleich," like God), could just as easily be taken at face value as Lenau's image of Zeus kissing Christ:[16]

---

[16] See Clemens Brentano, *Werke*, ed. Wolfgang Frühwald, et al. (Darmstadt: Wissenschaftliche Buchgesellschaft, 1968), 1:309ff.; and John F. Fetzer, *Romantic Orpheus: Profiles of Clemens Brentano* (Berkeley, Los Angeles, and London: Univ. of California Press, 1974), pp. 251ff.

> Nein ohne Sinne, dem Gott gleich,
> Selbst sich nur wissend und dichtend
> Schafft er die Welt, die er selbst ist
>
> ...
>
> Keinem ward alles, denn jedes
> Hat einen Herrn, nur der Herr nicht;
> Einsam ist er und dient nicht,
> So auch der Sänger!

(No, without senses, the same as God / Knowing and writing only himself / He creates the world, that is himself ... / No one has everything, since everyone / Has a master, except for the Lord; / He is lonely and does not serve / Thus, too, the poet and singer!)

Brentano makes a virtue out of Beethoven's plight, insofar as he transforms (indeed, transfigures) his deafness ("ohne Sinne," without senses) — that is, a human defect — into a divine attribute, a kind of acoustical equivalent of the blind seer. The motive recurs again later: for Hans Pfitzner, the defender of absolute music, Beethoven had to be deaf in order to compose the "Szene am Bach" (Scene at the Brook) without programmatic intentions,[17] while on the contrary for those such as Richard Wagner who considered Beethoven's *Pastoral* Symphony an example of music imitating nature, he had to be able to hear. Even the fate of an artist, the misfortunes of his physiological disposition can be introduced as an argument in the dispute over correct aesthetic theory. In so far as Beethoven composed despite his deafness — serving for many people apparently as a reason for amazement, but unnecessarily so — and that he therefore suffered, yet at the same time overcame his suffering, the association with Christ easily suggests itself, to be sure, but not the juxtaposition of Christ and Zeus which — without Lenau's image of the kiss — was taken up and varied by Nietzsche at the end of his poem "Beethoven's Tod," in which the motif of lightning-hurling Zeus is brought together with the Ascension of Christ:[18]

> Du [Beethoven] winkst — und deinem Wink entquillt
> Rings dämmernde Gewitterschwüle;
> Du winkst — und Lüfte forschend mild
> Umwehen mich in leichtem Spiele;
> Du donnerst — und hernniederschlägt
> Der Blitz, — ich starre unbewegt
> Und schaue dich mit lichten Schaaren
> In weissen Kleidern aufwärts fahren,

---

[17] Therefore in Pfitzner's interpretation, the tone paintings that were indisputably present cannot be an imitation.

[18] *Gesammelte Werke*, Musarion edition, 20:55.

Und fühle, wie die Ewigkeiten
Vor mich sich endlos, zeitlos breiten.

(You beckon Beethoven — and from your beckoning
Humid thunderstorms spring forth all around;
You beckon — and gentle breezes searchingly
Waft about me in their nimble play;
You thunder — and downward strikes
The lightening bolt, — I stare motionless
And see you with your radiant hosts
Traveling upward in white raiment,
And feel how eternities
Spread themselves endlessly, timelessly before me.)

These concluding verses, especially because of the elevation of time to eternity, offer still greater cause to suspect that Nietzsche used Lenau's poem as at least one of his sources for his — by comparison — not very self-assured poetic fragment. And the monument that Max Klinger created for Beethoven at the turn of the century which was shown at the 1902 Beethoven exhibit of the Wiener Sezession along with Gustav Klimt's Beethoven-frieze[19] and already in its model form inspired Richard Dehmel's poem "Jesus und Psyche" — there Beethoven is greeted rather hollowly as a "neuer Zeus" (new Zeus)[20] — this monument was satirized with biting sarcasm by Ferruccio Busoni in 1919, who demonstrated a strong aversion to the received image of Beethoven together with its chauvinistic under-tones:[21] "Schade, daß er [Klinger] so in der Musik pantschte und nur das 'entdeckte,' wovon seine Zeit und sein Land ihn brav und gemächlich führten. Er hatte Aspirationen, die Ketten zu brechen — und rasselte so an ihnen herum — Beethoven-Zeus! mit präraphaelitischen Engelsköpfchen und Christi Passion hinter dem Rücken — welches confuse Resume von Allem, was Deutschland 1875–95 gravitätisch verehrte! Welche Schwere. Und eigentlich komisch dabei. — (Alle Achtung vor der ernsten Absicht und der

---

[19] See Marian Bizanz-Prakken, *Gustav Klimt: Der Beethovenfries* (Munich: Deutscher Taschenbuch Verlag, 1980), pp. 17ff.

[20] See ibid., p. 24. (Aside from Beethoven's monument, Klinger's *Gesamtkunstwerk* "Christus im Olymp" also played a role.) See also Martella Gutierrez-Denhoff, "Max Klingers 'Beethoven': Ausschnitte aus der Rezeptionsgeschichte," *Beethoven und die Nachwelt*, pp. 142ff.

[21] "It's a pity that he [Klinger] just muddled around in music and was led by his time and country to 'discover' only that with which his time led him comfortably and well-behavedly around. He had aspirations to break the chains and rattled them a bit — Beethoven-Zeus! With Pre-Raphaelite angels' heads and the Passion of Christ behind his back — what a confused summation of everything that was solemnly revered in Germany in the years 1875–95! What ponderousness. And actually comic at the same time. — [All due respect for the seriousness of purpose and artistic exertion.]"; Ferruccio Busoni, *Briefe an seine Frau*, ed. Friedrich Schnapp (Erlenbach, Zurich, and Leipzig: Rotapfel, 1935), pp. 368ff.

künstlerischen Anstrengung).” Busoni, the Berliner by choice, was one of
the first to notice and then publicly declare that the relationship of the
Germans with “their” Beethoven had taken on curious features. It should be
remarked, moreover, that on closer inspection often those who rose up
against the “Romantic image of Beethoven” after World War I did nothing to
soften these tendencies criticized by Busoni, but out of precipitous
chauvinism indeed rather strengthened them. Lenau himself, who cannot be
suspected of nationalistic exaggeration, stands at the beginning of a chain,
a beginning that we can charitably call still innocent.

Lenau’s figure of Zeus kissing Christ unquestionably has profound
historical and philosophical meaning. It serves to overcome the concept of
“Wetterscheide der Zeiten” (weather divide of the times) and to prepare the
two closing lines of the poem, in which the old and the new world are
supposed to be combined to form an eternal one. As familiar a theme as it
may have been for Lenau’s time — one that, to be sure, is only really
intimately understood in our time — to see America as the new and Europe
as the old world (he himself in 1832 made an unsuccessful attempt to find
happiness in America), it will be advantageous here not to become prisoners
of our own patterns of thought, by either understanding “the weather
divide” to pit the old, pre-Beethovenian music against the new Beethovenian
or looking to some other then current tendency to distinguish between an
old and new time or world, but rather to take seriously and literally the hint
here about Zeus and Christ. As can easily be seen from Kierkegaard to
Nietzsche, an eminent theme in those classicistic and early historicistical
times was not only the religious difference between antiquity and Christianity, not only the reconciliation of God and man through Christ’s death and
redemption, but most of all the cultural differences between antiquity and
Christianity that were felt and conceived then, even before entering the
stage around 1902 which, inspired by Klinger’s Beethoven monument, saw
people talking about a synthesis of Zeus and Christ, antiquity and Christianity, that supposedly became symbolized by Beethoven and brought the
expression “Drittes Reich” (Third Reich) into use, a term to be sure that was
itself ancient[22] yet soon proved to be a self-destructive beacon lighting the
way towards the world’s demise.

---

[22] See, with references, Bizanz-Prakken, p. 25. Somewhat later Rudolf
Kassner, *Die Moral der Musik: Aus den Briefen an einen Musiker* (Leipzig:
Insel, 1912), p. 49, ironically takes issue with this: “‘Wir aber wollen das
dritte Reich gründen, und dieses wird sowohl schön [wie das Heidentum]
als auch gut [wie das Christentum] und so das Allerbeste sein und aus
Heidentum und Christentum zu gleichen Teilen bestehen. Welcher Vorteil,
welche Summe! Zwei ist mehr als eins und drei mehr als zwei. Umarmen
wir uns nur schnell!’” (But we want to found the Third Reich, and it will
be both beautiful [like paganism] and good [like Christianity] and thus be
the best of all and consist of equal parts of paganism and Christianity. What
a benefit, what a combination! Two is more than one and three more than
two. Quickly, let’s embrace!” The happiness thus promised Kassner explains
as resulting from anxiety: “Und nichts soll fehlen, und stets haben sie Angst,
daß etwas fehle.” (And nothing is supposed to be lacking, yet they are
constantly afraid that something is lacking.)

Even if the old world alludes to Zeus and the new world to Christ, the eternal avoids one-sided fixation on either the present or the future world. It is possibly a matter of the old and new worlds being subsumed in a religion of art, in any case of transporting them to an everlasting, divine, all-encompassing world, and as well as that the form of time (of Chronos) that surrounds us and applies also to music is subsumed in that of timeless, eternal time (of Aion). The appropriate verb for this, the final word "zerfließen" (melt away), reminds us once again how much movement the entire poem contains and to what extent movement itself is a theme in the poem — a movement that here, unlike in music by necessity, is no longer organized temporally, but instead diffusedly dissolves in the flow of time. How much the two forms of time are mirrored in one other also emerges from the fact that Lenau allows that eternal world to arise from its opposite, the point in time of "Jetzt oder Itzt" (the present), insofar as the entire conclusion of the poem remains tied to the "jetzo" in stanza XVII.

VI

In the final vision, Lenau returns one last time in stanza XVIII to the "I" form ("seh ich ...") that has not appeared since stanza VIII ("hör ich rasseln ...") and yet always remains indirectly present, so to speak, in the dialogue with Beethoven, or rather his music, just as the bust or the appearance of Beethoven was secretly there without being the direct object of observation. In Josef Weinheber's "Vor der Maske Ludwig van Beethovens" for the cycle *Kammermusik* (Munich, 1939) such digressions are not observable, since for him the facial features as set in the death mask themselves provide the inspiration to illuminate the characteristics of the phenomenon Beethoven. Notably, he prefaces his poem with Schiller's four line stanza, "Seid umschlungen, Millionen! / Diesen Kuß der ganzen Welt! / Brüder, überm Sternenzelt / muß ein lieber Vater wohnen" as its motto. The poem itself runs counter to the motto. The mask, denoting Beethoven's death (and Weinheber is referring here no doubt to Joseph Danhauser's famous death mask), contrasts as much with Schiller's words as with Beethoven's music, and it seems as though Weinheber in the face of death was unable to arrive at a conciliatory ending:

> Denn alle Klag und Anklag dieser Welt
> steht hinter diesen Zügen auf und *bleibt.*
> Die eingedrückten Augendeckel schrein
> die Marter und die Qual der Kreatur,
> es weidet sich an ihrem wilden Schrei
> das Wilde in sich selbst, die Grausamkeit
> der breiten Nase. Jener große Mund,
> zerpreßt vom Urgewicht der Traurigkeit,
> vertritt im Tod, wie so im Leben nie,
> den Menschen in der Kelter — Wo ist Gott,
> wo ist da noch Musik ... ?

(For every lament and complaint of this world
rises up behind these features and *remains*.
The sunken eyelids cry out
the torment and torture of creation,
upon their wild cry
graze wildness itself, the ferocity
of the broad nose. That large mouth,
pressed together by grief's primeval weight,
represents in death, as never in life,
mankind in the wine-press — Where is God,
where is there music anymore ... ?)

The second half of this eminently dark poem, elevated with part expressionism, part primitivism ("das Wilde in sich selbst") and full of terror and pain,
cracks and despair, tolerates neither rejoicing nor redemption and reconciliation. In literally closing in on Beethoven's body it is all too clearly
borrowed from the speech patterns and stereotypical thought of its time —
thus the disposition to say "down with everything" as well as the pleasure
in decline — and yet it remains out of season in its pessimism, in its refusal
to shout Hurrah.

Where Weinheber's eyes remain firmly fixed on Beethoven's mask,
Lenau's gaze distances itself from the bust — in general with much less
helplessness and perplexity; and this is said indirectly in many ways in the
poem: about the bust itself, about Beethoven's music, and again indirectly
through reference to Schiller. Even in Lenau's phrase in the last stanza "Hört
das Herz die große Liebe / Alles in die Arme schließen," we are reminded
once again from afar of the "liebe Vater" and the "seid umschlungen" that
Weinheber took as motto and used as a direct quote 100 years later. Even
though he chooses different words, in a mysterious way Lenau does not free
himself from Schiller or get around him. And yet Lenau's poem stands quite
apart from Schiller's "An die Freude." Despite everything Lenau offers in the
course of the poem, the "Freudenschimmer" (glimmer of joy) produced by
the vision of Beethoven's bust through the partly opened door is not
expanded upon. Not by accident is there talk in stanza XVII about the
"Zwiespalt dieser Töne" (discord of these tones). Schiller portrays joy as
being so overpowering that its rejoicing reaches to the ends of the earth.
Contrary to this stormy apotheosis of joy which reaches far and wide is
Lenau's apotheosis of a "großen Liebe" turned inward, but it remains
uncertain whether the listening heart — the "I" of the poem affected by
Beethoven's music — thereby comes entirely to itself, whether the transformation of the initial grief via the fantastic way stations in the middle, into the
love at the end has more to do with reality than to be simply an imagining,
whether the much desired therapeutic effect really occurs. Beethoven or his
music, thus the quintessence of the poem, sets free inner worlds — no
more, no less. The web of association into which the poetic "I" wanders on
the occasion of thinking about Beethoven outweighs the intention of
drawing a portrait of Beethoven himself.

Lenau's heroization of Beethoven is thus unmistakable, just as it remains
recognizable that he strives for a very personal, almost private treatment

that, to be sure, relies in large measure on concepts then current, yet goes far beyond them. This applies for example to the highly romantic atmosphere of the magic garden in the middle of the poem, which depends on the underlying topos of the composer as magician that was common in early Beethovenian reception. All in all, we should take into consideration not only that about which Lenau speaks, but also that which he passes over. The horizon of the ethical and moral that appears highly illuminated precisely at the moments when Beethoven and Schiller are viewed together remains otherwise dim. Traces are present to the extent that the attempt is made to see the phenomenon Beethoven as bettering the individual, but this is again placed into doubt — at least through the Coriolanus episode. There is no trace of the ideals of a republican sentiment — on a broad scale this was, to be sure, only later credited to Beethoven. In the end it remains unclear whether or not 'Beethoven' offers the support that Lenau's poetic "I" promises itself at the beginning, and whether the heroization of Beethoven, admittedly against Lenau's poetic intent, does not actually proceed hand in hand with the dismantling of that heroic image. As in all heroizations, the model recedes from view. Yet for Lenau it does remain close.

Lenau emphatically demonstrates how much music — Beethoven's music — can do in us. Elements of envy, at the same time, are not present. Nothing leads us to conclude that the poet perceived elements of rivalry on the part of the musical composer, rivalry that time and again flared up briefly in the mistrust on the part of poets from Goethe to Rilke, mistrust produced not only by music's supposedly or actually greater power over the soul or spirit, but also by music's broad success, for which reason, if we are not mistaken, even a poet of Hugo von Hofmannsthal's stature allowed his fragile words to endure the strong tones of Richard Strauss. Despite and perhaps precisely because of the one or the other questionable light in which Beethoven appears, Lenau accepts him evidently without reservation as exemplary. He transports Beethoven to such a height as that later derided by Grillparzer in order not to be overpowered by the composer, when in an epigram Grillparzer makes fun of the "Beethovenmania," and in another dedicated "To the Beethoven Enthusiasts" he writes,

> Wie ihr hab' ich Beethoven hoch geehrt,
> Wobei jedoch als Unterschied sich anhängt,
> Daß, wo eure Bewunderung erst recht anfängt,
> Die meinige schon wieder aufhört.[23]

---

[23] Franz Grillparzer, *Gesammelte Werke*, ed. Edwin Rollett and August Sauer (Vienna: A. Schroll, 1923), 2:47. (For the reference to "Beethovomanie" see p. 46.) The poem "Beethoven" referred to in footnote 2 is in vol. I (Vienna: A. Schroll, 1925), pp. 123–237, and is the most detailed attempt by Grillparzer to celebrate Beethoven. Others include one of the formerly popular poems "on the occasion of" a music work (not necessarily about it): "Clara Wieck and Beethoven (F minor Sonata)" (ibid., p. 127).

(Like you I greatly respected Beethoven, / Whereby however the difference is appended, / That where your veneration only really begins, / Mine already leaves off.)

Grillparzer clearly is lamenting that he does not have Beethoven to himself anymore, but has to share his true love with the cohorts of music enthusiasts. While Grillparzer tries only to defend Beethoven against his fans, Lenau undertakes to stand up to Beethoven's superiority and to penetrate and grasp it as far as his language and his times allow. Perhaps it is an indictment of his time, but certainly not an indictment of Lenau's poetic abilities, that a century and a half later a stale taste of embarrassment remains, at least regarding the poem's conclusion, with its aiming at a trinity of Zeus-Christ-Beethoven — a flat aftertaste that has accompanied the Beethoven ideal from the beginning. "Und eigentlich komisch dabei ..." (and actually comical at the same time ...).

Turn of the Century and Since

Round Dance and Dance as Symbols of Life in the Arts around 1900[*]

WALTER SALMEN

THE EPISODE OF THE "Tanzlied" (dance song, bar 409ff.) as well as the "trunkenen Lied" (drunken song, bar 875ff.) of Richard Strauss's symphonic poem *Also sprach Zarathustra* (1896) mark the culmination of one of the most ambitious orchestral works of the turn of the century — a work that together with its poetic model was to signal a new departure. Friedrich Nietzsche's often cited philosophy of the corporeal and spiritual — the dionysian Weltanschauung of 1870, with its uninhibited delight in existence ("Lust am Dasein") — was to manifest itself musically in the progressively wilder gestures of the superhuman beings ("Übermenschen") in his dance song ("Tanzlied") which promised, through the intoxication of purposeless play, to help overcome the principle of gravity ("Geist der Schwere"). Strauss, as composer, in order to liberate the orchestra and to answer the poet's antirationalistic call for expression of delight in existence, made free use of reminiscences from the fashionable Viennese waltzes of his namesake Johann Strauß. Thus, with such insufficient means, the composer was only seemingly able to fulfill Nietzsche's intended liberation from a world of purposes, of decaying ideals, and of sober facts. This pathos-laden orchestral music remained imprisoned in the ritual of the symphony concert to be received in a mood of serious concentration.[1] The dance that the creator of the vision utopically intended was a symbol for the liberated life of free spirits which move intoxicatedly like those in the motto from Nietzsche's dancing song "An den Mistral":

> Tanzen wir in tausend Weisen,
> Frei — sei unsre Kunst geheißen ...,
>
> (Let us dance in a thousand ways,
> Let our art be called — free).

It was a vision not realized by Strauss's music, which stuck with the passive enjoyment of implied pleasures; the piece offered no opportunity for provocative action. Just as a discrepancy appears in the relationship of the

---

[*] English translation of the German original by Ellen Gerdeman-Klein and James M. McGlathery.

[1] Walter Salmen, *Das Konzert* (Munich: Beck, 1988), pp. 114ff.

composer Strauss to his poet Nietzsche, for whom life was supposed to be a well of passion ("ein Born der Lust") enhanced by redemption through art, similarly, around 1900, other artistic dreams aiming at life's fulfillment remained unfulfilled, endeavors in which the dance and dancing were supposed to be a central experience. *Reigen* (round dance), *Paartanz* (pair dancing), and *Solotanz* (solo dancing) were models for part of a generation which — in rebellion against the times — set itself against the cultural pessimism, the reigning sexual repression, the sober patriarchally-ruled industrial world, the historically constraining rituals, but at the same time, to combat isolation and alienation, offered a more communicative, vital concept of life. Dance as the epitome of vitalistic joy in life, as a celebration of existence, was supposed to help lead the way back to lost origins; once again bodily movement — filled with feeling for life — was supposed to aid the suffering spirit. In keeping with this desire to reform life by exciting and intoxicating all the senses, the aim was for an artistic transfiguration in word as well as in tone, color, line, and movement. All of the arts, with their claims to absoluteness and their divisions, came together once again briefly in a shared conjuring of the vision of interweaving art and life through the arts' parallel commitment to the theme of "life," which was posited as an absolute. All of the fine arts were to contribute, as Heinrich Mann put it, to life's sanctification ("Heiligung") and emancipation by interweaving with, and into, each other. Dance as symbol as well as in its actuality held a special fascination for anarchists, futurists, therapists, aestheticists, and symbolists. Dance and round dance, as metaphors for the consuming will to live and for warding off pessimistic decadence, were raised to the level of a universal context beyond the realm of knowledge. Rudolf Pannwitz summed it up in his book *Kosmos Atheos*: "der tanz ist das erlebnis und die erlösung des leibes" (dance is the experience and redemption of the body). Let us now, with a concise comparative excursion through selected artistic phenomena of the times, call to mind how this quest for the elan vital, for nature-likeness, for rhythmic motion, manifested itself in works and activities around 1900.

The key words for this promise of happiness in the "Dance of Life" — which was "life itself," according to Havelock Ellis — were provided by Nietzsche, Henri Bergson, Wilhelm Dilthey, Georg Simmel, and several other thinkers who can be counted among the proponents of a philosophy of life and freedom. As one who experienced life as suffering, Nietzsche longingly shaped his Zarathustra (1883) as a spokesman for life ("Fürsprecher des Lebens") with the virtue of a dancer ("Tugend eines Tänzers") in "Die sieben Siegel" (III). Zarathustra's glorification of the body, of purposeless movement in dance, referred to the whole of life in its boundlessness as well as its limitedness, abandoning itself, without God and morality and in prodigal intoxication, to the all-embracing universe. Nietzsche wrote, "Im Tanze nur weiß ich der höchsten Dinge Gleichnis zu reden" (Only when dancing do I know how to speak in metaphor about the highest things). Accordingly, the synonymity between dance and life transcends the intellect; art animated by dance is capable of offering metaphysical solace.[2] The rapid adoption of these aphoristically formulated impulses with their biological nomenclature (life, dance, urge) was reflected after 1890 in a movement that found experience of the dynamics of life to be blissful. Vitalism, activism, "Jeunesisme," "Jugendstil" were some of the responses to the promised realm of freedom of a supposedly perpetual "energy of life" (Bergson), which was supposed to continue to flourish ecstatically to the end of time. All-exclusive intoxication, the erotic, should determine the aesthetic; according to Rudolf von Delius, dance had the task of bringing about a higher, erotic culture ("eine höhere erotische Kultur herbeizuführen"). What form did this feeling for life take as a compensation for a repressed Eros, this surrogate mediating between congruent impulses in all the arts?

I

The arts' response to the longing emanating from this philosophy of life for the realization of an intoxicating immediacy and antirational, Dionysian fullness of life was not only an impractically aesthetic one. It was accompanied by abrupt changes in the practice of dance itself, and indeed in social dance as well as in show dance. Suddenly after 1890 dances, rhythms, gestures, and dancing attire shattered the conventions of the upper middle-class ball culture that up to that time had been uniformly controlled — shattered it in such a way that it was feared to be an attack on propriety and accepted standards of modesty. A whirlwind of controversy broke loose around this "modern dancing," the "élan vital" on the dance floor demonstrated in corsetless, reform-inspired clothing — an "élan vital" that spread very quickly to almost every dance-hall with the exception of those such as at the imperial court in Berlin, which set itself against this trend threatening the social status quo and opposed it with strict regulations of a monarchistic-historicizing nature.[3] Those who defended "academic" dance and the previous norm universally diagnosed the development as a contagious neurosis that originated with dances like the Boston, Cakewalk, Tango, Onestep, or Ragtime. These so-called "moving dances" with their partners pressing uninhibitedly close to each other, wanting to liberate themselves sexually, too, filled the masses in all the large cities with the prospect of a socially dominant, libertine fashion. The end of the "social dance" in its traditional sense seemed to have arrived. This change was experienced paradigmatically by the Bohemians, especially, who gathered for Fasching (carnival) in Munich-Schwabing, and at their festivals did not perform dance

[2] Gunter Martens, *Vitalismus und Expressionismus* (Stuttgart: W. Kohlhammer, 1971), p. 49. Roger Garaudy formulated the maxim "danser sa vie."

[3] Walter Salmen, *Tanz im 19. Jahrhundert* (Leipzig: Deutscher Verlag für Musik, 1989).

pleasurelessly as a listless ceremonial social event, but rather as an expression of the joy of life and of free humor ("von Lebensfreude und freiem Humor," Carl Ehrenberg). This assessment of the socially divided situation, with its ever deeper divergences, was also confirmed by activities which originated with the *Wandervogel* movement and the *Jugendbewegung* or with representatives of a direction characterized by cults of nudity, longing for nature, and liberating corporeality, like those of Bess Mensendieck, Rudolf von Laban, or Émile Jaques-Dalcroze. The first-named trend reactivated the round dance in its groups as an expression of a strong communicative need for action in a time characterized by alienation. The Hellerau School for Rhythm, Music, and Physical Education ("Schule Hellerau für Rhythmus, Musik und Körperbildung") founded by Jaques-Dalcroze in 1911 near Dresden had as its goal the creation of a Golden Age utopia through communal life in a colony, and had some lasting success, as witnessed most recently in the activities of the dance therapist Christel Ulbrich in the former German Democratic Republic. The aim in the colony was to savor an existence devoted to beauty and experienced through communal, rhythmically pulsated activities. The constraints and conventions of civilization, the fetters of encapsulation in egoistic existences were to be overcome, and through rhythmical movement reconciliation of everyone with the cosmos was to take place. In Hellerau near Dresden they practiced dance as a re-educating exercise, which was supposed to provide the participants with a feel for the rhythm of life, and, as Jaques-Dalcroze put it, "to liberate driving forces" through spontaneous self-expression in movement and gesture. In this way, bodily forces were to be brought into harmony with those of the soul, a goal at which Rudolf von Laban aimed, too, with his school of the free and absolute art of movement ("Bewegungskunst") in Munich after 1910.

This outbreak of impulsive divestiture of, and turning away from, the "dance d'école," with its fixed choreography and coded movements, was just as clearly demonstrated on the show dance stage. Initiatives in this direction were taken beginning in 1889 by the American dancer Loïe Fuller (1862–1928) (Illus. 1) and Ruth St. Denis (who was admired by Hugo von Hofmannsthal among others), as well as Isadora Duncan, Grete Wiesenthal in Vienna, Nijinsky, and others. Supported by a transforming light show and dressed in voluminous silk costumes, Fuller made the uninhibited billowing of color, lines, and folds visually captivating. Her imitations of fire, serpents, or butterflies fascinated not only the public of the "Folies Bergère" in Paris, but also composers such as Claude Debussy and Florent Schmitt. She was the sensation of the nineties, whose performances were imitated or visually captured by such artists as William H. Bradley, Toulouse-Lautrec, or François Rupert Carabin.[4]

Isadora Duncan, above all, in opposition to every kind of Puritanism, presented herself as seeking to be freed from gravity through gestures imitating flight. Barefoot, dispensing with ballet's conventional tights, corsetting, and toe-training, and using models from antiquity, she gave expression to an emphatic experience of bodily freedom, striving for a mystic, cult-like enchantment of the surrounding world. The American painter John Sloan summarized his impressions with the words: "she lifted human movement to the level of the divine."[5] Through dance the profane was thus rendered sacred. Made closer to nature in this way, dance, as an autonomous art dispensing even with music, was supposed to help make liberation to a higher state of being possible. The ecstatic Dionysian language of bodily movement that was associated with this dancing quickly led to visions of an epiphany occurring through dance. The result was "free dance," of which Eleonora Duse expected in 1903 that it would become "the true art" that brings liberation. In keeping with such high esteem, both female and male dancers such as Nijinsky were raised to the level of goddesses and gods of dance in an otherwise godless world. In figures like the "Flight of Spheres" ("Sphärischen Schwung"), the "Maenad," or the "Dance of Pan," Grete Wiesenthal, beginning in 1908, reached out into seeming Infinity.[6] The new techniques of floating and spinning she introduced called forth associations that pointed to Sigmund Freud, active at the same time in Vienna, who likewise was devoting his therapeutic and scientific attention to uncovering the role of instinct and process in the psyche. As the last great solo dancer, Mary Wigman in 1921 was still praising the "dance of life" as that of pleasure, and which can interpret life's meaning through gesture and allow life like death to appear invincible.[7] With these and similar excessive claims, this phase of a euphorically transfigured dance art came to an end.

---

[4] Carl Hofer, *Erinnerungen eines Malers* (Munich: Paul List Verlag, 1963), p. 46; Paul David Magriel, *Chronicles of the American Dance* (New York: Da Capo Press, 1978), pp. 203ff.; Deirde Priddin, *The Art of Dance in French Literature* (London: Black, 1952), p. 110.

[5] David W. Scott, *John Sloan, 1871–1951* (Washington, D.C.: National Gallery of Art, 1971), illus. 72. Also see Isadora Duncan, *The Dance of the Future*, ed. Karl Federn (Leipzig: E. Diederichs, 1903).

[6] Erwin Lang, *Grete Wiesenthal: Holzschnitte* (Berlin: E. Reiss, 1910).

[7] Mary Wigman, *Die sieben Tänze des Lebens: Tanzdichtung* (Jena: E. Diederichs, 1921).

II

Let us now consider the answers that poets gave to Nietzsche's promise of a "paradise" of freedom and gaiety to be gained through dance. In several currents pluralistically coexisting around 1900, from historicism to futurism, they vehemently followed the inflammatory motto, "Hail, to him who invents new dances!" In poems, plays, dance plays, and stories, people abandoned themselves to a rapturous, intoxicated feeling for nature. They celebrated the blind urges of an uninhibited sensuality and raised their aims to the level of a deification of the body ("Vergottung des Leibes"). Everything was seen as happening in movement of colors, sounds, and lines, and the world was experienced pantheistically as an "eternal flow" ("ewige Flut," Hermann Bahr). The processes in nature as well as in man were understood through the symbol of the dance. Life, the pleasures of this world, spring, youth, love, round dance, and dance were often-used metaphors with which one lent expression to the striving for emancipation, the bon-vivant lasciviousness, the eroticized dynamic. In accord with Nietzsche's words: "Only when dancing do I know how to utter the metaphor for the highest things," the theme of dance encompassed life and death, existence, and the triumph of life ("Triumpf des Lebens," Julius Hart), the "salvation" of life sought through art and the "eternal truths" (Anatole France). Paul Valéry paradigmatically coined the apt formulation "All of life becomes dance" (*Toute elle devient danse*).

In the poem "Semiramis," Ernst Stadler penned the emphatic line: "Rot tanzt die Sonne" (The sun dances red); in the work "Das Haus am Meer" (UA Wien, 1912), Stefan Zweig wrote of "die Sterne / In ihrem stillen Tanz des Nachts" (the stars / In their quiet nocturnal dance); in "Herbst," Felix Dahn let the "Blätter tanzen in wirbelnden Reigen" (leaves dance in a whirling round dance); according to Carl Bulcke's "Der Geiger" (1901) even Arnold Böcklin's act of painting a self-portrait was a dance of the paint brush on the canvas.[8] The rhythm of dance was seen to inhabit all of nature's movements as well as all artistic endeavor.

Thus everything that could be perceived with the senses or experienced in dreams was defined in pictures taken from this — for a time dominant — atmosphere of dance and intoxication. The performances by the above-named dancers — rich in gestures, colors, and rhythms — provided stimulation through fascinating impressions. Loïe Fuller (Illus. 1), above all, came to be venerated by many writers. The co-founder of the "Insel," Alfred

---

[8] Carl Bulcke, *Die Töchter der Salome* (Stuttgart: J. G. Cotta, 1901), p. 122. Also see Bruno Hillebrand, *Nietzsche und die deutsche Literatur* (Tübingen: Niemeyer, 1978) and Wolfdietrich Rasch, *Zur deutschen Literatur seit der Jahrhundertwende* (Stuttgart: Metzler, 1967).

Walter Heymel, expressed his impressions of her serpentine dancing in the verses:

Muse tanzt im Kreis herum,	Muse dances in a circle,
Daß die Wangen glühen.	Until her cheeks glow.
Tanzt die dummen Sorgen um,	Dances around the stupid worries
Daß sie heulend fliehen.	Until they crying flee.
Schleierkleid und goldne Schuh,	Veiled gown and golden shoe,
Seidenwellen fließen.	Silken waves flow.
Farbenstrudel immerzu,	Incessant colored swirls,
Grellstes Lichtergießen.	Dazzling streams of light.
Tänzerin mit schlankem Leib —	Dancer with a slender form —
Brüste zum Entzücken —	Breasts to enchant —
Komm, und laß als nacktes Weib	Come, and as naked woman
Fest dich an mich drücken.	Firmly press yourself to me.
Tanzen wir im Kreis herum,	Let us dance in a circle,
Daß die Wangen glühen.	Until our cheeks glow.
Tanzen alle Sorgen um,	Dance around all worries,
Daß sie heulend fliehen!	Until they crying flee!

Emanuel von Bodman also glorified the sensual life of a woman in "Serpentinentanz" (serpent dance). Alfred Mombert gave tribute to a "Wunderweib" (woman of marvel) in a "Tanzlied" of 1896 with the words:

Es wieget und schmieget	It rocks and cuddles
Den lieblichen Leib	The winsome form
Auf Tönen getragen	Borne upon tones
Ein Wunderweib.	A woman of marvel.
Die Haare entflattern dem	The hair escapes the
fesselnden Band,	confining band,
Es woget wie Wellen das weite	Like waves the full gown
Gewand;	surges;
Wie Wellen wogt es	Like waves it surges
Ohne Rast ohne Ruh,	Without rest or calm,
Und wir, wir fiedeln	And we, we fiddle
Den Takt dazu.	The beat along.
Die Arme blinken,	The arms glitter,
Die Wangen glüh'n,	The cheeks blush,
Und Feuerfunken	And sparks of fire
Die Augen sprüh'n,	The eyes flash.
Die Lippen lechzen	The lips thirst

Vor Liebeslust,	With love's lust,
Es woget wie Wellen	Like waves billow
Die weiße Brust.	The white breasts.
Das wellet und woget	It surges and swells
Um Glück und Ruh,	Around happiness and calm,
Und wir, wir fiedeln	And we, we fiddle
Den Takt dazu.	The beat along.

Models for this expansive, intoxicated feeling for nature, in addition to the new types of dance performance, were provided increasingly by reminiscences and images from antiquity. Nietzsche, in the dualism "Apollinisch-dionysisch" (*Der Wille zur Macht*, III), had defined two opposing conditions, for which he appropriated the names of two gods from antiquity, of which the latter demanded from him the highest wonderment as the ecstatic expression of a triumphant will ("Ausdruck eines siegreichen Willens"). From then on, the praises sung to manifestations of the dancing followers of Dionysus multiplied — manifestations into which one wanted glowingly and jubilantly to plunge. Bacchants, maenads, fauns, satyrs, and Pans populated the pagan, artificial landscape which was drunk with life. Significantly, the magazine *Pan* was founded in 1895, and aimed predominantly to set the tone for glorification of life. All of these figures from antiquity represented models of vitality and eroticism that were supposed to produce a frenzy without purpose or any connection with worship of God. Poets such as Hermann Lingg, Stefan Zweig, Ernst Stadler, Alexander Blok, and Georg Heym lent eloquent expression in their dances to a primal urge, the life force. The major image of the frenzied maenad found its way even into Henrik Ibsen's play, *Nora* (Act II), where the heroine — with a tambourine as characteristic attribute — frees herself from an unhappy marriage and domestic oppression by dancing a tarantella — "with growing excitement ... as if her life were at stake."

Closely related to these concepts of the mythical figures from antiquity — but also of the North, was the round dance's pulling or turning as the collective fulfillment of dancing, which swept everything and everyone along and facilitated the acceleration of movement. In 1896 Paul Wertheimer, in his poem "Gastmahl," provided a pompous scene set in a spacious, luxurious palace with a bacchanal in which mad round dances ("närrische Reigen") were danced with thyrsus staffs ("Thyrsosstäben"). Hyperbolically, Felix Dörmann in his poetry repeatedly has erotic feeling expressed in frenzied round dance ("hochgepeitschten Reigen"). For Otto Julius Bierbaum, the entwined round dance ("geschlungene Reihen") corresponded to the line patterns of his milieu in Munich, as characterized by Jugendstil. In 1896 in "Vom neuen Jahr" he celebrated this optimistically accordant enticement:

Zu Flöten und Geigen	To flutes and fiddles
Hintanz' ich im Reigen	I dance in the round dance,
Habe Blumen im Haar.	With flowers in my hair.
Oh laßt euch bewegen,	Oh let you be roused,
Ihr Trüben und Trägen,	You gloomy and sluggish ones,
Im Tanze ist Segen,	In dance there is blessing,
Die Freude macht klar.	Joy makes all bright.
Auf, wagt es, zu springen!	Up, venture to leap!
Es muß euch gelingen,	You must be successful,
Was fröhlich ihr schafft.	In what joyfully you create.
Das grämliche Hocken	Peevish sitting around
Bringt Alles ins Stocken.	Brings everything to a stop.
Frei wehn meine Locken,	Freely my hair blows,
Die Freude macht Kraft.	Joy gives us strength.

In *Die versunkene Glocke* by Gerhart Hauptmann (1897), the elves perform a round dance, whereas in "Reihn" Ludwig Finckh paints for himself flighty butterfly-maids ("Faltermädchen") in a glittering world of gold and light. Hugo von Hofmannsthal expanded the metaphor of the round dance in "Sünde des Lebens" (1891) to an embodiment of wasted existence, thereby pillorying sins against life:

Jauchzend und schrankenlos,	Shouting and boundless,
Sorglos, gedankenlos	Carefree, thoughtless
Dreht sich der Reigen,	The round dance whirls,
Der Lebensreigen. —	The dance of life. —

We encounter the catch-word "life" everywhere, up to its thematization in "Lebenslieder" (songs of life), that are to be found in Stefan Zweig, Hofmannsthal, and many others. In "Pippo Spano," Heinrich Mann went to the hypertrophic extreme of assigning to art the task of "creating a second, more powerful life" ("ein zweites, mächtigeres Leben schaffen"), the artist accordingly becoming a creator in the full sense of the word. Dance served, in these contexts, as a means to combat death, for dance smells of life ("riecht nach Leben"), according to Karl Schönherr in "Der Weibsteufel." Carl Hauptmann, Selma Lagerlöf,[9] Max Halbe, Georg Kaiser (in the 1914 dance play, *Europa*), Arthur Schnitzler, August Strindberg, and Frank Wedekind used this symbol to have vitalistically characterized figures, in highly tense emotional situations, dance instead of speak, especially when

---

[9] Selma Lagerlöf, "Der Ball auf Ekeby" (1891); Gösta Berling "wollte sich brausende Lebenslust ins Blut tanzen."

words, when clear thought failed or were supposed to be outdone.[10] Figures such as Lulu or Salome were called upon to dance their minds right out of their heads ("Verstand zum Kopf hinauszutanzen"). In the play *Und Pippa tanzt!* of 1905, the playwright Gerhart Hauptmann gives the advice, "Tanze drauflos und tanze dich aus!" (Dance away at it, and dance yourself out!, Act IV). The dancers thus were supposed to become active in both directions, both pleasurably stamping down on the floor and elevatedly seeking to rise with gestures imitating flight. In the story, "Die Tänzerin und der Leib" (The Dancer and the Body), Alfred Döblin gave significant stimulus to this idea. The dancer Mary Wigman, who wrote the dance poem "Die sieben Tänze des Lebens" (The Seven Dances of Life, 1921),[11] drew choreographic conclusions for herself and her students from this duality of spirit and life. In this connection it should be noted that this progressing into life ("Zug ins Leben," Ernst Stadler)[12] through wild, racing dance did not originate with thinking at the turn of the century. Similar tones and rhythms were sounded in the poetry of the *Sturm und Drang* (Storm and Stress) around 1775, such as in Jakob Michael Reinhold Lenz's "Lied zum deutschen Tanz" (Song to German Dance), in which he effusively puts forth the motto "feel all desires" ("fühl' alle Lust"):

O Angst: o tausendfach Leben!	Oh fear: oh manifold life!
O Mut: den Busen geschwellt,	Oh courage: with swelled breast,
Zu taumeln, zu wirbeln,	To stagger, to whirl,
zu schweben,	to hover,
Als ging's so fort aus der Welt!	As though one went thus out of the world!

This longing for life in the rhythm of Dionysian passion, which allowed individuals in their isolation to dissolve into in a chorally animated exultation, was pointedly identified with areas of life such as springtime, youth, desire, and love. This apotheosis of a purposeless life and activity in supposedly eternal youthfulness was exemplified paradigmatically by Isadora Duncan. In this she was lastingly inspired during a stay in Florence, where she was plunged into meditation in front of Botticelli's painting "Primavera" and formed the resolution: "I will dance this painting and give to others this message of love, spring, engendering of life.... I will give them through dance this ecstasy.... Oh lovely, half-perceived, heathen life...." She actually did create this so-called "Dance of the Future," inspired by Nietzsche, thus

[10] See Rasch, *Zur deutschen Literatur* (1967) and Friedrich Rothe, *Frank Wedekinds Dramen: Jugendstil und Lebensphilosophie* (Stuttgart: J. B. Metzler, 1968).

[11] Mary Wigman, *Die Sieben Tänze des Lebens* (1921).

[12] Martens, *Vitalismus* (1971), p. 134.

marking the birth of modern dance. This innovative production was recast by Christian Morgenstern, among others, in the poem "Ewige Frühlingsbotschaft" (Eternal Message of Spring):

> Sieh mit weißen Armen, schwellenden Brüsten,
> purpurnen Lippen, blitzenden Augen dort
> der jungen Weiber hold erregte Reigen
> aus den immergrünen Toren der Jugend,
> gleich aus brechenden Körben rollenden Früchten,
> quellen — strömen — sich ergießen —
> des Lebens unversiegliche Bürgschaft selber ...

> See, with white arms, swelling breasts,
> purple lips, flashing eyes there
> the young women's sweet, excited round dance
> out of the evergreen gates of youth,
> just like fruits rolling out of breaking baskets,
> well up — gush — overflow —
> life's inexhaustible guarantee itself ...

During this time, "youth," as catchword and word to conjure with, had become a much used cipher, particularly after 1896 when it was taken as the title of a magazine and after 1899 when it passed its literary debut in the *Insel*. It made clear the search for an elementary, total experience of life, which was supposed to promise unending pleasure. In 1901 Carl Bulcke emphatically praised youth as an eternal right ("ewiges Recht"):

> Jugend, ihr goldenen Zeiten!   Youth, you golden times!
> Liebe, du brennendes Weh!   Love, you burning pain!
> Es tanzen durch Ewigkeiten   Through eternity dance
> Die Töchter der Salome.   The daughters of Salome.

In Stefan Zweig's play *Das Haus am Meer* (Scene 3, UA Wien, 1912), he has young, enticing Peter say to Christine:

> "Wir bleiben da, und wenn wir wieder wollen,
> Ist heute Tanz wie gestern, morgen wieder,
> Und so ein Leben lang, bis uns der Wirbel
>   zu Boden wirft...."
> (We'll stay here, and whenever we want to again,
> There's dancing today like yesterday, again tomorrow,
> And so all our lives, until the whirlwind
>   hurls us to the floor....)

Alfred Walter Heymel celebrated the hot dance of love in the castle of the god of love's frenzy ("des Gottes Liebesraserei"); in his poem "Begehren" Stefan Zweig alluded to the antithesis between the rushing after hot women ("heißen Frauen") and the heat of wild rhythms ("wilder Rhythmen Glut"), and the desire for quiet, peace, and happiness. With the outbreak of World War I, at the latest, this expressive antithesis inevitably led from a momentary, intoxicated engrossment to the sobering insight that in reality, dance was a reeling "between life and death" ("zwischen Leben, Sterben"; in "Lebenslust" by Ludwig Jacobowski), that dances can also mean a perverse turning of life into insanity, into death-like derangement. The thought that dancing not only could help attain a festively enhanced reality, but that it also belonged to life's opposite side, to dull stumbling about in the night, was drastically underscored by Stefan George (in the poem "Fest"), Georg Trakl (in "Die junge Magd"), and Hugo von Hofmannsthal (in *Elektra*). In this contrast between an optimistic life force and an uncannily destructive urge to ruin, the medieval theme of the Dance of Death was lent a renewed actuality. For Trakl this excessive dance itself represented leperousness purely and simply, while Baudelaire had experienced this "muse of time's end" as a sign of decline, ruin, and "disgust with reality," in the face of which only night could offer comfort.[13] Lastly, with many poets, the melancholy of decadence and return to realistic constraints again broke through the cult of exalted eroticism and irrational drunkenness. In uncannily paradoxical fashion, Emanuel von Bodman depicted this inevitable succumbing to death's power through dance in his poem "Totentanz" (Dance of Death):

Menschen, nur noch Haut und Knochen,
Kommen rings hervorgekrochen
Und verrenken ihre Glieder,
Glühn im Tanze auf und nieder,
Schleppen Brüder auf den Schragen,
Um ihr Fleisch zu Markt zu tragen.

Naht das Ende aller Zeiten?
Schreckliches will sich bereiten,
Dem wir jetzt entgegensehen.
Selbstmord möcht das Herz begehen,
Sieht es sich als armen Narren
Angespannt am Totenkarren.

Hättest du das Spiel erfunden,
Um beim Anblick unsrer Wunden

---

[13] Ibid., p. 231. The Norwegian novella by Sigbjörn Obstfelder, *Sletten in To Novelletter* (Bergen: J. Grieg, 1895).

Eine kluge Lust zu fühlen,
Mit dem Finger drin zu wühlen —
In den Himmel möcht ich greifen,
auf die Erde dich zu schleifen.

(People, now just skin and bones,
Come crawling forward in the round
And dislocate all their limbs,
Glowing in dance up and down,
Dragging brothers on the frames,
To carry to market their flesh.
Is the end of all times near?
Something terrible is preparing to happen,
Something to which we must look ahead.
The heart is wanting suicide,
Sees itself as a poor fool
Stretched upon a hearse.

If you had the game invented,
So that seeing all our wounds,
You could feel a clever joy,
Dig with your finger in them,
I would like to reach into heaven
To drag you down to earth.

III

Many visual artists spontaneously took up these poetic images from an art of motion, celebrating life in dance, and appropriated them as models for diverse imitative forms using the techniques of "Jugendstil," "Secessionsstil," "Style Moderne," as well as "Modernista." Comparing the motives and set-scenes applied by the two different arts, one sees an almost congruent parallelism emerge. A noteworthy magical power of association seized the artists of all fields in staging their mirrored paradises together with the contrasting worlds. Had not Heinrich von Kleist, in his dialogue "Über das Marionettentheater,"[14] emphasized, "Doch das (wirkliche) Paradies ist verriegelt und der Cherub hinter uns" (But, the [true] paradise is bolted and the cherub [is] behind us)? Still, artists struggled to recreate this lost, premoralistic paradise using art's imaginative means. In order to make this ideal omnipresent in life, they emphatically pursued unity in art, a "Synthèse

---

[14] H. Schwegerle, "Bewegung, Rhythmus, Stil und Tanz in der bildenden Kunst," *Die Plastik* 4, no. 3 (1914) and H. Theissing, "Tanzen: Zu einem Bildmotiv um 1900," *Aachener Kunstblätter* 41 (1971): 289ff.

d'Art" (van de Velde, 1895), in the service of an illusionary cult of the aesthetic that embraced all the senses.

Opposing the fatalism of the turn of the century, the Fin de siècle, they sought by means of the visual arts to combat this anxiety by inventing images of a giddy self-abandon in forbidden ecstacy and fleeting intoxication. They voluptuously staged illusory worlds of passionately viewed activity, of violently motivated extroversion. To this end they sought new artistic tricks of a formal nature in order to break through and destroy traditional limits of representation so they could effectively show the dynamics and speed of moving bodies or circle segments, of spirals and oscillations. The process became more important than the subject, which was freed from its immobility to become part of a sensual playing with form as expression of release, of desire or of an excessive enhanced feeling of life ("hohen Lebensgefühls"). Pictures and sculptures were given rhythmic structures polychromatically, or also abstractedly in the representation of "absolute rhythm" (Ezra Pound). Polyphonic or rhythmically complementary lines were experienced as signs for the power of life, of excitement, and of will.

As in poetry, there was in illustrative graphics, paintings, and small sculptures reproduction of reality alongside attempts to depict dance in symbols, all the way to the limit as represented, for example, by the "Rhythmical Spaces" (1902) of Adolphe Appia (1862–1928), enlivened as they were by light and movement. There were countless portrayals of the whirling, flaming performances of the "Serpent Dancer" Loïe Fuller (1862–1939).[15] Henri de Toulouse-Lautrec was as captivated by her fluttering hair, the gliding flow of the folds of her airy garments, and her contortions as were Jules Cheret, Thomas Theodor Heine (in "Die Insel," 1900), or Lovis Corinth. In 1892, the Paris magazine *L'Illustration* printed a series of eight graphics from the "danse serpentine ... et ses transformations" which had been extraordinarily successful in the Folies-Bergère there. Fuller's dancing was used commercially on bronze candlesticks (see Illus. 1),[16] or included as small sculpture in the Nippes Collection. Painters such as Franz von Stuck (1897) and Emil Nolde (Illus. 2) transformed the images of the unrestrained, fiery, whirling dance paradigmatically expressed in her dancing into general metaphors of longing,[17] whereby the dance character with its broadly sweeping expressive gestures as signs of individual liberation were delineated more than was the dancer herself. Wave lines conveyed the impression of power and positive orientation.

---

[15] Karl Storck, *Der Tanz* (Bielefeld: Velhagen und Klasing, 1903), illus. 102–104. Hans Hellmut Hofstätter, *Jugendstil, Druckkunst* (Baden-Baden: Holle, 1973), p. 50.

[16] Gabriele Sterner, *Jugendstil: Kunstformen zwischen Individualismus und Massengesellschaft* (Cologne: DuMont Schauberg, 1975), illus. 30.

[17] Curt Moreck (pseud. for Konrad Haemmerling), *Der Tanz in der Kunst* (Stuttgart: W. Seifert, 1924), illus. 140.

In accord with the idea of many graphic artists and painters who aspired to awaken again a concept of the whole, of the cosmic, in order to transcend particularity in representing individual things, everything in nature which moved was rhythmically articulated and dancingly interwoven. In the flight of clouds and play of waves there ruled the primal image of dancing power, into which rhythms of human life were supposed to be integrated as an aid to spiritual orientation. In 1897 Richard Riemerschmid had "Wolkengespenster" (Ghostly Clouds, see Illus. 3) appear in the process of flowing like a stormy leaping dance of raving women; in 1900 Edvard Munch, in his painting "Tanz am Strand" (Dance on the Beach), had nocturnal twirling, dancing girls merge into the harmoniously moving lines of the surrounding landscape and of the phallic sexual symbolism of the glittering moon. Finally, in the drawing "Tanz" (1910), Ludwig von Hofmann had the whirling of naked women's bodies dissolve into circular lines that suggested the sun, free nature, or the cosmos.

The key words "life" or "festival of life" occupied painters as early as the 1880s. In his 1888 painting "Die Lebensinsel" (The Isle of Life) in contrast to his "Toteninsel" (Isle of Death), Arnold Böcklin had dancers form a round dance as a sign of affirmation of life within time and earthly reality.[18] Life enjoyed to its fullest is consequently a dance in a fictitious earthly paradise on islands, in meadows, in forests, or at the beach. Pictorially appropriating a poetical metaphor, Edvard Munch has his "Tanz des Lebens" (Dance of Life) happen there in 1900. In 1905 Henri Matisse painted the scene "Joie de vivre" in front of a background of dancers happily enjoying free nature (see also Illus. 5). Ferdinand Hodler (1853–1918), in a study of movement anticipating the later dances expressive of the awakening of naked women, thematized their rhythm of life ("Rhythmus des Lebens"), as he did also in "Der Tag" (1899).

The will to live in social union, to overcome alienation, and to discover identity through action was manifested most clearly in pictures in which free people dancing the round dance bound themselves to one another. The favored nineteenth-century image of chaste, naive children's round dances (for example in Hans Thoma or Hans Richter)[19] was replaced by wildly executed children's dances (see for example Emil Nolde) and voluptuous adult round dances which let the body's natural language express itself through silent gestures untainted by convention. Round dance was presented either as an open chain (Illus. 4), thus as an aimlessly moving

---

[18] Arnold Böcklin (1827–1901), *Ausstellungskatalog des Kunstmuseums Basel* (1977), Nr. 178. As early as 1873 the Aargau Art Association announced an artistic competition with the motto "Lebensfreude" (joy of life)!

[19] See also Salmen, *Tanz im 19. Jahrhundert* (1989), illus. 1.

wave, or as a communally closed circle.[20] The first type was effected by Franz von Stuck (Illus. 6), among many others, and in 1909 by Hugo Höppener (called "Fidus") in his drawing "Tanz." The second type, the closed circle, was suggested in Max Klinger's throng of bodies and limbs in the 1894 etching "Fest,"[21] Henri Matisse's 1901 painting "Dance" (Illus. 5), and Albert Weisgerber's gouache "Pfauentanz."[22] In the primary colors red, green, and blue — as if tuned in a triadic chord — Matisse has five nude girls whirling as a garland to express vitalistic joy in living, whereas Klinger envisions the sexes (the men with horse tails tied-on) doing a round dance around a heathen altar with a blazing fire.

The vision of sexually mixed as well as single-sex round dances was associated chiefly with pictorial images which were assigned to pre-Christian antiquity. Remembrances from late mythology occasioned not only the imitation, but also the revival of bacchanals and of Pan as personifying urges, and of satyrs, fauns, and nymphs. Naked dances in the mode of antiquity were just as customary in the Fasching balls of the bohemians in the Schwabing district of Munich as in the parties of the studios in Paris, which, according to Karl Hofer, conveyed an orgiastic picture ("ein orgiastisches Bild") in the spirit of Paul Valéry's inflammatory motto: "Danse cher corps, ne pense pas." In the dance ecstacy of figures dressed as maenads, Dionysus, and sileni, there was presented a contrast to the existing, middle-class world, a contrasting world that reflected unfulfilled wishes. In setting this world apart, luxuriating fantasy permitted straying off into antiquity's groves, temple areas, and Mediterranean shores. The archaicist and symbolist Arnold Böcklin provided some models for this (see his 1872 "Tanz um die Bacchus-säule," Dance around the Pillar of Bacchus). Lovis Corinth, Paul Bürck, Franz von Stuck, and Otto Dix followed his models, increasingly splitting reality into the real and the imaginary.[23] In this regressive striving for unity, atheistic images of life, associated with the bucolic and the idyllic, were seen as sources of stimulation from the past which tied the unique rhythm of the

---

[20] See also Walter Salmen, "Ikonographie des Reigens im Mittelalter," *Acta Musicologica* 52 (1980): 14ff.

[21] Max Klinger, "Die graphischen Zyklen," *Ausstellungskatalog des Museums Villa Stuck* (Munich, 1980), illus. 130.

[22] For further examples see Hofstätter, *Jugendstil* (1973); Thomas Walters (ed.), *Jugendstil-Graphik* (Cologne: Dumont, 1980), illus. 51; Moreck, *Der Tanz in der Kunst* (1924), illus. 116; Wolfgang Brückner, *Elfenreigen* (Cologne: M. DuMont Schauberg, 1974), p. 93; *Staatliche Museen Preußischer Kulturbesitz, Kataloge des Kunstgewerbemuseums Berlin*, vol. 4 (Berlin, 1970), no. 136.

[23] Hofstätter, *Jugendstil* (1973), p. 162; "Von Wilhelm Leibl bis Lovis Corinth," *Ausstellungskatalog aus der Sammlung Georg Schäfer*, no. 131 (Schweinfurt, 1983); Heinrich Voss, *Franz von Stuck 1863–1928* (Munich: Prestel, 1973), pp. 119ff.; *"L'Illustration,"* vol. 99 (Paris, 1892), p. 53; Alfons Mucha (1860–1939), *Ausstellungskatalog Mathildenhöhe* (Darmstadt: Mathildenhöhe, 1980), illus. 234.

individual to the rhythm of all being. From cultic contexts of meaning images for the contemporary vitalism were borrowed.

In its dancing figures this new paganism, which propagated — with aesthetic intentions — the cult of nakedness without shame, celebrated youth (*Jugend*) above all. Symptomatic of this are the 1897 title pages for the magazine of that name done by Franz von Stuck and Ludwig von Zumbusch, both from Munich. In each work, the glorification of youthfulness was visualized — in the framework of a pleasurable world of wish fulfillment — through loosely girded dancers.[24] Streaming lines extending through space, linear rhythms, curves swelling up and down, were supposed to allow the pathos of youthful enthusiasm for life to affect the viewer suggestively and awaken the impulse to join in.

Consecration, paradise, dreamland, youth, and spring gardens were thematic images that set dominating accents above all in the extensive works of Ludwig von Hofmann (1861–1945),[25] also in collaboration with Hugo von Hofmannsthal.[26] In the spring, in the "Vers sacrum," the "Ballet du printemps"[27] of liberated bodies, a guiding image of dancing and of the desired closeness to our origins, found its incarnation. These spring pictures — portrayed by Mathieu Molitor (Illus. 8), Franz von Stuck, and others — also had an erotic meaning, for they were intended, as a preliminary exercise, to help prepare for the fully experienced pleasures of summer, of mature adulthood.

The last two decades before the beginning of World War I were inwardly at variance. A passion for decadence existed alongside the mood for fundamental change. To the restless hunger for life and intoxicating dance corresponded a flight from life to the point of apathy and longing for death. Excessive passionate pleasure gave way to revulsion. A luxuriating passion for life was interwoven with desire for destruction, somewhat as the motion of waves produces peaks and valleys. Life and love were fulfilled in death, for only in the losing of life did the intoxicating new wave arrive with macabre joy at its goal. The search for a new humanity exhausted itself in a dance to the death, from which redemption was brought for many by World War I. Just as dance was supposed to cause the torch of life to glow brightly, one experienced parallel to that the accompanying demonically consuming flame, for as Hugo von Hofmannsthal wrote, "überall alles. Alles im Reigen" (everything [is] everywhere. Everything in round dance), that is to say, no fulfilled life without death. As a figure symbolizing this giddiness in

---

[24] See Lovis Corinth, *Ausstellungskatalog der Museen der Stadt Köln*, ed. Siegfried Gohr (1976), table XIII.

[25] Oskar Fischel, *Ludwig von Hofmann* (Bielefeld: Velhagen und Klasing, 1903).

[26] Ludwig von Hofmann, *Tänze, mit Text von Hugo von Hofmannsthal* (Leipzig: Insel, 1905).

[27] Moreck, *Der Tanz in der Kunst* (1924), illus. 137.

uninhibited dance at the edge of the abyss, one experienced anew the morbidity of the legendary Salome, who, as the embodiment of unfathomableness in all the arts, illustrated the borderline character of the period.[28] The royal daughter Salome not only danced her way into personal catastrophe, bringing about a unity of love and death in an orgy of blood, she also personified, in her wanton seductiveness, the unfortunate destiny that hung over the times. Franz von Stuck and Max Slevogt seized upon the delirium of this lively deserter of conventions, locating it in a Munich dance hall in 1896 to symbolize the dance of death, which they saw and experienced[29] as the end of everyone's dance of life. Noteworthy in these paintings is that, contrary to the tradition familiar since Holbein, it is not the personification of death, but rather the frivolously aggressive individual herself that pushes on lustfully toward death, much as on the contemporary dramatic stage, the female characters Elektra and Pippa both die at the end of their dances. The Dionysian was endowed with suffering and ruin as well as with passion. In 1906 Gustav Adolf Mossa summed this up in the formulation: "Elle aimait trop le bal, c'est ce qui l'a tué...." In his oil painting, "Der Tanz des Lebens" (1900), Edvard Munch juxtaposed a closely snuggling dancing pair in the middle with a resigned older woman in mourning clothes standing lonesomely to their right. In a 1908 watercolor the Norwegian painter then even more directly and strikingly confronted a woman dancing impetuously in white with an isolated, benumbed man in black who takes no part in her vitalistic rapture.[30]

IV

To what extent did composers and the musical world take part in the pathos of life artistically portrayed in overflowing motion? Connection to this euphoric mood was sought in various ways. In the Lied the vitalistic current emphasizing rhythm and gesture expressed itself differently than in the ballet or in symphonic poems. Thus, a spectrum developed that stretched from the composition of the dance songs in Nietzsche's *Zarathustra* to the *danses sacrales* in Stravinsky's *Le sacre du printemps*; to Debussy's piano piece *Voiles*, written in memory of Loïe Fuller's performances in Paris; to Max Reger's *Bacchanal* on a picture from Böcklin, op. 128; and to Franz

---

[28] Hugo Daffner, *Salome: Ihre Gestalt in Geschichte und Kunst* (Munich: H. Schmidt, 1912); Carl Bulcke, *Die Töchter der Salome: Gedichte* (Stuttgart: J. G. Cotta, 1901); Erwin Koller, "Die Entwicklung der Totentanz-Tradition im 20. Jahrhundert," in *Festschrift für Eugen Thurnher*, ed. Werner M. Bauer, Achim Masser, and Guntram A. Plangg (Innsbruck: Institut für Germanistik der Universität, 1982), pp. 409ff.

[29] See also August Brömse (1873–1925), *Ausstellungskatalog der Ostdeutschen Galerie* (Regensburg: Ostdeutsche Galerie, 1978), pp. 16ff.

[30] Edvard Munch (1863–1944), *Ausstellungskatalog des Haus der Kunst* (Munich: Haus der Kunst, 1973), pp. 109ff.

Schreker's one-act opera *Das Spielwerk* of 1913, which portrays an unbridled throng in orgiastic revelry — saints and whores together with depiction of their annihilation. Just as influential musicians like Frederick Delius, Alban Berg, Alexander Zemlinsky, Richard Strauss, Max Reger, and Maurice Ravel were different from one another, they were involved heterogeneously and episodically in the consequences of Nietzsche's forceful thoughts, and of impressions particularly from Wagner's *Rheingold* (Act I) or of Impressionism and Art Nouveau as models. What remained empty gesture for one or another of them produced in others profound effects touching upon their philosophy of life. In this, the productive stimulus of a corresponding milieu that fostered a magic of connections ("Beziehungs-zauber," Thomas Mann) played a role, as can be seen with special clarity in the example of the city of Munich.

The general theme of "life," the goal of helping form a new humanity (a "neuen Menschen") out of a new attitude toward life and with the help of a "new art," did not fail to leave its trace on a number of musicians. In 1906, Maurice Ravel wrote in a letter to Jean Marnold, "j'éstime la joie de vivre exprimée par la danse...." This influence, together with the aesthetic excitation aimed at escaping morbidity, affected the English composer Frederick Delius, for example, who was throughout his life influenced by Nietzsche. Thus, Delius wrote the provocative tone poem, "The Dance Goes On" (1908); he had Fritz Cassirer gather texts for the hymnically elevated *A Mass of Life*, and wrote in addition two "Dance Rhapsodies" (1908 and 1916) as well as the orchestral work *Life's Dance, Ronde de la vie* (Cologne, 1912) and the late work *Fantastic Dance* (1932). The Swedish composer Wilhelm Peterson-Berger (1867–1942) thematicized his longings for beauty and Dionysian intoxication in his Second Symphony *Sunnanfärd* (1910), which ends in a tarantella. The mythical Pan was programmatically made a symbol of omnipresence and perpetual capability of transformation in an orchestral piece of that name (1910) by the Czech composer Josef Suk. The Polish composer Mieczyslaw Karlowicz (1876–1909), who belonged to the revolutionary group "Młoda Polska" (= Young Poland) and had studied philosophy with Wilhelm Dilthey in Berlin beginning in 1896, gave the third movement of his symphony *Auferstehung*, op. 7 (1899–1902), a scherzo waltz, with the literary motto "Auf! Hinein ins Leben ... " (Up! Rush into life ...). Besides his first and second symphonies, this Polish innovator, who fluctuated between abysmal pessimism and drunken sensuality, also composed in 1904 a symphonic poem *Wiederkehrende Wellen*, freely borrowed from Nietzsche, in which he portrayed the dance of life in waltz rhythms by using Richard Strauss as a model. This social dance was thereby transferred from its conventional ballroom usages to the realm of symphonic music, where it was made into a symbol of enthusiastic giddiness produced by whirling oneself around.[31] The accelerating waltz was generally accepted after 1890 as symbolizing enhanced joy in living. In poems such as Giraud's "Valse de Chopin" homage was paid especially to the ecstatic element in this dance; Camille Claudel, Felix Vallotton, and Hugo Höppener (Illus. 9) among others raised the turning dance to an emblem of intoxication with life.[32] In her solo dancing, Grete Wiesenthal created the waltz effect by using maximal whirling movements in every direction. Karlowicz also joined in this interpretation of waltz as a dance for life. He explained his fifth theme (bars 299–312) of *Wiederkehrende Wellen* with the commentary: "Es blitzten die schwarzen Brillanten der Augen auf, nach denen er sich, die ganze Welt vergessend, in den Strudel der Gelüste, Qualen und Tollheiten gestürzt hatte" (He saw flash those black diamond eyes for which, forgetting the whole world, he had thrown himself into the whirlpool of lust, torment, and madness). Here, too, we see the attempt to appeal to the readiness for euphoric surrender to the whirlpool of lust ("Strudel der Gelüste") as it was suggested with optic effect in the early years of the century, also in the many compositions in which dancers like Salome, Anitra, or the "Tanz der Aurora" were portrayed, inspired by the pioneering example of Loïe Fuller's serpentine dances on stage. Florent Schmitt aimed his "Feuertanz" in the ballet *La Tragédie de Salomé* (1907) directly at this fascinating soloist, as had Gabriel Pierne in his *Ballett de Salomé* of 1897.[33]

This call for realization of the dance of life and the musical creation of dancing movements infused with the spirit of Nietzsche did not remain completely without echo in the works of composers such as Gustav Mahler and Arnold Schönberg. The former reflected this trend of the time in the piano Lied, "Hans und Gret," which begins in a leisurely waltz tempo ("im gemächlichen Walzertempo") but accelerates to a fortissimo with the shouts of joy, "Juchhe! Juchhe!"; and for a subscription concert he conducted on 22 October 1903 the management of the Concert-Gebouw in Amsterdam had Antoon Molkenboer design a program in the middle of which were dancing pairs swaying in wave patterns, in the style of Jugendstil decor (Illus. 7).[34] Schönberg, meanwhile, in the song "Mädchenfrühling" (1897) with a text from Richard Dehmel, musically suggested the dancing move-

---

[31] See L. Polony, "Le programme litteraire et la symbolique musicale dans l'œuvre symphonique de Karlowicz," *Polish Art Studies* 6 (1985): 159.

[32] Hofstätter, *Jugendstil (1973)*, p. 142; Carlo Ludovico Ragghianti, *Mondrian e l'arte del XX secolo* (Milan: Edizioni di Comunitá, 1962), illus. 343.

[33] S. Sommer, "Loïe Fuller's Art of Music and Light," *Dance Chronicle* 4 (1982): 392. See also the opera *Semiramis* (1910) by Ottorino Respighi as well as the symphonic poem *Salome*, op. 55 (1906) by Henry Hadley and Edvard Munch. The drawings are in the *Ausstellungskatalog der Staatlichen Graphischen Sammlung München* (1971), no. 206f.

[34] Salmen, *Das Konzert* (1988), illus. 59.

ment of swiftly flowing lines inspired pictorially by Jugendstil;[35] and Alban Berg incorporated a round dance in the second number in his *Drei Orchesterstücke.*

In addition to Munich and Moscow, Vienna was definitely a place that led musicians toward this thematic of dance, because of a great variety of stimuli. The activities of the Viennese artists' group "Sezession," the offerings of the dancer Grete Wiesenthal, as well as the poetic enthusiasms of Hugo von Hofmannsthal combined to give rise to certain notable musical works in which the integration of various effective means was optimally achieved. In 1909, Wiesenthal commissioned the composition *Panstänze* (Pan's Dances) from Franz Schreker. In the opera *Die Gezeichneten* (Vienna, 1916), a world of glowing lust for life is represented in polarity with an abysmal tragedy. Nymphs, fauns, and bacchants dance in racing rhythms to an ecstatically excited music. Spirit and an uninhibited, glowing lust for life, erotic demonism, and orgiastic rites all confront a moderate humanity. An isle of beauty is repulsively placed in an atmosphere of tension with ugliness in order to elucidate the tragic alienation of art from the fulfilled life in the middle-class milieu.

Life in all its age-determined nuances and ties to time, as well as the battle between the sexes, was thematisized by Hugo von Hofmannsthal in the libretto for the ballet *Der Triumph der Zeit* (The Triumph of Time), which was set to music by Alexander Zemlinsky in Vienna in 1900–01. In the ballet the young poet comes to be torn by his relationships to an ingenue and to a femme fatale, "the dancer."[36] "Die Augenblicke" (The Moments), "Die Stunden" (The Hours), and "Die Jahre" (The Years) in life are figuratively and allegorically reflected and suggested musically in a manner borrowed from Jugendstil.

In Munich, the themes discussed here were taken up in their full range by musicians around 1900. The pictures by Franz von Stuck provided just as impressive inspiration as did the poetry of Otto Julius Bierbaum and Frank Wedekind, or also the Bohemian atmosphere in the city's Schwabing district. The composer and conductor Carl Ehrenberg (1878–1962) attested to this in his autobiography: "Tanz, nicht als abgezirkeltes Gesellschaftsspiel, sondern als künstlerischen Ausdruck von Lebensfreude und freiem Humor, das sah und erlebte ich zum ersten Male im Münchner Karneval" (Dance, not as a delimited social game, but as artistic expression of joy in life and free humor; that I saw and experienced for the first time at the Munich

---

[35] Arnold Schönberg, "Mädchenfrühling," in *Seven Early Songs*, ed. Leonard Stein (Los Angeles: Belmont Music Publishers, 1986).

[36] H. Weber, "Stil, Allegorie und Secession: zu Zemlinskys Ballettmusik nach Hofmannsthals 'Der Triumph der Zeit,'" in *Art Nouveau, Jugendstil und Musik*, ed. Jürg Stenzl (Zurich: Atlantis, 1980), pp. 135ff.

carnival).[37] Intoxicating costume balls were celebrated with all kinds of extravagances, life was enjoyed in a libertine atmosphere by rejecting metaphysical transcendence as the fulfillment of temporal existence. Emphasizing the hedonistic orientation, Carl Ehrenberg gave his tone poem for large orchestra a title that characterized the situation: "Memento vivere," thereby following Nietzsche by rejecting the Christian motto "Memento mori."

Inspired by the pictures of Franz von Stuck, compositions of a Dionysian and neo-pagan stamp appeared in Munich, such as the orchestral piece "Tanzende Faune" (1914) by Carl Orff; "Pan" by Hermann Bischoff (1868–1936), who was Richard Strauss's only composition student; the dance piece "Pan im Busch" (1900) by Felix Mottl with a libretto by Otto Julius Bierbaum; the symphonic waltz "Olafs Hochzeitsreigen" (1893) by Alexander Ritter; and in 1901 the "lustful round dances" in the opera *Die Rose vom Liebesgarten* by Hans Pfitzner. In the first act, spring's youthful power, the "Jugendkraft des Lenzes," is conjured up; boys and girls tease each other and play tag until they are exhorted by the water sprite "Minne-leide" (roughly "Suffering Love") to dance the round dance. James Grun wrote the following verses to this:

> Minneleide ruft! in funkelnder Pracht
> schlägt sie die Harfe zum Tanze.
> Waldweibchen und Männer in waldiger Macht
> sind trunken vor Glück und vor Glanze....

> Minneleide calls! in glittering pomp
> she strums the harp as a call to dance.
> Women of the forest and men under sylvan spell
> are drunk with delight and radiance....

Minneleide "ladet zur Lust, ladet zu brünstigem Reigen, zu schwebenden Kreisen, Brust gegen Brust" (summons [them] to pleasure, summons [them] to a lustful round dance, to floating circles, breast against breast). In this opera a Jugendstil theme is struck in the stimulating impetus introduced by the color magic of wave lines moving with youthful rapidity. Pfitzner thereby translated into music images of the times that the artistic milieu (to which he was then close) had to offer.

While this world of thoughts and images only produced in Pfitzner an intermezzo, Richard Strauss entered into this current of the times in a more long-term way. With the precipitous movement of wild arpeggios, he ornamentally set to music Otto Julius Bierbaum's poem "Wir beide wollen springen" (We Both Want to Leap) in 1896. With an ornamented frame

---

[37] See "Jugendstil — Musik?: Münchner Musikleben 1890–1918," *Ausstellungskatalog der Bayerischen Staatsbibliothek* (Munich, 1987).

designed by Julius Dietz, this song was published like a motto in the first volume of the magazine *Jugend* (1896, Nr. 42, 676) from which it was borrowed, for example, for the Ball Album of the Press Association of Berlin in 1899.[38] Likewise in songs such as "Frühlingsgedränge," op. 26, No. 1; "Frühlingsfeier," op. 56, No. 5; "Barkarole," op. 17, No. 6; and "Wenn ... ," op. 31, No. 2 with a text by Carl Busse, Strauss followed the Jugendstil movements suggested by dance and the waves in dance ("Wellen im Tanz"). Of lasting influence was Strauss's attempt to make a meaningful musical interpretation of one of Nietzsche's main works, the philosophical poem composed of speeches *Also sprach Zarathustra* (op. 30, 1896). Following Nietzsche's idea, Strauss first had planned a five-part ballet. Because this concept could not be realized, Strauss turned to a tone poem which musically suggested that the dance was a transition in the process of humanity's self-liberation from the fetters of religious dogmas. As a sign of the victorious conquest of sorrow and subjugation, the disciples and the fully evolved superhuman, the "Übermenschen" become ever wilder with drunken happiness as they perform the dance of life, the "Tanzlied" (bars 251ff. and 409ff.) with its musical alternation between C major and B major, the musical symbols for the enduring conflict between nature and reason. Strauss characterizes the *Übermensch*'s temporary elation over the achieved freedom with a Vienna waltz, which is employed here, as Mieczyslaw Karlowicz had done, as a means of achieving giddiness by spinning oneself around.

Strauss likewise used wild, intoxicating dance as the gesture and symbol of both triumph and downfall in his momentous stage works, *Salome* and *Elektra*.[39] In the opera *Salome* he requires a wild dance ("einen wilden Tanz") into which all the motifs of the work enter poetically and which thus represents the crucial point of the erotic seduction, the perversity, the dramatic employment of the flamboyant veil dances of Loïe Fuller. Here, as in the tragedy, *Elektra*, the immoderate dancing that produces an intoxication of fulfillment among the raging, vengeful femmes fatales leads to destruction. Elektra dances like a maenad ("Wie eine Mänade"), she stretches her arms far out, and face to face with death at her somber end, she issues the challenge:

Schweig, und tanze. Alle müssen herbei! hier schließt euch an!
Ich trage die Last des Glückes, und ich tanze vor euch her.

(Be silent and dance. All must join in! Here gather 'round!
I carry the burden of happiness, and I will lead the dance.)

---

[38] Hans Hollander, *Musik und Jugendstil* (Zurich: Atlantis, 1975), pp. 47ff.

[39] See also Rasch, *Zur deutschen Literatur* (1967), pp. 70f.

This pathos in dance leading to death, combined with its grandiose gesturing, was also an important component in the works of Russian and French composers. Out in front of all the rest, Alexander Scriabin was compelled to issue both the cry, "To life! to life! People, animals, flowers, and stones!" and the challenge to perform the orgiastic "Dance upon Corpses." Beginning in 1906 he aimed at the synthesis of all arts within the framework of a theosophical mystery, at the end of which an orgiastic dance was supposed to lead to ecstasy and therewith to a sacramental act of cosmic eroticism. To celebrate this, Scriabin outlined the esoteric project of a temple of sensual pleasure, of intoxicating inspiration, of a utopian redemption of man and God. In this "total art," dance that makes possible mystic ecstasy was indispensable. He appended to bar 298 of his Piano Sonata, No. 6, op. 62 (1911), the explanation derived from the dark, demonic idea of the Nietzschean God-man: "l'épouvante surgit, elle se mêle à la danse délirante." In the "Acte preable" that conjures up the world of pleasures, the "Chor der Gefallenen" (Choir of the Fallen Ones), rebelling against heaven and frenetically moved by apocalyptic visions, sings:

Zertrümmern wird der Tanz alle Wohnstätten
Der seelischen Qualen, der Dramen des Herzens....
Der Tanz ist die erste Ursache,
Und der gerechte Herr des Gerichtes.

The dance will destroy every abode
Of spiritual torment, of dramas of the heart....
Dance is the primal cause,
And the just lord of judgment.

With this, dance is accorded an infernal-eschatological meaning. This intended pathological cult of decadence was explained by the composer in an appendix to the "Flammes sombres," op. 73, No. 2, with the words: "This is very audacious music. This is the dance of fallen man. This borders on black magic. Already here there is an unhealthy eroticism, perversity, and finally an orgiastic dance ... a dance upon corpses." Just how unfulfilled this boundless scheme remained in the end is shown by his overly pretentious tone poem, "Le Poème de l'Extase," the grandiose gestures of which remained unfulfilled, and which failed to achieve the intended level of impact which was supposed to transform the listeners. The extent to which these hypertrophic notions of a deification through dance were of concern to his contemporaries, though, is shown by glancing into the score of Claude Debussy's "Martyre de St.-Sebastien" (1911) with the saint's "Danse extatique" or in Igor Stravinsky's "Le Sacre du Printemps" (1911–13), the images from pagan Russia with a spring-time round dance, the dance of the young girls and the earth, as well as the "Danse sacrale de l'élue" with its driving rhythm.

The radical conclusion to this over-enhancement of the demand to be fulfilled through dance was no doubt drawn only by its originator himself, namely Nietzsche, who applied that conclusion to his own life. His life was shattered by modes of thought that relativized everything, by the megalomania of the savior of the world ("Welterlösers," 1899), who wanted to make the earth into a holiday ("die Erde zu einem Festtag machen" — letter to Cosima Wagner). After he had admitted at the end of 1888, "Ich bin ein Verhängnis" (I am a misfortune), mental derangement befell him. In January 1889 Overbeck, his friend from Basle, found him in Turin, naked, ludicrously dancing and leaping, behaving like a satyr. He who wanted to be a ruler was withdrawn from the rational world dancing like a buffoon. In this way dance became existentially much more than simply a decoration of one's gait ("Schmuck des Ganges," 1886, Henri van de Velde). Dancing, this life — Nietzsche's — fulfilled itself both in the will to survive during the day and in perishing in the darkness of insanity.

Illus. 1

"Die Tänzerin Loïe Fuller" (around 1900)
Raoul Larche, bedside table lamp of bronze
Badisches Landesmuseum, Karlsruhe

Illus. 2

"Tänzerinnen" (1917)
Emil Nolde, woodcut

Illus. 3

"Wolkengespenster" (1897)
Richard Riemerschmid, oil
Städtische Galerie im Lenbachhaus, Munich

Illus. 4

"Reigen" (around 1900)
Franz Reiter, oil on canvas
Vorarlberger Landesmuseum, Bregenz

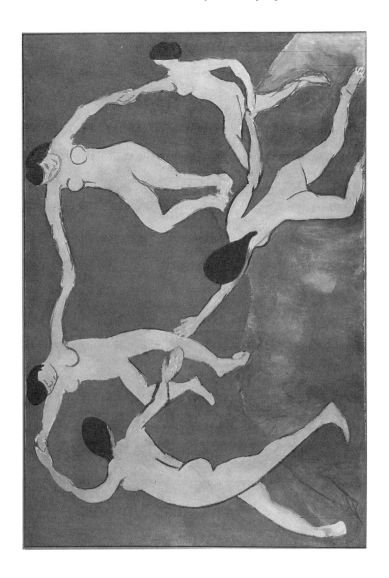

Illus. 5

"Dance" (1909)
Henri Matisse, oil on canvas
Collection, The Museum of Modern Art New York
Gift of Nelson A. Rockefeller
in honor of Alfred H. Barr, Jr.

Illus. 6

"Frühlingsreigen" (1909)
Franz von Stuck, tempera and oil
Hessisches Landesmuseum, Darmstadt

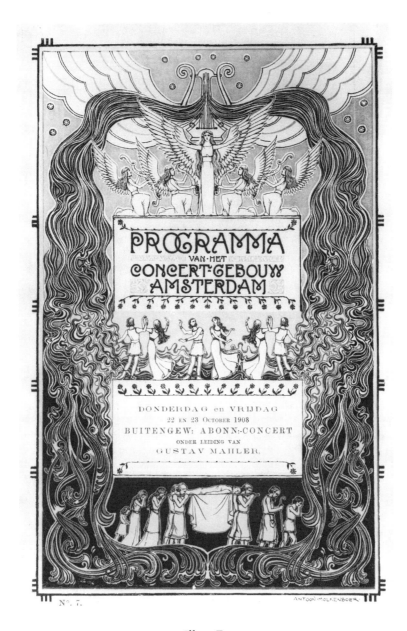

Illus. 7

Concert program (1903)
Antoon Molkenboer, designer
Gemeentemuseum, Den Haag

Illus. 8

"Tänzerin mit Kastagnetten" (1908)
Mathieu Molitor, bronze statuette
Private collection

Illus. 9

"Walzer III" (1894)
Hugo Höppener (called Fidus), color lithograph
from the portfolio "Tänze"

The Final Chapter of the Strauss-Hofmannsthal Collaboration on *Ariadne auf Naxos*

DONALD G. DAVIAU

As ORIGINALLY CONCEIVED *ARIADNE auf Naxos* had consisted of a severely abridged version of *Le Bourgeois Gentilhomme* of Molière, climaxed by the original opera *Ariadne* instead of, as in Molière's play, by the Turkish ballet. This version of *Ariadne*, which premiered in Stuttgart in 1912, was accorded such hostile criticism that Hofmannsthal eventually severed the play from the opera and replaced it by a *Vorspiel* of his own creation. It is this second version of *Ariadne auf Naxos* (1916) that remains the definitive text today.[1]

Even before the première of the revised version of *Ariadne* took place on 4 October 1916, Hofmannsthal had already devoted some thought to salvaging his adaptation of Molière's *Le Bourgeois Gentilhomme*. Actually, as he claimed later to Strauss, his decision to rewrite the Molière play was an act of generosity on his part, stemming from his wish to save Strauss's incidental music, which Hermann Bahr had praised as the finest thing Strauss had done. Although Bahr normally was given to talking in superlatives, Hofmannsthal in a letter of 24 July 1916 added that he would agree with this commendation "mit minder exclusiver Formulierung" (with a less exclusive formulation) and for that reason would like to see this music preserved:

> Vergeuden Sie doch, lieber Dr. Strauss, ja nicht voreilig diese Musikstücke, sicherlich wird es mir gelingen an Stelle der schematischen Nebenhandlung für diese Komödie eine zarte und musikable zweite Handlung (um die Tochter gruppiert) zu finden und das Ganze, mit einer burlesken Zeremonie am Schluß, wo Jourdain als Pascha schließlich auf einer türkischen Fastnachtsgaleere auf den Teich hinausfährt — die Liebenden im Mondschein zurückgeblieben —, zu einem richtigen phantastisch-realen Singspiel zu gestalten, wovon Reinhardt den Vorteil haben soll.[2]

---

[1] See Donald G. Daviau and George Buelow, *The Ariadne auf Naxos of Hugo von Hofmannsthal and Richard Strauss* (Chapel Hill: Univ. of North Carolina Press, 1974).

[2] *Richard Strauss-Hugo von Hofmannsthal Briefwechsel*, ed. Willy Schuh (Zurich: Atlantis, 1964), p. 256. All further citations are to this volume. This translation and those following are from *The Correspondence between Richard Strauss and Hugo von Hofmannsthal*, trans. Hanns Hammelmann and Ewald Osers (London: Collins, 1952), p. 256: "Please, dear Dr. Strauss, do not rashly waste these pieces of music; I am sure I shall succeed in inventing a second delicate action for this comedy (centered on the daughter) which lends itself to music, to replace that conventional subsidiary plot. I will make the whole thing into a genuine, half fantastic, half realistic Singspiel, with a burlesque ceremony at the end

This reference to Reinhardt is only one instance of how history repeated itself in connection with this drama. All through the collaboration on the opera, Hofmannsthal had warded off Strauss's every objection with the phrase that Reinhardt would handle all that. In fact the genesis and première of this adaptation follows the pattern of the original collaboration on *Ariadne* almost step for step. It virtually appears as if fate decreed that no aspect of this work should proceed easily and without complications, and this situation remained true to the very end.

Like every phase of the work connected with *Ariadne auf Naxos*, the collaboration of Hofmannsthal and Strauss on *Der Bürger als Edelmann* cost both men a great deal of effort and challenged to the utmost their ability to work together. Although the play ultimately proved unsuccessful, it is worthy of attention, for the stresses and tensions arising from this collaboration provide additional insights into the character of the two artists and their relationship to each other. In addition this adaptation provides a valuable illustration of Hofmannsthal's concept of comedy.

During the writing of the original opera, Hofmannsthal had dominated over Strauss's comments and criticisms, and he now wielded his sense of authority even more strongly in connection with this work which he considered fell into his area of expertise, that is, a drama with musical accompaniment rather than an opera. Hofmannsthal relished the fact that this time the composer had to play the secondary role and serve the needs of the dramatist for a change. As a result Strauss's suggestions were rejected out of hand by Hofmannsthal, who regarded them as irrelevant if not ridiculous and offensive. Strauss's patience was severely tested, but, except for a few occasions when he forcefully expressed his own annoyance at Hofmannsthal's behavior, he managed to control himself admirably in the face of his collaborator's unusual asperity. Finally, the misunderstanding about the nature of the work they were creating reached such a point that Hofmannsthal again was forced to write a lengthy analysis of his poetic intentions for Strauss's benefit in the manner of his previous "Ariadne letter" of July 1911 (132–35). Unfortunately, history repeated itself to the disappointing end of a failed première, for Hofmannsthal had possibly never misjudged anything he had written as badly as he did this adaptation.

After his initial letter to Strauss proposing the project, almost nine months passed before Hofmannsthal and Strauss discussed *Der Bürger als Edelmann* again. Strauss wrote on 10 April 1917 that everything was settled with Edmund Reinhardt (Max's brother) for the première on 1 April 1918, that is, approximately a year ahead, with the play scheduled for a run of two months. He added that although he had been looking through the works of Lully (who wrote the music for the original Molière play) to derive inspiration for the music, he had found nothing particularly useful there

where Jourdain as Pasha finally launches out on the pond in a Turkish carnival bark while the lovers remain behind in the moonlight — just the thing for Reinhardt."

(364). Then on 11 May 1917, Strauss notified his partner that he would like to work on *Der Bürger als Edelmann* at the beginning of June when he returned from a trip to Switzerland. He was working on the music for the Turkish comedy (which was taken over into the adaptation virtually intact) but would be glad to receive Hofmannsthal's manuscript soon (364–65).

Hofmannsthal replied on 19 May 1917 that he had been working hard for a month on the adaptation of the play:

> Es gibt sehr viel mühevolle Arbeit, wird mir trotz der Anonymität nichts wie Böses und Schiefes eintragen, aber es macht mir großen Spaß, denn es wird eine merkwürdige, gut gebaute burleske Komödie werden. Für Akt I haben Sie nichts Neues zu machen, für Akt II einiges, für Akt III ziemlich viel, vor allem die Cérémonie turque. Ich hoffe Ihnen alle drei Akte zum 10. bis 15. Juni schicken zu können.[3]

It is not possible in the space available to trace the fascinating genesis which illustrates the vast differences, artistic as well as personal, between these two supreme creative talents, each a master in his own field. One example will suffice. On 1 July 1917, since he had still not received the full text, Strauss innocently sent Hofmannsthal a few observations concerning the possibilities for musical exploitation offered by the play. He suggested that each act ought to be introduced by music and effectively concluded with music. Since the singers and the ballet were already involved in the action, he wished to use them to create a favorable final effect: "Da wir Sänger und Ballett schon haben, dürfen wir, glaube ich, nicht versäumen, uns ihrer zu einer freundlichen Schlußwirkung zu bedienen, um so mehr als die rein aufs Burleske gestellte türkische Komödie für den Musiker nicht sehr ergiebig und fürs Ohr der Zuhörer nicht sehr einschmeichelnd ist" (369).

Hofmannsthal responded immediately that Strauss's suggestions, while interesting and stimulating, had come too late, "… da alles mit großer Mühe und Überlegung zu einem glücklichen reizvollen Ganzen abgeschlossen ist" (370; he happily and attractively rounded off the whole thing and brought it to an end, 270). He informed Strauss that there was no point in his reading the original Molière play and basing an opinion on it, since everything had been changed in his revised version, and the musician could obtain no idea of how the whole thing would look until he had Hofmannsthal's text in his hands. Although this response would seem sufficient, Hofmannsthal then continued to explain in detail why Strauss's suggestions were either irrelevant or completely wrong headed. He concluded with the confident assurance to Strauss that there was no cause for concern, for he

---

[3] "It makes a great deal of laborious and minute work and, despite anonymity, will earn *me* nothing but unpleasantness and insinuations, but it will be a   remarkable, well constructed burlesque comedy. In Act II there will be a certain amount, in Act III quite a lot to do, especially the *Cérémonie turque*. I hope to send you all three acts by June 10th or 15th"; *Richard Strauss-Hugo von Hofmannsthal Briefwechsel*, p. 365.

had everything well in hand, including the musical development: "Seien Sie überhaupt ruhig, so wie ich bei Ihnen immer ruhig bin, wenn Sie sagen, daß etwas gut ist."[4]

Strauss, having been told unequivocally to mind his own business concerning the structure of the play since this was dramatist's work safely in the dramatist's hands, did not take kindly to such criticism. He no doubt felt, and with considerable justification, that he also knew a thing or two about writing for the stage. In his reply on 19 July 1917, he implored Hofmannsthal in strong terms to reconsider his plans, for he was able to state, even without seeing the text, that it would not be effective:

> Ihre Ausführungen über die Neubearbeitung interessieren mich natürlich gewaltig. *Ohne sie genau zu kennen*, möchte ich heute schon die stärksten Zweifel über alles *Melodram* äußern: das ist die unbeholfenste, blödeste Kunstform, die ich kenne. Da jede Musikübung im Melodram auf ein Minimum beschränkt sein muß, da man sonst dabei noch *weniger Text* versteht als in der Oper, bietet sie für den Musiker die am allerwenigst lohnende Aufgabe und in Folge dessen stets auch dem Publikum sehr wenig Ohrenschmaus. So ein kleines Stückchen am Schluß des II. Aktes sehr gut. Aber fast den ganzen dritten Akt *äußerst bedenklich!!!* sage ich heute schon *ungesehen!* Um so mehr als die türkische Komödie sehr wenig dankbar für den Musiker ist.[5]

However, just as Strauss was unable to convince Hofmannsthal in 1911 that the text was neither humorous enough nor explicit enough for an audience's comprehension, he faced the same problem again. He could not persuade the poet that the curtain scene without music would be ineffective. Hofmannsthal, partly standing on his pride as a dramatist, but mainly because he believed that his subtle approach was right, refused to be moved by Strauss's appeals and arguments. Instead, piqued by the criticism, he felt that Strauss was ungrateful for even raising objections since he had only undertaken this unrewarding project as a favor to his colleague. His five-page reply on 16 July 1917, including pointed reference to the financial

---

[4] "Altogether, you have nothing to worry about, just as I cease to worry when you say that something is good" (p. 271).

[5] "Your observations about the new arrangement naturally interest me tremendously. Even without knowing it in detail I should like to voice my strongest doubts about all melodrama right away: it is the clumsiest and most idiotic art form that I know. Since all music in melodrama must be limited to a minimum, as otherwise one would catch even less of the words than in an opera, it offers the least rewarding task of all to the musician, and, as an invariable consequence, not much of a treat to the audience's ears. A little of it at the end of Act II is excellent. But for nearly the whole of Act III extremely risky!!! I can tell you that right now, unseen! ... I implore you; curtains definitely based on music from the outset, and at the end of the piece some enjoyable vocal conclusion, a solo quartet — a dash of really pleasant music, not just a few stop-gap squeaks. I've had enough of these with the present endings of Acts I and II" (pp. 272–73).

arrangements that apparently were not at all to his liking, reiterated that Hofmannsthal had undertaken his adaptation only to save Strauss's music and that there was no benefit to him from such a work, to which he did not even intend to affix his name — indeed the work appeared anonymously and has to date never been included in his collected works. His explanation seeks to draw Strauss into his concept by clearly illuminating for him the work's originality:

> Es handelt sich um ein einmaliges Genre, weder Singspiel noch Operette, sondern eben ein Genre für sich, das aber in den schon bestehenden eineinhalb Akten klar und deutlich vorgezeichnet ist, dieses Genre lasse ich mir nicht verwirren, es nicht zur Operette hinüberbiegen, und alle Ihre Vorschläge gehen auf Verwirrung und Vermischung der Genres aus. Hier aber bleibe ich bei der Stange, denn Sie sind in vielen künstlerischen Gaben und Kräften mir überlegen, Stilgefühl aber habe ich mehr und eine größere Sicherheit des Geschmacks, das hervorzubringen, was zwar im Moment nicht ganz dem Geschmack der Masse gemäß ist, aber eine gewisse Dauer verbürgt.[6]

Nevertheless Strauss persisted in his view that the play ought to end grotesquely, either with Jourdain being cured of his delusions and turned into a sensible human being or as tragi-comedy with the achieving self-illumination followed by his collapse and possibly madness (380).

Patiently, almost as if resigned to misunderstanding, Hofmannsthal on 28 July 1917 replied that Strauss probably had not realized how much the whole play, as he had written it, aimed at a half-burlesque, half-sentimental finale, in short the same blend of worlds that formed the culmination of *Ariadne*. Just as they had argued then over the presence of the two worlds of Ariadne and Zerbinetta at the end of the opera, they disagreed now over the same problem:

> Das ganze Stück hindurch (in meiner Fassung) ist die Intention wirksam, den Endpunkt der Liebesintrige und den Höhepunkt in Herrn Jourdains närrischen Erdenleben wirklich poetisch in eine Einheit fallen zu lassen, während Molière diese beiden Dinge ganz stumpf nebeneinander sein läßt, ohne alle Synthese; dieser Schluß ist für unser heutiges Gefühl unmöglich: er muß entweder revoltieren oder er wird als "historisch" hingenommen und läßt ganz kalt. Auf meinen Schluß, die Bindung der beiden Motive zu

---

[6] "It is a work of a unique kind, neither Singspiel nor operetta, but in a genre of its own, though one which is already clearly and plainly mapped out in the existing act and a half. This genre I shall not allow to be adulterated or bent towards operetta, and all your suggestions tend towards such adulteration and confusion of the different genres. And on this point I shall stand firm, for although you are my superior in many artistic gifts and abilities, I have the greater sense of style and more reliable taste with which to create what is sure of enduring for some time though it is not for the time being wholly in line with the taste of the crowd ..." (pp. 274–75).

einer bitter-süßen Harmonie, hab ich die ganzen drei Akte hindurch hingearbeitet, insbesondere durch die Führung des Charakters der Lucile, durch die Nuance von weltmännischem Jesuitismus, die ich dem Cleonte gegeben habe u.s.f. Es kommt alles darauf an, das Musikfinale organisch mit diesem Schluß, dessen Intention ich Sie bitte, nachzuempfinden, zu verbinden.[7]

Strauss still did not approve and suggested adding a fourth act, an idea which received short shrift. This idea finally showed Hofmannsthal how far apart they were in their conception of the play, causing him to write a lengthy letter explaining his meaning, as he had previously done for the opera. Beginning with the observation that the great critics like Boileau, Fénélon, and Vauvenargues have always praised Molière's ability in his comedies of character in finely separating the foolishness of the protagonist from the pathological and from madness, he describes how he has tried to emulate Molière in this approach:

> Durch Berechnung jeder Nuance in Lucile und Cleonte (der nicht so schuldlos wie sie, sondern etwas von praktischem Jesuitismus tingiert), durch das Zusammenrücken zweier Festmomente: der Zeremonie der Kontraktunterzeichnung, durch Luciles ernste, schuldbewußte Ergriffenheit, worin Geständnis und Verzeihung des trotz allem doch geliebten Vaters vorweggenommen, habe ich getrachtet und erreicht, der Schlußsituation ihren schwebenden, buntgemischten, gleichsam schillernden Charakter (ohne den sie sogleich ins Bürgerlich-Schwere, Intrigante, Verletzende hinabfällt) zu wahren; durch die Erfindung der Sylphen mit ihrem Spiegel habe ich das Festliche noch durch die Beimischung des Phantastischen, das Leichte durch das Luftige erhöht: ... Weil hier Narrheit und Schicksalerfüllung, Lug und Trug der Welt und Liebesglück, gelungene Intrige und bittere Philosophie sich in einem Punkt, gleichsam auf der Spitze einer Nadel, treffen, darum, nur darum ist es auch schwer, für die Schlußcouplets, für ein von Ihnen gewünschtes Finale den richtigen Stil, die richtige Nuance zu finden.[8]

---

[7] "The whole drift and purport of the piece in the new version is to make the culmination of the love intrigue coincide with the climax of Jourdain's foolish experience so as to pull the play together, whereas Molière lets the two plots amble along stolidly side by side without attempting any synthesis. Such an end is impossible by our present-day notions; it is bound either to upset people or to be accepted as 'historically interesting' and so to leave them quite cold. My finale, that blending of the two themes in bittersweet harmony, is what I have aimed at throughout the three acts, especially by my treatment of Lucile, by that touch of worldly Jesuitry which I have given to Cleonte, and so on. What matters is to wed organically the musical finale with this ending, into the spirit of which I beg you to enter" (p. 280).

[8] "I have succeeded in this by calculating every shade of the characters of Lucile and Cleonte (who is not as blameless as she is, but has something of the practicing Jesuit about him); by telescoping two festive occasions, the ceremony and the signing of the contract; by Lucile's serious qualms of conscience which anticipate her confession and the

Other points discussed were Strauss's objections to the exclusion of Dorante and Dorimène at the end and also the omission of the philosopher's spelling lesson, which Reinhardt and he found clumsy and tedious. Hofmannsthal concluded that he was profoundly saddened by Strauss's reaction. He felt that with a lot of difficulty on his part he had taken an old, badly constructed summer house and turned it into a luxurious mansion without Strauss giving one word of approval or providing any indication that he even noticed any of the improvements. In his disappointment he asked Strauss to consider whether he wanted to continue the collaboration on the play before they held their planned meeting to reconcile their differences (387).

The offer by Hofmannsthal to relieve Strauss of any obligation to continue working on the adaptation forced the musician to moderate his criticism, but it by no means diminished his reservations. Despite Hofmannsthal's repeated insistence that Reinhardt, in whom he continued to have unlimited faith, would decide how best to end the various acts, Strauss persisted in questioning the effectiveness of the final curtain scene to Act I: "Schlußmelodramen mit Rührung sind auch ein ziemlich oft wiederholtes Rezept. Ich fürchte, so wie es heute ist, wird Reinhardt das Stück, auch mit Pallenberg, nicht einen vollen Monat durchspielen können."[9] Strauss undoubtedly still remembered the days prior to the Stuttgart première when he had heard so often that Reinhardt would settle all troublesome matters as Hofmannsthal's means to quiet his objections. He had not shared Hofmannsthal's adulatory opinion of Reinhardt then, and he saw no reason to change his opinion now.

Strauss had prepared a different ending of Act I with music, which he considered superior to Hofmannsthal's conclusion, which, as usual, he found too quiet and too subtle. For Strauss there was nothing worse than theatrically ineffective plays: "Sie können mich totschlagen, aber für mich gibt es nichts Schrecklicheres als Theaterstücke, die nicht wirken, die nur für die sogenannten fünf 'feinen' Leute im Theater geschrieben sind und *in solchen doch auf reinste Publikumswirkung geschriebenen Stücken wie diesem Molière* Szenen und Aktschlüsse so pflaumenweich, daß niemand

---

pardon from her father, whom, despite everything, she has always loved. In introducing the sylphs with their looking glass I have raised the festive element by an admixture of the fantastic and have lifted what was light-hearted to the ethereal plane; but so as not to fall out of Molière's style into Shakespearizing romanticism, they could not be real fairies or elves but, to remain within the Latin convention which derives from the classical stage, a machination of the servant who manages the whole intrigue (in this Coville). Folly and destiny, the duplicity of the world and the fulfillment of love, successful intrigue and bitter philosophy all come together here as it were on a needle's point, and this, only this is why it is so difficult to find the right style, the right shade for the final vaudeville, for a finale such as you want it" (pp. 283–84).

[9] "Melodramatic endings with pathos are also a rather often used recipe. I fear, the way things are today, Reinhardt will not be able to perform the play for a full month even with Pallenberg"; *Richard Strauss-Hugo von Hofmannsthal Briefwechsel*, p. 389

weder weint noch lacht, noch applaudiert, noch zischt. Dies ist mir direkt peinlich: ich kenne kaum etwas fataleres. Wer dazu zu fein veranlagt ist, der muß Romane und Gedichte lesen, aber nicht ins Theater gehen...."[10] In his opinion, although Hofmannsthal had improved the Molière play, it was still not strong enough to captivate the public. Unfortunately, Strauss's view proved all too correct.

Der Bürger als Edelmann premiered in Reinhardt's *Deutsches Theater* in Berlin 9 April 1918 with Pallenberg in the title role. There are no letters about the première, but the first hint of dissatisfaction arises in Strauss's letter dated 31 May 1918, reporting the same kind of problem with the play that they had experienced with *Ariadne*: other than at Reinhardt's theater the casts were not good, and the play failed to achieve any particular success. Thus, although this time their work *did* have its première in the theater for which it was designed, namely, Reinhardt's theater in Berlin, even the talented hand of the master magician of the theater could not save this adaptation of a classical comedy from an early death after a mere 31 performances and many of those to poorly-attended houses. Most likely the play would have closed even sooner if Reinhardt had not been such a close friend of the author.

On 8 July 1918 Hofmannsthal wrote at length to Strauss, reviewing the fate of their various joint works as a preamble to his main point, the errors he had made in the composition of this work and ultimately his condemnation of *Der Bürger als Edelmann* as a complete failure. Although initially he accepted the responsibility for the failure, the roots of which went all the way back to the original decision in 1911 to use a Molière play as a framework for *Ariadne* rather than a work of his own, ultimately he arrived at the curious conclusion that Strauss's music actually caused the problem because it acted as a retarding feature:

> Die dünne und schwächliche Handlung wäre beständig von musikalisch-untermalten Stellen unterbrochen, und der naive Grundsinn des Publikums, der am Faden der Handlung nach vorwärts will, gerät in Widerspruch gegen dieses Retardierende. Ja, indem die Handlung so oft unterbrochen wird, wird dem sonst ganz bewußtlosen Publikum die Dünne der Handlung erst ins Bewußtsein gebracht, die einer Entspannung, eines Retardierens nicht bedarf. So lege ich mirs zurecht, und man müßte mit sehr sachlichen Argumenten kommen, um mich zu überzeugen, daß es andere Ursachen haben könnte: wenn ein Molière mit Pallenberg am beliebtesten Theater der Großstadt, mit Musik vom ersten und in der obern Schicht auch

---

[10] "You can kill me, but for me there is nothing worse than plays which are not effective, which are written only for the so-called 'fine' people in the theater and *in such plays as this Molière, written for the purest effect on the public*; the scenes and the endings of the acts are as soft as mush, so that nobody either cries or laughs, or applauds, or hisses. That is almost embarrassing to me. I scarcely know anything more disastrous. Whoever has too fine a disposition must read novels and poems but not go to the theater"; ibid.

populärsten Komponisten, reizend ausgestattet, glänzend besetzt, zu einem unzweideutigen Mißerfolg führt.[11]

Hofmannsthal refused to give up on the play without a struggle. In accordance with his suggestion to Strauss to revive *Der Bürger als Edelmann* for presentation at special occasions, Hofmannsthal attempted to revive it in 1921 at the Salzburg Festival. From his letter of 16 May 1921, it would appear that he and Reinhardt had even considered the possibility of taking the play on tour after the production at Salzburg. Just as he had taken the lead in revising *Ariadne* after its failure in 1912, Hofmannsthal, with renewed enthusiasm, now indicated to Strauss that he intended to recast the play in an endeavor to revive it on the stage, an enterprise which Reinhardt endorsed (466).

The Vienna première of *Der Bürger als Edelmann* took place in the Redoutensaal on 1 October 1924, with Strauss conducting. Again their letters make no mention of the performance, but, judging by the reviews, it was not very successful. A short time later Strauss resigned from the Vienna opera company, and perhaps for that reason he simply passed over the whole event. Hofmannsthal could not comment, for he had not attended the première. He had felt so confident of the outcome that he had left Vienna for a vacation at Bad Aussee. His only mention of the performance was a letter to Strauss expressing his sudden concern at the last minute that the music critic for the *Neue Freie Presse*, Julian Korngold, who had been carrying on a campaign against Strauss in his reviews, might prejudice public opinion against their work. Hofmannsthal therefore took steps to insure that the play would be reviewed also by the drama critic for the *Neue Freie Presse*, Raoul Auernheimer, a friend who could be counted on to present a fair judgment (392).

To insure that Auernheimer would understand his artistic intentions, Hofmannsthal from Bad Aussee took the liberty of addressing a detailed letter of explanation to the critic on 28 September 1924.[12] As he had

---

[11] "The meager and rickety action is constantly interrupted by passages of descriptive music and the audience, whose unsophisticated impulse is to get on with the plot, becomes restive and chafes at these retarding moments. It is, indeed, the constant interruption of the action which brings home to the public what otherwise it might not notice at all, I mean how meager the plot is; they feel there is no need here for any relaxation of tension, for any retarding passages. This is my own explanation, and it would take pretty solid factual arguments to convince me that there could be any other reason why a Molière comedy with Pallenberg, produced at the most popular theater in the Metropolis, with music by the foremost and at the highest level even the most popular composer — why a comedy charmingly staged and brilliantly cast should turn out an unequivocal failure"; ibid., pp. 413–14.

[12] Donald G. Daviau, ed., "The Correspondence of Hugo von Hofmannsthal and Raoul Auernheimer," *Modern Austrian Literature* (Special Hofmannsthal Issue) 7, nos. 3/4 (Dec. 1974): 260–63.

mentioned to Strauss, Hofmannsthal explained that since the work was primarily a play, he preferred Auernheimer as drama critic to judge him rather than allowing Korngold to review the performance alone, particularly since he felt that Korngold was less competent to cover theater productions and moreover was so prejudiced against Strauss.

Hofmannsthal then entered into a justification of his adaptation of Molière along the lines of his earlier analysis for Strauss's benefit and explained in detail what he had changed in the play and his reasons. Hofmannsthal explained how *Der Bürger als Edelmann* fulfilled his general theory of rewriting masterworks, namely, that they should be true to the period in which they were written, but at the same time they should be appropriate to their own day. After describing Molière's hurried composition and careless construction, Hofmannsthal continued,

> Wenn ich es nun gewagt habe, an einem Molière zu ändern, und *viel* zu ändern (freilich nichts an den berühmten Hauptszenen, wohl aber an den schwächeren Teilen des Stückes): wenn ich die etwas schematische Ehefrau durch die ausgeführte Gestalt der Tochter ersetzt, den Philosophen aus einer bloßen Andeutung zur vollen Figur entwickelt, den Cleonte eine Physiognomie (die mit seiner etwas zweideutigen Handlungsweise übereinstimmt) und dem Abenteurerpaar mehr sociale Bestimmtheit und sogar ein paar pittoreske Gefährten gegeben habe, so habe ich bei diesem allen, und den noch mehreren Freiheiten die ich mir mag gegeben haben, dies eine im Auge gehabt: die verschiedenen gar zu lose nebeneinander hängenden Fäden der Intrigue in einen stärkeren zusammenzudrehen, und die Einwirkungen der beiden ihre selbstsüchtigen Figurengruppen auf die Hauptfigur zu einer consistenten Handlung zu verbinden — durch welche eine Lebensatmosphäre entstehen, in deren Mitte der betrogene Selbstbetrüger zur tragi-komischen Culmination geführt wird.[13]

Hofmannsthal also explained why he was not signing his name to this work in more complete terms than were used in his earlier comments to Strauss on the same point: "daß ich meinen Namen nicht unter eine solche Arbeit setze, mögen Sie mir als Stolz oder als Bescheidenheit auslegen: es ist von beiden etwas darin. Ich finde, daß man eine schöpferische, nicht nur

---

[13] "If I have dared now to change a Molière, and to change a *great deal* (to be sure nothing in the famous main scenes but rather in the weaker parts of the play): if I have replaced the somewhat schematic wife through the fully drawn figure of the daughter, have developed the philosopher from a mere presence to a full figure, have given Cléonte a physiognomy (which corresponds to his somewhat ambiguous behavior) and the adventurer couple more social direction and even a few picturesque companions, then I have, with all this and the several additional liberties which I may have allowed myself, had one thing in view: to pull together the various much too loose threads of the intrigue hanging side by side into a stronger one, and to unite the effects of the two groups of figures pursuing their selfish aims in terms of the main figure into a consistent plot — through which an atmosphere of life will result, in the middle of which the deceived self-deceiver is led to a tragi-comic conclusion"; ibid., p. 262.

dramaturgische Arbeit unterzeichnet, und weiß mich lieber in der Tradition des lebendigen Theaters — mögen auch die alten Auffassungen des Augenblicks, die von Literaten und halbgebildeten Philologen in Umlauf gesetzt wird, davon abweichen."[14]

The reviews of both Auernheimer and Korngold appeared sequentially in the Feuilleton section of the *Neue Freie Presse* on 3 October 1924. While Auernheimer, a man of great sincerity and probity, and highly regarded by Arthur Schnitzler,[15] was possibly flattered by the personal attention from Hofmannsthal, it did not influence his review perceptibly. Contrary to Hofmannsthal's expectations, Auernheimer's comments were less than laudatory and contained a number of well-founded reservations, while — also contrary to expectations — Korngold praised Strauss's music in general but was very negative about the play.[16] Moreover, Auernheimer destroyed Hofmannsthal's desire for anonymity not only by designating him as the author of the work, but also by quoting in his review from the letter which the poet had sent him. Auernheimer, who was knowledgeable about Molière, devoted fully half of his review to a discussion of how Molière had originally come to write *Le Bourgeois Gentilhomme*, describing how this diversion was quickly improvised at the order of the king, who wanted to be entertained. He thus supported Hofmannsthal's opinion that this was not a vintage Molière play but an occasional work hastily written within a specific period of time and for a specific purpose. In describing the adaptation,

[14] "That I do not put my name on such a work you may interpret as owing to my pride or my modesty; there is something of both in it. I find that one is signing a piece of creative work, not only a dramaturgical one, and see myself rather in the tradition of a living theater — even if the views of the moment that have been put into circulation by literary types and half-educated philologists may deviate from this perception"; ibid., p. 261.

[15] See *The Correspondence of Arthur Schnitzler and Raoul Auernheimer Together with Auernheimer's Unpublished Aphorisms*, ed. Donald G. Daviau and Jorun B. Johns (Chapel Hill: Univ. of North Carolina Press, 1972).

[16] "Richard Strauss, der selbst dirigierte, unterstrich das rhythmische Element; im Verlaufe des Abends schien ihm die Teilnahmslosigkeit des Publikums zu verstimmen. Seine Musik wirkt, losgelöst von Wort und Szene Molière-Hofmannsthal's, jedenfalls stärker. Sie leidet schon — siehe die Tisch-Szene — als melodramatische Musik. Grillparzer's Ausspruch, daß die Worte die Musik verderben, scheint hier in einem übertragenen Sinne Geltung zu haben. Vielleicht beeinträchtigt aber auch die Musik die Worte ... Straussens Suite durfte lebenskräftiger bleiben als die Komödienmusik, der sie entnommen ist, die Komödie selbst mit eingeschlossen" (Richard Strauss, who himself was conducting, emphasized the rhythmic element. In the course of the evening the audience's lack of interest seemed to put him in a bad mood. The effect of his music in any case, separated from the text and staging of Molière-Hofmannsthal, is stronger. It suffers to begin with — see the scene at table — as melodramatic music. Grillparzer's pronouncement that the words spoil the music seems to have validity here in a figurative sense. But perhaps the music gets in the way of the text, too. Strauss's pieces may remain alive longer than the music for comedy from which they derive, and longer than the music for comedy itself); Julius Korngold, "Der Bürger als Edelmann von Molière — Musik von Richard Strauss," *Neue Freie Presse*, 3 October 1924, p. 2.

Auernheimer pointed out that Hofmannsthal had cut the original Molière play from five acts to three, dispensing with inessential material to achieve a stricter economy. Yet, he commented, the eliminated features were not always replaced by inventions of any greater essential value. He particularly missed the "juicy" (*saftige*) scene in which the philosopher became angry as well as the folksy figure of Jourdain's wife, whose healthy common sense, he felt, was a necessary counterweight in the play to the insipid foolishness of her husband. Hofmannsthal, by eliminating the wife and transposing all of her speeches to the daughter, had given the latter a mind of her own and a cleverness that no girl of her age ever possessed in a Molière play. The specific gravity of the daughter, now so heavily weighted, was too great, he felt, for the medium of comedy.[17]

In the remainder of the review, Auernheimer then praised the various additions which he felt were particularly successful, such as the form given to the banquet scene. Citing Hofmannsthal's letter again, he also praised the more tightly-knit structure which tied the various loose elements of the original comedy together in a more dramatically effective manner. He devoted the conclusion to commentary on the performance of the various actors, without, however, presenting any summation concerning the reception of the play by the audience. Auernheimer's critique was on balance favorable and served less as an analysis than as a cautiously written appreciation. Nevertheless, Hofmannsthal expressed his satisfaction with the fairness of the review in a second letter to Auernheimer.[18]

Thus the circle was rounded with the unfortunate result in this case that it encircled very little. Despite the change from a two-act adaptation of a Molière play with an opera to a three-act version with musical accompaniment, the result was still considered a bad text with good music. This one aspect of a work begun so optimistically in 1911 ended in failure in 1924. Among those works which he completed, *Der Bürger als Edelmann* might be considered the greatest failure of Hofmannsthal's career. Precisely for this reason the work has been worthy of consideration, for in this failure, perhaps even more clearly than in his successes, can be seen Hofmannsthal's particular talents as a dramatist and as a human being. Possibly, had he listened to Strauss's suggestions, as he did along with those of Harry Graf Kessler for *Der Rosenkavalier*, he might have found greater success with this work that even Reinhardt in his own theater could not save. However, if he had been capable of following Strauss's theatrical ideas, so antipodal to his own, he would not have been Hofmannsthal.

There is little point here in making a detailed comparison of Hofmannsthal's adaptation with the original Molière, but some of the more pertinent aspects of the revised version are worth noting in order to understand why

---

[17] Ibid.

[18] Daviau, ed., "The Correspondence of Hugo von Hofmannsthal and Raoul Auernheimer," pp. 263–64.

this work failed, even though Hofmannsthal's intentions were fully realized in it.[19]

Hofmannsthal, in undertaking to adapt *Le Bourgeois Gentilhomme*, correctly recognized it as a hurriedly written work containing one strong, central character around which all of the other elements were loosely grouped, providing ample opportunity for the insertion of dances and songs. This was not so much a play as a *divertissement* and was presented in this form originally with music by Lully. As Hofmannsthal himself had stated in 1911, only because the play did not conclude with any real point, ending as it did with the Turkish ballet, was it possible for him to combine it with their opera. In his first adaptation of the play for the opera Hofmannsthal had retained the casual spirit and intent of the Molière original. However, in revising the play to be performed independently, Hofmannsthal, who had in the interim completed his masterful comedy *Der Schwierige*, virtually abandoned his model to bring the work into line with his own sophisticated ideas of comedy. He tightened the structure considerably, unified the action by binding the various plot lines together, and gave the play a conclusion instead of leaving the action unresolved. In short, he attempted to raise what was a light farce to the level of high comedy.

As Auernheimer had pointed out, this shifting of the play to a denser atmosphere than Molière had intended these characters to breathe destroyed most of the work's comic vitality. However, Hofmannsthal, who eschewed all boisterous humor — hence his inability to accept any of Strauss's suggestions —, was simply incapable by temperament of working in terms of farce. By improving the structure of the play, as he unquestionably did, Hofmannsthal sacrificed its farcical essence, which alone was the source of the original work's enduring success. The poet's attempt in his rationalizing letter to Strauss to blame the retarding effect of the music for the failure of the play overlooks the salient fact that the original had been conceived from the beginning with music and dance involved. To cite Oswald's pertinent comment: "Odd that it did not occur to him [Hofmannsthal] to wonder how Molière's play had survived the retarding effects of Lully's music for two and a half centuries."[20] This oversight on Hofmannsthal's part is particularly striking, for the great Viennese tradition of folk comedy, which flourished in the nineteenth century in the works of Raimund and Nestroy, featured, as he well knew, interludes of dance and music without detriment to the plays.

The reason for the failure, as Oswald has rightly indicated, must be attributed directly to Hofmannsthal:

---

[19] See Helmut Wocke, "Hofmannsthal und Molière," *Neuphilologische Zeitschrift* 2 (1950): 127–237; and Victor A. Oswald, Jr., "Hofmannsthal's Collaboration with Molière," *Germanic Review* 29, no. 1 (Feb. 1954): 18–30. Of the two articles, Oswald's is by far the more penetrating and informative.

[20] Oswald, p. 26.

The prime reason for the play's failure can be traced to Hofmannsthal's fundamental aversion to the burlesque, and, indeed, for all the more robust kinds of humor. Not even the smashing success of *Der Rosenkavalier* could reconcile him to the slapstick of Act III, where the borrowings from *Monsieur de Pourceaugnac* are capped by even more drastic horseplay. It was Strauss who had kept prodding him to make the audience laugh, and almost two decades later Hofmannsthal still resented it.... Hence the deletion of all simply rib-tickling incidents from his *Bürger als Edelmann*; and hence, no doubt, Hofmannsthal's fatal inability to see that Jourdain is a viable stage figure only upon the condition that the rest of the play constantly verge upon the farcical.[21]

As mentioned earlier, Hofmannsthal both in his works and in his theorizing about drama conceived of comedy in terms of sophisticated high comedy, of a refinement which invokes smiles but not laughs and often borders on the tragic. The fruition of this theory, the only fully realized example of it in his work, is *Der Schwierige*, completed shortly before the adaptation. His theory of comedy involved a substantial use of irony — not verbal irony but irony resulting from the relationships of the characters — for in his view comedy juxtaposes its characters in such a fashion that each casts an ironic light on the other: "Aber die wirkliche Komödie setzt ihre Individuen in ein tausendfach verhäkeltes Verhältnis zur Welt, sie setzt alles in ein Verhältnis zu allem und damit alles in ein Verhältnis der Ironie."[22] As has been shown, even in *Ariadne*, which is classified among the comedies, the two opposing worlds are brought together finally through ironic misunderstanding. For Hofmannsthal felt that loose form was impossible for comedy, hence his tightening of the plot, his deletion of key characters such as Jourdain's wife, and his decision to bring all of the remaining characters into ironic relationship with one another. However, while loose form is incompatible with his kind of comedy, it is a prerequisite for farce. Inability to adapt to the kind of play he was dealing with was the source of Hofmannsthal's problem. He unified Molière's play and won the battle of form, but ended by losing the war of genre. Instead of a loose-knit but highly successful farce carried along substantially by the songs and dances, he created a tightly-unified comic melodrama that was a failure. Strauss had correctly recognized the flaw in Hofmannsthal's conception when he suggested that there needed to be a fourth act either to allow Jourdain to be vindicated or to show him driven mad. Since Hofmannsthal had revised the text, not to high comedy but more to the level of melodrama, the play needed to be resolved rather than leaving it open-ended, as Molière had done. While Hofmannsthal resolved the plot in terms of the two genera-

---

[21] Ibid.

[22] "Real comedy places its characters into a thousandfold complicated relationship to the world, it places them in a relationship to everything and thus everything into a relationship of irony"; Hugo von Hofmannsthal, *Die Ironie der Dinge*, in *Prosa IV*, ed. Herbert Steiner (Frankfurt am Main: S. Fischer, 1955), p. 40.

tions, that is, in terms of Jourdain and his daughter, he says nothing about the outcome of Jourdain's folly. However, by bringing the action out of the never-never land of Molière's original into contact with the real world, as Hofmannsthal had done, the problem of Jourdain could not be left without resolution. As Oswald pointed out:

> What makes it a failure is the sorry incompatibility between Hofmannsthal's characters and Molière's unique, immemorial M. Jourdain. It is the *sine qua non* of Jourdain's very existence on the stage that no one take him seriously. Everyone, even the members of his own family, must accept him without reflection as an amiable zany. The emotional involvement of even one character — and Hofmannsthal's Lucile is emotionally deeply involved with her father — blocks the "anaesthesia of the heart" and makes us see Jourdain, not as a figure of comedy, but as a "case of pathology."[23]

Hofmannsthal had been unable to achieve the fine line between the merely foolish and the pathological that he had earlier claimed to Strauss constituted Molière's genius. He had also weakened the humor by eliminating incidental bits of comedy, including the sure-fire quarrel between the philosopher and the other masters (which Auernheimer also had missed), as well as the famous spelling scene, which Strauss had defended and which had always proved a hit in this play.

Hofmannsthal may have been right that the primary purpose of comedy is not to generate laughs, but it is certainly the purpose of farce, which is what Molière's *Le Bourgeois Gentilhomme* was originally. Furthermore, he had not succeeded in creating a true comedy but had only advanced the play to the level of melodrama, a form he usually shunned. It is ironical that this play, in which the poet so completely attained his dramatic intentions, should have proved so unsuccessful. His effort reminds one of Kafka's *Hungerkünstler*, who when left to his own desires could only self-destruct. Judged in its own terms, Hofmannsthal's *Der Bürger als Edelmann* is an excellently crafted work of solid proportions and finely-tuned comic rhythm. Its only flaw, unfortunately fatal, is that the play no longer possesses the verve, life, and sparkle of Molière's *Le Bourgeois Gentilhomme*. For that reason it has disappeared virtually without a trace, while — one final irony — Strauss's incidental music, to save which was Hofmannsthal's sole purpose in undertaking this adaptation, has survived on its own merits and continues to be performed.

---

[23] Oswald, pp. 24–25.

In Praise of "Culinary" Art?:
On the Libretto Discussion between Hugo von Hofmannsthal and Richard Strauss, with a Glance at Walter Felsenstein's Music Theater[*]

Sybille Hubach

DISCUSSIONS ABOUT OPERAS ARE like conversations about fine meals. What remains in the memory, and becomes a secondary enjoyment as a possible topic of conversation, is a certain flavor or series of remembered palatal pleasures, without such memories allowing of precise verbal expression. Now, in a sense the art of cooking is reproduced by means of this secondary enjoyment: one knows the ingredients, the ways they are prepared; by the so-called act of tasting one divines the accumulated experience that lies behind the certain trick — and knows immediately that only that process which leads to the successful unity of all the ingredients creates true pleasure. That the process usually cannot be repeated and the hope for confirmation through its repetition usually remains disappointed surely is a function of temporality. For this reason, the gluttons, to whom Dante assigned a special place in hell, are often enough melancholy and sometimes suffer like medieval monks from "acedia," from a kind of *acedia tabulae*. The enjoyment of opera appears comparable to such culinary pleasures. A happy synthesis of different elements also constitutes the event here. Thus opera lovers speak about pleasure, and so do the detractors of "culinary theater," who are thus equally well its — deficient — connoisseurs. Since culinary art appears related to the essence of opera, opera's aim is decidedly to be a feast for the senses.

In its almost four-hundred-year history, opera has developed special laws, special possibilities and limits, and has found a special public, indeed lovers. Limited for a short time at first only to courtly circles, it soon reached a larger public and became finally a large middle-class social event, principally after, as a result of fashion, theaters devoted exclusively to opera began to be opened, bringing with them discovery of the orchestra stalls. From the beginning opera lived in and through a desire to keep up appearances, with music as the dominating element, with beautiful voices and pleasant staging, a festival produced deliberately for the eye and ear.

A festival not so much for spirit and intellect, to use, by way of contrast, Paul Valéry's definition of poetry as "fête de l'esprit." Despisers of the genre

[*] This translation of the German original into English is by Ellen Gerdeman-Klein and James M. McGlathery.

tend to focus their antipathy on the libretto, which as a rule is a pretty sad piece of literature, illogical, disconnected, chaotic, with a tendency to pathos, stereotypes, even to "Kitsch" (trash), as well as being unrealistic and therefore unbelievable. And when Schiller, a born man of the theater, defends opera with the same argument used by its opponents in writing to Goethe that opera is the highest form of the dramatic genre precisely because it does not come to terms with base reality,[1] it is difficult for the connoisseurs and lovers to disarm the genre's critics. So the libretto appears to deserve little more than the lowest rank as a necessary evil, simply enabling the music to serve the purpose of keeping up appearances without standing in its way. Thus it is merely a play the words of which are sung, but are for the most part, however, unintelligible (which usually doesn't matter, since well-known material serves as the model). The opera text surely must appear overtaxed by all the stricter requirements for the art of language, for logic and rhetoric, for polished, clever dialogue, by complicated constellation and dramaturgy — that is, by all the qualities of higher spoken theater. The effective aesthetic laws of opera as a genre require that the background fable from which the libretto comes be simplified and shortened, that psychological problems be rendered perceptible to the senses, that the characters be reduced to clearly circumscribed exponents of emotion. Even libretti that were not based on previous material and were therefore written for a "new" opera (which was an anomaly) were supposed to conform to these obviously iron rules.

Although the relative position of word and music in opera appears clear considering that often one and the same libretto was set to music by several composers one after another, there has nevertheless existed since the birth of this theatrical hybrid a repeated contest — mostly hidden but at times open — between the arts involved, fought out on opera's very own turf. One need only think of Salieri's *Divertimento theatrale*, "Prima la musica, poi le parole" or of Mozart's comedy with music, *Der Schauspieldirektor*, or especially of Richard Strauss's late piece of shadow-boxing entitled *Capriccio*. And when one remembers that the creators of opera from the beginning of the genre onwards were astoundingly devoted to the Orpheus myth, historical interpretation can see in this a repeated attempt to have the singing poet or the poetic singer become the genre's ideal, symbolizing a reconciliation of the two sides.

---

[1] *Der Briefwechsel zwischen Schiller und Goethe*, ed. Emil Staiger (Frankfurt am Main: Insel, 1966), p. 529; the letter to Goethe of 29 December 1797: "In der Oper erläßt man wirklich jene servile Nachahmung, und obgleich nur unter dem Namen der Indulgenz könnte sich auf diesem Wege das Ideale auf das Theater stehlen. Die Oper stimmt durch die Macht der Musik und durch eine freiere harmonische Reizung der Sinnlichkeit das Gemüt zu einer schönern Empfängnis, hier ist wirklich auch im Pathos selbst ein freieres Spiel, weil die Musik es begleitet, und das Wunderbare, welches hier einmal geduldet wird, müßte notwendig gegen den Stoff gleichgültiger machen."

Still, to remind ourselves how things really look within the genre, it is well to remember that in the aforementioned *Capriccio* the words, "Ton und Wort sind Bruder und Schwester" (Tone and words are brother and sister), is met with the ironic reply, "ein gewagter Vergleich!" (a daring comparison!).

A daring comparison? Hardly. Where is it written that siblings must get along, even if they should — which the psalmist praised as being a "lovely" thing? (Psalm 133, 1). In the history of opera one cannot speak of family considerations when it comes to the arguments about hegemony or balance of the two arts. Also, the problem of the "dramma per musica" appears less a burning issue until about the time of Richard Wagner: the structure of music, built on threes and fours and their multiples, simplifies the understanding of the text by its repetitions. The through-composed melody — or as Wagner called it, the "unendliche Melodie" — and its symphonic construction does not provide this assistance. Although a few "stimulating" words like love, revenge, mercy (even better in Italian: *amore! vendetta! pietà!*) along with stock scenes such as prayers, oaths, conjurations, drinking songs, and arias about loss of sanity suffice to sketch the situation, the librettists just starting out incline toward flights of literary fancy but soon have their wings clipped. In the end, a simple maxim rules: the easier the text, the less intrinsic literary worth, so much the better for the opera. Nevertheless, even less gifted librettists have been known to insist on the importance of their contribution.

It was almost inevitable that under these problematical circumstances the collaboration between such two self-willed, brilliant people as Hugo von Hofmannsthal and Richard Strauss would be fraught with particular difficulties. And a number of critical studies (in the etymological sense) have been done on this in equal measure productive and precarious relationship: from the respective positions the collaboration has been criticized, defended, or denounced. Noteworthy among others are the studies of Richard Alewyn, Hans Mayer, Willi Schuh, Jakob Knaus, Karl Joachim Krüger.[2] It is hard to say whether or not Theodor W. Adorno's bon mot, that Strauss may have caused a lot of damage to Hofmannsthal's poetry but that Hofmannsthal unintentionally paid him back in full, is justified.[3] In any case when the composer gloats at one point that the words lend themselves to musical composition "like oil and butterfat" ("wie Öl und

---

[2] See the *Forschungsbericht* by Hans-Albrecht Koch, "Hugo von Hofmannsthal," in *Wege der Forschung*, 265 (Darmstadt: Wissenschaftliche Buchgesellschaft, 1989).

[3] Theodor W. Adorno, "Richard Strauss," in *Gesammelte Schriften*, vol. 19: *Musikalische Schriften I–III*, ed. Rolf Tiedemann and Hermann Schweppen (Frankfurt am Main: Suhrkamp, 1978), p. 601.

Butterschmalz"),[4] when Hofmannsthal then complains in reply that Strauss was pouring a superfluous symphony ("entbehrliche Symphonie") over the text like sauce on a roast ("Sauce über den Braten")[5] — the culinary comparison appears here unavoidable — these are the fiercely ironic asides emanating from a double workshop not exactly lacking in conflict.

The work in question was *Der Rosenkavalier*, by far the most popular and successful product of this collaboration. As regards the librettist, no one would wish to claim that his text is lacking in ingenious ideas and their development. It may, however, be contended that through its musical setting the text does not necessarily come into its own, but rather turns into an opera entitled *Der Rosenkavalier*.

Superfluous "sauce" naturally does not mean that the music is really superfluous. After all, both artists aimed to create "eine neue Spieloper" (a new opera-as-play), although later in Vienna, *Der Rosenkavalier* was occasionally also performed as a comedy without music. "Superfluous" implies the suspicion that the music develops a domination which falsifies the text and with it the entire play and its aesthetic aim. For if characters, when they sing, often move in a completely different direction than the librettist planned, this does not apply only for the Fausts, the Mephistos, and Gretchens, the Hamlets, and the Maids of Orleans, but also for the figures which Hofmannsthal, in the service of Richard Strauss, created to come to life on stage.

On the musical stage these characters appear and live in a different region. Hofmannsthal clearly admitted this to himself, entirely in keeping with his concept of theater in general: "Wer sondert, wird unrecht tun. Wer eines heraushebt, vergißt, daß unbemerkt immer das Ganze erklingt. Die Musik soll nicht vom Wort gerissen werden, das Wort nicht vom belebten Bild. Für die Bühne ist dies gemacht, nicht für das Buch oder den einzelnen am Klavier." This was written in 1911 as an unwritten afterword to *Der Rosenkavalier* ("Ungeschriebenes Nachwort zum Rosenkavalier").[6] It must be understood also as a calm before the storm favored by success, namely a respite before the next collaborative, problematical task, which was an aesthetic endeavor of a totally different nature: *Ariadne auf Naxos*. It is precisely in the staging, specifically the practicalities of production, that the

---

[4] Letter of 21 April 1909. *Richard Strauss-Hugo von Hofmannsthal: Briefwechsel. Gesamtausgabe*, ed. Franz Strauss and Alice Strauss; rev. ed. Willi Schuh (Zurich: Atlantis, 1952), p. 49.

[5] Letter of 30 May 1909. *Hugo von Hofmannsthal — Harry Graf Kessler. Briefwechsel 1898–1929*, ed. Hilde Burger (Frankfurt am Main: Insel, 1968), p. 234.

[6] "He who divides is guilty of wrongdoing. He who emphasizes one thing forgets that, unnoticed, the whole always sounds. The music should not be torn from the word, the word not from the animated scene. The thing is made for the stage, not for a book or an individual at the piano"; Hugo von Hofmannsthal, *Gesammelte Werke in Einzelausgaben. Prosa III*, ed. Herbert Steiner (Frankfurt am Main: S. Fischer, 1952), p. 43.

problem of the supposed and intended unity presents itself — all the more so if one wants to make the opera fit a staging concept that is directed against an artistic purpose suspect as being purely culinary.

That was the aim, too, of the program of so-called "Realistisches Musiktheater" (realistic music theater) founded by Walter Felsenstein as a decided and clear rejection of unreflective pleasure — a concept not to be confused with Ferruccio Busoni's theory of "musikalisches Theater" (musical theater) which calls for non-Aristotelian structure and thereby insists on theater's "Spielcharakter," or principle of playfulness, that is, its artificiality and remoteness from everyday reality.

The fact that the stage which experimented with this new realistic style was called "Komische Oper" (comic opera) has an historical background. The style is reminiscent of the "opera comique," the lighter, truer-to-life, thus "more realistic" type of opera. As we know, this type of opera mixed spoken dialogue with musical numbers; it let song, at certain points, develop from the plot; and demanded a new quality of presentation. The form found its culmination in Bizet's *Carmen*. Thus it was a *Carmen* production which Felsenstein, after a number of earlier experiments, offered in 1949 as the model of his working style, thereby creating a breakthrough in staging. The production not only pointed the way for his own later efforts towards universality in musical theater, it was also the model that his collaborators and pupils Joachim Herz and Götz Friedrich developed further and applied to works in operatic literature which did not directly correspond to the "comique"-ideal.

Felsenstein's concept, based on the vision of a humanly truthful theater experience ("menschlich wahrhaftes Theatererlebnis"), was thus not meant to be the style of a time or epoch (such as the turning away from stage naturalism) or an identification of theater with reality beyond the theater. The political situation in 1947 naturally played a role in the founding of the "Komische Oper" in East Berlin: in agreement with socialist doctrine, one wanted "nicht den Beifall der gebildeten Kreise, sondern die Zustimmung des werktätigen Volkes, das sich um die Realität und Glaubhaftigkeit eines theatralischen Vorgangs nicht mehr betrogen fühlen sollte."[7] Felsenstein pinpointed the deception, the considerable lack of believability on stage as resulting from the function of song: it was unnatural, up to now just coincidental, leaving the audience uninvolved, and degrading the opera evening to a pleasant show without deeper meaning. To change that, it would be necessary to arrange the production so that the singing would emerge by itself as the "natural" consequence of a believable situation.

---

[7] "not [want] the applause of the educated circles, but rather the approval of the working class, which should no longer feel cheated out of the reality and believability of the action on stage"; The quotation and the ones following are from Walter Felsenstein, Götz Friedrich, and Joachim Herz, *Musiktheater: Beiträge zur Methodik und zu Inszenierungs-Konzeptionen*, ed. Stephan Stompor (Leipzig: Reclam, 1970).

Reworking based on critical examination of the text and its sources; faithful translations; and musical revisions put an end to the tradition Gustav Mahler had once spontaneously called slovenliness "Schlamperei." Accordingly, routineness, mental lassitude, and intellectual indolence were to be banned from the theater, both from on stage and from in the audience. Out of the necessity of being able to speak about music beyond its emotional content, beyond the formal, the technical and historical, Felsenstein made a virtue of a dialectical reversal of relationships: the basic preoccupation with the word, the fable, the dramatic substance of the piece, the history of the work itself and cultural history, formed the basis of his concept of staging. Once the plausibility of the dramatic situation was established, the music entered again into its rights wholly as a matter of course; it grew out of the event portrayed, song was just the enhancing, indispensable affirmation. Felsenstein thus formulated in his own way an old objective of theater practice: play, song, and music become an identical unity ("Spiel, Gesang, und Musik werden zur identischen Einheit").

Do they really? That would mean that the debate over the primacy of music or text would be determined solely by the scene, by the whole, "das Ganze," as Hofmannsthal called it. And since he characterized Strauss as a so fabulously unrefined person ("so fabelhaft unraffinierter Mensch") in a letter to Harry Graf Kessler on 12 June 1909,[8] since he did not see himself as music's obedient servant, one can suppose that this "whole" was the secret stimulus for their unparalleled partnership. Their collaboration was to lead to a "concordia discors," to a unity which transcended the individual medium to reach that secret point where art becomes absolute. And since with the question of what makes art art the claim surely still holds true that all great artists say the same thing, it is easy to cite testimony from transmitted reflections on art which understand this intentional transcendence of the art form (to speak with Schiller) as the victory of form as such over artistic elements. Hofmannsthal was therefore surely aware of such a tradition in his introductory comments (his "Geleit") to the *Rosenkavalier*: "Nichts ist schwieriger, als sich das Existierende als nicht existierend vorzustellen. Diese Figuren haben sich längst von ihrem Dichter abgelöst, ... das ganze Gewebe des Lebens zwischen ihnen, es ist, als wäre dies alles längst so gewesen, es gehört heute nicht mehr mir, nicht mehr auch dem Komponisten, es gehört jener schwebenden, sonderbar erleuchteten Welt: dem Theater, in der es nun schon eine Weile, und vielleicht noch für eine Weile, sich lebend

---

[8] *Hofmannsthal-Kessler Briefwechsel*, p. 242.

erhält"[9] — thus Hofmannsthal courted that mysterious texture of the aesthetic in his "Ungeschriebenes Nachwort zum Rosenkavalier" (1927).

All the same, Hofmannsthal's further collaboration with Strauss, too, was accompanied by sketches of a possible poetics for opera, which again and again take into account the effect and function of music as an indeterminable and yet empirical factor — above all how his linguistic consciousness of music might be transposed into the composer's consciousness of speech.[10] If, as Hofmannsthal formulated it in reference to his basic belief of the "individuum ineffabile," the ineffability or "Unaussprechlichkeit" of the individual, "daß im Leben durch Reden nie etwas entschieden wird" (in life nothing is solved by talking),[11] then poetic form does not show its essence through direct communication — through words, concepts, and reflection — but through its being, through its bearing or attitude that through the music and the scene is complementarily enlarged and thereby rendered perceptible. The recognition that in this process the characters detach themselves from their creator, that literary figures and constellations of figures become theatrical figures with scenically individual existences of their own, showed the librettist Hofmannsthal the way from *Konversationsoper* (conversational opera), the derivative of word comedy (*Wortkömodie*), to a "lyrical" formulation of the text which the music intended and contained from the start. That the hermeneutic balance can then work to the disadvantage of the librettist can be seen in the history of the work *Die Frau ohne Schatten*. This is probably the only known case in the history of opera in which a prose work, namely the fairy tale "Die Frau ohne Schatten," was created chronologically after the libretto. Idea and plot of the fairy tale focused, as we know, superficially on fertility in the biological sense, but allegorically on the poetic portrayal of an artistry which has fallen in danger of sterility — presumably with critical overtones referring to the case of Stefan George.[12]

---

[9] "Nothing is more difficult than to imagine that which exists as not existing. These figures have long ago distanced themselves from their poet, ... the whole pattern of life between the figures is as if it had long been so, it no longer belongs to me nor to the composer, but to that floating, strangely illuminated world: to the theater, in which it already has survived for a while, and perhaps will for a while longer"; Hugo von Hofmannsthal, *Gesammelte Werke. Prosa IV* (Frankfurt/Main: S. Fischer, 1955), p. 426.

[10] According to Stephan Kohler in his essay "'Worte sind Formeln, die können's nicht sagen': Musikbegriff und Musikalität Hugo von Hofmannsthals," *Hofmannsthal-Blätter* 31/32 (1985): 68.

[11] Hugo von Hofmannsthal, "Die ägyptische Helena," *Werke. Prosa IV*, p. 458.

[12] See the essay by Arthur Henkel, "Beim Wiederlesen von Hofmannsthals 'Die Frau ohne Schatten' notiert," in *Für Rudolf Hirsch zum siebzigsten Geburtstag am 22. Dezember 1975*, ed. J. Hellmut Freund (Frankfurt am Main: S. Fischer, 1975), pp. 235–38. Rpt. in Henkel, *Der Zeiten Bildersaal: Studien und Vorträge. Kleine Schriften Band 2*, (Stuttgart: J. B. Metzlersche Verlagsbuchhandlung, 1983), pp. 219–23.

In a letter before the premiere of the *Rosenkavalier*, Hofmannsthal describes how sensitive such a life of one's own is, and how dependent upon the favor of the moment: "ein rundlicher Octavian rankt sich mangelhaft um eine rundliche Marschallin, alle sind rundlich, nur nicht der Ox, der weder noch buffo, weder humoristisch, noch behaglich, noch drastisch ist, sondern ein 'edler' Comödiant, der in Bayreuth den Amfortas singt, man muß das alles mit Humor auffassen"[13] — an experience which leads up to the later *Ariadne auf Naxos* and its ironic reflection of dependencies and professional and psychological limitations of the musical and theatrical industry, which too must earn its daily bread.

Let us focus, however, on the theory of a realistic music theater, thinking of its ideal form as opposed to its realizations in the everyday world. It is a commonplace in critical study of the evolution of *Der Rosenkavalier*, that, as regards the exact interpretation of the text, Hofmannsthal hardly felt that his partner Strauss understood the essence of his poetry. When he pointed out to the composer, who had found the text fine, but perhaps a little too fine for the masses ("aber vielleicht ein bißchen zu fein für den großen Haufen"),[14] the plot's maximal simplicity ("non-plus-ultra an Einfachheit"), Hofmannsthal was acting on his famous maxim learned from Nietzsche that one must hide the deeper meaning beneath the surface. But what if the deeper meaning is hidden so well that one has to be content with the surface? Since viewed superficially *Der Rosenkavalier* deals with — here I indeed quote the author — a fat, old, arrogant suitor ("einem dicken, älteren, anmaßenden Freier"), who, although favored by her father, is outdone by a young, beautiful one ("von einem jungen, hübschen ausgestochen wird"), as Hofmannsthal wrote to Strauss on 12 May 1909.[15] Actually, however, it is a matter of conventions: marriage as a business, trading money and love, Eros and Ethos, faithfulness and unfaithfulness, if, as Hofmannsthal said, the point of the piece is that a charming but actually ordinary young gentleman ("ein im Grund gewöhnlicher junger Herr") takes for his wife a pretty, middle-class, lively, but basically ordinary girl ("ein hübsches, bürgerlich lebhaftes, aber im Grund gewöhnliches Mädchen").[16] She is thus the first acceptable young woman ("die erste beste Junge") for whom his relationship with the intellectually and socially superior lover

---

[13] "a plump Octavian twines himself incompletely around a plump Marschallin, everyone is plump except Ochs, who is neither basso nor buffo, neither humorous nor cozy nor drastic, but rather a noble comedian who sings the role of Amfortas in Bayreuth. One must retain a sense of humor about the whole thing"; Letter to Graf Kessler of 11 January 1911. *Hofmannsthal-Kessler Briefwechsel*, p. 319.

[14] Letter to Hofmannsthal, *Werke. Prosa IV*, p. 426.

[15] *Strauss-Hofmannsthal Briefwechsel*, p. 52.

[16] Letter to Graf Kessler of 20 May 1909. *Hofmannsthal-Kessler Briefwechsel*, p. 51.

must give way: that is the joke that unifies the whole ("Das ist der Witz, der das Ganze zu einer Einheit macht").[17]

Because of the decision to name the piece "Der Rosenkavalier" (for the opera was after all first supposed to be called "Ochs auf Lerchenau"), the — invented — ceremony of the bridal courtship à la rose becomes the centerpiece, and with it the "basically ordinary" ("im Grund gewöhnlicher") young man, who through the musically created silver-white atmosphere suddenly takes on the role of one of those radiant fairy-tale princes who sought and found their princesses. The omnipotence of the music in this scene produces a metamorphosis of the characters which the makes one forget their intended grouping: namely that Octavian's ancestry reaches from Mozart's "Cherubino d'amore," the embodiment of immanent erotic rapture, to the seducer and adventurer à la Casanova, and that we are thus dealing with a rather heartless male character type, to whom the Marschallin, with her perception of the inconstancy of life and love, correctly predicts: "Da steht der Bub ... und mit dem fremden Mädel dort wird er so glücklich sein, als wie halt Männer das Glücklichsein verstehn" (there the boy stands ... with that new girl he'll be as happy as he can be, seeing how men understand happiness).[18] The music also lets one forget that the naive Sophie has only her youth to thank for her good match. And when the Marschallin ends Sophie's chatter with the reproof: "Red sie nur nicht zu viel, sie ist ja hübsch genug" (Just don't talk too much, you are after all pretty enough),[19] one is again reminded of what Hofmannsthal said about Sophie's middle-class, silly, affected, acquired demeanor ("bürgerlich albernes, gespreiztes, angelerntes Wesen"),[20] that she is a mixture of an immature convent schoolgirl and a daughter eager to rise to the nobility and looking forward to marrying, because it is after all quite different than being single ("weil das doch was andres ist als der ledige Stand") and who needs a man for social fulfillment, namely, "daß ich was bin" (so that I am somebody).[21]

These and certain other components that are important for the personalities of the characters are canceled by the music, however. Already in the second act the music has arrived at the place that the text reaches only through the art of tying things together, in the ecstasy of the moment of fulfillment. If one wanted properly to stage only the psychological

---

[17] Letter to Strauss of 12 July 1910. *Strauss-Hofmannsthal Briefwechsel*, p. 89.

[18] Hugo von Hofmannsthal, *Sämtliche Werke*, vol. 23: *Operndichtungen 1. Der Rosenkavalier*, ed. Dirk O. Hoffmann and Willi Schuh (Frankfurt am Main: S. Fischer, 1986), Act 3, p. 99, l. 26ff. All subsequent references are to this edition.

[19] *Der Rosenkavalier*, p. 99, l. 7.

[20] Letter to Strauss of 13 July 1928; *Strauss-Hofmannsthal Briefwechsel*, p. 363.

[21] *Der Rosenkavalier*, p. 48, ll. 13 and 18.

appropriateness of these two figures as based on the text, one would have to do it in opposition to the music, which could hardly result in a congruence of word, tone, and action. How little Strauss concerned himself with the contrived finer points of Hofmannsthal's inventory of the types of human relationships ("Inventar der Formen menschlicher Beziehungen") is shown, too, by some of the wishes expressed in his letters to the librettist. On 16 May 1909 he writes, "Wollen Sie mir dazu noch etwas nachdichten? Die Musik ist schon fertig, ich brauche nur Worte zur Begleitung und zum Ausfüllen."[22] Or the letter of 26 June 1909, in which he writes, "Für den Schluß des dritten Aktes, das ausklingende Duett von Sophie und Octavian habe ich eine sehr hübsche Melodie: Wäre es Ihnen möglich, mir circa 12 bis 14 Verse zu schreiben in folgendem Rhythmus:

> Süße Eintracht du / holdes Band,
> voll treuer Liebe / Hand in Hand
> fest ver/eint für / alle Zeit
> fest ver/eint in / Ewigkeit.[23]

Going along with such silliness — but not completely without ironic reserve, which seems to substantiate Adorno's bon mot — Hofmannsthal makes the following out of it: "Ist kein Traum, kann nicht wirklich sein" (it's not a dream, it can't really be) and "Spür nur dich, spür nur dich allein und daß wir beieinander *sein*" (I feel only you, just you alone, and that we together be). And here one can perceive a final echo of the artistically mixed, totally invented ("völlig erfundenen") speech of *Der Rosenkavalier* in the dialectical coloring of the indicatively meant "sein" (to be) instead of "sind" (are).

The example is illuminating since from this ending, the happiness of "being together," thus of marriage by a love which lets us forget all the intrigues and burlesque "Qui pro quo" that led up to it, means that the composer understood the essence of the piece better than it may appear to experts on the text and readers of the letter exchange. Strauss did so namely by anticipating the ending in the beginning, by musically celebrating the victory of love over temporality. When in that blissful range which Strauss's music is capable of reaching, the silver rose is presented in accord with

---

[22] "Would you like to write a little more text for me? The music is already finished; I just need words for accompaniment and filling it out"; ibid., p. 54f.

[23] "I have a very pretty melody for the end of the third act, the concluding duet by Sophie and Octavian. Would it be possible for you to write for me about 12 to 14 lines with the following rhythm:
> Sweet harmony you / charming bond,
> full of true love / hand in hand
> firmly united for / all of time
> firmly united in / eternity."
Ibid., p. 58.

rituals that aim at happiness, the metamorphosis occurs that Hofmannsthal surely had in mind: the blissfulness of a fairy-tale scene, the most beautiful concentration of the story upon I and thou. The scene depicts — as he esoterically called it — the allomatic ("allomatische") metamorphosis of two rather unimportant young people through love, with a suggestion of the secret of the transmigration of souls when both sing: "Wo war ich schon einmal und war so selig?" (Where was I once before and was so bliss-ful?).[24] That the young man from a good family ("junge Mann aus gutem Haus") appears as an archangel ("Erzengel"),[25] that the strong fragrance of the rose appears as a greeting from heaven ("Gruß vom Himmel"), that as though on its own accord the comparison is made by the former convent girl Sophie to celebrate him as heavenly roses, not earthly ones, like roses from a most sacred paradise ("himmlische, nicht irdische, wie Rosen vom hochheiligen Paradies")[26] — all this belongs likewise to the series of discreetly ironic hints about the psychology of the figure, which presents itself only to the reader, not to the opera's listeners or audience. Even in the stage directions which, here as always with Hofmannsthal, are to be read carefully, we find: "Sophie und Octavian stehen einander gegenüber, einigermaßen zur gemeinen Welt zurückgekehrt, aber befangen" (Sophie and Octavian stand opposite one another, somewhat restored to the everyday world, yet preoccupied).[27] What can be gleaned from such a tenderly ironic stage direction? It seems to me that despite the persistent burlesque amidst all the turbulence of the third act, the archetypical truth of the text which, to put it somewhat solemnly, speaks about the experience of transcendence, finding its way to a higher language — in the music. The transition of the language, particularly the erotic language, to the "higher" expression of the music — even if a sobering up quickly follows — embodies the old romantic theme, and the theme of German Romanticism. This theme not only provides the pathos for the opera of the nineteenth century, it is above all the quasi-liturgical idea of the Wagnerian *Liebestod*. But this touching of the spheres ("Berührung der Sphären") is nowhere recognized so discreetly, so knowingly melted in a naive and melancholy way into a synthesis of word and tone as in this scene of *Der Rosenkavalier*.

Here, too, the negative use of the adjective "culinary" becomes meaning-less when a performance unites the aforementioned elements of word, scene, and tone, thus approaches the completeness at which the concept of "realistic music theater" aims. What counts is the degree to which the conflict of the categories of the aesthetic and the ethical momentarily are

---

[24] *Der Rosenkavalier*, Act 2, p. 46, l. 20f.

[25] Ibid., Act 2, p. 45, l. 11.

[26] Ibid., Act 2, p. 46, l. 10f.

[27] Ibid., Act 2, p. 47, l. 11f.

reconciled. Goethe once memorably described this experience metaphorically. In his novel *Die Wablverwandtschaften* he has his mysterious heroine
Ottilie write the following in her diary: "Alles Vollkommene in seiner Art
muß über seine Art hinausgehen, es muß etwas anderes Unvergleichbares
werden. In manchen Tönen ist die Nachtigall noch Vogel; dann steigt sie
über ihre Classe hinüber und scheint jedem Gefiederten andeuten zu
wollen, was eigentlich singen heiße."[28] Exaggerated? Can it yet be denied
that we today — excepting those who make a profession of being naive —
experience art as no longer beautiful, so that we hear that possible harmony
as being "still" there or "never again," as a remembrance of the times when
beauty was allowed to be truth's splendor? And if opera was pressed into the
service of morality, pedagogy, and politics as so it might be — even in the
highest windings of the culinary spiral, to which Felsenstein's concept may
belong, i.e., reflective culinariness — even such a posture as this remains
only apparent, that is, aesthetic. Then, too, the fusion that is produced in us
with the rose, nightingale, and the human voice, still has the power to
remind us of what has been lost. Still remind us it could be: once again. Or
even: timelessly for those who are responsive to it.

---

[28] "Everything of one kind that is a perfect specimen of its kind must transcend that kind,
it must become something incomparably other. In some tones, the nightingale is still a
bird; but then she rises above her class, and seems to want to indicate to every feathered
being what singing really is"; "Weimarer Ausgabe" of *Goethe's Werke*, I, 20, (Weimar: H.
Böhlau, 1887– 1919), pp. 310ff.

Rilke and Music: A Negative View

GEORGE C. SCHOOLFIELD

MOVING TOWARD HIS FORTIETH birthday, Rilke began to confess his ignorance about music. On 25 November 1912, he wrote to Alexander von Thurn und Taxis about his "vollkommene[n] Analphabetismus in der Musik,"[1] after having heard a "Salve" in a little Mozarabian parish church in Toledo; to Ilse Sadée, on February 8 of the same year, he had already spoken with (for him) unaccustomed plainness: he thanked her (called "gelehrtestes Mädchen") for having made him acquainted with *Harzreise im Winter* — "nicht die Brahmssche (ich kenne fast keine Musik), aber das Goethesche Gedicht."[2] To Magda von Hattingberg, the pianist and temporary queen of his heart, he made a similar lament some two years later, about his inability to remember (or to carry?) a tune: "Wirklich, ich behalte keine Melodie, ja ein Lied, das mir nahe ging, das ich dreißigmal hörte, ich erkenn es wohl wieder, aber ich wüßte auch nicht den mindesten Ton daraus anzusagen, das ist wohl die dichteste Unfähigkeit selber."[3] Such self-denigration would be repeated. After a visit to Muzot by Werner Reinhart and his two musical protegés, the violinist Alma Moodie and the composer Ernst Křenek (whom Rilke, ever mindful of great connections, described as "mit der Tochter Mahler's verheirathet"), Rilke told Maria von Thurn und Taxis of the instant creation of "ein Klima von *Musik*, in dem ich, tauber Berg, mich recht felsig ausnahm, immerhin dankbar für die melodischen Angriffe und Zärtlichkeiten an allen Hängen meines Gefühls."[4]

---

[1] "total illiteracy in music"; *Briefe*, ed. Karl Altheim with Ruth Sieber-Rilke (Wiesbaden: Insel, 1950), 1:410. Hereafter *B* (1950).

[2] "most learned girl"; "not the Brahms [setting] (I know almost no music) but Goethe's poem"; *B* (1950), 1:359.

[3] "Really, I cannot retain any tune; indeed, a song which affected me, which I had heard thirty times — I'll recognize it, of course, but I wouldn't know how to intone even the slightest note from it, it's a case, after all, of the densest incapability, personified"; *Briefwechsel mit Benvenuta*, ed. Magda von Hattingberg and Kurt Leonhard (Esslingen: Bechtle, 1954), p. 27 (4 February 1914). Hereafter *Benvenuta*.

[4] "married to Mahler's daughter"; "a musical climate, in which I, a deaf mountain, cut an altogether stony appearance, grateful, to be sure, for the melodic assaults and caresses on all the slopes of my emotions"; Rainer Maria Rilke and Marie von Thurn und Taxis, *Briefwechsel*, ed. Ernst Zinn (Zurich: Niehans und Rokitansky, 1951), 2:801 (12 May 1924). Hereafter *RMR/MTT*. Cf. Rilke's definition of Křenek in the same fashion in the *Briefe an Nanny Wunderly-Volkart*, ed. Rätus Luck (Frankfurt am Main: Insel, 1977), 2:997 (25 April 1924): "sa femme est la fille de Mahler ... " (his wife is Mahler's daughter). Hereafter *NW-V*.

Such statements, albeit striking, are relatively few in the epistolary corpus; more often, Rilke — as was only natural — made efforts, sometimes very successful ones, thanks to his wonderful stylistic art, to adorn his musical shortcomings, or to turn them into virtues of sorts. The letters to Magda, or Benvenuta, provide some nice specimens of this way out. There is the repeated description (having found a catchy device, Rilke, like Puccini, was reluctant to let it go) of the innocence, or the freshness, of his musical hearing. (The suggestion reflects the child's rôle he so often took in his correspondence with female friends, from Ellen Key — "dein Kind" [your child] he had called himself to her — to Nanny Wunderly-Volkart.) In his second letter to Magda, from 26 January 1914, he recalled music he had heard from an adjoining room in his hotel at Ronda; "[ich] empfand wie in jenes wunderbare Element (ich kenne es kaum, auch war es immer zu stark für mich) die Welt gelöster übergeht, und es gab mir ein überfülltes, fast müheloses Glück, sie von dort her hereinzufühlen, denn mein Gehör ist neu wie eines Tragkindes Fußsohle."[5] He came back to the image a little more than a week later, again describing his pristine hearing, "wie eines Saug-kindes Fußsohle ... : das will nicht nur heißen: so neu, so ungebraucht, so *vor* aller Verwendung, sondern auch so ungeschickt, so unbrauchbar und unbeholfen und am Ende, (was man mir schon als Kind immer versicherte) gar nicht fähig, zu gehen, außerstande, auch nur drei Schritte zu lernen."[6] The statement quoted above (footnote 3) about his inability to keep a tune follows directly. The strategy is meant to sow the seed in Magda of the notion that her *métier* will reach (and enrich) his unused hearing: "Mein Gott, die Musik; Sie können sich denken, daß es Momente gab, wo ich auf sie hoffte...."[7]

To frankness about musical ignorance and/or an inherent lack of musicality, and, then, a virgin auditory sense are added, frequently, excuses about a fear of music. The disclosure of January 26 to Benvenuta is interrupted by the parenthesis: "ich kenne [jenes wunderbare Element] kaum, auch war es immer zu stark für mich ... " (I scarcely know [that marvelous element], also, it was always too strong for me). The same revelation comes up in letters to another of Rilke's pianist friends (although not a professional, as Magda was), Sidonie von Nádherný; whether a trace

[5] "I felt how the world passes over more relaxedly into that marvelous element (I scarcely know it, also, it was always too strong for me), and it gave me a surfeited, almost effortless happiness, to feel it coming toward me from there, for my sense of hearing is like the sole of a babe in arms"; *Benvenuta*, p. 18 (26 January 1914).

[6] "like the sole of a suckling babe ... : that doesn't only mean: so new, so unused, so *previous* to any application, but rather, too, so clumsy, so useless and awkward and finally (something people always assured me of as a child) not at all capable of walking, unable even to learn a mere three steps"; *Benvenuta*, p. 27 (4 February 1914).

[7] "My God, music: You can imagine that there were moments when I set my hopes in it ... "; *Benvenuta*, p. 35 (7 February 1914).

of wooing helplessness can be found, as in the case of Magda, must be left to the reader (or Rilke-watcher) to decide. He tells Sidie (again, early in the correspondence) that he would like to hear music together with her some day, "Musik (die mir zu stark ist, zu sehr Essenz, so daß ich sie nie zu hören wage)."[8] He repeats the phrase, in variation (just as he did the one about the babe-in-arms), after having heard what he describes (with a heavy-handed play on words) as "Beethovens drittes Quartett mit Joachims letzter Geige"; not able to say more about the piece in question (but wishing, all the same, to expatiate upon it to the musical Sidie), he continues: "Aber es war wie immer: Musik ist schon viel zu viel für mich: ein Jenseits; sie übersteigt alle meine Sinne."[9] For the Countess Margot Sizzo, in 1923, he returned to his musical anxiety, now somewhat softening its expression: "Ich hatte Musik hier zu Ostern, muß ich noch erzählen, herrliche Musik — ein Ereignis für mich, der ich so selten dazu komme, Musik aufzunehmen (und vielleicht mir auch gar nicht wünschte, oder es nicht wagte, ihr öfter offen zu sein)."[10] The occasion was a visit of Alma Moodie to Muzot: "Muzot hat seine große Musik-Taufe empfangen...."[11]

Particularly during the time of his Rodin-*raptus* (and of "learning to see"), Rilke had been strongly deprecatory of music. Malte, we may assume, speaks for Rilke as he describes the distrust he felt for music as a child, and then exempts the song of his aunt, Abelone, from this unease: "Ich, der ich schon als Kind der Musik gegenüber so mißtrauisch war (nicht, weil sie mich stärker als alles forthob aus mir, sondern, weil ich gemerkt hatte, daß sie mich nicht wieder dort ablegte, wo sie mich gefunden hatte, sondern tiefer, irgendwo ganz ins Unfertige hinein), ich ertrug diese Musik, auf der man aufrecht aufwärtssteigen konnte, höher und höher, bis man meinte, dies müßte ungefähr schon der Himmel sein seit einer Weile."[12] The sharpest

---

[8] "Music (which is too strong for me, too much an essence, so that I never dare to listen to it)"; *Briefe an Sidonie Nádherný von Borutin*, ed. Bernhard Blume (Frankfurt am Main: Insel, 1973), p. 45 (14 November, 1907). Hereafter *SNB*.

[9] "Beethoven's Third Quartet with Joachim's last violin"; "But it was the way it always was, music is simply too much for me: a realm beyond, it surpasses all my senses"; *SNB*, p. 57 (18 December 1907).

[10] "I had music here at Easter, I must add, splendid music — an event for me, who so seldom has the chance of receiving music (and perhaps, too, did not at all wish, or did not dare, to be open to it more often)"; *B* (1950), 2:410 (12 April 1923).

[11] "Muzot has received its great musical baptism"; *NW-V*, 2:886 (11 April 1923).

[12] "I, who even as a child was so distrustful toward music (not because it lifted me out of myself more strongly than everything else, but rather because I had observed that it did not set me down again where it had found me but rather at a deeper point, somewhere wholly into incompleteness), I bore this music, on which one, standing upright, could climb upwards, higher and higher, until one imagined that this must already have been heaven, more or less, for a while"; *Sämtliche Werke* (Wiesbaden and Frankfurt am Main: Insel, 1955–66), 6:824–25. Hereafter *SW*.

expression of dislike is in a letter of 8 August 1903, to Lou Andreas-Salomé, as a comparison in Rilke's effort to define Rodin's art: "Seine Kunst war von allem Anfang an Verwirklichung (und das Gegentheil von Musik, als welche die scheinbaren Wirklichkeiten der täglichen Welt verwandelt und noch weiter entwirklicht zu leichten, gleitenden Scheinen."[13] The attack on music then shifts, directly, into an attack on its listeners: "Weshalb denn auch dieser Gegensatz der Kunst, dieses Nicht-ver-dichten, diese Versuchung zum Ausfließen, so viel Freunde und Hörer und Hörige hat, so viel Unfreie und an Genuß Gebundene, nicht aus sich selbst heraus Gesteigerte und von außen her Entzückte …)." Hard words indeed. The classic instance of an assault on the musical audience occurs in the praise of Beethoven in *Die Aufzeichnungen des Malte Laurids Brigge*, the eulogy in whose course, by the way, Rilke attributes the quality to Beethoven which he has listed in the negative ("dieses Nicht-ver-dichten"; this not-taking-shape), in the "anti-musical" letter to Lou: "Diese unerbittliche *Selbstverdichtung* [italics added] fortwährend ausdampfen wollender Musik."[14] Subsequently in the apostrophe, Malte calls for a giant "Hammerklavier" to be placed in the Egyptian desert, the home of anchorites, where Beethoven would pour out music *without* a willingly seduced and self-indulgent audience; of such listeners, Malte (or Rilke) gives a vicious depiction: "Denn wer holt dich jetzt aus den Ohren zurück, die lüstern sind? Wer treibt sie aus den Musiksälen, die Käuflichen mit dem unfruchtbaren Gehör, das hurt und niemals empfängt? da strahlt Samen aus, und sie halten sich unter wie Dirnen und spielen damit, oder er fällt, während sie daliegen in ihren ungetanen Befriedigungen, wie Samen Onans zwischen sie alle."[15] The conclusion of the entry is also notable, related as it is to the image of the infant's untried foot Rilke would use to Magda: "Wo aber, Herr, ein Jungfräulicher unbeschla-

---

[13] "From the very beginning, his art was realization (and the opposite of music, as [the art] which transforms the apparent realities of the diurnal world and takes away their reality still further, [changing them] into light, gliding appearances"; "On which account, then, too, this opposite of art, this not-taking-shape, this temptation to outpourings, has so many friends and listeners and slaves [Rilke's pun on 'Hörer und Hörige' is untranslatable], so many vassals and addicts of enjoyment, [beings] not elevated out of themselves but enraptured from without …)"; Rainer Maria Rilke and Lou Andreas-Salomé, *Briefwechsel*, ed. Ernst Pfeiffer (Frankfurt am Main: Insel, 1975), p. 94.

[14] "This unrelenting *solidification* of music that perpetually wishes to evaporate"; *SW*, 6:779.

[15] "For who will now retrieve you from those ears that are lascivious? Who will drive them from the concert halls, those venal beings with their barren hearing, which fornicates and never conceives? Seed comes streaming out there, and they pull themselves aside like whores and play with it, or it falls, as they lie there in their unaccomplished gratifications, like the seed of Onan between them all"; "Where though, lord, a virginal man with uncopulated ear would lie with your sound: he would die of bliss or he would carry something infinite to full term and his impregnated brain would have to burst from sheer birthing"; *SW*, 6:780.

fenen Ohrs läge bei deinem Klang: er stürbe an Seligkeit oder er trüge Unendliches aus und sein befruchtetes Hirn müßte bersten an lauter Geburt." This art that seduces listeners into "unaccomplished gratifications" is produced, mostly, by artists who have discovered its genius for easy solutions. Writing to Clara Rilke from Sweden on 24 July 1904, Rilke told about his memories of Egon Petri, a pianist and, although Rilke did not mention it, a disciple of Busoni. Once he had had an excellent conversation with Petri about Poe, and he still remembered Petri's whimsical temperament (which caused some friction between the earnest poet and the pianist) and, more important, Petri's chronic despair: "Es war viel Wesentliches darin, wenngleich es auch, besonders nach der Seite des Humorhaften hin, Mißstände gab, die wir nicht beseitigten. Er wächst ohne Zweifel, darum ist er auch in Not, und das ist das Sympathische an ihm: daß er in Not bleibt. Seit Jahren in immer neuer Not, in aufrichtiger (wenngleich vielleicht selbst aufgesuchter, angerufener) Not. Möge er nie aus ihr herausfinden: Musiker sind voller Auswege, entsprechend den leichten Auflösungen, die ihre Kunst ihnen nahe legt. Nur wenn sie, wie Beethoven als Lebender oder Bach als Betender, Auflösung um Auflösung verachten und ablehnen, wachsen sie. Sonst nehmen sie einfach an Körperumfang zu."[16] Most musicians are no better than their listeners; the latter — as Rilke would tell his Danish translator Inga Junghanns, in his explanation of the Beethoven passage in *Malte* — "lassen sich, unverdient gewissermaßen, von der Musik befriedigen, ohne die ungeheure Aufnahme, die die Musik verlangt, eigentlich zu leisten."[17]

The Petri-passage not only reveals (as does the Rodin-passage in the letter to Lou) Rilke's odd condescension toward the musical art, its creators and its recipients, but lets slip a weakness of Rilke's own for "leichte Auflösungen" (facile resolutions) in many of his declarations about it. The phrase, "Beethoven als Lebender oder Bach als Betender" (Beethoven as a living [creator] or Bach as a praying [one]) is surely an all too facile characterization of these two composers — who, for the rest, were far and away the most favored members of Rilke's exclusive musical club. The searcher for

---

[16] "There was a great deal of the essential in it, even though, especially toward the humorous side, there were difficulties we did not eliminate. He is growing, without doubt, that is why he is in distress too, and that is the appealing quality in him: that he remains in distress. For years in an ever new distress, in sincere (even though perhaps self-sought, self-invoked) distress. May he never find a way out of it: musicians are full of ways-out, corresponding to the facile resolutions which their art urges on them. Only when they, like Beethoven as a living [creator] or Bach as a praying [one], scorn and reject resolution upon resolution, do they grow. Otherwise, they simply increase in physical circumference"; *B* (1950), 1:94–95.

[17] "let themselves, to a certain extent without having earned it, be gratified by music, without really accomplishing the enormous act of reception that music requires"; Rainer Maria Rilke and Inga Junghanns, *Briefwechsel*, ed. Wolfgang Herwig (Wiesbaden: Insel, 1959), p. 42 (4 July 1917; Fragebogen). Hereafter *RMR/IJ*.

Rilke's musical statements will (or should) be struck by the almost bathetic fashion in which he adduces Beethoven's name in the diary-poem from the autumn of 1900 to Paula Becker, one of the several echoes of the musical evenings at Worpswede — the poem beginning: "Ich weiß euch lauschen: eine Stimme geht, / und Sonntag-Abend ist im weißen Saal," with its trifold invocation of Beethoven:[18] "Beethoven sprach ... mir zittern noch die Sinne, / und alles Dunkel in mir rauscht noch nach," and "[wir] saßen sanft und mit gesenktem Kinne: / Beethoven sprach ... ," and "fast mütterlich schien alles Ungemach — / Beethoven sprach." Compare, then, the equally empty rhetoric of a letter to Magda: "so kommt mir Beethoven wie der Herr der Heerschaaren vor, der Macht hat über die Mächte und der die Gefahren aufreißt, um die Brückenbogen strahlender Rettungen drüber zu werfen."[19] Or, later still, the vapidity of the description of the Valais landscape to Nanny Wunderly-Volkart: "welches Land hat soviel Einzelheiten in so großem Zusammenhang; es ist wie der Schlußsatz einer Beethoven-Symphonie."[20] A celebration of Bach as a kind of magic figure appears in the letter to Sidie Nádherný, where he proposes that they hear music together, "Bach, vor allem, von dem Sie so innig wissen, daß er 'reicher ist als das weiteste Meer.'"[21] Further, "Bach" as an underlined semi-outcry comes up in the postscript to a letter of 7 April 1923, about the first of the Easter-time visits of Alma Moodie to Muzot: "Ich habe eigenthümlich feierliche Ostern gehabt: durch zwei Tage hat lauter *Bach* bei mir geklungen in der herrlichen Geigenstimme, die die junge, auch in Wien bekannte Geigerin, Alma Moodie, zu erwecken weiß."[22]

May we suspect that "Beethoven and Bach" assumed a ritualistic function for Rilke in part because he never took the trouble to acquire other names? The *correspondantes* send out signal upon signal about admired composers of their own, or pieces they have heard, as if wanting to get an opinion, and receive no reply. Marie von Thurn und Taxis brings up Schubert: "Letzthin

---

[18] "I know you are hearkening: a voice passes / and it is Sunday evening in the white salon"; "Beethoven spoke ... my senses still are trembling, / and all the darkness still murmurs within me," "[we] sat gently and with sunken chin: Beethoven spoke"; "all adversity seemed almost maternal — / Beethoven spoke"; *SW*, 3:703–4; *Tagebücher aus der Frühzeit* (Leipzig: Insel, 1942), pp. 358–59. Hereafter *TadF*.

[19] "Thus Beethoven appears to me as the Lord of hosts, He who has power over the powers and wrenches perils open, in order to cast the arching bridges of shining salvations across them"; *Benvenuta*, p. 26 (1 February 1914).

[20] "what land has so many particular details in such a great cohesion; it is like the final movement of a Beethoven symphony"; *NW-V*, 1:510 (15 July 1921).

[21] "Bach above all, of whom you have such intimate knowledge, that 'he is richer than the broadest sea'"; *SNB*, p. 45 (14 November 1907).

[22] "I have had a remarkably solemn Easter: for two days, *Bach* alone has rung out for me in the splendid violin-voice which the young violinist Alma Moodie, well-known in Vienna too, knows how to awake"; *RMR/MTT*, 2:751 (7 April 1923).

das Forellenquintett von Schubert — entzückend wiedergegeben — und so wohlthuend, beruhigend, *une paix si douce et si délicieuse.*"[23] Inga Junghanns offers her long eulogy of Bruckner, in her letter of 2 August 1922, about the F-Minor Mass, which she compares to Beethoven's *Missa solemnis* (although she did not know it, Rilke had written a poem about the Beethoven mass once upon a time): "wo Beethoven sich vor dem Mächtigen in den Staub wirft und die Augen schließen muß, gleitet Bruckner still, entblößten Hauptes, mit in den Himmel hinein, und steht, wie ein Kind vor dem Weihnachtsbaum, lichtempfangend ...,"[24] and so forth. Rilke does not bite. Mailing a book about Chopin to Sidie Nádherný (he knew that Chopin was her special favorite), he passes quickly to another early-dead artist on whom he could claim, as a poet, some authority: "Der 'Chopin' kommt nächster Tage.... Kennen Sie die Zeichnung aus dem kleinen Museo Keats in Rom, Keats im Tode vorstellend?; sicher. Sie hat etwas wunderbar rein Ergreifendes. Soll ich sie Ihnen senden?"[25]

To be sure, Mozart turns up in passing, incidentally as it were — i.e., the performance of *Die Zauberflöte* Rilke heard in Hamburg in September 1900, as a member of the Worpswede delegation; he made the traditional complaint about the Schickaneder libretto and its "komische Menschen," who stand "unglaublich plump, dumm und albern in diesem lichten, schimmernden Pavillon [des] reichen harmonischen Klanges."[26] Rilke's mind seems to have wandered during the performance: "Die Musik war etwas unendlich Wohltuendes an diesem Abend. Leise Schleier breitete sie über die Gedanken aus, die nicht mit Papageno sich beschäftigten, und wie Rosenblätter legten sich die Töne auf unser spiegelndes Gefühl." The salute to the graceful, soothing quality of Mozart is a *hapax legomenon* in Rilke. (We may remember, as well, his strong reaction against the consolatory text

[23] "Latterly, the Trout Quintet of Schubert — enchantingly rendered — and so comforting, calming, une paix si douce et si délicieuse [so sweet and so delicious a peace]"; *RMR/MTT*, 1:287–88 (14 April 1913).

[24] "Where Beethoven casts himself into the dust in the presence of the Mighty One and must close his eyes, Bruckner quietly glides, with bared head, along into Heaven, and stands, like a child before the Christmas tree, receiving light ... "; *RMR/IJ*, p. 212 (2 August 1922).

[25] "The 'Chopin' will come during the next few days.... Are you familiar with the drawing in the little Keats Museum in Rome, showing Keats in death? Of course. It has something marvelously and purely touching about it. Shall I send it to you?"; *SNB*, p. 214 (14 February 1914).

[26] "comical people"; "unbelievably coarse, stupid, and foolish in this rich, shimmering pavilion of rich, shimmering sound"; "The music was something infinitely comforting on this evening. It spread gentle veils over one's thoughts, which did not concern themselves with Papageno, laying themselves like rose petals on our mirroring feeling"; *TadF*, p. 318 (27 September 1900).

of Schubert's *An die Musik,* heard at Worpswede.)[27] For Rilke, music was not to be a comfort but a tremendous and upsetting force. Is the pendant to Princess Marie's appreciation of the Trout Quintet meant as a correction of her momentary apostasy from Rilke's standpoint: "généralement pour moi la musique ce n'est pas du tout la paix — Beethoven p[ar] e[xample] on dirait qu'il me tord tout le coeur comme avec des mains cruelles et adorées" (For me, generally, music is not peace at all ... Beethoven, for example, one would say that he twists my heart with cruel and beloved hands)? The other Mozart references of substance concern the performance of the *Requiem* Rilke heard in Paris, in October 1913. The context in which the performance is mentioned is significant: he tells Sidie Nádherný that he has been in Rouen and Beauvais and thus knows "zwei Kathedralen mehr," and then goes on: "[ich] habe Sonntag das Requiem von Mozart gehört, — und da glaubt man doch einen Moment, daß man das Leben hier ablehnt sei eine Kleinigkeit, wenn man es dort nur tausendmal hervorbrächte, liebendsten Herzens."[28] The syntax is peculiarly strained, and betrays, perhaps, with what subliminal unwillingness Rilke confronted the Catholic-Christian ambiance out of which the *Requiem* had sprung. Elsewhere, writing about the same performance to still another musical amateur, Helene von Nostitz, he is impelled to allude to the composition's flaws, telling how he has heard "Mozarts (zum Theil) herrliches Requiem,"[29] as if almost in apology for what he has done.

Willy-nilly, Rilke had a weakness for sacred music. (A cultural conservatism is at work here, not unlike the attitude represented by the aesthetic decadents of the 1880s and 1890s, that the ancient music of the church is the only true music; we think of Huysmans' Des Esseintes or George Moore's Mr. Innes, Evelyn's father.) The report on the Toledo "Salve" to Alexander von Thurn und Taxis makes this clear, as do several accounts for Princess Marie: "Ich höre heute und gestern alte italienische Musik von den Sängern in der Kirche St. Gervais; Vittoria, Palestrina, Ingegneri."[30] A favorite piece of his, as Marie reminded him, was a "Lied" by Pergolesi: could it have been a portion of the *Stabat Mater*? She had sung it to him on his birthday, at Duino in 1911, he remembered it in 1912, in Spain, and mentioned it to her ("Vor einem Jahr an diesem Tag sangen Sie mir den

---

[27] *TadF,* p. 255 (10 September 1900).

[28] "two more cathedrals"; "On Sunday [I] heard the Requiem by Mozart — and there one believes for a moment, after all, that it may be a small matter [that] one rejects life *here,* if *there* one might bring it forth a thousand times, with a most loving heart"; *SNB,* p. 201 (31 October 1913).

[29] "Mozart's (partly) splendid Requiem"; Rainer Maria Rilke and Helene von Nostitz, *Briefwechsel,* ed. Oswalt von Nostitz (Frankfurt am Main: Insel), p. 57 (4 November 1913).

[30] "Today and yesterday I hear old Italian music, [performed] by the singers in St. Gervais' church: Vittoria, Palestrina, Ingegneri"; *RMR/MTT,* 1:281 (21 March 1913).

Pergolesi, der mich so an Greco denken ließ").[31] He had told Sidie Nádherný about the performance when it happened, carefully — behaving like a lover, even when he was not one — omitting the name of the singer: "Ich feierte gar nichts, es ist wahr, ein bischen Musik hörte ich und ein *unendlich trostloses Lied* [italics added] von Pergolesi, das ich auch heute habe singen hören, das ich jeden Tag hören könnte, ein Lied voll gebrochener Strahlen, von einer sinnlichen Geistigkeit wie ein Greco."[32] (Without mentioning Pergolesi, Rilke associates ecclesiastical music with ecclesiastical art in a letter to Magda, as he makes one of his several efforts to explain what music means to him: "Abends, vor ein paar Tagen, schlug ich den Band Abbildungen zum Greco-Werk auf, 'Die Kreuzigung,' und versuchte daneben aus dem Katalog des 'Prado' zu entziffern, was ich dort, vor dem Bilde, mit Bleistift, mehr schauend als schreibend, angemerkt hatte. Da las ich das Wort 'Musik.'")[33]

The fixation of Rilke on the tragically or starkly sublime (in a church setting) readily produced a blanket admiration for medieval music, or, as he had written to Alexander von Thurn und Taxis, about the "Salve" in Toledo: "Es geht mir sehr nah, wie alle ganz alte Musik...."[34] Warming up for the tribute to Beethoven in the letter of February 1 to Magda, he remembered "was an unmittelbarer Gewalt anstand in irgend einem Stück abgebrochener uralter Musik, wie ich dergleichen in Italien oder Spanien, auch im südlichen Rußland manchmal, zu hören bekam...."[35] In another of his reports to Clara from Rodin's studio, in November 1909, he told of his encounter with Gregorian chant, as it emerged from a phonograph; it demanded the exertion from him he thought true listeners to music should make. "[Es] hatte immerzu eine frische Bruchstelle, aus der es austrat wie der Saft eines Astes. Man war hernach wie nach schwerer Arbeit körperlich

---

[31] "A year ago on this day you sang the Pergolesi for me, which made me think so much of Greco"; *RMR/MTT*, 1:241 (4 December 1912). On 7 April 1914, Rilke wrote to the Princess that he had heard Pergolesi's *Stabat Mater* in the Schola Cantorum at Paris: " ... wie erkannt ich ihn in den schmerzlichen Stellen" (how I recognized him in the painful passages; *RMR/MTT*, 1:372).

[32] "I celebrated not at all, it's true, I heard a little music and an *infinitely inconsolable song* by Pergolesi, which I've heard sung today, too, which I could hear every day, a song full of shattered rays, with a sensuous spirituality like a Greco"; *SNB*, p. 139 (8 December 1911).

[33] "In the evening, a couple of days ago, I opened the volume of reproductions from Greco's work, *The Crucifixion*, and, in addition, tried to decipher from the catalogue of the Prado what I had noted there, in pencil, looking more than writing, [standing] in front of the picture. There I read the word, 'Music'"; *Benvenuta*, p. 67 (13 February 1914).

[34] "It affects me deeply, like all very old music"; *B* (1950), 1:410.

[35] "what there was of direct power gathered in some piece of fragmentary age-old music or other, of the kind that I had had the chance to hear in Italy or Spain, sometimes, too, in southern Russia ..."; *Benvenuta*, p. 26.

und in der Seele, als sollte man gleich die äußerste, schwerste tun."[36] A third and annoying party was in the room as the chant was played, Madame de Choiseul, Rodin's mistress, who led the sculptor down from the heights, putting on "immer dümmere Platten" (ever more stupid records) to Rilke's dismay. Finally, on purpose or accidentally, Rilke intervened: "Durch meine Unvorsichtigkeit kam aber darnach nochmals ein gregorianisches Lied, ein ungeheures; nur in Rußland hab ich Ähnliches gehört, auch die Gesänge in der armenischen Kirche waren noch neumodisch und verschwächt gegen diese erste, unüberlegte Musik" (Through my carelessness there still came, after this, one more Gregorian chant, a tremendous one: only in Russia have I heard something similar, even the singing in the Armenian church was still new-fangled and vitiated, compared to this primal, heedless music").

Understandably, a tension arose in Rilke between his devotion to music associated with the church and his announced distaste for Christianity. His uneasiness may have prompted the awkwardness of the aperçu, quoted above (footnote 28), on the Mozart *Requiem*; to a degree, it spoiled the performance of the *St. Matthew Passion* he heard in the Basel cathedral in March 1920. He had felt at some distance, he wrote to Nanny Wunderly-Volkart, from the passion's first part, but was more and more caught up by the second — yet drew back, even while appreciating the performance of the distinguished tenor, Karl Erb, as the evangelist, for its lack of naiveté: "die Erb'sche Auslegung und Führung verlangte nicht durchaus den Gläubigen sich gegenüber, sie ging selber aus Betrachtung und Abstand hervor, nicht aus dem Erlebnis, für den heutigen Hörer mochte sie die richtigste und entsprechendste sein."[37] Then he was captivated once more, but only momentarily: "In den größesten Stellen stand man indessen doch im Gefühle Bachs, das mir unendlich herrlich wurde, wo es, um sein Großartigstes zu erweisen, seine schlichtesten und strengsten Erfahrungen in Gebrauch nahm: ein unermüdlich gekonntes Handwerk und einen ununterbrochen geübten Glauben" (Meanwhile, at the greatest passages, one stood nonetheless in Bach's feeling, that became infinitely glorious for me where, to show its greatest grandeur, it made use of its simplest and sternest experiences: an untiringly skilled artisanship and an uninterruptedly practiced faith). Nevertheless, his own growing inability, Rilke continued, directly to take part in the Christian experience, prevented him from

---

[36] "[It] continuously had a fresh point of fracture, from which it emerged like the sap of a branch. Afterwards, one was physically and spiritually exhausted, as after hard labor, as if one must directly perform the most extreme, most difficult [task]"; *Briefe aus den Jahren 1907–1914* (Leipzig: Insel, 1939), pp. 80–81 (3 November 1909). Hereafter *B 1907–1914*.

[37] "Erb's interpretation and demeanor did not wish to have the true believer as its recipient, it emerged, itself, from observation and distancing, not from the experience, for the contemporary listener it might well be the most correct and suitable [approach]"; *NW-V*, 1:193–94 (22 March 1920).

knowing "diejenige Hingerissenheit ..., die die Aufnehmung des Ganzen zum Ereignis machen müßte" (that rapture ... which would have to turn the reception of the whole into an event). Even for Rilke, the long passage is tortuous in its arguments. He repeats his familiar doctrine of the rejection of an intermediary between God and his own heart, and says that "dieses elementarische Zu-viel Gottes" (this elementary too-much-ness of God), which he does *not* wish to have channeled for him, possesses such a great relationship "mit der Natur der Musik, daß ich dieser größesten protestantischen [Musik] immerhin das programmatisch eingeschränkte Gemüth vorwerfen möchte, aus dem sie hervorgegangen ist ... " (with the nature of the music, that I would like all the same to reproach this great Protestant [music] with [the] programmatically limited spirit from which it has emerged"). Music, like God, must be unlimited and unattached to a faith; but the sublime music to which Rilke was drawn had originated, here as elsewhere, in a "programmatically limited spirit." Does the dedicatory poem to the violinist Lucie Simon, the daughter of the director of Bad Ragaz, who (together with another lady, the pianist Countess Hartenau) played "Bach, Mozart and Bruch" for him in the summer of 1924, contain a pun faintly derogatory about Bach? The possibility is at least worth considering:

Wüßte ich für wen ich spielte, ach!
immer könnt' ich rauschen wie der Bach.[38]

Daring to criticize even Bach, Rilke was of course intolerant (as purist amateurs often are) of music that did not fit into his category of elementary splendor: giants of the nineteenth century are reduced to comical anecdotes. He recounted to Ilse Sadée,[39] after the disclaimer about Brahms' *Harzreise im Winter*, how, as a seventeen-year-old, he had literally bumped into Brahms on a mountain path near Bad Aussee, and had been held at (symbolic?) arm's length by the portly gentleman, who behaved — in Rilke's amusing account — like a bear, "plötzlich brummend," and then, somewhat placated, uttered "ein sanftes Gebrummse," which at length turned into a warning. Wagner, readily enough, served as the object of a verbal joke: "Wie war Winterthur?" Rilke asks Frau Wunderly, adding: "eine Zeile alliterierend wie aus der 'Götterdämmerung'!"[40] (Rilke would not have wanted to be reminded that he himself had constructed, in the past, numerous Wagnerian-sounding alliterations, not least in his musical imagery. In the unpublished *Dir zur Feier*, there are: "Leg du auf meine Lebensgeige / die Hände

---

[38] "If I knew for whom I played, oh! / I could rustle forever like the brook [Bach]"; *SW*, 2:262–63.

[39] "suddenly growling," "a gentle sort of growl"; *B* (1950), 1:360–61 (8 February 1912).

[40] "What was Winterthur like?"; "a line alliterating like one from *The Twilight of the Gods*"; *NW-V*, 1:361 (17 December 1902).

an des Schicksals Statt" and "Knaben, die auf Flöten bliesen, / so friedlich, still und feierlich,"[41] or, published in *Traumgekrönt*, "empfand ich, wie der Feierabend / in meiner Seele Saiten griff.")[42] Sometimes his musical witticisms slide over into the realm of doubtful taste. Having heard the Berlin Cathedral Choir sing Bruch in September 1920 — at the Basel cathedral, together with Frau Wunderly — Rilke shortly tendered painful remarks about the composer's passing: "Der arme Compositeur Bruch, dessen Daten wir am vorigen Sonntag mit Befremdung konstatierten (im Münster), ... dieser Bruch ist auf der Stelle gestorben, da wir fanden, es sei schon zu lange...."[43] Demotic composers fared still worse. Having put up at Brissago's Grand Hotel in October 1919, he told Frau Gudi Nölke that a certain Herr Amrhyn from Lucerne directed the hotel from "seiner oberhalb gelegenen Villa aus, die die Villa (ach!) Leoncavallo's war. Der Edel-Schweiß des Maestro (verzeihen Sie) klebt noch an den Palmen."[44] (Was this invitation to merriment prompted by the news of Leoncavallo's recent passing?) Rilke had only contempt for lesser breeds of music, a contempt to which he had given full rein long ago, in the family dinner of *Ewald Tragy*; there, the major's widow plays requests, by ear and with arthritic fingers. She is apparently not up to the *Cavalleria rusticana* number (Mascagni's *Intermezzo*, doubtless) that the "four cousins" demand, but she can deal with Tragy senior's request for "An object all sublime" from *The Mikado*, and selections from *Der Bettelstudent* and *Les cloches de Corneville*. "Die anderen schlafen darüber ein, und die Majorin selbst kommt ihnen nach. Da hält es Ewald nicht länger aus, er muß es aussprechen um jeden Preis; und als ob das die selbstverständliche Folge der 'Glocken von Corneville' wäre, sagt er: 'Der letzte Sonntag.'"[45] The scene ridicules both "light music" and music's all too comfortable reception. The parlor-concert prompts Ewald once more (heard only by Mademoiselle Jeanne) to announce his decision to leave the bourgeois world: at Muzot a quarter of a century later, in Alma

---

[41] "Lay upon my life's violin / your hands in destiny's stead"; "Lads who blew on flutes, / so peacefully, stilly, solemnly"; *SW*, 3:183.

[42] "I felt how the leisured evening / reached into my soul's strings"; *SW*, 1:76.

[43] "The poor *compositeur* Bruch, whose dates we ascertained last Sunday to our astonishment (in the cathedral) ... this Bruch died on the spot, when we found that it had been going on too long ..."; *NW-V*, 1:325–26 (3 October 1920).

[44] "from his villa located up above, which was (alas!) the villa of Leoncavallo. The maestro's exalted sweat (forgive me!) still clings to the [fronds of the] palms"; *Briefe an Frau Gudi Nölke*, ed. Paul Obermüller (Wiesbaden: Insel, 1953), p. 19 (3 November 1919).

[45] "The others fall asleep in the process, and the major's widow herself keeps up with them. Then Ewald can bear it no longer, he must declare it at any cost, and, as if it were the self-evident consequence of 'The Bells of Corneville,' he says: 'The last Sunday'"; *SW*, 4:527–28.

Moodie, Rilke found an acceptable replacement for the major's widow, her repertoire, and her pianistic art.

Rilke despised the opera, as he told his diary in 1898; little reason exists to think the opinion ever changed. (However, in 1920, having heard an aria from *Alceste*, "Divinités du Styx," in "der herrlichen Kathedrale" of Lausanne, he told Frau Wunderly: "C'était sublime; combien je voudrais un jour entendre tout un opéra de Gluck.")[46] To the diary, the young man confided that: "Nur ein so willfähriger und grober Rahmen wie die Bühne konnte ... eine Vereinigung von Text und Musik befürworten, wie sie in der Oper und Operette zu Tage tritt. Daß dabei die Musik als das naivere Element das Sieghafte bleibt, spricht nur für die Ungerechtigkeit einer derartigen Vermählung."[47] (Rilke had just stated: "Ein Gemälde darf keines Textes, eine Statue keiner Farbe — im malerischen Sinn — und ein Gedicht keiner Musik brauchen, vielmehr muß in jedem alles enthalten sein.") Moreover, the union of text and music in the opera (still another sidewipe at the public that lazily liked "die leichten Auflösungen" of music) is called the product of "einem Zugeständnis an das Publikum ..., das sich in seiner Trägheit am liebsten eine Kunst von der zweiten kommentieren lassen möchte." (That Rilke himself would use another art in order to suggest music is a matter on which we have found some evidence elsewhere; see the Pergolesi/El Greco case.) For several reasons, Rilke could scarcely have entertained the affection of his fellow Praguer, Werfel, for Verdi.

Thus much of the nineteenth century's musical culture fell outside Rilke's tight limits, as did the world of Strauß and Hofmannsthal; the Rilke-Hofmannsthal correspondence makes no mention whatsoever of music, or of the Hofmannsthal libretti. The contemporary composers who came within his ken did so through personal connections. Magda von Hattingberg, who had been one of the so-called caryatides around Busoni, furthered a (shadowy) acquaintanceship between her two mentors, and gave the poet a copy of the first edition, published at a little house in Trieste in 1907, of Busoni's pamphlet, *Entwurf einer neuen Ästhetik der Musik*; Rilke recommended it to Anton Kippenberg for the Insel-Bücherei, where it appeared in 1916, expanded and revised, with a dedication to "Dem Musiker in Worten" (To the Musician in Words). What must have appealed to the technically unsophisticated Rilke in the *Entwurf* was its simple champion-

---

[46] the splendid cathedral of Lausanne"; "It was sublime; how much I'd like to hear a whole opera by Gluck some day"; *NW-V*, 1:335 (5 November 1920).

[47] "Only such a complaisant and coarse frame as the stage ... could favor a union of text and music, as it appears in the opera and operetta. That the music, as the more naive component, remains victorious in the process, only speaks for the inequitability of such a marriage"; "A painting may need no text, a statue no color — in the painterly sense — and a poem no music; rather, everything must be contained in each of these"; "the facile resolutions"; "a concession to the public ... which in its laziness most prefers to have one art commented on by another"; *TadF*, p. 57.

ship of a genuine "absolute music." "Was die Gesetzgeber darunter meinen, ist vielleicht das Entfernteste vom Absoluten in der Musik. 'Absolute Musik' ist ein Formenspiel ohne dichterisches Programm, wobei die Form die wichtigste Rolle spielt. Aber gerade die Form steht der absoluten Musik entgegengesetzt, die doch den göttlichen Vorzug erhielt zu schweben und von den Bedingungen der Materie frei zu sein."[48] Earlier in the text, Rilke had come across the following: "Das Kind — es schwebt! Es berührt nicht die Erde mit seinen Füßen. Es ist nicht der Schwere unterworfen. Es ist fast unkörperlich. Seine Materie ist durchsichtig. Es ist tönende Luft. Es ist fast die Natur selbst. Es ist frei."[49] ("Tönende Luft" [Sounding air] is reminiscent of a phrase Rilke had used to Magda about music: "Fast ist sie wie eine höhere Luft...."[50] Later, he enhanced the image in a strophe from *Aus dem Nachlaß des Grafen C.W.*: "Musik, Musik, gesteh, ob du vermagst / ihn zu vollziehn den unerhörten Hymen? / Ach, du auch weißt am Ende nur zu rühmen, / *gekrönte Luft*, was du uns schön versagst.")[51] Rilke must have liked the pamphlet, too, because it supported his principal choices for his tiny Parnassus, composers whose work lies closest to the freest and most elemental sound: "Neben Beethoven ist Bach der 'Ur-Musik' am verwandtesten."[52] Nor could Rilke, with his belief in the importance of childhood for artistic creation, and his equally strong belief in a never-ending future of artistic development, rather than a static and finished art, have overlooked Busoni's emphasis on music's youthfulness, a child compared to the other arts, and "eine jungfräuliche Kunst, die noch nichts erlebt und gelitten hat."[53] Recommending the book to Kippenberg on 3 March 1914, Rilke was moved to say that it had become "wunderbar unentbehrlich" for him: "nur in Beethovens Briefen noch, scheint mir, gibt es solches Bewußtsein

---

[48] "What the makers-of-rules mean thereby is perhaps the farthest thing from the absolute in music. 'Absolute music' is a playing with forms without a poetic program, in which the form has the most important role. But it is precisely the form that stands opposed to absolute music which, after all, was vouchsafed the divine advantage of soaring and being free from the conditions of the material world"; Ferruccio Busoni, *Entwurf einer neuen Ästhetik der Musik* (Wiesbaden: Insel, 1954), pp. 12–13.

[49] "The child — it soars! It does not touch the earth with its feet. It is not subject to gravity. It is almost incorporeal. Its material is transparent. It is sounding air. It is almost nature itself. It is free"; *Entwurf*, p. 11.

[50] "It is almost like a higher [kind of] air"; *Benvenuta*, pp. 66–67 (13 February 1914).

[51] "Music, music, confess, whether you are able / to consummate it, that unprecedented marriage? / Alas, you too, at last, know only how to praise, / [oh] *crowned air*, what you so beautifully deny us"; *SW*, 2:129.

[52] "Next to Beethoven, Bach is most closely related to 'primal music'"; Busoni, *Entwurf*, p. 15.

[53] "a virginal art, which as yet has experienced and suffered nothing"; *Entwurf*, p. 11.

um Musik."[54] (Magda had given him Beethoven's letters the month before.)

Other contacts with contemporary creative musicians were no less brief and fortuitous. The acquaintanceship with Schönberg, during Rilke's military service in Vienna in 1916, has left no accessible epistolary evidence sturdy enough to bear interpretation, however tempting it is to reflect on what Rilke meant by a sentence to Lou Albert-Lasard, written when he was becoming acquainted with Oskar Kokoschka's art: "Nun will ich Kokoschka gut ansehen und darauf achten, ob ich Schönbergsche Musik zu hören bekomme."[55] At Geneva in the summer of 1920, he was introduced to Othmar Schoeck, and noted that Schoeck was in the company of a particularly handsome young woman; to Frau Wunderly, Rilke observed that he would have liked to see Schoeck again and to ask him about Scriabin — but forgot to inquire where he was staying, and he made no effort to find out.[56] In May of 1922, he mentioned Schoeck's opera, *Venus*, to Frau Wunderly, and sent her clippings from the *Journal de Genève* about it, but did not try to see it himself, claiming, all the same: "Wie gerne wäre ich mit Ihnen dabei gewesen."[57] "Schoeck'sche Musik geht mich ganz gewiß an, — ich glaube, die kommt noch vor für mich, wieder und wieder,"[58] but it did not, and he evidently made no effort to find out about it.

The acquaintanceship with Ernst Křenek, arranged by Werner Reinhart, led to Rilke's writing "O Lacrimosa" for Křenek, which — so Rilke's accompanying letter implied — might "am Liebsten einen imaginären italiänischen Ursprung vorgeben, um noch *anonymer* zu sein, als [die Trilogie] schon ist."[59] (The "Italian source," of course, recalls Rilke's affection for Italian composers of the sixteenth century, and for Pergolesi.) To Frau Wunderly, he had described the composer thus: "Křenek paraît être

---

[54] "wondrously indispensable," "only in Beethoven's letters, then, it seems to me, is there such awareness concerning music"; *Briefe an seinen Verleger*, ed. Ruth Sieber-Rilke and Carl Sieber (Wiesbaden: Insel, 1949), 1:264.

[55] "Now I mean to have a good look at Kokoschka, and to pay close heed to whether I'll get the chance to hear Schönbergian music"; Lou Albert-Lasard, *Wege mit Rilke* (Frankfurt am Main: S. Fischer, 1952), p. 129 (8 March 1916), quoted in Joachim Storck, "*Haßzellen, stark im größten Liebeskreise ...*": *Verse für Oskar Kokoschka* (Marbach: Deutsches Literaturarchiv, 1988), p. 24, p. 59.

[56] *NW-V*, 1:303 (14 August 1920).

[57] "How much I'd have liked to attend with you"; "Schock's music quite surely concerns me, — I believe it will still occur for me, again and again"; *NW-V*, 2:745 (16 May 1922).

[58] *NW-V*, 2:747 (17 May 1922).

[59] "most preferably pretend to having an imaginary Italian source, in order to be more anonymous, as [the trilogy] already is"; letter of 5 November 1925, quoted in Ernst Křenek, "Zur Entstehungsgeschichte der Trilogie 'O Lacrimosa,'" in Gert Buchheit, ed., *Stimmen der Freunde* (Freiburg im Breisgau: Urban, 1931), p. 159.

un très grand musicien et qui, comme compositeur, promet *beaucoup*";[60]
he subsequently revealed to her that he had gotten his opinion of Křenek's
talents from Reinhart — how could he himself have judged? In September
1924, Křenek was in Sierre, and met Rilke again, who "erzählte unermüdlich"[61] — not the only indication of Rilke's growing loquaciousness toward
the end of his life. Křenek was also keenly aware of Rilke's belonging to a
different generation from his own, and of being somehow "nicht fünfzig,
sondern sechshundert oder zweitausend Jahre alt."[62] Presumably, Křenek
expected no understanding of modern music from him.

It might be asked why Rilke never decided to include a course on music
among those many projects he undertook for his improvement — studying
Danish, studying art history, studying Egyptology. That he contemplated
such a plan may be indicated by the Florentine diary: "...ich werde die
Musik suchen," this pronouncement coming on the heels of another about
the distance at which he stood from the art: "Ich habe [der Musik] noch nie
auf irgendeinem Wege mich nahen dürfen."[63] Somehow, music fascinated
him, and he wanted, when in the company of musical friends, to react
intelligently to it; witness the several poems on music he wrote during the
Worpswede days, when he was confronted by the art in a social setting, or
his remarks in connection with Marie von Thurn und Taxis and her Duino
concerts, or his moving, in Switzerland, in circles that contained such
respected amateurs as Werner Reinhart, about whom he wrote to the
Princess Marie (in the letter where he called himself a "tauber Berg") that:
"Musik steht ihm doch offenbar näher als alles übrige, und ich konnte auch
jetzt wieder merken, wie alle diese produktiven und ausübenden Künstler
sein Urtheil schätzen und zu Herzen nehmen."[64] The causes for his failure
to act on whatever musical resolve he had (and better to prepare himself for
that strenuous reception of music he demanded) may only be guessed at.
Perhaps he truly believed that he lacked the normal musicality of others
(even the ability to carry a tune), perhaps he had become convinced that an
effort to grasp the essence of music was, in the last analysis, hopeless, for
him or for anyone else. The letter of 13 February 1914, to Benvenuta might
imply this, in which music is called a higher air. Compared to the other arts,
"da ist die Musik freilich ein näheres Wesen, sie strömt herbei, wir stehn ihr

---

[60] "Křenek would seem to be a very great musician and someone who, as a composer,
promises *much*"; *NW-V*, 2:997 (25 April 1924).

[61] "told stories untiringly"; Křenek, p. 157.

[62] "not fifty but six-hundred or two-thousand years old"; Křenek, p. 155.

[63] "I have still never been allowed to approach music on any path at all"; *TadF*, p. 56, p.
55.

[64] "deaf mountain"; "Obviously, music is closer to him, after all, than anything else, and
now I could notice once again, too, how all these productive and practicing artists value
his judgment and take it to heart"; *RMR/MTT*, 2:801.

im Weg, da geht sie durch uns. Fast ist sie wie eine höhere Luft, wir ziehen sie ein in die Lungen des Geistes und sie giebt uns ein größeres Blut in den heimlichen Kreislauf. Aber *was* reicht sie nicht über uns fort! Aber *was* drängt sie nicht neben uns hin! Aber *was* trägt sie nicht mitten durch uns und wir fassen es nicht! Ach wir fassen es nicht, ach wir verlieren's!"[65] Or perhaps Rilke entertained a belief in his special and untrammeled musical perception (for all his protestations of musical ignorance and musical fear) and was determined to keep it unspoiled.

A poem from the ambiance of the Worpswede music room may well hint at a conviction that he had the makings of music's savior. The refrain in "Strophen"[66] from the Schmargendorf diaries ("ich bin bei euch," I am with you) repeated seven times, inevitably makes us think of the words of Jesus in Matthew 28:20: "Und siehe, ich bin bei euch alle Tage, bis an der Welt Ende." (A sentence in *Malte*'s Beethoven-apostrophe — "Wer treibt sie aus den Musiksälen, die Käuflichen ..." [Who will drive them from the concert halls, those venal ones ...] — is likewise reminiscent of John 2:15, Christ driving the money-lenders from the temple.) Far away from Worpswede now, in Berlin, the poet may understand music more fully than those present at Vogeler's house, "ihr sanften Aufmerksamen" (you gentle attentive ones) and "ihr Lauschenden des Klanges" (you harkeners of the tone); he gives definitions of music ("Musik! Musik! Ordnerin der Geräusche, / nimm, was zerstreut ist in der Abendstunde"; Music! Music! Orderer of sounds, / take what is dispersed in the evening hour) and instructions to it ("Geh hin, Musik, zu jedem Ding und führe / aus jedes Dinges jeder Türe, / die lange bange waren, — die Gestalten"; Go forth, music, to every thing and lead / from every door of every thing / those which long were anxious — the forms), and tells it its purpose ("Musik ist Schöpfung, Seele des Gesanges, / du machst aus vielen Dingen *einen* Bau, / indem du steigst in diese vielen Dinge"; Music is creation, soul of the song, / you make from many things one edifice, / in that you climb into these many things). Music is a unifier and a helper for others: "Und Knaben giebst du ein Gefühl zu finden / und eine Stelle, wo die Welt sich dehnt, / und Greise, welche schon dem Tag erblinden, / leben nur noch, an dich gelehnt" (And to boys you vouchsafe the finding of a feeling / and a place where the world expands, / and old men, who already are blind unto the day, / are only alive still, [when] leaned against you"). Yet the speaker of the poem makes his utterance out of his

---

[65] "thus music, of course, is a being nearer [to us], it comes streaming toward us, we stand in its way, then it goes through us. It is almost like a higher [kind of] air, we breathe it into the lungs of the spirit and it provides [our] secret circulation with a greater sort of blood. But what does it not carry beyond us! But what does it not thrust past us! But *what* does it not bear through our very center, and we do not grasp it! Oh, we do not grasp it, oh, we lose it!"; *Benvenuta*, pp. 66–67.

[66] "I am with you"; "And lo, I am with you always, even unto the end of the world"; *SW*, 3:704–7; *TadF*, pp. 360–63.

"Schweigsamkeit" (silentness) which is superior to the ordered and comforting sounds the gentle listeners in Worpswede hear. (In his account of the phonograph performance at Rodin's studio, Rilke tells how Rodin was much impressed by Rilke's remark, which the sculptor then repeated, about the Gregorian chant: Rilke had said "'C'est large comme le silence.'")[67] Already, Rilke — or the poem's speaker — had acted as a teacher, admonishing against music's dangerous charms, in "Musik" from the summer of 1899; a boy, playing a musical instrument, is warned not to let his spirit become the prisoner of music: "Der Klang ist wie ein Kerker, / darin sie [die Seele] sich versäumt und sich versehnt."[68] The soul will be exhausted by being poured out in music (that seductive art), and needs the refuge of silence ("Gieb ihr ein Schweigen"); otherwise, it will become mutilated and earthbound ("so wirst du, Träumer, ihren Flug vergeuden, / daß ihre Schwingen, vom Gesang zersägt, / sie nicht mehr über meine Mauern trägt, / wenn ich sie rufen werde zu den Freuden"), unfit to attend those numerous festivals of beauty which Rilke so often announces in both the prose and poetry of the time.

Again, in Schmargendorf following the Worpswede days, Rilke wrote "Im Musiksaal,"[69] after he had heard a concert of music by the Norwegian composer, Christian Sinding. Although hidden in the last row, the speaker of the poem feels himself to be the object of the yearning which has arisen, sentimentally enough, in the violins ("Eine Sehnsucht stand auf in den Geigen"); this "yearning" finds the speaker-listener in a state of withdrawn silence, the silence of creation ("und mein Schweigen schuf sich Stimmen, Schreie, / die es wie ein Flüchtender erstieg"). The music and the poem end with the listener once more excluded from the world of images the music has elicited: "Wieder war ich hinter hundert Türen" — but music has been allowed to stir the outsider's imagination, and (behind the last door, the strongest) lies the promise of the images it could bring forth ("Und es klang

---

[67] "It is broad, like silence"; *B 1907–1914*, p. 80.

[68] "The sound is like a dungeon, / in which it [the soul] tarries and wastes itself in yearning"; "Give it a silence"; "Then you, oh dreamer, will squander its flight, / so that its wings, sawed up by song, / will bear it no more over my walls, / when I shall summon it to joys"; *SW*, 1:379–80. See the interpretation by Christoph Petzsch, "Musik: Verführung und Gesetz," *Germanisch-Romanische Monatsschrift* 41 (1960): 65–85; on p. 65, note 1, Petzsch gives a listing of previous literature on Rilke and music; Clara Mágr, *Rilke und die Musik* (Vienna: Amandus, 1960), appeared the same year as the article. Petzsch's proposal, "Kann Rilke die Verse auf Hanno Buddenbrook geschrieben haben?" (Can Rilke have directed the verses at Hanno Buddenbrook?) seems untenable if Zinn's dating of the poem (22 July 1899) is correct. Thomas A. Kovach also addresses the poem in his essay on the later "Bestürz mich, Musik" (see note 71).

[69] "A yearning arose in the violins"; "and my silence created voices for itself, cries, / up which it clambered like someone in flight"; "Once more I was behind a hundred doors"; "And it sounded from within / as if someone were playing with strings of pearls"; "My fear fell like a child to rest"; *SW*, 3:462–63; *TadF*, pp. 370–71.

von innen / so als spielte wer mit Perlenschnüren"). As in the case of *Zauberflöte*, the listener's wandering mind, his "Schweigen," has been moved to produce its own world, but — in contrast to "rose petals laid on the emotions" by Mozart's music, and to the sense of security felt at the present poem's opening: "Meine Angst kam wie ein Kind zu Ruh" — it has been pursued by the frightening "Stimmen, Schreie" of the imagination in the poem's middle. (In Rodin's studio, Rodin would hear — does Rilke impute his own idea to Rodin? — the voices of the damned in the Gregorian chant.) Of the three poems from the turn of the century just adduced and (too hastily) discussed, the third, "Im Musiksaal," is perhaps the most important — if, as literature, the weakest.

Directly addressed by music, Rilke expected and wanted to be over-whelmed. (His fear of the power of music — and his derogatory remarks about it — are other aspects of the same complex: he did not dare too often to be "open" to it, in the words he used to Countess Sizzo.) The plea is expressed unabashedly in the paralipomenon to the elegies, "Bestürz mich, Musik, mit rhythmischem Zürnen,"[70] which Thomas A. Kovach has characterized, in an excellent essay, as Rilke's "Wendung zur Musik" of 1913,[71] on the eve of the experience with Magda. Often, Rilke chooses the most overpowering of instruments, the organ, for the poetic instrumentation of his urge — and the organ, as well, is the primary ecclesiastical instrument. In the fragment just quoted, the arches wait: "Die Wölbungen warten, / die obersten, daß du [Musik] sie füllst mit orgelndem Andrang."[72] With its tremendous sound, the organ is to be found early and late in the Rilke-corpus; in *Advent*, the "verträumte Heiligenbilder" wait, again, "warten auf den Sonntag mit den vollen / Gestühlen und dem großen Orgelrollen";[73] the hands of the beloved, in *Dir zur Feier*, "warten wie auf Orgeltasten / einer neuen Hymne zu";[74] in *Die weiße Fürstin*, when the plague comes, "an Siebenhundert und die Orgel schrien";[75] waiting, "we" in a fragment of 1913 turn into the organ itself: "Wir ahnen kaum, / wie wir uns nach unermessnem Rate / um zur Orgel bauen, horchend, leis, / für den Sturm

---

[70] "Startle me, music, with rhythmic raging"; *SW*, 2:60.

[71] "Turn to music"; Thomas A. Kovach, "Rilkes Wendung zur Musik: Das Gedicht *Bestürz mich, Musik*," in Roland Jost and Hansgeorg Schmidt-Bergmann, eds., *Im Dialog mit der Moderne: Zur deutschsprachigen Literatur von der Gründerzeit bis zur Gegenwart: Jacob Steiner zum 60. Geburtstag* (Frankfurt am Main: Athenäum, 1986), pp. 170–78.

[72] "The arches wait, the topmost ones / for you [music] to fill them with an organing rush"; *SW*, 2:61.

[73] "statues of saints, lost in dreams"; "wait for Sunday with the full / pews and the great rolling of the organ"; *SW*, 1:107.

[74] "wait as on organ keys / toward a new hymn"; *SW*, 3:183.

[75] "wellnigh seven-hundred and the organ cried out"; *SW*, 1:216.

der kommenden Kantate";[76] the young worker of Rilke's feigned letter of 1922, as leery of Christianity as Rilke himself, is aware, in the church of St. Eustache, of "diese Angriffe von der Orgel her";[77] in a sketch from 1925, the weaker voices in a church concert are subdued by the organ's storm, "Stimmen, Flöten, und Fiedeln / ordnet der Orgel Föhn."[78] In *Vergers*, the overriding experience of love is prepared by the growling of organs: "Il faut que les Orgues grondent, /pour que la musique abonde / de toutes les notes de l'amour,"[79] and in the fragment "Notre Dame," "Menacées par l'approche du calme divin, / les orgues se déchaînent. / Saura-t-on dompter à la fin / ces forces indigènes?"[80] From Ragaz, in Rilke's last summer, the whole song may be deduced from the first note of the organ: "so hört man in dem ersten Orgelton / das ganze Lied sich unaufhaltsam heben. / Das ganze Lied mit Opfer, Wandlung, Sieg...."[81] Rilke remarks to Princess Marie, from the Toledo cathedral, on "die herrlichen Orgeln"[82] and adds that the trumpet-shaped pipes stand out from them like weapons — like harquebusses.

To the Countess Alexandrine Schwerin, Rilke suggests an experiment with the organ: "wie manchmal, beim Versuchen einer Orgel, aus dem Anschlag zweier Tasten ein ganzer Sturm von Klang hervorbricht."[83] Two keys are pressed down (as a prank or in a test) and a whole storm breaks forth, without purpose, without program. The lines may call to mind the recollection Rilke sent to Magda von Hattingberg about an initial musical adventure — how he learned that (like the experimenter with the two organ keys) he could produce a free and elementary music all his own. The tale comes as the climax of a series of letters stretching from 16 February 1914, on, which repeatedly bring up the themes of childhood and motherhood, and the role Magda (whom he calls "Du mein wirkliches Kind und meine

---

[76] "we scarcely surmise / how, in accordance with unmeasured council, / we rebuild ourselves as an organ, listening, quiet, / for the storm of the coming cantata"; *SW*, 2:394.

[77] "these attacks from the organ"; *SW*, 6:1120.

[78] "the spring storm of the organ puts / voices, flutes and fiddles in order"; *SW*, 2:503.

[79] "it is necessary that the organs growl / so that music may abound / with all the notes of love"; *SW*, 2:529.

[80] "Threatened by the approach of the divine calm, / the organs unchain themselves. / At the end, will one know how to tame / these native forces?"; *SW*, 2:722.

[81] "Thus, in the first note of the organ / one hears the whole song arise, unstoppable. / The whole song with sacrifice, transformation, victory ..."; *SW*, 2:510.

[82] "the glorious organs"; *RMR/MTT*, 1:230 (13 November 1912).

[83] "as sometimes, at the testing of an organ, a whole storm of sound breaks forth from the striking of two keys"; *B* (1950), 2:362 (16 June 1922).

wirkliche jungfräuliche Mutter, liebes Mädchen")[84] will play in leading him into a fruitful relationship to music. He also tells her about the musical experience of his own daughter, Ruth, who has performed the cuckoo-part in Haydn's *Children's Symphony*; since Ruth was going on thirteen, Rilke stretches things by making her seem younger, more the child, than she was: "Ruth machte den Kuckuck, der es, wie es scheint, furchtbar genau nehmen muß und gar nicht leicht hat."[85] The climax is likewise couched in an arch style, telling about a passion little René had entertained for dusting the furniture. Recently, by chance, the old enthusiasm has come over him again, "aus dem Stegreif." "Du mußt wissen, daß das fast die größeste [Leiden- schaft] meiner Kindheit war, sogar meine älteste Beziehung zur Musik, denn unser Pianino fiel in mein Abstaubebereich, es war einer der wenigen Gegenstände, der sich leicht dazu hergab und sich doch nicht langweilig unter dem Eifer des Staubtuchs benahm, sondern ganz plötzlich so metallisch brummte und überdies schön dunkel spiegelte, jemehr man sich Mühe gab. Was mochte man dabei alles erlebt haben?"[86] It was this aleatory, unprepared appearance of sound which seems most to have allured him, beyond Beethoven and Bach, beyond the stark Gregorian chant; no training was necessary to produce the pure sound, no training was necessary to let it sweep through and over the listener (who nonetheless had discovered the trick of eliciting it) — only the open and virgin ear.

May it be proposed that the well-known sound-perceptions the mature Rilke took pains to describe are descended from the little boy's dusting of the spinet? The sound of the bat's wing scraping along the sphinx's profile, in the famous scene described to Magda,[87] and then in the Tenth Duino Elegy ("und [die Eule], / streifend im langsamen Abstrich die Wange entlang, / jene der reifesten Rundung, / zeichnet weich in das neue / Totengehör, über ein doppelt / aufgeschlagenes Blatt, den unbeschreiblichen Umriß"), touches — in the elegy — a hearing that is new and virginal in death.[88]

---

[84] "You, my real child and my real virginal mother, dear maiden"; *Benvenuta*, p. 91 (16 February 1914).

[85] "Ruth played the cuckoo, which, so it seems, must be terribly exact and does not have an easy time at all"; *Benvenuta*, p. 100 (17 February 1914).

[86] "on the spur of the moment"; "you must know that it was almost the greatest [passion] of my childhood, indeed my oldest relationship to music; for our parlor piano fell into my dusting's realm, it was one of the few objects which easily offered itself and yet did not behave in a boring fashion under the dustcloth's zeal, but rather, quite suddenly, gave out such a metallic growl and, besides, provided such a handsomely dark mirror, the more effort was applied. What all one must have experienced in the process!"; *Benvenuta*, p. 136 (22 February 1914).

[87] *Benvenuta*, p. 25 (1 February 1914).

[88] "and [the owl] / grazing in a slow stroke along the cheek, / that of the ripest rounding, / softly designs in the new / hearing of the dead, across a doubly / opened page, the indescribable contour"; *SW*, 1:724.

Or, in the essay *Ur-Geräusch*, from the summer of 1919, Rilke presents —
the physiological conceit is known to every Rilke-reader — an almost
Meyrinkian notion of turning the patterns of the coronal suture into sound
by means of a phonograph needle drawn along it.[89] These acoustical
discoveries, these changes of shapes into sounds, will make a new kind of
music, or a very old kind, a primal sound. (In this connection, Rüdiger
Goerner's analyses of the gong-poems from 1925 and 1926 should be examined.)[90] Rilke had inventively employed a traditional musical-emotional
imagery in the poetry up to and including *Neue Gedichte*, with all those
fiddlers and fiddles and strings, which sometimes turned out aptly and to
great effect, as in the line "Fremde Geige, gehst du mir nach?",[91] and in
the famous *Liebes-Lied*:

> wie ein Bogenstrich
> der aus zwei Saiten *eine* Stimme zieht.
> Auf welches Instrument sind wir gespannt?
> Und welcher Geiger hat uns in der Hand?
> O süßes Lied.[92]

and sometimes mawkishly, when the components of the image fit less well
together:

> Du hast mich wie eine Laute gemacht;
> so sei wie eine Hand.
> Du hast den Abgrund meiner Nacht
> mit Saiten überspannt.[93]

---

[89] *SW*, 6:1085–93.

[90] Rüdiger Goerner, "'… und Musik überstieg uns …': Zu Rilkes Deutung der Musik,"
Blätter der Rilke Gesellschaft 10 (1983): 50–69, esp. pp. 65–69.

[91] "Strange violin, do you pursue me?"; *SW*, 1:392.

[92]   "like the stroke of a bow
which draws *one* voice from two strings.
Upon what instrument are we stretched?
And what violinist has us in his hand?
Oh sweet song."
SW, 1:482.

[93] You have rendered me like a lute;
   now be like a hand.
   You have stretched strings
   over the abyss of my night.
SW, 3:676.

Similarly, the efforts in the early poetry to create the effect of traditional sublimity are grandly mellifluous, if not always remarkable in their conformations, for example, in "Nach Beethovens Missa Solemnis":[94]

Aus dem hohen Jubelklanggedränge,
welches durch des Himmels Tore will,
steigen steile Stimmen, Übergänge —
und auf einmal sind die Stürme still.

Only when, at last, Rilke is confident enough to confront his double sense — of musical ignorance on the one side and virginal hearing on the other — can he write the original 'musical' poetry of "An die Musik" of 1918,[95] a poem with its lapidary address to "Du Fremde: Musik," this "andre / Seite der Luft: / rein, / riesig, / nicht mehr bewohnbar," and of "Musik" from 1925, dedicated to the cellist Lorenz Lehr, in which music is "Du mehr als wir ..., von jeglichem Wozu / befreit,"[96] a compression of what Rilke had written to Alexander von Thurn und Taxis about the "old music" heard in the Toledo church: "es stößt wie der Wind in die Welt hinein, ganz als bliese es so für sich, auch wenn wir nicht da wären. Und das ist doch wohl Musik!"[97] Perhaps a musical training, a knowledge of music, would have stood in the way of reducing music to primal sound, heard by the virgin ear. Rilke's musical judgments resemble Zuleika Dobson's: "'I don't know anything about music, really, but I know what I like.'" (To which might be added the narrator's voice in Beerbohm's incomparable novel: "People who say it are never tired of saying it.") But Rilke thought a great deal harder than Zuleika about what it was that enchanted and baffled him.

---

[94] From the high sound-throng of jubilation,
which wants to go through heaven's gate,
steep voices ascend, transitions —
and suddenly the storms are still.
SW, 3:677; *TadF*, p. 213.

[95] "To Music"; "other / side of the air: / pure, / gigantic, / no longer inhabitable"; *SW*, 2:111; see Thomas A. Kovach, "'Du Sprache wo Sprachen enden': Rilke's Poem 'An die Musik,'" *Seminar: A Journal of Germanic Studies* 22 (1986): 206–17.

[96] "You [who are] more than we ..., from every purpose freed"; *SW*, 2:266–67.

[97] "it thrusts like the wind into the world, altogether as if it were blowing for itself, even though we were not there. And that, nonetheless, is surely music!"; *B* (1950), 1:410.

Music and the Subversive Imagination

MARC A. WEINER

BETWEEN 1900 AND THE rise of fascism, the cultural vocabulary of German-speaking Europe associated music of a pure and/or primitive nature with visions of alternative, sometimes violent societies not yet contaminated by the failings of the modern age. Both in diverse extra-literary manifestations and in the literature of the period which drew its motivic repertoire from pervasive cultural motifs (many of them receiving such currency through the popularity of Nietzsche's *Die Geburt der Tragödie aus dem Geiste der Musik*), the image of fantastic and bizarre collectives opposing an idealized lost paradise, or even a violent yet genuinely free world, to the reality of contemporary social despair conflated with the notion of music as an art of subversion. The motif of a culturally, and hence musically superior lost social order is discernible, for example, in the rhetoric of the aesthetic debates from 1907 to 1926 between Hans Pfitzner, Ferruccio Busoni, and Paul Bekker, and appears repeatedly in Oswald Spengler's *Der Untergang des Abendlandes* of 1918–22.[1] For a variety of reasons, music at this time suggests insurrection and implies a threat to the status quo, and as such becomes closely tied to expressions of a desire for social change. Out of this ubiquitous perception of music in the culture of the German-speaking countries in the early twentieth century, music's role as a literary motif took on associations of subversion and danger in narrative texts of the time. While recent scholarship has focused attention on the emancipatory impetus inherent in images of alternative (and often primitive) societies found in

---

[1] Bernhard Adamy, *Hans Pfitzner: Literatur, Philosophie und Zeitgeschehen in seinem Weltbild und Werk* (Tutzing: Hans Schneider, 1980), pp. 90, 372; Johann Peter Vogel, "Pfitzner und Busoni: Eine ästhetische Auseinandersetzung im Lichte der Gegenwart," *Mitteilungen der Hans Pfitzner-Gesellschaft* 33 (1974): 10–22, here 10, 14; Antony Beaumont, *Busoni the Composer* (Bloomington: Indiana Univ. Press, 1985), p. 97; Jürgen Kindermann, "Zur Kontroverse Busoni-Pfitzner: Futuristengefahr — Mißverständnis einer Kritik?" in Ludwig Finscher and Christoph-Hellmut Mahling, *Festschrift für Walter Wiora* (Kassel: Bärenreiter, 1967), pp. 471–77; Winfried Zillig, *Von Wagner bis Strauss: Wegbereiter der neuen Musik* (Munich: Nymphenburg, 1966), pp. 145–58; Paul Bekker, "Futuristengefahr?" in *Kritische Zeitbilder* (Berlin: Schuster & Loeffler, 1921), 265–69; Oswald Spengler, *Der Untergang des Abendlandes: Umrisse einer Morphologie der Weltgeschichte* (Munich: C. H. Beck, 1950), I ("Gestalt und Wirklichkeit"), pp. 34–47, 362–64. I would like to thank my colleague Breon Mitchell for bringing these passages by Spengler to my attention.

numerous manifestations of German literary modernism, the role of music as a motif accompanying these images has been ignored.[2]

In the following pages I would like to offer some examples of the way music, as a motif in German and Austrian narrative texts from 1900 to 1930, unobtrusively suggested socio-critical issues, and in so doing implied a desire for social change. This essay is divided into three sections: the first seeks to characterize the ubiquitous connection between music and extra-musical issues in the early twentieth century by focusing on two works of Thomas Mann, each concerned in different ways with music as a cultural construct or code signifying social position; the second addresses different images of subversion evoked through music in a number of literary works from the period; and the final section, based largely on the cultural criticism of the Frankfurt School, discusses the clichéd nature of these manifestations of a longing for a different world as examples of an ideological impasse that results whenever one attempts to envision social relations operating outside existing ideological forms. My concluding remarks concern the irony involved in musical images of social difference which are limited to an aesthetic repertoire representative of existing social configurations.

I

The location of a superior society in an indeterminate past is a pervasive feature of the cultural vocabulary of the early twentieth-century cultural imagination in Germany and Austria, manifested in both literary and extra-literary writings of the time. It is found for example in the sociological works of Ferdinand Tönnies and Ernst Troeltsch, and in such politically diverse texts as the leftist socialist reflections of Gustav Landauer and the conservative cultural criticism of Hans Pfitzner.[3] Consonant with the widespread imaginative gesture that nostalgically locates perfection and difference in the

---

[2] The best analysis of the relationship between various forms of modernism and the diverse alternative communities they imply is found in: Russell A. Berman, *The Rise of the Modern German Novel: Crisis and Charisma* (Cambridge: Harvard Univ. Press, 1986).

[3] On Tönnies and Troeltsch, see Harry Liebersohn, *Fate and Utopia in German Sociology, 1870–1923* (Cambridge: MIT Press, 1988), pp. 11–77; on Landauer, see Russell A. Berman and Tim Luke, "Introduction," in Gustav Landauer, *For Socialism*, ed. Russell A. Berman and Tim Luke (St. Louis: Telos Press, 1978), pp. 1–18; for evidence of Pfitzner as a cultural critic, see Hans Pfitzner, *Futuristengefahr: Bei Gelegenheit von Busonis Ästhetik* (Leipzig and Munich: Süddeutsche Monatshefte, 1917), reprinted in *Gesammelte Schriften* (Augsburg: Benno Filser, 1926–29), 1:185–223; his "Die Verpöbelung des Lebens in Geräuschen," in *Konzerttaschenbuch für die Saison 1908/9*, I (Munich: Emil Gutmann, 1908), reprinted in *Gesammelte Schriften*, vol. 4, ed. Bernhard Adamy (Tutzing: Hans Schneider, 1987), 185–86; and his *Die neue Ästhetik der musikalischen Impotenz* (Munich: Verlag der Süddeutschen Monatshefte, 1919), reprinted in *Gesammelte Schriften*, 2:99–281; see Marc A. Weiner, "Der Briefwechsel zwischen Hans Pfitzner und Felix Wolfes, 1933–1948," in *Jahrbuch für Exilforschung*, ed. Wulf Koepke and Thomas Koebner (Munich: Text + Kritik, 1984), 2:393–411.

past, music highlights within the cultural vocabulary of the time a desire for social change, be it conservative, leftist, or politically ill-defined.

Why should music accompany the expression of social dynamics? In part the answer is historical and concerns both the privileged position of the art in bourgeois life in the late nineteenth and early twentieth centuries and the increasing conflation of social issues with music in the course of the nineteenth century. The projection in German literature from 1900 to the 1930s of social issues onto various kinds of imagined music is determined by social pressures different from those influencing visions of an alternative society associated with music in German literature of the early and mid-nineteenth century; this is underscored by the fact that in the twentieth-century narrative music often evokes such extra-musical, social issues as anarchy and an alternative community opposed to the alienating, rigidly structured society of the modern age. This is the case in works by Thomas Mann, Gerhart Hauptmann, Hermann Hesse, Franz Werfel, Arthur Schnitzler, Hugo von Hofmannsthal, and others at this time. Earlier depictions of music offering an escape from the trials of everyday life were far more concerned with the individual than with an ideal or different community, as seen in the works of E. T. A. Hoffmann (*Ritter Gluck* and *Don Juan*), Eduard Mörike (*Mozart auf der Reise nach Prag*), Franz Grillparzer (*Der arme Spielmann*), Adalbert Stifter (*Turmalin*), and to a lesser extent in the mid-nineteenth-century Parisian novellas of Richard Wagner (*Eine Pilgerfahrt zu Beethoven, Ein Ende in Paris*, and *Ein glücklicher Abend*).

By the late nineteenth century, the connection between music and social themes became embedded in the cultural imagination and in the literature that drew upon it for its content, and the evocation of another world through music would increasingly assume an aura of a lost — past — paradise. Music as an evocation of an alternative world would come to imply a longing for a pre-industrialized, pre-capitalistic collective. From such diverse thinkers as Wagner and Paul de Lagarde writing in the mid-nineteenth century, to Julius Langbehn in the 1880s, to Pfitzner in the first third of the twentieth century, and to Theodor W. Adorno afterwards, a leitmotif in reflections on imagined past paradise is the notion that in these long-lost communities the individual and the arts would not yet have suffered alienation.[4]

Yet this historical dimension in the development of music's role in German literature cannot by itself adequately explain music's function as a harbinger of alternative collectives in early twentieth-century writings. In the literary production of this time, the connection between music and imagined societies different from those of contemporary reality is based on both the culturally pervasive equation of music and social problems and,

---

[4] On Lagarde and Langbehn, see Fritz Stern, *The Politics of Cultural Despair: A Study in the Rise of the Germanic Ideology* (Berkeley: Univ. of California Press, 1961), pp. 27–70, 116–52.

perhaps more importantly, on music's traditionally ill-defined *metaphorical* function in narrative texts in general. For a number of theoreticians of the relationship between music and society, such as Ernst Bloch and Adorno writing in the 1950s, music's comparative resistance to mimetic association makes it a superior vehicle for analyzing the role of ideology in aesthetics.[5] Similarly, and certainly less self-consciously, the art provided the early twentieth-century author with a metaphorical locus within the narrative text, a locus open to a variety of authorial concerns, because music aroused less visually standardized, less visually specific and easily anticipated associations in the reader.

These notions — music as resistant to mimesis, as a vehicle for the expression of (imagined) desire, and as somehow fundamentally *different* from the other arts — are all notions deeply entrenched within the cultural imagination of the German-speaking countries in the early twentieth century. They all highlight music's role in this culture as providing an imaginative space in which visions of alternative social configurations could emerge to underscore the limitations of contemporary social reality. Just as music takes on, in the reflective and socio-critical imagination, a privileged and different quality against which the immediate and visible world implicitly appears impoverished, so within the narrative text music as another art proportionally devoid of mimetic association forms the negative space, the blank screen, upon which social concerns are projected. With music as the silent art brought to imaginary sound during the reader's thoughtful attention, a space is provided within the reader's fantasy for the acoustical backdrop to the literary portrayal of social problems. It is in this space that the battle is waged between an entrenched status quo and visions of an alternative society. No wonder, then, that music so often appears at the time as a motif signifying difference, exoticism, strangeness, volatility, licentious desire, and danger. Perhaps these more clandestine, less obvious extra-aesthetic (socio-political) messages implied by music (music as subversive, as danger, as anarchy, music as a reflection of the status quo, or of competing socio-political agendas, etc.) may have been masked by a more conscious attention to purely aesthetic matters cultivated in the reception of music in German cultural life in general, yet such subliminal and socially determined attendant messages may have actually propelled interaction with

---

[5] Cf. Ernst Bloch, "The Artistic Illusion as the Visible Anticipatory Illumination," in *The Utopian Function of Art and Literature: Selected Essays*, trans. and ed. Jack Zipes and Frank Mecklenburg (Cambridge: MIT Press, 1988), pp. 141–55; Wayne Hudson, *The Marxist Philosophy of Ernst Bloch* (New York: St. Martin's Press, 1982), pp. 27–28, 175–76; music as metaphor provides the basis for much of Adorno's social criticism of the art; see Adorno, *Einleitung in die Musiksoziologie*, in *Gesammelte Schriften*, ed. Rolf Tiedemann, (Frankfurt am Main: Suhrkamp, 1975), 14:178–447, especially the section on "Kammermusik," pp. 271–91.

the art, both in the everyday musical reception in Germany and Austria and in the reception of music as a literary motif as well.[6]

In much of the literature of the early twentieth century, one kind of aesthetic form is set against another, because each operates as a sign of a given social and ideological position. An appreciation of this pervasive equation is central to an understanding of the way music could function as a sign of a different collective order. Usually this opposition of two kinds of art juxtaposes music and language, but at times it invades even the interpretation of music itself. The tension between classical music and the romantic music of Wagner in Thomas Mann's *Buddenbrooks* of 1900, for example, is representative of an ubiquitous aesthetic polarity in the literature of the time. Here, a musical polarity is based on the diametrically opposed socio-political orientations of the foreign, non-German violinist and impassioned Wagnerite Gerda Buddenbrook, and of her accompanist, the conservative Prussian organist Edmund Pfühl, whose musical proclivities are described in terms redolent with social implications:[7]

> Edmund Pfühl war ein weithin hochgeschätzter Organist, und der Ruf seiner kontrapunktischen Gelehrsamkeit hatte sich nicht innerhalb der Mauern seiner Vaterstadt gehalten.... [S]eine Fugen und Choralbe-arbeitungen ..., sowie auch die Phantasien, die er sonntags in der Marienkirche zum besten gab, waren unangreifbar, makellos, erfüllt von der unerbittlichen, imposanten, moralisch-logischen Würde des Strengen Satzes.... Es sprach aus ihnen, es triumphierte sieghaft in ihnen die zur asketischen Religion gewordene Technik, das zum Selbstzweck, zur absoluten Heiligkeit erhobene Können.... "Palestrina" sagte er mit einer kategorischen und furchteinflößenden Miene.

The key terms here are "unerbittlich," "imposant," "moralisch-logisch," and "asketisch"; they delineate Herr Pfühl's love of severity and control. A given

---

[6] This is the basis of Adorno's argument in his *Einleitung in die Musiksoziologie*.

[7] Thomas Mann, *Buddenbrooks: Verfall einer Familie*, in *Gesammelte Werke in dreizehn Bänden* (Frankfurt am Main: S. Fischer, 1974), 1:495–96. This translation and the ones following are from Thomas Mann, *Buddenbrooks*, trans. H. T. Lowe-Porter (New York: Vintage, 1952), pp. 390–91; all subsequent translations of *Buddenbrooks* are likewise from this edition: "Edmund Pfühl was an organist of no small repute, whose reputation for contrapuntal learning was not confined within the walls of his native town. His ... fugues and chorals ... as well as the voluntaries he played on Sundays at Saint Mary's, were flawless, impeccable, full of the relentless, severe logicality of the *Strenge Satz*. What spoke in them, what gloriously triumphed in them, was a technique amounting to an ascetic religion, a technique elevated to a lofty sacrament, to an absolute end in itself.... He would utter the name of Palestrina in the most dogmatic, awe-inspiring tone. But even while he made his instrument give out a succession of archaistic virtuosities, his face would be all aglow with feeling.... This was the musician's look; vague and vacant precisely because it abode in the kingdom of a purer, profounder, more absolute logic than that which shapes our verbal conceptions and thoughts."

form of aesthetic expression (here contrapuntal music) brings with it associations of repression, and hence is deemed *morally* superior to other forms of art. The repressive, ascetic, and by implication conservative nature of this art evokes a socio-political dimension; indeed, such extra-aesthetic associations characterize all passages devoted to Herr Pfühl's relationship to music. In the discussions between this traditional Prussian and the foreign Gerda Buddenbrook, one kind of music — be it that of Palestrina in the passage above, or of Haydn, Mozart, or Beethoven below — represents clarity, decency, and honesty, and hence functions as an Enlightenment emblem of accepted taste in the ruling Prussian order, while another — invariably Wagner — represents licentious desire, a lack of diligence and discipline, and foreign chaos threatening to the male German social status quo. Pfühl's reaction to a foreign, threatening art is made clear in the following passage:[8]

> Ein Satz Haydn, einige Seiten Mozart, eine Sonate von Beethoven wurden durchgeführt....
> Gerda Buddenbrook war eine leidenschaftliche Verehrerin der neuen Musik. Was aber Herrn Pfühl betraf, so war sie bei ihm auf einen so wild empörten Widerstand gestoßen, daß sie anfangs daran verzweifelt hatte, ihn für sich zu gewinnen.
> Am Tage, da sie ihm zum ersten Male Klavierauszüge aus "Tristan und Isolde" aufs Pult gelegt und ihn gebeten hatte, ihr vorzuspielen, war er nach fünfundzwanzig Takten aufgesprungen und mit allen Anzeichen des äußersten Ekels zwischen Erker und Flügel hin und wider geeilt.
> "Ich spiele dies nicht, gnädige Frau, ich bin Ihr ergebenster Diener, aber ich spiele dies nicht! Das ist keine Musik... glauben Sie mir doch ... ich habe mir immer eingebildet, ein wenig von Musik zu verstehen! Dies ist das Chaos! Dies ist Demagogie, Blasphemie und Wahnwitz!"

In *Buddenbrooks*, Mann's fictitious musician discerns a threat to the values of his Hanseatic heritage in the contours of a foreign musical aesthetic. Calling upon morality as the backbone of his civilization, Herr Pfühl rejects an art whose social implications threaten to cast the world as he knows it into chaos through the rule of the people, for Wagner's music, representing

---

[8] Mann, *Buddenbrooks*, pp. 497–98: "They played a movement of Haydn, some pages of Mozart, a sonata of Beethoven....

Gerda Buddenbrook was an impassioned Wagnerite. But Herr Pfühl was an equally impassioned opponent — so much so that in the beginning she had despaired of winning him over.

On the day when she first laid some piano arrangements from *Tristan* on the music-rack, he played some twenty-five beats and then sprang up from the music-stool to stride up and down the room with disgust painted upon his face.

'I cannot play that, my dear lady! I am your most devoted servant — but I cannot. That is not music — believe me! I have always flattered myself I knew something about music — but this is chaos! This is demagogy, blasphemy, insanity, madness!'" (p. 392).

in the novel unbridled sensuality, is immediately associated by the organist with an imagined demagogue, a leader championing the cause of the common people. (It is in keeping with the cultural vocabulary of the period that this foreign music is introduced to the severe man by a woman, a fitting detail in the sexual metaphors surrounding different kinds of aesthetic form at the time.)

Pfühl's privileging of classical severity over a loss of control, as well as his guilty conscience engendered through a titillating fascination with Wagner's *Die Meistersinger*,[9] foreshadows a similar motif in *Der Tod in Venedig* of 1911, though the aesthetic representations of Pfühl's and Gustav von Aschenbach's psycho-social orientations — classical music and epic writing, respectively — are different. The fictional musician Pfühl, and Aschenbach the writer of epics, both fear a psychological condition replete with social connotations of insurrection exemplified for them in a form of art diametrically opposed to the art with which they identify themselves. Extra-aesthetic concerns propel their aesthetic affiliations. Thus the very conflation of moral inferiority, sexualized music, the masses, egalitarianism, illness, and the dissolution of the body and of the social organism later found in *Der Tod in Venedig* is already apparent in the opposition of classical and Wagnerian music in *Buddenbrooks* of 1900.

Such aesthetic opposition has less to do with the innate formal features of the arts — different kinds of music or music and writing — than with the social tensions to which they allude. In *Der Tod in Venedig*, for example, different arts are signs of different ideological positions and even of different social levels.[10] Classicistic writing emerges in this text as the emblem of a repressive and morally conservative Protestant Prussian order, while music per se functions much like Wagner in *Buddenbrooks* — it represents potential anarchy and the lower orders of both the psyche and of society. In the novella, Gustav von Aschenbach's texts of a classicistic and epic nature are accepted into the Prussian educational system because they exemplify its moral standards of repression and obedience to a higher authority.[11] As a representative of his society, Aschenbach is terrified of the sexual and

---

[9] Mann, *Buddenbrooks*, p. 497: "Dann jedoch, während Gerda, die Geige unterm Arm, neue Noten herbeisuchte, geschah das Überraschende, daß Herr Pfühl, Edmund Pfühl, Organist an Sankt Marien, mit seinem freien Zwischenspiel allgemach in einen sehr seltsamen Stil hinüberglitt, wobei in seinem fernen Blick eine Art verschämten Glückes erglänzte.... Das Meistersinger-Vorspiel zog vorüber." ("Then, while Gerda was picking out some music, with her violin under her arm, a surprising thing happened: Herr Pfühl, Edmund Pfühl, organist at St. Mary's, glided over from his easy interlude into music of an extraordinary style; while a sort of shamefaced enjoyment showed upon his absent countenance.... It was the overture to *Die Meistersinger*," p. 392).

[10] Cf. Marc A. Weiner, "Silence, Sound, and Song in *Der Tod in Venedig*: A Study in Psycho-Social Repression," *Seminar* 23, no. 2 (May 1987): 137–55.

[11] Thomas Mann, "Der Tod in Venedig," in *Gesammelte Werke in dreizehn Bänden*, 8:456.

social forces music represents, forces that emerge with attendant musical motifs as his breakdown progresses, challenging both his social position and the high culture which has been its fetishized banner.

It is in Aschenbach's nightmare that the social superiority of a culture based on words and power (and excluding music) is threatened; his dream is a terrifying Dionysian vision filled with acoustical phenomena, noise, screams, and lascivious choral and flute music, that threaten the representative of a rigid and morally hypocritical world:[12]

> Angst war der Anfang ... und seine Sinne lauschten; denn von weither näherte sich Getümmel, Getöse, ein Gemisch von Lärm: Rasseln, Schmettern und dumpfes Donnern, schrilles Jauchzen dazu und ein bestimmtes Geheul im gezogenen u-Laut, — alles durchsetzt und grauenhaft süß übertönt von tief girrendem, ruchlos beharrlichem Flötenspiel, welches auf schamlos zudringende Art die Eingeweide bezauberte. ... Weiber ... schüttelten Schellentrommeln über ihren stöhnend zurückgeworfenen Häuptern ... Männer ... ließen eherne Becken erdröhnen und schlugen wütend auf Pauken.... Und die Begeisterten heulten den Ruf aus weichen Mitlauten und gezogenem u-Ruf am Ende, süß und wild zugleich wie kein jemals erhörter: — hier klang er auf, in die Lüfte geröhrt wie von Hirschen, und dort gab man ihn wieder, vielstimmig ... und ließ ihn niemals verstimmen. Aber alles durchdrang und beherrschte der tiefe, lockende Flötenton. Lockte er nicht auch ihn, den widerstrebend Erlebenden, schamlos beharrlich zum Fest und Unmaß des äußersten Opfers? ... Aber mit ihnen, in ihnen war der Träumende nun und dem fremden Gotte gehörig. Ja, sie waren er selbst.

Here, music is the corrective to the pressures in late-Wilhelminian society that limit the personality; it is the terrifying, negative aesthetic space in which an alternative society can be imagined. While the noble author is revered in Venice even as the musicians and street singers are seen as

---

[12] Mann, "Der Tod in Venedig," pp. 516–17. The following translation is from: Thomas Mann, *Death in Venice*, trans. Kenneth Burke (New York: Alfred A. Knopf, 1925); subsequent translations of *Death in Venice* are likewise from this edition: "It began with anguish, anguish and desire.... It was night, and his senses were on the watch. From far off a grumble, an uproar, was approaching, a jumble of noises. Clanking, blaring, and dull thunder, with shrill shouts and a definite whine in a long-drawn-out *u*-sound — all this was sweetly, ominously interspersed and dominated by the deep cooing of wickedly persistent flutes which charmed the bowels in a shamelessly penetrative manner.... Women ... were holding up tambourines and beating on them, their groaning heads flung back.... Men clashed brass cymbals and beat furiously at kettledrums.... And the bacchantes wailed the word with the soft consonants and the drawn-out *u*-sound, at once sweet and savage, like nothing ever heard before. In one place it rang out as though piped into the air by stags, and it was echoed in another by many voices ... and it was never silent. But everything was pierced and dominated by the deep coaxing flute. He who was fighting against this experience — did it not coax him too with its shameless penetration, into the feast and the excesses of the extreme sacrifice? ... But the dreamer now was with them, in them, and he belonged to the foreign god. Yes, they were he himself" (p. 112–14).

rabble, the figures in Aschenbach's dream form a collective free from political and moral oppression and from the adulation of the individual in Wilhelminian society that constitutes the basis for Aschenbach's career. In this text from 1911 reflecting the culturally ubiquitous connection between music and social issues per se, music is part of an alternative counter culture opposed to the world of the dreamer in the late-Wilhelminian Empire; music attends a negative vision of a different social order.

II

Both the bifurcation of music — in *Buddenbrooks* — and the polarization of the arts — in *Der Tod in Venedig* — project onto a given kind of music a longing for the transformation of a procrustean ideology. From the general equation of music and social concerns emerges the connection between music and counter-cultural impulses. Suffering from dissatisfaction with the modern world, the imagination at this time often projects music onto a superior past. While this imaginary vision is of a profoundly negative character in *Der Tod in Venedig*, many other texts of the period employ similar imagery in more positive contexts. The specific character of the alternative musical vision changes, but the intellectual gesture, the imaginative escapist mechanism associating music with a lost and different collective, remains nearly identical.

The Mediterranean setting of an alternative music implying spontaneity, freedom, social equality, and a release from the strictures of turn-of-the-century moral repression reappears in Gerhart Hauptmann's novella *Der Ketzer von Soana* of 1918. For Francesco, the priest in Hauptmann's text who comes to question institutional grace, music provides an emblem for a superior, more natural and spontaneous social exchange than that found in the modern Church, which reflects and furthers alienation in the modern world. This is at first only suggested when Francesco beholds a Greek frieze on a rustic sarcophagus in the mountains:[13]

> Zum erstenmal, ... ließ sich der junge Priester herbei, den Orna-mentfries des Sarkophages zu betrachten, der in einem Bacchantenzuge bestand und hüpfende Satyren [und] tanzende Flötenspielerinnen ... zeigte.... [Z]eitweilig kam es ihm vor, als ob er selbst von berauschten Mänaden umjauchzt war.

---

[13] Gerhart Hauptmann, "Der Ketzer von Soana," *Sämtliche Werke*, ed. Hans-Egon Hass (Frankfurt am Main and Berlin: Propyläen, 1963), 6:85–169, here 128–29. The following translation is from Gerhart Hauptmann, *The Heretic of Soana*, trans. Bayard Quincy Morgan (London: J. Calder, 1960); subsequent translations of *Der Ketzer von Soana* are likewise from this edition: "For the first time, ... the young priest condescended to inspect the ornamental frieze on the sarcophagus, which consisted of a bacchanalian procession and showed prancing satyrs, dancing female flutists.... At ... times it seemed to him that he himself was surrounded by shouting intoxicated mænads" (pp. 67–68).

That this Dionysian (and hence Nietzschean) music is associated with nature, uncivilized spontaneity, and sensuality opposed to the strictures of the modern world is suggested through the art's metaphorical connection to Agata, the young Italian heathen who, like the foreign and musical Tadzio for Aschenbach, so bewitches a representative of modern morals and causes his rejection of modern social norms:[14]

> Jeder Zug in der Musik dieses kindlichen Hauptes war zugleich Süße und Bitterkeit, Schwermut und Heiterkeit. In seinem Blick lag schüchternes Zurückweichen und zugleich ein zärtliches Fordern: beides nicht mit der Heftigkeit tierischer Regungen, sondern unbewußt blumenhaft.

As Hauptmann's novella progresses, music implying nature, sexual freedom, and emancipatory spontaneity located in a different kind of community conflates with primitive sounds of nature that break through the acoustical art of institutionalized turn-of-the-century Catholicism:[15]

> Immer, Tag für Tag, gegen die Zeit der Abenddämmerung, hielt er, hauptsächlich vor den Frauen und Töchtern Soanas, einen kleinen Diskurs, der die Tugenden der gebenedeiten Jungfrau zum Gegenstand hatte. Vorher und nachher erscholl das Schiff der Kirche, bei offener Tür, in den Frühling hinaus, zu Ehren Mariens von Lobgesang. Und in die ... köstlichen, nach Text und Musik so lieblichen Weisen, mischte sich von außen fröhlicher Spatzenlärm und aus den nahen, feuchten Schluchten die süßeste Klage der Nachtigall. In solchen Minuten war Francesco, scheinbar im Dienste Mariens, dem Dienste seines Idols ganz hingegeben.

Finally, the passage in which Francesco and Agata consummate their love is replete with musical motifs signifying a revolt against the corruption of the modern world, a return to nature, and a loss of individuation implicitly suggestive of an alternative collective not based on modern modes of competition, like those in *Der Tod in Venedig* reinforced through moral

---

[14] Hauptmann, *Der Ketzer von Soana*, p.133. "Every strain in the music of this childlike countenance was at once sweet and bitter, melancholy and gay. In her glance was a shy retreat and at the same time a tender challenge, unconscious, flower like, innocent of the violence of animal passions" (p. 74).

[15] Hauptmann, *Der Ketzer von Soana*, pp. 137–38. "Regularly, every day, at about the hour of twilight, he delivered a little discourse, principally to the women and daughters of Soana, which had for its subject the virtues of the Blessed Virgin. Before and afterward the nave of the church resounded with songs of praise in honour of Mary, which rang out through the open door into the springtime. And with the delicious old airs, so beautiful in both text and music, there mingled from without the cheerful chirping of sparrows and the sweet plaint of the nightingales in the damp gorges of the neighborhood. At such moments Francesco, while apparently serving Mary, was wholly given over to the service of his idol" (p. 80).

rectitude and righteous individuality, but on a less repressive mutual exchange:[16]

> Nie hatte Francesco, nie hatte der Priester ein solches Nahesein bei Gott, ein solches Geborgensein in ihm, ein solches Vergessen der eignen Persönlichkeit gefühlt, und im Rauschen des Bergbachs schienen allmählich die Berge melodisch zu dröhnen, die Felszacken zu orgeln, die Sterne mit Myriaden goldner Harfen zu musizieren. Chöre von Engeln jubilierten durch die Unendlichkeit, gleich Stürmen brausten von oben die Harmonien, und Glocken, Glocken, Geläut von Glocken, von Hochzeitsglocken, kleinen und großen, tiefen und hohen, gewaltigen und zarten, verbreiteten eine erdrückend-selige Feierlichkeit durch den Weltenraum. — Und so sanken sie, ineinander verschlungen, auf das Laublager.

The motif of a natural and primitive music opposed to a more modern and corrupted civilization and to its aesthetic signs of discontent was of course already a cliché after the appearance of *Der Tod in Venedig*; indeed, its location in Nietzsche had made it part of a pervasive cultural imagery from which Thomas Mann had drawn.[17] As a cliché, the conflation of a superior lost society and its music appears as a staple of the conventional motivic inventory and thus often crosses the border separating cliché and kitsch (as seen in the passage above), both in works that have entered the literary canon and in texts now forgotten or considered trivial. Music of this kind appears for example in Max Dauthendey's novel *Raubmenschen* of 1911, where problems of the modern age are projected into past paradisiacal settings in which music plays a key role.[18] As an action-packed thriller describing murder, sexual escapades, and figures from the upper classes of Europe, *Raubmenschen* can be seen as a second-rate literary document of

[16] Hauptmann, *Der Ketzer von Soana*, p. 161. "Never had Francesco, never had he as priest felt such a nearness to God, such a security in Him, such an obliviousness of his own personality, and gradually, in the rushing of the mountain brook, the mountains seemed to boom melodiously, the rock-crags to peal like an organ, the stars to make music with myriads of golden harps. Choirs of angels shouted through infinite space, like tempests the harmonies came roaring down from above, and bells, bells, chimes of bells, wedding-bells, small and large, deep and high, immense and delicate, diffused an oppressive, blissful solemnity throughout the universe. And so they sank, locked in each other's embrace, upon their leafy bed" (p. 113).

[17] See Roger A. Nicholls, *Nietzsche in the Early Works of Thomas Mann*, University of California Publications in Modern Philology, no. 45 (Berkeley: Univ. of California Press, 1955), pp. 85–88; Hans Wysling, *"Mythos und Psychologie" bei Thomas Mann* (Zurich: Eidgenössische Technische Hochschule, 1969), pp. 11–12; T. J. Reed, *Thomas Manns "Der Tod in Venedig": Text, Materialien, Kommentar*, Literatur-Kommentare, no. 19, ed. Wolfgang Frühwald (Munich: Hanser, 1983), p. 129.

[18] Cf. George C. Schoolfield, *The Figure of the Musician in German Literature*, University of North Carolina Studies in the Germanic Languages and Literatures, no. 19 (Chapel Hill: Univ. of North Carolina Press, 1956), pp. 128–30.

cultural conservatism. Yet its literary value is of less importance here than the topicality of its cultural vocabulary. The fact that it was so popular at its appearance underscores the widespread function of its motifs.

Within the machinations of the slightly pornographic, blood-and-guts narrative there are passages symptomatic of a tension between technologically advanced, modern society and a vision of a primitive simplicity lost in the hectic and modern world, a motif that was not new when the novel appeared. In a number of passages, Hanna, one of the many heroines in the novel suffering from the turbulence and bustle of turn-of-the-century Europe, imagines a peaceful life she believes must have existed in Aztec Mexico and in classical Greece. These imagined civilizations serve a nearly identical function in this text. They both provide imaginary settings for the expression of early twentieth-century desires, and they both contain music. The most prominent musical emblem of Hanna's dissatisfaction with the modern world is a hymn to Apollo that is discovered during an excavation in Delphi. Rennewart, the narrator and main protagonist, reflects upon this hymn and on the failings of modern Europe that cause such devotion to a lost civilization and to its representative music:[19]

> Europa ist so wunderbar sentimental, dachte ich. Alle anderen Erdteile, so schien es mir, müßten uns verlachen, weil bei uns das Leben zu einer zweitausendjährigen Apollohymne zurückkehren kann, zu einer ausgegrabenen Melodie, für die wir plötzlich eine Liebe empfinden können, eine Melodie, die unser Leben heute nicht hervorbringen kann, wegen der wir deshalb unser Leben, das diese Melodie nicht fertigbringt, beinah verachten können, auswandern und ruhelos werden und uns um zweitausend Jahre zurücksehnen können.

Remarkable here is the erasure of Nietzsche's distinction between the Apollonian and the Dionysian that are so fundamental to Thomas Mann's works and that had attained such currency in the cultural vocabulary of the time. Now, the fact that this music is lost, past, and Greek is of greater significance than the specific nature of its aesthetic contours, which would have had such far-reaching implications to other writers of the time. Nietzsche's distinction between Apollonian clarity and Dionysian passion, transposed by Mann from the realm of music alone to the juxtaposition of distinct aesthetic genres, epic writing and music, vanishes here because the

---

[19] Max Dauthendey, *Raubmenschen* (Berlin: Deutsche Buchgemeinschaft, 1911), pp. 113–14. This translation and the following one from *Raubmenschen* are by the author of this essay: "Europe is so wonderfully sentimental, I thought. It seemed to me that all other parts of the earth must be laughing at us, because our life can return to a two-thousand-year-old hymn to Apollo, to a dug-up melody, in which we can suddenly fall in love, a melody, which our life cannot produce, and because of which we therefore can nearly despise our life, which cannot create this melody, and can emigrate, become restless and can yearn for a two-thousand-year-old past."

function of the motif of music as a vehicle for the expression of social dissatisfaction supersedes attention to the nature of the musical material itself. Already in this work a streamlining is discernible, a movement towards standardization and cliché.

Hanna, too, projects her longing for an anti-modern alternative community onto a cultural cliché, an impoverished image that characterizes all manifestations of music in this popular text. Her dream of an ancient Aztec civilization is remarkably similar to her image of ancient Greece. When traveling through twentieth-century Mexico, she describes to Rennewart the role of music in the life of the Aztecs:[20]

> da fragte sie mich, ob ich wüßte, daß die Indianer zur Aztekenzeit hier rund um diesen Platz ihre Hauptgebäude gehabt hätten. Die Kathedrale sei der Tempel der Sonne gewesen, links davon die Tanzakademie, rechts die Musikakademie und an der vierten Seite der Königspalast. Und es sei damals Sitte gewesen, daß jeder Bürger sein Examen im Spielen irgendeines Musikinstrumentes ablegte, um die Bürgerrechte zu erlangen. Denn die Indianer seien ein sehr musikalisches Volk gewesen.

Clearly this vision of a musically rich past is determined by the social forces of the bourgeoisie in early twentieth-century German society, in which music was privileged and a musical education was deemed a sine qua non. As the self-understanding of this class is called into question, its image of itself is transferred to a wish that is projected onto a lost age: Dauthendey, Hanna, and the early twentieth-century reader unconsciously see themselves reflected in these images of "lost" civilizations, an example of the way modern social forces imbue musical visions of imagined social alternatives disguised as lost collectives. The description above is far more a thinly-veiled evocation of the *Gründerjahre* under Wilhelminian rule or even a make-believe fin-de-siècle Vienna than a description concerned with archaeological verisimilitude.

If one did not know that this vision was Mexican, one could easily imagine its locus as Greek. Edward Said has suggested that the European interpretation of the East and of ancient Greece has served more to express ideological desires of Western scholars than to paint an objective picture of these locales and civilizations.[21] Much the same can be said for these projections of music onto literary visions of the past in early twentieth-century German literature. In Dauthendey, again, an alternative, foreign

[20] Dauthendey, *Raubmenschen*, p. 125: "[Then] she asked me if I knew that the Aztec Indians had had their main buildings around this square. The cathedral was the temple of the sun, to the left of which was the dance school, to the right the school of music, and on the fourth side the palace of the king. And at that time it was the custom that every member of society passed an exam in playing an instrument in order to receive the rights of citizenship, because the Aztecs were a very musical people."

[21] Edward Said, *Orientalism* (New York: Vintage, 1979).

collective replaces the existing collective of the present, while this innately imperialist vision is accompanied by a mysterious and chimerical music evoking difference and desire in the fantasy of the modern reader.

Music's function as a forum for the expression of social discontent thus supersedes or masks its status as an aesthetic construct itself worthy of interest. Another example of this is found in Franz Werfel's novel *Verdi: Roman der Oper* of 1923, which exploits a musical past in order to portray socio-political problems of the 1920s in Austria. In this text, the works of Verdi, Monteverdi, and Wagner have little to do with the music with which modern audiences and readers are familiar. Instead, they serve as a forum for the discussion of such extra-musical issues as the decline of liberalism, the conservatism of the German-speaking powers, and the way the Austro-Hungarian Empire had failed to heed the longing for Slav and Czech national autonomy prior to World War I.

Beneath the surface of the text a connection is established between aesthetic works and political developments, so that when the former are addressed the latter are implied as well. Remarks on nationalism are presented in passages devoted to artistic traditions and, similarly, these are discussed in terms of their connection to the make-up of a nation's people. As in the works of Thomas Mann and Hauptmann, extra-aesthetic polarities are expressed through opposing kinds of music, and this opposition conflates with images of superior lost collectives. In Werfel's novel, Verdi and Wagner evoke two opposing political philosophies, one pragmatic, humanitarian, liberal, and folkish, the other theoretical, inhumane, and megalomaniacal, imposed upon those subjected to its influence. In chapter II the following passage announces the political-aesthetic polarity which functions behind the figures of Verdi and Wagner:[22]

Keiner historischen Generation geschieht in unseren Tagen so viel Unrecht als der unserer Großväter, deren Geburtsstunde in das erste und zweite Jahrzehnt des abgelaufenen Säkulums fällt. — Ihr reiner Begriff der Freiheit, ihr Streben nach Autonomie des Einzelnen und Ganzen, all das wird mit

---

[22] Franz Werfel, *Verdi: Roman der Oper* (Frankfurt am Main: S. Fischer, 1979), p. 26.; this translation and the following one are by the author of this essay: "Today no historical generation is treated so unjustly as that of our grandfathers, whose birth fell in the first and second decade of the past century. — Their pure conception of freedom, the simplicity of their soul, their healthy hunger for battle and daring, their striving for the autonomy of the individual and of the whole, all of this is stamped with the political pejorative 'liberalism.' — The spirit of romanticism has conquered the spirit of '48. The spirit of romanticism, comrade in arms of all Holy Alliances, servant of every dubious authority, this spirit of madness, insofar as madness represents a flight from reality, this demon of stagnant and bloated souls, this Narcissus of the deep, to whom the depths are a sensuous tickling, this god of complication and obfuscation, this idol of necrophilic sensuality, forbidden pleasures, sanctimonious gestures, and sick rapes, the evil spirit of romanticism, terrorist from right to left, this plague of Europe has conquered a generation of youth endowed with the strongest will to live, and still is ruling today."

dem politischen Schimpfwort "Liberalismus" niedergeschlagen. — Der Geist
der Romantik, Verbündeter aller heiligen Allianzen, Knecht jeder zweifelhaf-
ten Autorität, ... der böse Geist der Romantik, terroristisch von rechts und
links, diese Pest Europas hat die lebenswilligste Jugend besiegt, um heute
noch zu herrschen.

Werfel can argue here that an aesthetic school has triumphed over a
political movement because in his novel the two are interchangeable; they
are two expressions of the same phenomenon. Thus, Wagner's romantic
total works of art are equivalent to the desire of the German-speaking
political regimes to form alliances through which to exercise political power
over vast areas of Europe, while Verdi's operas express the desire of Italian
liberalism to resist such external control. The liberal objectives of 1848
(national autonomy and democratic representation) are conquered by an
aesthetic evoking the political reality of nineteenth-century Europe: Prussia,
Austria, and Russia form their "Holy Alliance" in 1815 even as German
romanticism, presented in this text as the aesthetic emblem of Metternich's
oppressive conservatism, spreads over Europe. It is no coincidence that the
description of this "terrorist" aesthetic camp begins on the conservative side
of the political spectrum and moves "from right to left," for romanticism is
opposed here to the liberalism that forms the foundation for Verdi's art and
for the lost society it represents.

Italy's national-political desire for the resurrection of humanitarian ideals
once central to a vanquished social collective is represented in the aesthetic
sphere by Verdi. The equation between Verdi and the politics of this lost
society is made explicit when Verdi's friend the Senator reflects[23]

... daß in der Menschenblüte von 1848 ein neuer Messias gewandelt habe,
unbekannt und heute noch nicht gewußt, der dieser Epoche den freudig-
stürmischen Charakter gegeben. Mochten auch die großen Menschen dieser
Jugend besiegt, gefallen, gestorben sein, unüberholt, göttlich und von der
Menschheit noch nicht genossen lebte ihr niemals alternder Geist, der jetzt
verachtet wurde.... Dieses Geistes reinste Erscheinung lebte nur noch in
Giuseppe Verdi.... Dieser allein noch schwenkte die Fahne über dem
Leichenfeld der niedergebrochenen Jugend von damals.

---

[23] Werfel, *Verdi: Roman der Oper*, p. 218: "that in the flowering of mankind in 1848 a
new Messiah had walked the earth, unknown and still unknown today, who gave to this
epoch its joyful and stormy character. Even though the great men of this generation had
been beaten, had fallen, and had died, its never-aging spirit, despised now, lived on,
unsurpassed, god-like, [though it still] was not yet shared by all of mankind. Since [the
Senator] himself was filled with this spirit, why should he be satisfied with the weak
present age, inactive and gray with the passing of the years?
    The purest expression of this spirit lived only in Giuseppe Verdi. The love of the Senator
for Verdi was the most passionate result of this generation's fanaticism. He clung to the
maestro with an almost perverse intensity. [Verdi] alone still waved the flag over the
battlefield strewn with the corpses of the downtrodden youth of the past."

Against this temporal and political background, the antipodal aesthetic philosophies of Wagner's music dramas and Verdi's operas take on paradigmatic proportions. Wagner, as the quintessential German, represents both the musical and the political opposite of Verdi, the embodiment of the Italian "spirit." Their rivalry is not simply that of two vain musicians or even of two aesthetic schools, but constitutes the competition between two political philosophies, one oppressive and theoretical, one folkish and down-to-earth. German abstract political power is manifested in and supported by a modern and alienating romanticism, while the lost paradise of the Italian nationalist agenda finds expression in the *realpolitische* situations and musical forms of Verdi's operas.[24] In Werfel's novel, the past musical traditions of Italy form the only hope for the present societies threatened by a different music and a different socio-political reality. Thus, here again a narrative text of the early twentieth century evokes socio-political issues through the music of a past age, and conflates music with the longing for a different social reality.

These examples from Thomas Mann, Hauptmann, Dauthendey, and Werfel establishing such connections between music and social issues could easily be replaced by others. Of particular interest is Max Brod's little-known utopian novel *Das große Wagnis* of 1918, which both incorporates the cliché of music-as-danger and, at the same time, presents a partial motivic reversal of this clichéd material by denouncing music as mere bourgeois culture. Here, music no longer threatens a given status quo, but represents a society that has already been overthrown through revolution. The novel is a fantastical discussion of a number of social issues of the early twentieth century, and presents alternatives to the values and social and governmental structures preceding and leading up to the First World War. At one point a socialist figure named Biber envisions a collective utopia in which music is rejected because of its non-utilitarian participation in the glorification of the individual:[25]

> Nur so viel weiß ich, daß mir nichts anmaßender vorkommt, als wenn heutzutage die Musik sich herausnimmt, selbstständig, ganz für sich, wie ein leibhaftiges Wesen, wie eine körperliche Stimme unter anderen Natur-

---

[24] For a discussion of Verdi's works as examples of *Realpolitik* see Paul Robinson, *Opera and Ideas: From Mozart to Strauss* (New York: Harper & Row, 1985), pp. 155–209.

[25] Max Brod, *Das große Wagnis: Ausgewählte Romane und Novellen*, VI (Leipzig — Vienna: Kurt Wolff, 1919), p. 20; the following translation is by the author of this essay: "I only know that nothing seems more pompous to me than when, as nowadays, music tries to be something special and to sound independent, like a living being, a bodily voice among other voices of nature. Where does it get the right to take up so much space in the real world? Is it more than a mere invention, a fiction? Does it have something to do with the direction of the war? — Well then! It is right and fitting that it has finally been suppressed."

stimmen zu erklingen. Woher nimmt sie denn das Recht, so viel Raum in der wirklichen Welt auszufüllen? Ist sie denn mehr als eine bloße Erfindung, eine Fiktion? Hat sie einen Zusammenhang mit der Kriegführung? — Nun also! Es ist gut und durchaus gemäß, daß man sie endlich untergekriegt hat.

Within Brod's ironic vision of a utopian (or, more precisely, dystopian) community, music functions as the emblem of the private sphere, and hence evokes elitism and a preoccupation with the individual; in Biber's opinion it cannot participate in a public, socialist collective. The narrator himself at times appears to share Biber's evaluation of the art as shameful in an egalitarian society. For nearly the first thirty pages of the novel he conceals from the reader the fact that he himself is interested in music, and often when he mentions the art it appears to emerge as a remnant of his former existence in a world disinterested in political developments and devoted only to study and pleasure. Music's potential as a socially volatile force has not been realized, has failed.

The resulting attack on music may stem in part from frustration with the art's unrealized potential as a signal for social reform. When the narrator states: "Musik muß gedämpft werden, das ist gleichsam die Lösung unserer Generation" music signifies social privilege, and therefore must be destroyed to make way for utopia.[26] Yet, because the society depicted in this text is supposedly intended to reflect an overly repressive world and, in Brod's opinion, the fact that the communist revolution had been transformed in a degenerative way, the absence of music ultimately parallels its initial suppression in other texts of the time, such as *Der Tod in Venedig* and *Der Ketzer von Soana*, that equate the power of the word with the status quo and view music as a danger to that social order. Once again, music represents a negative alternative community, but ironically that community is here bourgeois society itself.

Finally, an additional work merging social issues with music that both draws upon the collective pool of motifs already described and at the same time suggests resistance to the uniformity of such clichéd material is found in Hermann Hesse's *Der Steppenwolf* of 1927. Projection of current tensions onto a past music suggesting both anarchy and an alternative community characterizes many of the passages devoted to music in this work. When Hesse's protagonist Harry Haller compares the present age of decay with primitive past ages, music accompanies his vision:[27]

---

[26] Brod, p. 20.

[27] Hermann Hesse, *Der Steppenwolf* (Frankfurt am Main: Suhrkamp, 1975), pp. 42–43. This and the following translations are from Hermann Hesse, *Steppenwolf*, trans. Basil Creighton, Joseph Mileck, and Horst Frenz (New York: Bantam, 1988): "From a dance hall there met me as I passed by the strains of lively jazz music, hot and raw as the steam of raw flesh...."

Aus einem Tanzlokal, an dem ich vorüberkam, scholl mir, heiß und roh wie der Dampf von rohem Fleisch, eine heftige Jazzmusik entgegen.... Untergangsmusik war es, im Rom der letzten Kaiser mußte es ähnliche Musik gegeben haben.

Natürlich war sie, mit Bach und Mozart und wirklicher Musik verglichen, eine Schweinerei — aber das war all unsere Kunst, all unser Denken, all unsre Scheinkultur, sobald man sie mit wirklicher Kultur verglich. Und diese Musik hatte den Vorzug einer großen Aufrichtigkeit, einer liebenswerten unverlogenen Negerhaftigkeit und einer frohen, kindlichen Laune. ... War das, was wir "Kultur," was wir Geist, was wir Seele, was wir schön, was wir heilig nannten, war das bloß ein Gespenst? ... War es vielleicht überhaupt nie echt und lebendig gewesen?

In this passage so reminiscent of Spengler's equation of Rome with contemporary civilization and of Mozart with *Kultur*, Haller projects a purportedly superior cultural essence onto past music in opposition to the modern world, though the link to the jazz idiom is an innovative variation of this standard motif.[28] Haller ultimately comes to reject the cultural conservatism with which this projection onto the past is linked, but the intellectual gesture of lost socio-cultural superiority remains manifest, underscored even in the xenophobic racism of the passage. Haller perceives jazz to be an agent effecting a dissolution similar to that which befell ancient Rome, for the music is judged by him to be innately sensual, and thus immoral; the reference to the "Rom der letzten Kaiser" implies a time of both political and ethical decay. In this respect the function of jazz resembles that of music per se in *Der Tod in Venedig*. As in that text, a threat to an established culture is a threat to the social make-up because culture is a society's longed-for image of itself. Just as Gustav von Aschenbach's notion of *Kultur* is an elitist sign comprised of a hallowed classical canon besieged by forces deemed socially, aesthetically, and morally inferior — (immediately prior to Aschenbach's nightmare Mann's narrator states: "[die] Geschehniss[e] im Raume ... brachen von außen herein; seinen Widerstand — einen tiefen und geistigen Widerstand — gewalttätig niederwerfend, gingen hindurch und ließen seine Existenz, ließen die Kultur seines Lebens verheert, vernichtet zurück.") — ,[29] so Haller's revered Mozart and the social prestige the composer implies are threatened initially

---

I stood for a moment on the scent, smelling this shrill and blood-raw music, sniffing the atmosphere of the hall angrily.... It was the music of decline. There must have been such music in Rome under the later emperors. Compared with Bach and Mozart and real music it was, naturally, a miserable affair; but so was all our art, all our thought, all our makeshift culture in comparison with real culture" (p. 43).

[28] Spengler, pp. 41–47, 59, 144, 217, 267, 298, 363, 448.

[29] Mann, "Der Tod in Venedig," pp. 515–16.

through the musical cacophony of jazz suggesting to him a rowdy, plebeian, un-elitist and implicitly immoral crowd. Jazz as a danger to the status quo thus recalls a motivic cliché, already discussed, in other literary examples of the time. That Mozart and jazz are initially opposites in Hesse's text is a social statement couched in an aesthetic topos related to the rigid opposition of epic writing and romantic music in *Der Tod in Venedig* and to different kinds of music in *Buddenbrooks*, in *Der Ketzer von Soana*, and in *Verdi: Roman der Oper*.

And yet Hesse's text takes up topoi apparent in Mann's works and elsewhere and expands upon them; whereas the procrustean nature of the word-music polarity is so entrenched in *Der Tod in Venedig* that its dissolution is seen as cultural collapse, *Der Steppenwolf* presents alternatives to the procrustean status quo suggestive of different relationships between a society and its culture. The movement from the topos of rigid cultural elitism to the breakdown of aesthetic and social polarities constitutes a movement central to Hesse's novel, which both employs and develops the topoi on which Mann's novella is based. Haller, unlike Aschenbach, is at times able to question the very significance of the cultural icons found in Mann's texts connecting moral, social, and aesthetic decay; he is able momentarily to question the values of an oppressive society which fears decline and a loss of purported cultural superiority. In so doing, he transforms and expands upon a cultural cliché.

It is at the scene of the masked ball in Hesse's novel that the topoi connecting social unrest, xenophobia, the breakdown of sexual repression, and a foreign, penetrating, and sexualized music found in *Der Tod in Venedig* reemerge with greatest familiarity, all, as in the earlier text, signifying a vision of an alternative social make-up deemed chaotic by conservative standards.[30] Yet in this scene Haller finally abandons the elitism associated with his former life (which also attended Aschenbach's social position) and achieves a vision of a different kind of society that eschews the racism discernible in the passage above and in his many remarks concerning the foreign (Latin American?) saxophonist Pablo, whom he had repeatedly described as naive and unintellectual, possessing the eyes of an animal.[31] The masked ball is a parallel to Aschenbach's Dionysian nightmare vision of an alternative world that the epic writer is able to accept only in secret, at the conclusion to his dream, but one that Hesse's protagonist experiences as a real and publicly shared triumph over his previous life. The motifs associated with Aschenbach's Venetian decay and

---

[30] Cf. Berman, *The Rise of the Modern German Novel*, pp. 193–95.

[31] Hesse, pp. 136–37, 189.

Haller's revery are remarkably similar, but Mann's negative images are imbued here with a positive sense of acceptance:[32]

> ich ... fühlte die Luft voll Zauber, wurde gewiegt und getragen von der Wärme, von all der brausenden Musik, vom Taumel der Farben, vom Duft der Frauenschultern, vom Rausch der Hunderte, vom Lachen, vom Tanztakt, vom Glanz all der entzündeten Augen.... Mir aber ward allmählich dies ganze tönende Haus voll tanzbrausender Säle, dieses berauschte Volk von Masken zu einem tollen Traumparadies, Blüte um Blüte warb mit ihrem Duft, Frucht um Frucht umspielte ich suchend mit probenden Fingern, Schlangen blickten mich aus grünem Laubschatten verführend an, Lotosblüte geisterte über schwarzem Sumpf, Zaubervögel lockten im Gezweige, und alles führte mich doch zu einem ersehnten Ziel, alles lud mich neu mit Sehnsucht nach der Einzigen.

Clearly the import of motifs nearly identical to those in Mann's novella is now different. Through the influence of music, Aschenbach joins the riotous orgy of Dionysian worshippers, yet once he awakens he never appears as a member of any social realm but the cultural elite to which he has been accustomed throughout the novella. In *Der Steppenwolf*, however, Haller openly and overtly embraces a new kind of social interaction, and comes not merely to accept, but to resemble his one-time musical adversary Pablo. Under the influence of jazz and the social experience it has accompanied, Haller no longer treats the musician as a foreign and inferior *Musikanten*, but is shown to have a deep-seated affinity with the figure. His transformation in the course of the ball is more than private, it is carried out within a dismantling of prejudice and a reorganization of social experience portrayed in the public forum. Unlike Aschenbach, who fears the street musicians and secretly associates Tadzio with music, Haller publicly becomes a brother of the formerly despised and feared foreign musician:[33]

---

[32] Hesse, pp. 180, 183: "The warmth embedded me and wafted me on, and so no less did the riotous music, the intoxication of colors, the perfume of women's shoulders, the clamor of the hundred tongues, the laughter, the rhythm of the dance, and the glances of all the kindled eyes.... For my part, the whole building reverberated everywhere with the sound of dancing, and the whole intoxicated crowd of masks, became by degrees a wild dream of paradise. Flower upon flower wooed me with its scent. I toyed with fruit after fruit. Serpents looked at me from green and leafy shadows with mesomeric eyes. Lotus blossoms luxuriated over black bogs. Enchanted birds sang allurement from the trees. Yet all was a progress to one longed-for goal, the summons of a new yearning" (pp. 188–91).

[33] Hesse, 183–85. "An experience fell to my lot this night of the Ball that I had never known in all my fifty years, though it is known to every flapper and student — the intoxication of a general festivity, the mysterious merging of the personality in the mass, the mystic union of joy.... It was known, I knew, to every servant girl.... I had seen it ... in great artists in the enthusiasm, perhaps, of a musical festival.... Even in recent days I had marvelled at and loved and mocked and envied this gleam and this smile in my friend, Pablo, when he hung over his saxophone in the blissful intoxication of playing in the orchestra, or when, enraptured and ecstatic, he looked over to the conductor, the drum,

Ein Erlebnis, das mir in fünfzig Jahren unbekannt geblieben war,
obwohl jeder Backfisch und Student es kennt, wurde mir in dieser
Ballnacht zuteil: das Erlebnis des Festes, der Rausch der Festgemeinschaft,
das Geheimnis vom Untergang der Person in der Menge, von der Unio
mystica der Freude.... [Jeder] Dienstmagd war es bekannt, und oft hatte ich
... [es] gesehen ... an großen Künstlern, etwa im Enthusiasmus festlicher
Aufführungen ... und noch in jüngster Zeit hatte ich dies Strahlen und
Lächeln des glücklich Entrückten bewundert, geliebt, bespöttelt und
beneidet an meinem Freunde Pablo, wenn er selig im Rausch des Musizie-
rens im Orchester über seinem Saxophon hing oder dem Dirigenten, dem
Trommler, dem Mann mit dem Banjo zuschaute, entzückt, ekstatisch. Solch
ein Lächeln, solch ein kindhaftes Strahlen, hatte ich zuweilen gedacht, sei
nur ganz jungen Menschen möglich oder solchen Völkern, die sich keine
starke Individuation und Differenzierung der einzelnen gestatteten. Aber
heute, in dieser gesegneten Nacht, strahlte ich selbst, der Steppenwolf
Harry, dies Lächeln, schwamm ich selbst in diesem tiefen, kindhaften,
märchenhaften Glück, atmete ich selbst diesen süßen Traum und Rausch
aus Gemeinschaft, Musik, Rhythmus, Wein und Geschlechtslust, dessen
Lobpreis im Ballbericht irgendeines Studenten ich einst so oft mit Spott
und armer Überlegenheit mit angehört hatte. Ich war nicht mehr ich, meine
Persönlichkeit war aufgelöst im Festrausch wie Salz im Wasser.... Ach,
dachte ich zwischenrein, mag mit mir geschehen, was da wolle, einmal bin
doch auch ich glücklich gewesen, strahlend, meiner selbst entbunden, ein
Bruder Pablos.

Because jazz represents that which is fundamentally foreign to European
white middle-class society, it offers here an alternative to that society; the
positive character of its difference is experienced as racial, aesthetic, and
social in nature. Haller as elitist initially reacts to Pablo as a member of a
race deemed inferior by the writer's world, but he nevertheless comes to
locate in this racial difference and in its music an emancipatory, positive
dimension. Music accompanies a vision of social difference, associated with
notions of primitivism and emancipatory abandon.

Nevertheless, despite the significance of Hesse's transformation of
standard motifs, it is clear that his novel still operates with a standard

or the man with the banjo. It had sometimes occurred to me that such a smile, such a
childlike radiance could be possible only to quite young persons or among those peoples
whose customs permitted no marked differences between one individual and another. But
today, on this blessed night, I myself, the Steppenwolf, was radiant with this smile. I myself
swam in this deep and childlike happiness of a fairy tale. I myself breathed the sweet
intoxication of a common dream and of music and rhythm and wine and women — I, who
had in other days so often listened with amusement, or dismal superiority, to its panegyric
in the ball-room chatter of some student. I was myself no longer. My personality was
dissolved in the intoxication of the festivity.... Ah, thought I ... let come to me what may,
for once at least, I, too, have been happy, radiant, released from myself, a brother of
Pablo's" (pp. 192–94).

motivic repertoire firmly established in early twentieth-century German and Austrian culture. For example, the texts of both Werfel and Hesse no longer employ Greek imagery in their evocation of lost musical alternatives, but in them music serves much the same function as in those works whose counter-cultural motifs are Greek, whether Dionysian or Hellenistic. In *Der Tod in Venedig, Der Ketzer von Soana, Verdi: Roman der Oper*, and *Der Steppenwolf*, a figurehead of the moral ideals of the turn-of-the-century German-speaking world — Gustav von Aschenbach, Francesco, Verdi, and Harry Haller — undergoes a profound transformation linked with a music that functions in a different kind of social relationship. Again, music itself is less important in these novels than its ability to allow for the expression of extra-musical concerns. Ironically, the different and dangerous music that functions as a vehicle for the expression of emancipatory desire in this literature is itself ultimately undermined by the equalizing power of the standardized cultural imagination: alternative social visions are locked within communal imaginative forms and appear as clichés. What is intended as the messenger of freedom and of social difference — music — emerges, ironically, as so uniform in its function as to be trivial, and even the motivic expansion apparent in *Der Steppenwolf* remains locked within a given formula.

III

How might we explain the remarkable uniformity in the function, and, in part, even in the images of foreign alternative musical communities found in the literature from this period so overwhelmed by political and social change? Clearly music as the acoustically absent sign of difference and as the emblem of subversion is little more than a cliché in these texts and in others like them from the time. One provocative explanation for this uniformity may be found in Adorno's *Einleitung in die Musiksoziologie* and in Max Horkheimer's and Adorno's *Dialektik der Aufklärung*, the Frankfurt School's most persuasive analyses of the institutionalization of the arts in early twentieth-century society.[34] Horkheimer and Adorno have suggested that the culture industry furthers a standardization of thought and of social relations, thereby masking the tensions in modern society and creating a false sense of community, a *falsches Bewußtsein*. For them, the uniformity of aesthetic material and aesthetic judgment both propels and reflects the ideological standardization in western consciousness. The impact of such standardization is apparent in the appearance of clichéd musical collectives in these very texts. While the institutions of culture consume aesthetic material as interchangeable commodities, and thereby disregard the formal

---

[34] Cf. fn. 5; see Horkheimer's and Adorno's chapter on "Kulturindustrie: Aufklärung als Massenbetrug," in Theodor W. Adorno and Max Horkheimer, *Dialektik der Aufklärung: Philosophische Fragmente*, in Adorno, *Gesammelte Schriften*, 3:141–91.

characteristics of the works they channel into society, they also underscore social stratification and inequality even as they purport to operate in a democratic fashion furthering the collective. Thus, for the theorists of the Frankfurt School, the public comes to interact with aesthetic signs of social concerns under the guise of an interest in art even as these aesthetic signs are streamlined into interchangeable fodder for the culture-industrial mill. This observation is particularly applicable to the literature of the early twentieth century. Due to the prominence of social, extra-musical pressures in the consumption of art, the specific kind of art chosen as the vehicle for counter-cultural visions in the literature of this time becomes insignificant. The musical art works themselves are interchangeable in the institutions of culture, in the collective imagination they foster, and thus in its literary production as well; within the conformist socio-cultural context, any kind of music will do, so long as it remains within a given, accepted aesthetic vocabulary and fulfills a given social function.[35] Thus images of nonexistent musical societies in the literature of the early twentieth century are themselves exchangeable clichés: their form is less important than the social desires they negatively express. Palestrina in *Buddenbrooks* functions similarly to epic writing in *Der Tod in Venedig*, and Wagner can be replaced by a Dionysian Greek chorus that itself signifies issues evoked through a vision of ancient Mexico in a popular thriller: they each present a past music opposed to the modern world, while the juxtaposition of Haydn and Wagner in one work evokes notions discernible in the polarization of Wagner and Verdi and of Mozart and jazz in other texts from the period.

Because even the aesthetic vehicles used to express a desire for a different social order themselves emerge upon examination as a product of conformity, the clichéd or false image of an alternative collective can only evoke community through a process of negation. Social longing, after all, concerns a desire to resist a given conformity, to imagine what is not, and music is the aesthetic space in the narrative whose contours ironically highlight the limitations of the conformist imagination seeking a realm beyond the conformist status quo. Music for Aschenbach is terrifying, because it is everything that his world refuses to be; his imagination cannot conceive of the art in a form wholly divorced from the collective cultural imagery of his age. The impoverishment of Aschenbach's imaginative portrayal of music (closely linked to that of the narrator of the novella) is shared by many authors of the early twentieth century. Just as Thomas Mann's conventional writer can only draw upon clichés to imagine music, so the visions of other worlds found in the writings of Mann's contemporaries are impeded by the ideological limitations of the time; the creative imagination is shaped by, cannot escape, its cultural vocabulary and its own imaginative boundaries. As early twentieth-century Europe repeatedly

---

[35] Cf. Marc A. Weiner, *Arthur Schnitzler and the Crisis of Musical Culture* (Heidelberg: Carl Winter, 1986), pp. 50–51, 62–67.

projects its desires onto musical difference, its longing for an alternative world emerges only in the genuine, negative silence of the community it itself cannot imagine and cannot hear.

This would change in the 1930s. With the rise of fascism, the conflation of music and social desire would be transformed, leading to the erection of an imagined self-glorifying utopia in which music would play an integral role. Under such a transformation of the collective imagination, the relationship between the cultural vocabulary of the time and the desires it negatively expressed would shift from negation to affirmation. And yet, following the War, the alternative community would again negatively reemerge in Thomas Mann's *Doktor Faustus* in the silence of an imagined music that a world had already refused to hear, in Schoenberg's real and in Adrian Leverkühn's fictional dodecaphonic, negative appeals to a future society able to accept the primitivism that German culture until then had only viewed as a nightmare vision opposed to the status quo, a vision of a cultural content that had been repressed, but had reemerged as social chaos in the form of Nazism.[36] The alternative society, again, was a negative space, but the question remained whether this negative reflective space of resistance would once again end in cliché in its modern aftermath.

---

[36] Thomas Mann, *Doktor Faustus: Das Leben des deutschen Tonsetzers Adrian Leverkühn, erzählt von einem Freund*, in *Gesammelte Werke in dreizehn Bänden*, vol. 6.

Hearing, Speaking, Singing, Writing:
The Meaning of Oral Tradition for Bert Brecht[*]

ALBRECHT DÜMLING

I

DESPITE THE COARSENESS THAT Bert Brecht often openly displayed, he was a person who reacted with great sensitivity to sounds and noises. When his grandmother read to him from the Bible or friends played classical music for him, he was a very attentive listener. The sensitivity with which he reacted to music even as a schoolboy can be seen from an episode related by his classmate Georg Geyer.[1] When Geyer once played the slow movement of Mozart's F-Major Piano Sonata KV 280 for him, Brecht was impulsively inspired to write a poem about death, which he subsequently sketched into the music. He heard instrumental music in the sense of a symphonic poem, as entirely poetic-programmatic; it excited his "Klangbilderphantasie" (Heine), and thus became a source of his artistic productivity.

In the case of the F-minor adagio movement of the Mozart sonata, the dotted rhythms suggestive of a funeral march may have reminded him not only of the World War going on then, but also of his own uncertain health. Still in American exile in 1944, he mentioned the exceptionally strong effect of the *Matthäuspassion*,[2] which he had, as a schoolboy, indeed feared. Certain music affected the "Stückeschreiber" (Brecht's term for himself as playwright) like a drug which immediately altered his body temperature. When he later spoke of the fixed, gaping stares of the sweating concertgoers,[3] he was describing his own physical response to great symphonic music. He identified this kind of reaction with the middle class and saw in

---

[*] The translation of the German original into English is by Ellen Gerdeman-Klein and James M. McGlathery.

[1] Werner Frisch and K. W. Obermeier, *Brecht in Augsburg* (Frankfurt am Main: Suhrkamp, 1976), p. 133.

[2] See Bertolt Brecht, *Arbeitsjournal*, ed. Werner Hecht (Frankfurt am Main: Suhrkamp, 1973), 16 August 1944.

[3] Brecht, "Über die Verwendung von Musik für ein episches Theater," in *Gesammelte Werke* (Frankfurt am Main: Suhrkamp, 1967), 15:480.

the preeminence of the musical arts — as did the poet Stefan George[4] — a threat to literary arts and theater. (One can perceive the secret rivalry between opera and dramatic theater also in his critiques of the Augsburg Theater.)

Brecht battled against the seductive power of music so vehemently because he was himself so completely ensnared by it.[5] Music affected his emotions subliminally and was thus less controllable for him than literature. Its effect was therefore — and this he did experience — stronger at least for the short term. On 25 September 1920 he noted in his diary: "Immerfort beschäftigt mich die geringe Macht, die der Mensch über den Menschen hat. Es gibt keine Sprache, die jeder versteht. Es gibt kein Geschoß, das ins Ziel trifft. Die Beeinflussung geht anders herum: sie vergewaltigt (Hypnose)."[6]

The narcotic effect, particularly of late Romantic music, was based essentially on blocking out reality as demanded by the proponents of so-called absolute music; the mundane should remain excluded from the special world of the concert hall. The music historian Heinrich Besseler set this middle-class form of "Darbietungsmusik" against the historically earlier form of "Umgangsmusik," i.e., functional arts like the folk song or the music of church and school, which were still bound to life, to human activity.[7] Like the "Jugendbewegung" and with a similar activistic impulse, Brecht also demanded a return to functional musical forms. Against the vague generality of instrumental music which allowed itself to be misused so easily, he opposed a concrete designation of purpose; and against the socially unspecific music-making groups in the "Jugendbewegung" (which later decayed into "Volksgemeinschaft"),[8] he insisted on a specific target group, a particular person, an occupation, or even a class.

As opposite pole to the prevailing middle-class concept of art, to the much too broad and general human pathos of Classicism (but also of Expressionism), Brecht emphasized the concrete social place of every art, including texts and their music. Already in his hometown of Augsburg

---

[4] See Albrecht Dümling, "Umwertung der Werte: Das Verhältnis Stefan Georges zur Musik," *Jahrbuch des Staatlichen Instituts für Musikforschung Preußischer Kulturbesitz 1981/82*, ed. Dagmar Droysen-Reber (West Berlin: Merseburger, 1982), pp. 9–92.

[5] See Albrecht Dümling, *Laßt euch nicht verführen: Brecht und die Musik* (Munich: Kindler, 1985), pp. 97ff.

[6] "I am still occupied with the limited power that human beings have over themselves as human beings. There is no language that everyone understands. There is no bullet that hits the mark. The influence works the other way around: it overpowers us (hypnosis)"; Brecht, *Tagebücher 1920–1922* (Berlin and Weimar: Aufbau, 1976), p. 68.

[7] Heinrich Besseler, "Grundfragen des musikalischen Hörens," *Jahrbuch der Musikbibliothek Peters für 1925* (Leipzig: Peters, 1926), pp. 35–52.

[8] See Johannes Hodek, *Musikalisch-pädagogische Bewegung zwischen Demokratie und Faschismus: Zur Konkretisierung der Faschismus-Kritik Th. W. Adornos* (Weinheim and Basel: Beltz, 1977).

Brecht had turned towards the culture of the proletarian, small-town suburb. That culture was rarely preserved in written form since it essentially rested on oral tradition; it did not exist on paper, but rather all the more in reality, in the practice of life. Because there were neither books nor music stands on the street, listening was more important than reading. On special occasions people played music, sang, and spoke spontaneously or from memory. An important part of this suburban culture were the folk songs which Brecht mentioned in his essay, "Wo ich gelernt habe." He had happily not only read, but also heard them sung by the people with their special intonation and on the proper occasion ("glücklicherweise nicht nur gelesen, sondern auch gehört, ... gesungen von der Bevölkerung mit der besonderen Intonation und bei der richtigen Gelegenheit").[9] As in the case of the songs of the suburbs, Brecht hoped also that his songs would not just be read.

In the suburbs the songs were not the result of abstract instruction but were rather expressions of specific interests; they were tied to occasions. Folk songs achieved their worth and their meaning first through their realistic utilization. With this, Brecht distanced himself from the middle-class concept of the art work, which supposedly retained an unchangeable worth independent of its use. For him the term "Gelegenheitswerk" (occasional work) was in no way a negative stamp since it contained the connection with social activity, which for him had priority before art. "Gelegenheitswerke" had to subordinate themselves to their practical function, which included the possibility and even necessity of permanent change and spontaneous invention. Thus in his essay "Wo ich gelernt habe" he stressed that the women workers of a nearby paper factory did not always remember all the verses of a song, and therefore improvised certain passages from which much could be learned ("wovon viel zu lernen war"). Because social interaction stood in the forefront, literary as well as musical texts were secondary, derivative forms of singing, speaking, and music-making. They represented merely provisional versions, comparable to a tape recording. As it pertained to the readers, "literature" was just a stage direction, comparable to a score.

In Brecht's simple notations, similar to medieval neumes, this idea of temporariness is aptly expressed: it aspires to be no more than a memory aid, a basis for improvisation. The famous laxness of the "Stückeschreiber" in questions of copyright had its roots in the belief that art belongs to everyone and comes alive only in the individual's appropriation of it. Because his works — like true folk art — had to survive in oral tradition, they had to be alterable. Written forms represented for him in any case "Versuche" (attempts). Under this label he published those works he considered decidedly not "classical."

In contrast to Stefan George, for example, who valued expensive materials and durable bindings, Brecht preferred temporary stuff. This son

[9] Brecht, "Wo ich gelernt habe," in *Gesammelte Werke*, 19:502–7.

of a paper manufacturer showed a notable reserve regarding paper. He wanted to have his "Lautenfibel" published on newspaper or wastepaper: It will fall apart in three or four years so that the volumes will wind up on the junk heap after people have assimilated them ("Der zerfällt in drei, vier Jahren, daß die Bände auf den Mist wandern, nachdem man sie sich einverleibt hat").[10] Art achieved worth only through its use. As with the rough linen ("Rupfen") costumes and sets of his early stage productions, Brecht preferred provisional, perishable materials for his texts. He sketched his songs and poems on thin paper because he hoped his friends would soon learn them from memory anyway. The written form, this way, was supposed to become superfluous. A certain mode of speaking ("Sprech-haltung") was fixed in the melody of the poem which made possible its becoming a configuration of sound, a "Klanggestalt."

II

Moreover — and this has perhaps too seldom been noted — the process just described often corresponded to the actual productive procedure. Many of Brecht's texts arose through speaking aloud, through free fantasizing. Even when later, as Dessau reports, Brecht only murmured while writing, the texts still derived from speaking aloud. Both the actor Erwin Faber[11] and the radio reporter and director Alfred Braun have reported that Brecht needed music while working. Braun describes the creation of the radio play "Macbeth" in 1927 as follows: "Die gemeinsame Arbeit begann damit, daß das Grammophon eingeschaltet wurde, und die Rhythmen moderner Schallplattenmusik untermalten pausenlos unseren Arbeitstag. Dazu ging Brecht im Zimmer auf und ab und probierte laut die Überschriften der Moritaten, scharf skandierend: Macbeth — reitet — in der Nacht — über — die Heide."[12] This text was then immediately typed out by the secretary sitting in the background, no doubt Elisabeth Hauptmann.

Many of the texts were therefore not written down by Brecht himself, but rather spoken and dictated; they are in this way transcripts of speech ("Sprechprotokolle"). Accordingly he wanted to publish his "Lesebuch für Städtebewohner" as a speech recording, a work in which he took up the subject of the strongly opposing attitudes conveyed in big city slang. The written text represented only a secondary, derivative form, perhaps farther

---

[10] Brecht, *Tagebücher*, p. 37.

[11] Unpublished interview with the author, 1 January 1979.

[12] "The communal work began with the gramophone being turned on, and the rhythms of modern record music ceaselessly accompanied our work day. Meanwhile Brecht paced back and forth in the room and tested out loud the headings of the 'Moritaten,' sharply scanning the verse, 'Macbeth — reitet — in der Nacht — über — die Heide'"; Alfred Braun, *"Achtung, Achtung, hier ist Berlin!": Geschichte des Deutschen Rundfunks in Berlin 1923–1932* (West Berlin: Haude und Spenger, 1968), p. 42.

from the spoken "original" than those musical settings in which the original sound design ("Klanggestalt") was preserved. Because Brecht's fantasy apparently was inspired more vividly through acoustical than through optical stimuli (whence his enduring interest in radio and telephone), the dimension of sound is a vital part of his art, which includes more songs and radio plays than previously thought.

If therefore a great number of Brecht's poems take singing and speaking — a sound concept ("Klangvorstellung") as their starting point, we need to ask not only about literary traditions involved, but also about those of song and speech. For Brecht the great reciters of the time, such as Joseph Kainz or Ernst von Possart, were in no way the standard. As attested by the few sound recordings he made, his models were more likely the "Moritaten" and ballad singers ("Bänkelsänger") at the fairs, as well as Frank Wedekind and Karl Valentin. In the tradition of the ballad singers, he used for his songs above all only simple, easily remembered melodies which had a certain rhythm that was neutral in relation to the poetic content. An example would be in addition to "Baals Lied" above all the "Legende vom toten Soldaten."

Characteristic for the "Moritat" style of the ballad singer is the frequent repetition of a simple, easily remembered melody. It does not overwhelm one as does a great work of art, but rather serves as a "neutral" vehicle for the text. The modest melodies of the ballads were used on various occasions and could inspire the listeners to provide their own additional stanzas. Precisely the repetition of a known melody was thus an essential pedagogical tool; it enabled the author as well as the recipient to take up the melody, rhythm, and rhyme and add something of their own — to become productive themselves. If Brecht played records ceaselessly while working, he did not do it because he believed in the uniqueness of the songs. Rather, the constant repetition could expose for him the model character of a melody or rhythm and inspire him to ideas of his own: the model impressed on his consciousness became an object for critical evaluation and therewith a basis for inspiration. For this reason undoubtedly Brecht added in his "Lesebuch für Städtebewohner": Playing the record once is not enough ("Einmaliges Abspielen der Platte genügt nicht").[13]

The point of departure for his "Legende vom toten Soldaten" (Legend of the Dead Soldier) was not only a very simple melody, but also the experience of the World War familiar to his listeners of that time. Belonging further to these premises was the genre of heroic ballad, which he had called into question with his moritat-like "Legende." Point by point he carried to their logical extreme the methods with which a good fighting morale is instilled. In view of the hard sacrifices the soldiers had to make, he critically examined the gratitude shown by the Fatherland. Step by step, stanza by stanza Brecht showed in his song how a man, devoid of will, is

---

[13] Brecht, *Gesammelte Werke*, Vol. 8: *Gedichte*, ed. Elisabeth Hauptmann (Frankfurt am Main: Suhrkamp, 1967), p. 285.

transformed into a fighting machine. The song exposes manipulation by the military apparatus, it shows that almost every war depends on deception and false promises.

Brecht sketched a very simple melody for the "Legende vom toten Soldaten," and also performed the work publicly himself. This melody, which can hardly be called particularly delicate and sentimental ("besonders zart, sentimental")[14] consists of a fifth in descending oscillating steps within the minor chord, a model which returns twice in every stanza. The first time, the melodic phrase ends on the tonic note; the second time, astonishingly on the fifth. With this, the normal relationship of antecedent and consequent is reversed. The fifth leaves the ending open, at the same time emphasizing and calling into question the word "Helden-Tod" (a hero's death).

Brecht published the text and melody of his "Legende vom toten Soldaten" in the fifth lesson of his "Hauspostille," but also accepted revised adaptions by Hanns Eisler[15] and Kurt Weill.[16] Besides Brecht himself, the actor and singer Ernst Busch also made the "Legende" known to the public. Busch developed his own melodic version.[17] He kept the final fifth interval, but developed a three-part ABA song form in which each part included two stanzas. He was thereby able to diminish the danger of the monotonous organ-grinding in the stanzas, without completely severing the tie to the tradition of the "moritat" singer.

III

We must differentiate clearly between the Brecht songs that originated vocally and those for which the starting point, rather, was speaking aloud. The "Chorale vom Manne Baal" would be included in the first group, the much stronger, recitative-like, rhythmically free "Ballade von den Abenteuern" in the second. As an example, the hit tune "Verlorenes Glück" by Sprowacker was undoubtably the origin for the melody of the well-known "Erinnerung an die Marie A." and therefore parodied by it. From the combination of melody and text, sentimental love song and sober commentary, a peculiar emotional brokenness results.

Very many Brecht songs developed in this way through criticism or parody of a model. Already as a schoolboy he wanted to travesty *Des Knaben*

---

[14] Werner Mittenzwei, *Das Leben des Bertolt Brecht oder Der Umgang mit den Welträtseln* (Berlin and Weimar: Aufbau, 1986), 1:80.

[15] See Grabs 1.56 in Manfred Grabs, *Hanns Eisler, Kompositionen — Schriften — Literatur: Ein Handbuch* (Leipzig: VEB Deutscher Verlag für Musik, 1984), p. 38.

[16] David Drew, *Kurt Weill: A Handbook* (London: Faber, 1987), p. 222.

[17] Fritz Hennenberg, ed., *Das große Brecht-Liederbuch* (Frankfurt am Main: Suhrkamp, 1984), 1:10f.

Wunderhorn (the collection of supposed folk songs by the German Romantics Achim von Arnim and Clemens Brentano) with a "Plunder-horn."[18] For example, the "Marsch ins Dritte Reich" is based on the melody of the English soldiers' song, "It's a long way to Tipperary,"[19] whereas in the "Hitler-Chorälen" the devout attitude of the Nazis is compared to a church congregation. The "Ballade vom Stahlhelm" depicts a then current variant of the song about Prince Eugen, and the "Moritat vom Reichstagsbrand" represents a continuation of the "Moritat von Mackie Messer." Eisler composed a biting parody of the National Socialist "Horst Wessel Lied" in the "Kälbermarsch."

Kipling's works provided the models for the "Ballade vom Weib und vom Soldaten" and the "Kanonensong." In the "Ballade vom Weib und dem Soldaten" Brecht even borrowed Kipling's third stanza word for word. Kipling's instructions for performance, "A soldier's song which people love to sing during a fast march," inspired Brecht to write a new refrain in a fast tempo. In this form the song was used for the 1923 premiere of *Im Dickicht der Städte*, then revised again in 1925 in collaboration with Franz Bruinier for a melodramatic chanson, a dialogue between a soldier who sings and a woman who speaks. But that was not the final form. Hanns Eisler changed the song in 1928 for his stage music to the Feuchtwanger piece, *Kalkutta, 4. Mai* (Calcutta, fourth of May). In this form the song was borrowed for the Zurich premiere of *Mutter Courage*, and finally re-composed once again in 1946 by Paul Dessau in the United States. The vitality of the most important Brecht songs shows itself in their variability. This principle of the variability of art came from the desire to adapt it to the respective occasion. The principle corresponded moreover to the revision of songs through singing ("Umsingepraxis") characteristic of the folk song in the suburbs of Brecht's time.

IV

If in the melodramatic version of the "Ballade vom Weib und dem Soldaten" singing and speaking stand opposed to one another, reference is thereby made to two levels of feeling. The singing embodies — as opposed to the speaking — the area of emotional or even intoxicated urgency that Brecht considered dangerous. That he himself on the one hand employed such stimulation while on the other protecting himself from it, can be clearly seen from the melody he composed for the "Barbara Song."[20] An emphatic

[18] Hanns Otto Münsterer, *Bert Brecht: Erinnerungen aus den Jahren 1917–1922* (Berlin and Weimar: Aufbau, 1977), p. 140.

[19] In Brecht's collected poems this text is published under the title "Der Führer hat gesagt."

[20] Hennenberg, *Das große Brecht Liederbuch*, 1:62ff.

Puccini-like arioso in the refrain contrasts with a dry recitative style in the stanzas. The text of the refrain warns explicitly against surrender to feeling, however: "Ja, da kann man sich doch nicht nur hinlegen.... Ja, da muß man kalt und herzlos sein" (Yes, you can't just lie down then.... Yes, you have to be cold and heartless).

This opposing of dry parlando and critically contradicted arioso, which originated with the author himself, became a model for many Brecht-Weill songs. Certain songs from the play *Happy End* can be used here as examples. Like most of Brecht's theater pieces, this one resulted from a model and a particular occasion. Among the models, in addition to the *Dreigroschenoper*, was the parodistic poem "Vorbildliche Bekehrung eines Branntweinhändlers," which dates from September 1920. The timely occasion was the one-hundredth anniversary, in May 1929, of the founding of the Salvation Army. Brecht's collaborator, Elisabeth Hauptmann, who at his suggestion undertook the reworking of the material, was indeed familiar with this milieu.

A theme of the play and of most the songs is the clash of sober realism, looking to the present, with sentimental nostalgia. This clash is fully evident in the "Bilbao Song" in which the gangster boss Bill Cracker looks back sadly to the simple but romantically adventurous beginnings of his dance hall. He mourns the loss of the genuine, raw gangster life which has been replaced by middle-class sterility. The separation between the sober present and the nostalgically longed-for past can be found in the contrast of stanzas and refrain. The music underscores the two levels of feeling in the poem. It produces the intoxication that was reflected in the previous stanza.

The Viennese composer Friedrich Cerha, who composed among other pieces a "Baal" opera, reminisced about a conversation with the philosopher Ernst Bloch, who apparently was present at the beginnings of *Happy End* and was particularly impressed by the collective work: "Das habe ja niemand 'gemacht,' das hätten alle gemacht! Brecht hat improvisiert und dazu sofort gesungen, und Weill saß am Klavier. Die Leute haben Witze und Blödsinn gemacht, und es wurde gelacht und getrunken. Dann sind alle nach Hause gegangen. Der Weill hat den Kopf voll gehabt und hat sich am nächsten Morgen hingesetzt und hat dann geschrieben."[21] This report, which resembles the reminiscence by Alfred Braun quoted earlier, is further evidence for the close connection that singing and speaking had for Brecht. Art developed with him through improvising on a model, a process that was often collective. One can easily imagine Brecht becoming inspired by the ringing assonances like "Bills Ballhaus in Bilbao," while Elisabeth Haupt-

---

[21] "No one really 'made' it, everyone made it! Brecht improvised and sang simultaneously, too, and Weill sat at the piano. The people told jokes and talked nonsense, laughed and drank. Then they all went home. Weill had gotten filled with new ideas, and sat down the next morning to write"; Interview with Friedrich Cerha. Published in Dümling, *Laßt euch nicht verführen*, p. 657.

mann then penned the text and Kurt Weill noted down the melodic and rhythmic gestus.

The music in the "Bilbao Song" is a very effective agent of text illumination, but to be sure is not commentary. The opposite is the case, though, with the "Song of Mandelay," which along with the "Bilbao Song" and the "Ballade von der Höllen-Lili" was one of the few songs portraying the gangster world in *Happy End*. The "Mandelay Song" also has a lengthened and musically emphatic refrain following a very fast stanza, but here with a very self-contradictory text. First come the words, "Liebe ist doch an Zeit nicht gebunden" (Love isn't bound to time), followed by the cold thought of the expensive bordello price, "Johnny, mach rascher, es geht um Sekunden" (Johnny, hurry up, seconds are ticking). Thus the "timeless" love-emphasis is questioned and commented on. The lengthened melody of the refrain yearns to enjoy full pleasure in blissful oblivion, while the text reminds us of the temporal and material limitations.

More devoted to singing than the gangsters in *Happy End* are the conscripts of the Salvation Army for whom it is a means to conversion, such as in the traditional *Heilsarmee* songs like "Geht hinein in die Schlacht," "Bruder, gib dir einen Stoß," "Fürchte dich nicht," or "In der Jugend goldnem Schimmer," which the Chicago gangsters smile upon as high-minded religious trash. The play's main character, the Salvation Army lieutenant Lilian Holiday, therefore strives for more modern, less obvious means. The "Matrosen Song" belongs above all in this category. The first stanza, in which sailors dream of the pleasures of whisky and cigars, of Far Eastern "Schiffsromantik" and sensual pleasures in life, as expressed in the swinging tango rhythm, does not permit religious thoughts to surface. Text, rhythm, and the polished harmony make the song one of ambience. The refrain has an rapturous character corresponding to the words, "Ja das Meer ist blau so blau" (Yes the sea is blue, so blue), but is oddly aimless in tonality. After beginning in a disguised A minor it ends surprisingly in C major. This corresponds to the continuation of the text, "Und wenn die Chose aus ist, dann fängts von vorne an" (And when the thing is over, then it starts from the beginning). In the unexpected softening to C major the transition to the last refrain is possibly hinted at. In the South Sea paradise a storm begins, bringing the sailors back to faith. Weill musically hints at this upheaval by deleting the tango rhythm for a few measures and introducing a kind of funeral march rhythm.

Observing the effect of the sailor song on the gangster Bill Cracker, the Salvation Army lieutenant sees that she can get him to change his ways with sentimental songs. She purposefully uses the song "Surabaya Johnny" to stop a planned bank robbery, for example. The theme of this song is seduction's triumph over reason. The woman recognizes the crudeness of her friend but still succumbs to him. At the same time, in the "Matrosen Song" one can interpret the melody of the refrain as a hidden allusion to this conflict. The blues tempo is retained. Specifically at the words, "Mein

Gott, und ich liebe dich so" (My God, and I love you so), the singing changes to speaking against all traditional conventions for such a passage. The music interprets the woman's confession of love as grief — she cannot extricate herself from the relationship. The music clarifies the attitude hidden behind the text. The second time the words "Ich liebe dich so" are sung however, the harmony modulates to an unexpected key on the word *so*, again emphasizing the abnormality of this love.

Bill Cracker is so moved by this song that he forgets his planned robbery and converts. In the end both the *Heilsarmee* and the gangsters declare themselves for modern capitalism and strike up the "Hosianna Rockefeller" together. Good and evil, early church choral and secular dance music are reconciled with one another here. Accompanied by harmonium and bell tones and interrupted by "hosanna" cries from the chorus, the adoration of the great capitalist then turns, however, into a crass foxtrot rhythm. For this Weill borrowed the melody of his earlier song, "Berlin im Licht," which he composed in 1928 for a week's festivities celebrating the electric lighting industry. With this, he provided a connection between Chicago and Berlin and in addition reduced the halo of Rockefeller & Co. to what it was — an illuminated advertisement.

V

In the Brecht settings by Hanns Eisler, a student of Schoenberg's, there was only rarely such melodic emphasis as in the "Seeräuber Jenny," "Alabama Song," or "Matrosen Song." More strongly than did Weill, the Marxist-schooled Eisler protected himself against misunderstandings and against a purely musical consumerism at the price, to be sure, of lesser success with the middle-class public. In Brecht's collaboration with Eisler the Bach *Passions* became the poetical-musical models. On this model are based the text and music of the proletarian "Lehrstück" *Die Maßnahme*, parts of the "Mutter," the "Deutsche Sinfonie," and the "Lenin Requiem." The change from the model of the ballad song to that of the Bach *Passions* was not only an aesthetic decision, but primarily a political one; it signified the change from the individual to the party. Eisler emphasized this superimposed aspect through the rhythmical symbol of the anapest, which since *Die Maßnahme* had stood for class struggle.[22] It was Eisler who in these years around 1930 also acquainted Brecht with a new form of speaking, that of the "Agitprop-Truppen." In his "Ratschlägen zur Einstudierung der Maßnahme"

---

[22] See Dümling, pp. 301ff.

he demanded of the chorus that they not sing with expression, but as if giving a lecture at a mass meeting.[23]

Although this was certainly not the only form of speaking that served as a starting point for the Eisler settings of Brecht, it is crucial that such forms were included at all in Brecht's texts. While in his poems and songs the early Brecht, as ballad singer, still recorded essentially his own ways of speaking, later he made use of outside impulses more and more. One of the most important speaker/singers for him and for Eisler came to be Ernst Busch, who enjoyed popularity among the working class.[24] His method of speaking imprinted itself, for example, on the text and melody of the "Solidaritätslied." While Brecht usually slipped poems to be set to Eisler without commentary — trusting him to give an exact reading — he often read them aloud to Dessau, "ruhig, zart und ganz auf Sinn, so musikalisch, wie kaum ein Dichter wohl je vorgelesen hat" (softly, tenderly, and entirely with regard to the meaning, more musically than probably any poet had ever read aloud).[25]

In order to increase the useful value of his poems, Brecht wanted them to be tied to melodies. Not only in his *Hauspostille*, but also in the collection *Lieder Gedichte Chöre* and the *Wiegenlieder für Arbeitermütter* he placed great value on the melodies being published as well.[26] The music conveyed his poems in sound, in social situations; it made them easily remembered and at the same time invited variation and change.

---

[23] Hanns Eisler, "Einige Ratschläge zur Einstudierung der Maßnahme," *Musik und Politik: Schriften 1924–1948*, ed. Günter Mayer (Leipzig: VEB Deutscher Verlag für Musik, 1973), p. 168.

[24] See Ludwig Hoffmann and Karl Siebig, *Ernst Busch: Eine Biografie in Texten, Bildern und Dokumenten* (Berlin [West]: Das Europäische Buch, 1987).

[25] Paul Dessau, *Notizen zu Noten*, ed. Fritz Hennenberg (Leipzig: Reclam, 1974), p. 41.

[26] See Brecht, *Briefe* (Frankfurt am Main: Suhrkamp, 1981), p. 173.

Epilogue

Musicopoetics or Melomania: Is There a Theory behind Music in German Literature?

STEVEN PAUL SCHER

COMMITTING SACRILEGE AS A Germanist, but also hoping for instant absolution as a comparatist, I begin by calling attention to a recent work of literature that is decidedly non-German:

> But what about [his] music?
> It doesn't get very good marks, because musicians don't like dabblers, and literary men don't like people who cross boundaries — especially musical boundaries. If you're a writer, you're a writer, and if you're a composer, you're a composer — and no scabbing.[1]

This allusive passage comes from Canadian novelist Robertson Davies's delightful new book *The Lyre of Orpheus* (1988); and the dabbler whose music "doesn't get very good marks" — and whose presence in a piece of contemporary Anglo-Saxon fiction comes as a pleasant surprise — is none other than the German romantic writer and composer E. T. A. Hoffmann! As a matter of fact, Davies's novel abounds in true delights for the initiated; for example, his title *The Lyre of Orpheus* derives directly from Hoffmann's celebrated 1810 critique of Beethoven's Fifth Symphony which, along with his other reviews of Beethoven's music, was recast as fiction and, under the title "Beethoven's Instrumentalmusik," then became part of Hoffmann's first published collection of narratives, the *Fantasiestücke in Callot's Manier* (1814).

To be sure, this essay will not trace the quaint details of Hoffmann's late-twentieth-century reincarnation from limbo in Robertson Davies's novel, however tempting such a critical task might be. That I shall not be rehearsing here the many concrete instances where music and German literature intersect needs no apology, I think, especially in view of the panorama of the relevant authors, composers, and topics explored in considerable detail throughout the present volume. The fact alone that a splendid international conference could be organized on "Music and German Literature" confirms that there is no dearth of enduring musically inspired literary works and literarily inspired musical works. My concern here, as intimated in my quizzical title, is more comprehensive and general and thus more open to speculation: Is it possible to discern and articulate, however tentatively, certain currents and tendencies in aesthetic theorizing that underlie the

---

[1] Robertson Davies, *The Lyre of Orpheus* (New York: Viking, 1988), p. 36.

evidently symbiotic relations between the two arts? In other words, I am interested in contemplating rather sweeping questions such as: What is the role of poetic and music theory, if any, in bringing about the reciprocal interaction that results in musico-literary practice? To what extent is the symbiotic relationship between music and literature something typically German? Is this latter question legitimate at all? To put it another way, how profitable — or even justifiable — would it have been to hold a symposium comparable to ours on "Music and French Literature" or "Music and English Literature"? What is it, then, that makes our topic a matter of course, a topic that needs no apology, nor elaborate explanation? Could it be perhaps the plain fact that music as an art form has traditionally been taken more seriously in the German-speaking lands than in other countries — especially by poets, writers, and critics, but also by the art-consuming public at large? Or would it be too simplistic to assert that since the German mind-set has always been more aesthetically inclined, the influential German philosophers like, say, Kant, Schelling, Hegel, Schopenhauer, Nietzsche, and Adorno — or even Lukács — have all made a special, if not always felicitous effort to integrate closer scrutiny of the phenomenon of music into their aesthetic speculations, more so than thinkers of other nations?

Clearly, there are no easy answers to such complex questions, but they do provide the larger philosophical and socio-political framework for our rather hermeneutically determined context. In the exploratory remarks that follow, inspired by the fine recent critical work on the subject, I shall try to be more specific. I am particularly indebted to the stimulating books and articles by the late Carl Dahlhaus, Lawrence Kramer, Norbert Miller, John Neubauer, and Ulrich Weisstein.[2] Above all, I share with them — and

---

[2] Each of these five scholars has written widely on musico-literary topics relevant to this essay, so I shall only mention here the studies that I found most directly useful. By Carl Dahlhaus: *Musikästhetik* (Cologne: Gerig, 1967); *Die Idee der absoluten Musik* (Kassel: Bärenreiter, 1978); "Musik und Text," in *Dichtung und Musik: Kaleidoskop ihrer Beziehungen*, ed. Günter Schnitzler (Stuttgart: Klett, 1979), pp. 11–28; "E. T. A. Hoffmanns Beethoven-Kritik und die Ästhetik des Erhabenen," *Archiv für Musikwissenschaft* 33 (1981): 79–92; *Musikalischer Realismus: Zur Musikgeschichte des 19. Jahrhunderts* (Munich: Piper, 1982); "Kleists Wort über den Generalbass," *Kleist Jahrbuch* (1984): 13–24; and *Klassische und romantische Musikästhetik* (Laaber: Laaber Verlag, 1988). By Lawrence Kramer: *Music and Poetry: The Nineteenth Century and After* (Berkeley: Univ. of California Press, 1984) and "Expressive Doubling: Beethoven's Two-Movement Piano Sonatas and Romantic Literature," *Studies in Romanticism* 27 (1988): 175–201. By Norbert Miller: "Musik als Sprache: Zur Vorgeschichte von Liszts Symphonischen Dichtungen," in *Beiträge zur musikalischen Hermeneutik*, ed. Carl Dahlhaus (Regensburg: Bosse, 1975), pp. 223–87; "Hoffmann und Spontini: Vorüberlegungen zu einer Ästhetik der romantischen *opera seria*," in *Wissen aus Erfahrungen: Werkbegriff und Interpretation heute. Festschrift für Herman Meyer zum 65. Geburtstag*, ed. Alexander von Bormann (Tübingen: Niemeyer, 1976), pp. 402–26 and "E. T. A. Hoffmann und die Musik," *Akzente* 24 (1977): 114–35. By John Neubauer: *The Emancipation of Music from Language: Departure from Mimesis in Eighteenth-Century Aesthetics* (New Haven and London: Yale Univ. Press, 1986) and "Die Sprache des Unaussprechlichen: Hoffmanns Rezension von Beethovens 5.

intend to substantiate further — their conviction, stated succinctly by John Neubauer in the concluding paragraph of his 1986 study *The Emancipation of Music from Language*, that "reflections on literature and music are interdependent."[3] This notion is certainly not new. But it needs to be stressed and reasserted, particularly in literary circles, for many literary critics and theorists who are not actively involved in musico-literary scholarship are still skeptical (because insufficiently aware) of the substantial cross-disciplinary connections that exist — implicitly as well as explicitly — between musical and literary aesthetics. To demonstrate at least partially that there is indeed a theoretical dimension to our field, with considerable consequences also for literary theory, I would like to call special attention to one of these cross-literary connections which, as an influential theoretical construct, has been central to aesthetic debates for the last two centuries. The connection I mean is in fact a dichotomy; it is the perdurable conflict between absolute music (i.e., pure instrumental music) and vocal music (i.e., texted or text-dependent music). More precisely I mean the radically polarized, mid-eighteenth century version of the age-old word-tone dichotomy that found an extraordinary poetological echo in romantic aesthetics.

Critics generally agree that modern music theory is rooted in the literary and philosophical traditions of the late eighteenth and early nineteenth centuries, that it evolved together with the momentous changes in the long-standing hierarchy of the arts, and that it culminated around 1800 in the conceptualization of a poetically inspired "metaphysics of instrumental music" (to borrow Carl Dahlhaus's phrase)[4] — in the articulation of a new, romantic aesthetics of music which in expressive content was more literary than musical. Here is how Norbert Miller posits the essence of this development: "Die Apotheose der reinen Musik (und damit die Ablösung der Oper durch die Symphonie als richtungweisender Gattung innerhalb der Musik) wird außerhalb der Musikästhetik vorbereitet: in der Dichtung der Empfindsamkeit und der frühen Romantik."[5] A new language was created

Symphonie," in *E. T. A. Hoffmann et la musique*, ed. Alain Montandon (Bern: Lang, 1987), pp. 25–34. By Ulrich Weisstein: "Librettology: The Fine Art of Coping with a Chinese Twin," *Komparatistische Hefte* 5/6 (1982): 23–42 and "Was ist die romantische Oper?: Versuch einer musiko-literarischen Begriffsbestimmung," in *Einheit in der Vielfalt: Festschrift für Peter Lang zum 60. Geburtstag*, ed. Gisela Quast (Bern: Lang, 1988), pp. 568–88.

[3] Neubauer, *Emancipation*, p. 210.

[4] "Die 'eigentliche' romantische Musikästhetik ist eine Metaphysik der Instrumentalmusik." The "truly" romantic aesthetics of music is a metaphysics of instrumental music; Dahlhaus, *Die Idee der absoluten Musik*, p. 68.

[5] The apotheosis of pure music (which also meant that the symphony replaced opera as the leading musical genre) occurred outside of musical aesthetics: in the literature of the Age of Sensibility ("Empfindsamkeit") and early romanticism; Miller, "Musik als Sprache,"

to talk about music, and the inventors (as well as the avid first practitioners) of this new discourse were for the most part "melomaniacs," writers such as Jean Paul, Wackenroder, Tieck, Novalis, Kleist, and E. T. A. Hoffmann. The term "melomaniac" is not meant here pejoratively, even though it does have a ring of the amateurish about it. On the contrary! It is true that, except for Hoffmann (who was a professional musician) and possibly Wackenroder (who studied music and might have become one, had he lived longer), these writers were musical amateurs.[6] But they were music lovers in the best sense of the word, for whom experiencing and contemplating a symphony bordered on religious devotion and who sincerely believed that music — and only music — could express the inexpressible.[7] They were melo-maniacs, because they were — each in his own, distinctively individual way, yet remarkably interdependent in their musico-poetic diction — "enamored with the expressive power of pure instrumental music and firmly convinced of the supremacy of music over the other arts, including poetry."[8] Their genuine, infectious enthusiasm for music enabled them to create a literature *about* music that corresponded to their conception of an ultimately unattainable literary semblance of music, of a literature *as if* it were music. As M. H. Abrams in his classic 1953 study *The Mirror and the Lamp: Romantic Theory and the Critical Tradition* perceptively observes, "the attempt to make literature aspire to the condition of music motivated the description by German writers of sounding forms, musical fragrance, and the harmony of colors...."[9] These melomaniacs' predecessor was none other than Johann Gotttfried Herder, the first in the long line of writer-cum-critic literati in the modern sense, who claimed, as early as 1769, that poetry, unlike painting and sculpture, "is the music of the soul. A sequence of thoughts, pictures, words, tones is the essence of its expression; in this does

---

268–69.

[6] Cf. Steven Paul Scher, "Temporality and Mediation: W. H. Wackenroder and E. T. A. Hoffmann as Literary Historicists of Music," *JEGP* 75 (1976): 492–502.

[7] "Die romantische Musikästhetik ist aus dem dichterischen Unsagbarkeits-Topos hervorgegangen: Musik drückt aus, was Worte nicht einmal zu stammeln vermögen.... Die Entdeckung, daß die Musik, und zwar als gegenstands- und begriffslose Instrumentalmusik, eine Sprache 'über' der Sprache sei, ereignete sich, paradox genug, 'in' der Sprache: in der Dichtung" (Romantic aesthetics of music originated from the poetic topos of the unsayable: music expresses what words are not capable of expressing, not even when stammered.... Paradoxically enough, the discovery that music — specifically instrumental music which cannot be objectified or conceptualized — was a language "above" language occurred "in" language itself: in literature); Dahlhaus, *Die Idee der absoluten Musik*, p. 66.

[8] Steven Paul Scher, *Verbal Music in German Literature* (New Haven and London: Yale Univ. Press, 1968), p. 159.

[9] M. H. Abrams, *The Mirror and the Lamp: Romantic Theory and the Critical Tradition* (New York: Norton, 1958), p. 94.

it resemble music.... Ode and idyll, fable and the speech of passion, are a melody of thoughts...."[10] Abrams concludes this seminal subchapter entitled "Expressive Theory in Germany: Ut Musica Poesis" by stating that "literature was made to emulate music by substituting a symphonic form — a melody of ideas and images, a thematic organization, a harmony of moods — for the structural principles of plot, argument, or exposition."[11] And Thomas Mann — musical connoisseur and Wagnerite par excellence, for whom music constituted "das reinste Paradigma" of his novelistic universe and who said about his own works in retrospect, "urteilt darüber wie ihr wollt und müßt, aber gute Partituren waren sie immer"[12] — is no doubt the most representative twentieth-century literary heir to this melomaniacal romantic disposition — whether or not we judge his *pro domo* sincerity to be genuine.

Valid, historically substantiated critical insights of such a straightforward, descriptive nature abound in scholarly treatments of our topic. But to my mind the real challenge lies in contemplating the possibility of a coherent theoretical construct or unifying principle which would account for the mutually fruitful interplay of the inherently contradictory thought patterns and aesthetic utterances that comprise the realm of musicopoetics. Within the last decade, two important studies have taken up precisely this challenge, albeit in very different ways: Carl Dahlhaus's *Die Idee der absoluten Musik* (1978) and John Neubauer's *The Emancipation of Music from Language* (1986).[13] As their titles intimate, both the musicologist Dahlhaus and the literary critic Neubauer are primarily concerned with the ideational background of instrumental music's newly gained autonomy and its impact on subsequent aesthetic theorizing. Neubauer persuasively claims that it was above all the continuous tradition of mathematical and Pythagorean approaches to music that prepared the ground for the triumph of autonomous instrumental music in the eighteenth century and beyond and that, in turn, this "instrumental music aided the resurgence of certain mathematical and Pythagorean notions of music that formed the basis of a new aesthetics in Romanticism."[14] Dahlhaus, in a magisterial anatomy of the idea of absolute music, traces the complex origins of what he calls the "metaphysical prestige" of absolute music[15] back to specific late eigh-

---

[10] Quoted by Abrams, ibid., p. 93.

[11] Ibid., p. 94.

[12] the purest paradigm and however you may want to and must judge them, they were always good scores. Thomas Mann, *Gesammelte Werke in 13 Bänden* (Frankfurt am Main: S. Fischer, 1974), 12:319.

[13] See note 2 above.

[14] Neubauer, *Emancipation*, p. 8.

[15] Dahlhaus, *Die Idee der absoluten Musik*, p. 144.

teenth- and early nineteenth-century philosophical and poetological utterances. When it comes to literary sources to support his argument, Dahlhaus invariably invokes the melomaniacs named earlier: Jean Paul, Wackenroder, Tieck, Novalis, Kleist, and most often E. T. A. Hoffmann. For Neubauer's mathematical orientation Novalis serves as chief German literary witness.

I find these two studies to be complementary rather than mutually exclusive; and while I endorse their solid conceptual framework and convincing critical insights, I should like to venture a step beyond and propose that we entertain a related, and perhaps no less rewarding notion which requires only a slight shift in critical emphasis. I believe that the potential aesthetic relevance for musical and poetic theory and practice of the dichotomy between instrumental music and vocal music has yet to be fully assessed and appreciated. I suggest therefore, that instead of focusing more or less exclusively on the idea of absolute music as "das ästhetische Paradigma der deutschen Musikkultur des 19. Jahrhunderts"[16] — as Dahlhaus has done with such inimitable aplomb — , we now focus on *both* components of the dichotomy *together* as a dialectic entity: on wordless instrumental music *together* with its counterpart, which is never far away, word-dependent vocal music. For ultimately, the persistent creative tension in this dichotomy is always between music without and music with language, where language connotes referentiality and can mean, of course, both poetic language or literature in general ("Dichtung"). Once we begin to contemplate the meaning and nature of this dichotomy, we find it omnipresent in aesthetic theorizing from the middle of the eighteenth century to the present. In its capacity as an influential theoretical construct or paradigm, it also helps to explain and interpret the motivating forces behind the subtle changes in musical and literary genres around 1800 that signal the advent of modernism. Dahlhaus himself is surely aware of the far-reaching implications of the dichotomy for the history of aesthetics when he maintains,

War die Instrumentalmusik zunächst, im 18. Jahrhundert, für die Common-sense-Ästhetiker ein "angenehmes Geräusch" *unter* der Sprache gewesen, so wurde sie in der romantischen Metaphysik der Kunst zu einer Sprache *über* der Sprache erklärt. Der Drang aber, sie in die mittlere Sphäre der Sprache hineinzuziehen, ließ sich nicht unterdrücken.[17]

---

[16] "the aesthetic paradigm of nineteenth-century German musical culture"; ibid., p. 15.

[17] "If instrumental music had been a 'pleasant noise' *beneath* language to the common-sense aestheticians of the eighteenth century, then the romantic metaphysics of art declared it a language *above* language. The urge to draw it into the middle sphere of language could not be suppressed"; ibid.

This model statement defines in bold strokes the three phases occasioned by the two crucial transformations that the dichotomy underwent until the end of the last century. It first changed from a mid-eighteenth-century instrumental music still subservient to textual dominance (as reflected in opera, oratorios, and early lied composition) to an instrumental music that — thanks largely to poetic mediation — shed its word-dependence and reigned supreme. This second phase is exemplified by the classical symphony. The third phase resulted from the irrepressible urge of nineteenth-century composers of symphonic music to reintegrate poetic content into instrumental music in the form of program music; an urge that is latently present even in Wagner's through-composed music dramas, which Nietzsche still conceived of as symphonic music.[18] For Nietzsche, *Tristan und Isolde* constituted "das eigentliche *opus metaphysicum* aller Kunst."[19]

Focusing on the continuous struggle between the two components of our dichotomy provides illumination for aesthetic problems where we least expect it. For example, it may put into question the hitherto obvious assumption that clearly mixed genres comprising music *and* literature like opera and other kinds of vocal music like oratorios, cantatas, masses, madrigals, and the lied are considered primarily musical. But in all honesty, will, say, librettology — a relatively recent branch of musico-literary study[20] — eventually be able to correct this perceptual imbalance convincingly enough so that we will conceive of opera spontaneously as a musico-literary genre? I wouldn't count on it; the original pull of autonomous instrumental music in the dichotomy remains just too strong. Also, most likely, a recital of, say, Hugo Wolf's Mörike lieder will always be regarded first and foremost as a musical event.

To take another example, even a cursory glance at the evolution of the lied — according to Liszt the most characteristically "intrinsic product of the

---

[18] "Nietzsche hörte das Musikdrama als Symphonie; der Rest ist 'Gaukelei' oder Schutzwehr. Er übertrug also die — von Wackenroder, Tieck und E. T. A. Hoffmann über Schopenhauer tradierte — These, daß die Instrumentalmusik die 'eigentliche' Musik sei, auf Wagners Musikdrama (wie Schopenhauer sie auf Rossinis Oper übertragen hatte)" (Nietzsche heard the music drama as a symphony; the rest is "trickery" or defenses. Thus he applied the thesis that instrumental music was the "true" music — as transmitted by Wackenroder, Tieck, and E. T. A. Hoffmann via Schopenhauer — to Wagner's music drama [as Schopenhauer had applied it to Rossini's operas]); ibid., p. 38.

[19] "the true *opus metaphysicum* of all art"; Friedrich Nietzsche, "Richard Wagner in Bayreuth," *Unzeitgemässe Betrachtungen*, Viertes Stück, in Nietzsche, *Werke in drei Bänden*, ed. Karl Schlechta (Munich: Hanser, 1966), 1:408.

[20] For initial orientation, see Patrick J. Smith, *The Tenth Muse: A Historical Study of the Opera Libretto* (New York: Knopf, 1970); Klaus Günther Just, "Das deutsche Opernlibretto," *Poetica* 7 (1975): 203–20; and Ulrich Weisstein, "Librettology."

Germanic Muse"[21] — suffices to bear out the validity of focusing on the dichotomy as a dialectic entity. Only recently have scholars more securely at home in both literature and music begun to realize that it is precisely the inherent and persistent creative tension between the lied's musical and verbal components — reflecting in miniature the relentless conflict within our dichotomy between absolute music and vocal music — that has propelled this symbiotic construct into prominence as the representative German genre of nineteenth-century music (thus Dahlhaus),[22] making it an influential catalyst and artistic manifestation of the Romantic movement. Lawrence Kramer's 1984 study *Music and Poetry: The Nineteenth Century and After* is symptomatic of this innovative view of song interpretation. Kramer, a literary critic and musical analyst who is also a practicing composer, persuasively argues that

> the primary fact about song is what might be called a topological distortion of utterance under the rhythmic and harmonic stress of music: a pulling, stretching, and twisting that deforms the current of speech without negating its basic linguistic shape. The art song as a genre is the exploitation of this expressive topology — its shaping both as a primary musical experience and as a reflection of the contest between musical and poetic meaning.[23]

To be properly understood as the fundamental driving force in the lied which shaped the course and stages of the genre's transformation throughout the nineteenth century, this "contest between musical and poetic meanings" must be seen in an evolutionary perspective.[24] Not surprisingly, pre-Schubert song exhibits virtually none of the "pulling, stretching, and twisting" that Kramer finds so energizing in the lieder of the "nineteenth century and after." Echoing Gottsched's opinion of 1730 that "singing is nothing more than a pleasant and emphatic reading of a poem,"[25] Johann Friedrich Campe's *Wörterbuch* of 1809 still defined the lied as "a poem

---

[21] "Das Lied ist poetisch wie musikalisch ein der germanischen Muse angehöriges Erzeugnis" (The lied is, poetically as well as musically, an intrinsic product of the Germanic Muse); Franz Liszt, "Robert Franz" (1855), in Liszt, *Schriften zur Tonkunst* (Leipzig: Reclam, 1981), p. 253.

[22] Cf. Carl Dahlhaus, *Die Musik des 19. Jahrhunderts* (Wiesbaden: Athenaion, 1980), pp. 4, 44.

[23] Kramer, *Music and Poetry*, p. 130.

[24] For a more detailed critical treatment of this topic, see Steven Paul Scher, "The German Lied: A Genre and Its European Reception," in *European Romanticism: Literary Cross Currents, Modes, and Models*, ed. Gerhart Hoffmeister (Detroit: Wayne State Univ. Press, 1990), pp. 127–41.

[25] Johann Christoph Gottsched, *Versuch einer Critischen Dichtkunst*, 4th ed. (Leipzig, 1751), p. 725.

which is intended to be sung."[26] It is well known that for Goethe, an arch-conservative in musical matters, the desirable balance between poem and music in the lied still meant the primacy of word over tone; and Reichardt and Zelter, his loyal composer friends, supplied him with just the kind of unobtrusive strophic settings he envisioned. Goethe had good reason to resist, or outright dismiss, truly inspired settings of his poetry by Beethoven and Schubert. He realized instinctively that more adventurous exploration of the musical potentialities of the genre would lead to a freer, more expressive musical component which would eventually outshine the poetic component and even claim independence. By the end of the eighteenth century the lied as a genre was well on its way to becoming what Goethe feared it would: an act of "composed reading," comprised decidedly more of music than of poetry.[27] Indeed, from Schubert on, the typical pattern of musical foreground versus poetic background constituted the irreversible norm for the nineteenth-century lied. The musical shape and mood of the lied became so vivid and primary that the recollection of the poem itself, however memorable as great poetry, pales in comparison, as, for example, in Schubert's setting of Goethe's "Erlkönig" or Schumann's setting of Eichendorff's "Mondnacht." Schumann even seems to have "thought of the Lied as a form of lyric piano piece — a 'song without words' but with words — and his habit of doubling the vocal melody of his lieder on the piano bears this definition out."[28] Further into the century, lied composers yielded more and more to the genuinely romantic impulse of transforming the lied into pure instrumental music, as reflected in Liszt's famous piano transcriptions of Schubert songs or in the tendency on the part of composers like Wolf, Mahler, and Richard Strauss to score lieder for voice and symphonic orchestra.

The complexities of the theory and practice of nineteenth-century lied composition provide perhaps the most telling illustration for the presence of a creative tension between instrumental and vocal music, a notion central to musico-literary study which continues to be profitably explored by musicologists as well as literary critics. Another larger topic of related interest, which holds fascinating implications for genre theory in particular and late twentieth-century literary theory in general, also merits closer scrutiny: the elevation of the critical act by the melomaniac German romantic writers around 1800 to a status comparable to the privileged status

---

[26] Quoted in Walter Salmen, *Haus- und Kammermusik: Privates Musizieren im gesellschaftlichen Wandel zwischen 1600 und 1900* (Leipzig: VEB Deutscher Verlag für Musik, 1969), p. 32.

[27] See Steven Paul Scher, "Comparing Poetry and Music: Beethoven's Goethe-Lieder," in *Sensus communis: Contemporary Trends in Comparative Literature. Festschrift für Henry Remak*, ed. János Riesz, Peter Boerner, and Bernhard Scholz (Tübingen: Gunter Narr, 1986), pp. 155–65.

[28] Kramer, *Music and Poetry*, p. 131.

occupied by the creative act of producing works of art and Friedrich Schlegel's pivotal mediating role in this privileging process. Specifically in this context, Schlegel's few and scattered musings on music promise to yield important new insights: no matter how diffuse, dilettantish, and inconsequential they seem at first, they are very much in line with contemporary mainstream aesthetic theorizing and also cut to the core of his own, unsystematic philosophical system. The creative artist who emerges alongside Schlegel as the other prominent mediator in the privileging process is the multiply talented storyteller, composer, and music critic E. T. A. Hoffmann. His music criticism and music-inspired fiction possess a self-referential coherence that exemplifies the unifying theoretical foundation upon which interdependence of reflections on music and literature rests. Looking back to eighteenth-century and earlier musical and poetic theories as well as pointing forward to later (both nineteenth- and twentieth-century) ideas, Hoffmann's musical writings occupy a seminal mediating position in the history of aesthetics: they successfully conjoin romantic musical and poetic theory and practice. Thus it is only fitting that Hoffmann was chosen as the model for the quintessential dabbler and conscious violator of the myopic, compartmentalized thinking code that Robertson Davies's succinct phrase "no scabbing" — in the passage quoted earlier from his novel *The Lyre of Orpheus* — so aptly captures. After all, more often than not, it is creative dabblers like Hoffmann — practicing artists and theorists in one — who function as prime catalysts of innovation and progress in the arts and art criticism and, as it happens, also in charting the course of musicopoetics and melomania that underlies modern German literature.

About the Contributors

The Middle Ages

RONALD J. TAYLOR, Professor Emeritus of German, University of Sussex, is author of books on the songs of Neidhart von Reuental (1959, with A. T. Hatto), on the melodies of the secular songs of the Middle Ages (1963), *The Art of the Minnesinger* (1968), the Romantic author and composer E. T. A. Hoffmann (1964), *Richard Wagner: His Life, Art and Thought* (1979), *Robert Schumann: His Life and Work* (1982), *Franz Liszt: The Man and the Musician* (1986), and *Kurt Weill: Composer in a Divided World* (1991).

HUBERT HEINEN, Professor of German, The University of Texas at Austin, is the author and editor of books and articles on a variety of subjects, primarily in German literature of the Middle Ages. His latest book, *Mutabilität im Minnesang: Mehrfach überlieferte Lieder des 12. und frühen 13. Jahrhunderts* (1989), represents the first of three volumes. The remaining two, "Minnesongs and their Permutations: Mutability and Coherence" and "MaP: Texts and Contexts," will treat literary and text-critical implications of the ubiquitous phenomenon of multiple and varying transmission of medieval song.

Baroque

DIANNE M. MCMULLEN, Assistant Professor of Music, Adelphi University, is investigating the effect of dance rhythms on textual phrasing in dance songs.

JUDITH P. AIKIN, Professor of German, University of Iowa, is the author of *German Baroque Drama* (1982, including a chapter on opera) and articles on "Creating a Language for German Opera" and "The Lyre and the Liar in Lyrical Poetry of the German Middle Ages." She is currently writing a book on the development of verse forms for German opera.

GARY C. THOMAS, Assistant Professor of Humanities and German, University of Minnesota, is author of "Dance Music and the Origins of the Dactylic Meter" (*Daphnis*, 1987) and has just completed an edition of Constantin Christian Dedekind's *Aelbianische Musenlust* (1657), a collection of 175 German songs.

Enlightenment

HANS JOACHIM KREUTZER, Professor of German Literature at the University of Regensburg and President of the Heinrich-von-Kleist-Gesellschaft, has written widely on German literature in general and is specially interested in the relationship between music and literature. Among his essays on this subject are studies on the libretto of Handel's *Messiah*, on realizations of the Don Giovanni theme in European drama, on images of Mozart in nineteenth-century literature, on the reception of Mozart's operas, on Schubert in his relations with the literary world of his time, and on the poet Wilhelm Müller and Schubert. He is also co-editor of a collection of papers (1977) on the works of Heinrich von Kleist (1777–1811) and their adaptations for the opera.

GLORIA FLAHERTY, Professor of German, University of Illinois at Chicago, is the author of *Opera in the Development of German Critical Thought* (1978) and articles on the relationship between music and German literature in the seventeenth and eighteenth centuries. Her most recent book, *Shamanism and the Eighteenth Century* (1991), includes a chapter on Mozart.

MARGARET STOLJAR, Reader in German and Head of the Department of Modern European Languages at The Australian National University, Canberra, is the author of *Poetry and Song in Late Eighteenth Century Germany: A Study in the Musical Sturm und Drang* (1985). She has recently been named a Fellow of the Australian Academy of the Humanities.

JOHN NEUBAUER, Professor of Comparative Literature, University of Amsterdam, the author of *The Emancipation of Music from Language: Departure from Mimesis in Eighteenth-Century Aesthetics* (1986), has been concentrating recently on institutional aspects of the arts.

Nineteenth Century

HELMUT GÖBEL, Member of the Faculty (Akademischer Oberrat) of the Seminar for German Philology at the University of Göttingen, has written on the Romantic author and composer E. T. A. Hoffmann, in addition to his other publications on Lessing, Herder, Dürrenmatt, and Canetti.

ULRICH WEISSTEIN, Professor Emeritus of German and Comparative Literature and Chair of Comparative Literature, Indiana University, is a leading authority in the field of librettology. He edited *The Essence of Opera* (1964) and has published many essays on opera and librettology.

ALBRECHT RIETHMÜLLER, Professor of Musicology and Head of the Musicological Institute at the University of Frankfurt am Main, has published extensively on music and literature, from his doctoral dissertation on music as a representation of reality (*Die Musik als Abbild der Realität*, 1976), *Ferruccio Busonis Poetik* (1988), and *Gedichte über Musik* (Poems on Music, 1991).

Turn of the Century and Since

WALTER SALMEN, Professor of Musicology and Head of the Musicological Institute, University of Innsbruck, is the foremost expert on German song. Among his recent books are *The Social Status of the Professional Musician from the Middle Ages to the 19th Century* (1983), *Das Konzert: Eine Kulturgeschichte* (The Concert: A Cultural History; 1988), and *Tanz im 17. und 18. Jahrhundert* (Dance in the 17th and 18th Centuries, 1988), *Tanz im 19. Jahrhundert* (Dance in the 19th Century, 1989), *Mozart in der Tanzkultur seiner Zeit* (Mozart in the Dance Culture of His Time, 1990), and *... denn die Fiedel macht das Fest: Jüdische Musikanten und Tänzer 13.–20. Jahrhundert* (... the Fiddle Makes the Feast: Jewish Musicians and Dancers from the 13th to the 20th Century).

DONALD G. DAVIAU, Professor of Austrian and German Literature, University of California, Riverside, is the author of *The "Ariadne auf Naxos" of Hugo von Hofmannsthal and Richard Strauss* (1975) and has authored or edited other books on Austrian authors, including editions of the correspondence of Arthur Schnitzler, Hermann Bahr, and Stefan Zweig and two studies of Bahr, as well as volumes on *Exilliteratur* (1985) and *The Major Figures of Contemporary Austrian Literature* (1986), among other publications. He has been editor of the journal *Modern Austrian Literature* since 1971.

SYBILLE HUBACH has had practical experience in the production of opera and drama, including positions with theaters in Mannheim, Hagen in Westphalia, and Dortmund. After ten years as Musikdramaturgin and Regieassistentin, she is now Research Assistant at the Academy of Sciences of Heidelberg, where she is working on the commentary to an edition of the letters of Johann Georg Hamann. She edited *75 Jahre Städtisches Theater in Dortmund* (1979) and is the author of *Galizische Träume: Die jüdischen Erzählungen des Karl Emil Franzos* (1986).

GEORGE C. SCHOOLFIELD, Professor of German and Scandinavian Literature, Yale University, has published *The Figure of the Musician in German Literature* (1956), *The German Lyric of the Baroque* (1961), *Rilke's Last Year* (1969), and *Janus Secundus* (1980), as well as many articles, particularly on Baroque poetry, both German and Neo-Latin, and on Rilke. In Nordic studies, he has written life-and-works volumes on *Edith*

Södergran (1984) and the poet, prose writer, and music critic *Elmer Diktonius* (1985). He has edited and introduced Eino Friberg's translation of the *Kalevala* (1988) and has translated selected poems of the Finland-Swedish *poeta laureatus* Lars Huldén, *The Chain Dance* (1991). Previously he turned books about Hans Christian Andersen (1961) and Kierkegaard (1980) into English, as well as a novel by Hagar Olsson (1966) and an historical anthology of Finland-Swedish short stories (1974).

MARC A. WEINER, Assistant Professor of German, Indiana University, is the author of *Arthur Schnitzler and the Crisis of Musical Culture* (1986), and articles on E. T. A. Hoffmann, Wagner, Hauptmann, Hugo von Hofmannsthal, Schnitzler, Proust, Mahler, Pfitzner, Felix Wolfes, Thomas Mann, and Adorno. He has a forthcoming book, *Undertones of Insurrection: Music, Politics, and the Social Sphere in the Modern German Narrative*, and is currently writing a monograph on Wagner and the iconography of the body.

ALBRECHT DÜMLING, Music Critic of the newspaper *Der Tagesspiegel*, Berlin, wrote *Die fremden Klänge der hängenden Gärten: Arnold Schönberg und Stefan George* (The Strange Sounds of the Hanging Gardens, 1981), *Laβt euch nicht verführen: Brecht und die Musik* (Don't Let Yourselves Be Led Astray: Brecht and Music, 1985), and several articles on George, Garcia Lorca, Brecht, and on problems of the Lied. He is editor of the series *Lied und Lyrik* (Song and Lyric Poetry) and co-author of the exhibition "Entartete Musik: Eine kommentierte Rekonstruktion" (Degenerate Music: A Reconstruction; Düsseldorf, 1988 and Los Angeles, 1991).

Epilogue

STEVEN PAUL SCHER, Professor of German and Comparative Literature, Dartmouth College, is the author of *Verbal Music in German Literature* (1968), and many articles on music and literature. He edited *Music and Text: Critical Inquiries* (1991); *Literatur und Musik: Ein Handbuch zur Theorie und Praxis eines komparatistischen Grenzgebietes* (1984); a volume of interpretations of E. T. A. Hoffmann (1981); and with Ulrich Weisstein co-edited *Literature and the Other Arts* (1981).

Index